12 MUSLIM REVOLUTIONS, AND THE STRUGGLE FOR LEGITIMACY AGAINST THE IMPERIAL POWERS

12 MUSLIM REVOLUTIONS, AND THE STRUGGLE FOR LEGITIMACY AGAINST THE IMPERIAL POWERS

Carl Max Kortepeter

To order additional copies of this book, contact:
Xlibris
1-888-795-4274
www.Xlibris.com
Orders@Xlibris.com
751064

Contents

Preface

To discuss revolution in any social system requires that a sharp break takes place between the prevailing system and a new system. This sharp division or change may take place in a political, social, economic, or religious sphere. In Islam, legitimacy is very closely defined. Only those institutions or rulers deriving from or related to the Prophet Muhammad and His message are deemed legitimate in the early centuries of Islam. Traditionally, only two legitimate strains are recognized, both of which derive from the Prophet's family, the chosen descendants of Abu Hashim (please note the genealogy on page viii). Islamic governments up to the twentieth century tried very much to make their governments acceptable to the norms of either the Prophet's family or the descendants of Ali bin Abi Talib.

The baseline for a study of the origins of Islam is pre-Islamic Arabia, the so-called *Jahiliyya*, "the Age of Ignorance," as noted in the Quran by the Prophet Muhammad. In this essay, we look first at the social structure of pre-Islamic Arabia to determine how the Prophet Muhammad, by introducing the Quran and his commentaries (*the Sunna*), brought about *the first Islamic Revolution*. The Umayyads, who succeeded the rightly guided caliphs (Abu Bakr, 'Umar, 'Uthman, and 'Ali) in AD 661, were considered kings (*mulūk*) and were content to permit the *'ulamā'* (the savants of Islam) to create the norms of Islamic law (*Shari'ah*). Meanwhile, by designating as their successors their own descendants, the Umayyads introduced hereditary rule into the Islamic State. This was considered the *Second Revolution*, as the *First Revolution* was the Prophet declaring

Al-Islam. The mere fact of the Umayyad family coming to power after being the richest merchants in Mecca, who initially had opposed the Prophet's message, caused a bitter reaction among the Shi'ites.

Genealogy of the Prophet

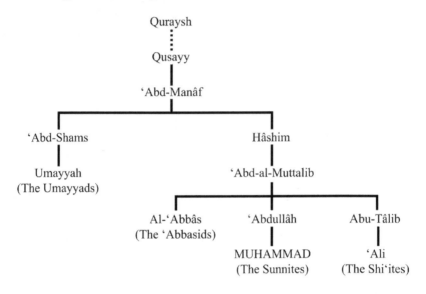

Philip K. Hitti, <u>History of the Arabs</u>, Palgrave/Macmillan, 10th ed., Preface by Walid Khalidi, pb, London, 2002, p. 111.

Because the Shi'ites had a much more legitimate claim to charismatic leadership of the Islamic believers (*the ummah*) through the descendants of Muhammad's daughter, Fatimah, who was married to the Prophet's first cousin and son-in-law, 'Ali bin Abi Talib.

The *'Abbasid Revolution* of AD 750, by restoring a line of direct descendants of the Prophet's Uncle 'Abbas, brought the leadership of the caliphate back to the Hashemite family. This revolution was considered the *Third Revolution*. The 'Abbasids basically faced four problems:

1. The Shi'ites, although the direct descendants of the Prophet, were persecuted and left out of the power elite.
2. The second problem developed from the escape of 'Abd ur-Rahman al-Umaiyah from the 'Abbasid bloodbath of the Umayyad rulers in AD 750. Eventually, 'Abd ur-Rahman arrived

in *Al-Andalus* ("Islamic Spain"), where very soon, he declared a rival Imarate (Ar., *I'marah*) in AD 755.

3. Very debilitating also for the Arab caliphs was a financial system set up by 'Umar, the second caliph, the *Diwan,* requiring the payment from the state treasury of stipends to those Arab tribes who had established the Islamic State. This enactment meant that as Arabs became rich from the treasury, they no longer wished to serve in the Muslim army or cavalry or in the Baghdad Guards Regiments. They preferred to live on their estates and enjoy the high life of Al-Madinah.

4. Equally destructive of 'Abbasid power were the far-flung boundaries of the empire, forcing the 'Abbasid caliphs to give full investiture and absolute power to distant provincial governors (*'amirs*).

In consequence of their difficulties, the 'Abbasid caliphs were forced to rely mainly on young Turkish males to fill the ranks of their armies and guards regiments. The Turks had only in recent decades become converts to Islam. As the caliphs themselves retreated from active management of the empire, they came to rely on *wazirs*, virtually deputy caliphs, given full powers to manage affairs of state and to lead the armies. Furthermore, as noted above, the various amirs assumed the powers of absolute rulers, only reluctantly recognizing the overlordship of the caliph. Hence, we note here the *Era of the Amirates*, counted here as the *Fourth Revolution*. Elsewhere, the Era of the Amirates was dubbed by Professor Vladimir Minorsky as the "Persian Intermezzo" because the Persian governorates ('amirates), such as the Tahirids in Khurasan, the Saffarids of Sijistan, the Samanids of Transoxiana, the Ghaznavids of Afghanistan and Punjab (originally Turkish), and the Buwayhids of Daylam, Shiraz and Baghdad, all of whom were of Persian origin, played such important roles in weakening the 'Abbasid caliphate. The Buwayhids, given status equal to the caliph in AD 945, were Shi'ites that eventually accepted Twelver Shi'ism in keeping with the majority of their Shi'ite followers. But it would be a major mistake to leave out of our picture the many amirates that sprung up in Egypt and North

Africa, the Aghlabids, the Tulunids, and the Ikshidids, to mention only a few. These amirates became subject to the propaganda from the Isma'ilis.

The *Fifth Revolution* relies upon our understanding of Isma'ili doctrine. The doctrine holds that it was Isma'il, the son of the Seventh Imam, Ja'far al-Sadiq, who possessed Muhammad's "Divine Spark." Eventually, in this belief system, Isma'il would return as *Al-Mahdi*, the savior, who would release his followers from all religious and political restrictions. This belief system advocated help to the poor and favored the merchant and artisan classes and became the philosophic underpinnings of the *Qarmatian and Fatimid Revolutions.* One would not be wrong to conclude that these beliefs were influenced by Christian docrines.[1]

With the weakness of the 'Abbasid caliphate after its first century (that is, approximately from AD 750 to 861), the empire was clearly heading for an ideological demise under the successful proselytizing of the Isma'ilis. Before the tenth century, however, other ideologies had influenced the 'Abbasid Dynasty. *The Mu'tazilites*, fostered by a famous theological school in Basrah, occupied a major ideological position in the early 'Abbasid caliphate and was favored by Al-Ma'mun, caliph from AD 813–833, a son of Harun ar-Rashid (AD 786–809). The Mu'tazilites were described by their enemies as *Al-Manzila bayn Al-Manzilatayn* (the position between two positions, belief and unbelief), but perhaps the earliest meaning was "to take up a neutral attitude in the quarrel between 'Ali and his adversaries." They had basically remained neutral in the disputes of the Shi'ites about 'Ali's succession and had been enemies of the Umayyads. They lost official support when they adopted the position that the Quran was created, not uncreated—that is, God gave the Quran to Muhammad, and he dictated what he heard; hence, the Prophet is sometimes described as the "mouthpiece of God." "God is just; all that he does aims at what is best for his creation; he does not desire evil and does not ordain it. He has nothing to do with man's evil deeds; all human actions result from man's free will." In later times, the Mu'tazilite beliefs were deemed the most rational of the medieval philosophies influencing Islamic belief.[2]

The Isma'ili doctrine of the Sevener Shi'ites gave rise to the political organizations of the *Qarmatian and the Fatimid Revolutions*, noted here as the *Fifth Revolution*. This revolution, as noted above, was rather likened to a social democracy wherein the poor received special care from the state and among the merchant class, and the craft guilds international trade was fostered. This movement temporarily expanded to Syria, Iraq, and Yemen by gaining some Bedouin support for raids on town dwellers but was most successful on the island of Bahrain. The concept of a Fatimid Revolution has aroused strong objections. The inhabitants of Egypt remained largely Sunni or Coptic. One can thus argue that the Fatimids largely adopted the practice of previous dynasties and amirates such as the Ikshidids, Aghlabids, and Tulunids. They did improve the food production of the Nile Basin, aided the poor, and also favored the merchant and artisan classes, as had the Qarmatians.[3]

The Umayyads had earlier defeated the Visigoths of Spain in AD 711, but their momentum flagged greatly until 'Abd ar-Rahman al-Umaiya escaped from the clutches of the 'Abbasid bloodbath in AD 750 to rejuvenate Islam in Spain counted here as the *Sixth Revolution*. The eras of the amirates were concentrated in the Eastern caliphate and Iran, and as the Isma'ilis were concentrated in Egypt, Syria, the Arabian Peninsula, and North Africa, gave the opportunity for the revitalization of Islam in Islamic Spain, Al-Andalus, with the arrival of 'Abd ar-Rahman. As the Persian amirates were concentrated in the Eastern caliphate and failed to develop large armies, except for Mahmud of Ghazna, their relative weakness provided a strong incentive for the Seljuk Turks to sweep them all away in the eleventh century; hence, the Seljuks must be counted the *Seventh Revolution*. Although Seljuk leaders tried to marry into the caliphal family, this ploy was unsuccessful; hence, they had to rely for their legitimacy on official investiture from the captive 'Abbasid caliphs, and the Seljuks served as their "sultans." The Great Seljuks in their overlordship emphasized once again Sunni Islam.[4]

As we shall see, a branch of the Great Seljuks, the Rūm Seljuks in Asia Minor (here Rūm refers to East Rome (i.e., Byzantium), attained their legitimacy from fighting the *Ghazawāt*, the wars against infidel

Byzantium, and gaining converts. Later, the Ottomans would follow this type of legitimacy and would generate new forms of legitimacy. But below, we shall deal with the Mongols who initially cared nothing for Islamic legitimacy. Their might and power conquered all enemies in the thirteenth century. They constituted the *Eighth Revolution* before the Ayyubids and the Mamluks of Egypt were forced to deal with the Crusaders from European Dynasties and the Papacy, here identified as the *Ninth Revolution*. Before the European powers were able to penetrate and exercise control in the Middle East in the eighteenth to the twentieth centuries, it was the Ottoman Empire that managed to hold sway in the central lands of Islam. We here count the Ottoman Empire as our *Tenth Revolution*. But it is important that one mentions also the sudden rise of the Twelver Shi'ite–dominated Safavid Persian Dynasty, here noted as the *Eleventh Revolution*.

The *Twelfth Revolution* is one of gradual retreat of Ottoman power. At first, the Austrian and Russian Empires made territorial gains against the Ottomans in the seventeenth and eighteenth centuries. The British attempted to stem this retreat with the Palmerston reforms of the navy and military in the nineteenth century, and Imperial Germany made great strides in training graduates of Harbiye, the Ottoman military academy, under General von der Goltz. But the Ottomans were fighting an uphill battle against Western European advances in technology that were largely not available to the Ottomans. These advantages have been summarized in the excellent study by Daniel R. Headrick, *The Tools of Empire: Technology and European Imperialism in the Nineteenth Century* (New York, Oxford University Press, 1981).

Acknowledgments

Unlike our distinguished classmate at Harvard, Henry Kissinger, I did not fall under the shadow of William Yandell Elliott in Government but was influenced by Professor Myron Gilmore, senior tutor in the History Department, and Professors Frederick Merk and Arthur Schlesinger Jr. in American History.

Before graduation, I trained for two summers in the U.S. Marine Corps Reserve and received the second lieutenant bars upon graduation in 1950. Of profound influence on my future career, I took a job teaching biology at Robert College in Istanbul, Turkey. After three years of studying Turkish and Russian and traveling in the Mideast on holidays, I applied to the Institute of Islamic Studies, McGill University in Montreal. I graduated with an MA in 1954 and promptly joined the U.S. Army. At McGill, I had come under the influence of three scholars: Dr. Fazl ar-Rahman, an Islamic historian from Pakistan, Dr. Niyazi Berkes, a sociologist from Turkey, and Wilfred Cantwell Smith, the director.

The U.S. Army sent me to Germany because I spoke German. Meanwhile, I had resigned my commission in the Marine Corps. After two years in Germany, I had planned to teach Turkish at the University of Michigan and study for a PhD in economics. In actuality, I made the best decision of a lifetime by marrying my wife, a Michigan art student, and applying for a PhD in Ottoman history, at the School of Oriental and African Studies in the University of London. At Michigan, I had taken a rigorous course in Arabic taught by Dr. George Makdisi but came under the influence of economists in the Department of Economics, headed by Dr. Kenneth Boulding.

Spending four years at the University of London, 1957–1961, I had prepared a thesis under the guidance of Professor Bernard Lewis and the Reader, Vernon Parry, on the topic *Ottoman Imperialism during the Reformation: Europe and the Caucasus* (published by NYU Press, 1972) and took up residence at the University of Toronto with a wife and three children. Thereafter, we spent six challenging years in the University of Toronto under the influence of Professor Michael Wickens, an Arabist, and Professor Roger Savory, a Persianist. Finally, we spent almost thirty years at New York University as colleagues of Dr. Bayly Winder, Dean of the College of Arts and Science and Dr. Frank Peters, Department Chairman.

"12 Centuries of Muslim Revolutions and the Struggle for Identity against the Imperial Powers," was originally a course I first taught at New York University. I have consulted a number of scholars while completing this study. I mention here Dr. Halil Inalcik of Princeton University and Bilkent University in Ankara, Dr. Abbas Hamdani of the University of Wisconsin, Dr. Salah Al-Askari of New York University, Dr. Mounir Farah of the University of Arkansas, and Dr. Teresa Anthony of the University of Georgia. Any errors of fact or interpretation are, of course, my own. I would here also mention our printers, Mr. Roger Moylan and Cynthia Bissonette. They and their staff have made every effort to print an accurate manuscript.

In conclusion, I mention, first and foremost, the tireless contributions of my wife Cynthia, for the sleepless nights, the meager salaries and daily worries of marriage to an academic. The computer skills of our sons, Karl and Adam Kortepeter, and grandchildren, Alena Ragan and Sean Kortepeter, have been indispensable. Adam worked tirelessly on the index and did all the art work for the front cover. My daughter, Erica Kortepeter-Ragan, and my son, Mark Kortepeter, did extensive work on the entire manuscript. I would also like to mention the staff of Xlibris and its contact persons, Greg Griffen, Ann Famor, Emman Villaran, Sam Clarke, Rachelle Mosley and the excellent work of Erin Morrison editing the manuscript.

I. Pre-Islamic Arabia and the Prophet's Message

Professor Michael Marmura, early in his career at the University of Toronto, wrote an important essay entitled "The Quran and the Jahiliya Temper." Part of this essay I intend to paraphrase as an introduction to our theme: "Revolutions and Legitimacy in Islam." Dr. Marmura chose to depict the "Jahiliyah Temper" as expressed in the Arabic poetry of the pre-Islamic period. As the majority of these poets were either nomads or expressed the ideals and the aspirations of the Bedouin, the term *Jahiliyah* is used in a narrower sense than its use in the Quran. The Quran addressed the people of Mecca and Medinah, where the atmosphere of commerce predominated. The Bedouin are specifically mentioned and rather unfavorably in three suras of the Quran:

1) *Sura xlviii (al-Fath)*—in this surah, the Bedouin are admonished for not helping Muhammad in a campaign.
2) *Surah xlix (al-Hujurat)*—verse 14: the Bedouin say, "We have believed." But I (Muhammad) say, "Ye have not believed but (the Bedouin should) say rather, 'We have become Muslims,' for belief has not entered your hearts."
3) *Sura ix (at-Tawbah)*—verse 98: "The Bedouin are even stronger in unbelief and in hypocrisy and more apt not to know the limits of what Allah has sent down to His messenger. Allah is knowing, wise."

1

Marmura notes that this does not mean that the Quran is irrelevant to the Jahiliyah spirit. The difference lies in the subject matter. The Quran implicitly negates the Jahiliyah ideal, though it transmutes many of its moral values, which were the common values of all Arabs. But the Quran remains incompatible with the Jahiliyah Temper.

What Are the Distinctive Features of the Jahiliyah Temper?

1) *Particularism:* particularism is exhibited in the tribal spirit, *al-'Asabiyah,* and in the assertion of the individual. Marmura illustrates this feeling in the poetry of Bishr ibn Abi Khazm wherein blood kinship is all-important: "Ancient glory and renown undimmed forbid the sons of Khuzaimah to yield in nought." The poet Jarir also attacks his adversary, a man from the Banu Numayr with biting satire: "Cast down thine eyes for shame! For thou art from Numayr—no peer of Ka'ab nor yet Kilab. (*Kilab* means "dogs.")

2) *Blood relationships* are of vital importance in tribal affairs; hence, tribal genealogies are essential. If one is not in a blood feud with a sister tribe, then one practices *ta'assub,* or fanatical devotion to that sister tribe against an outsider.

3) *Self-assertion:* a deed of valor or generosity brings honor upon one's self and also on one's tribe. In the words of the famous poet 'Antarah:

   "Those who witnessed the battle will testify that I attend the combat but stand aloof from the looting."

   Marmura notes that this is an example of *'izzat al-nafs,* or self-respect, an example of *muru'ah* (of "manliness"), expressing the Jahiliyah moral ideal.

4) Other aspects of *Muru'ah,* or manliness, include being generous, protecting the weak and defying the strong, and behaving

justly. The defense of the weak is associated with the concept of *'istijarah*, the asking for neighborly protection.

The Bedouin also exhibit a very naturalistic attitude toward life. In the time of Jahiliyah, they believed in pagan gods, and some of those beliefs persisted in many superstitions. They believed in *jinn*, the malevolent creatures that could intervene in ordinary life. Even the poets were believed to be inspired by devils, or *shayatin*, because poetry tended to have a very secular outlook on life. The Arabs believed in fate, *ad-Dahr or al-Qadar*, not a passive surrender, but an acknowledgment of the unpredictable in nature. The poet Zuhayr wrote:

> *"Death is like a night-blind camel stumbling on; The smitten die but the others age and wax in weakness whom he passes by."*

There is an absence in the belief of an afterlife. The hedonism and pessimism of some poets lead them to indulgence in the pleasures of the senses, gambling, drinking, and womanizing. One needs only to refer to the *Rubaiyat* of the eleventh-century Persian poet Omar Khayyam to find this persistent trait of Islamic poets:

> "Here with a Loaf of Bread beneath the Bough, A Flask of Wine, A Book of Verse and Thou, Beside me singing in the Wilderness. And Wilderness is Paradise enow."
>
> —Fitzgerald Translation

The Prophet Muhammad, wherever possible, enriched the lives of Muslims by introducing them to the "Miracle of the Quran," the beautiful and often poetic nature of the Quran that inspired the creation of Islamic law, *the Shari'ah*. The Prophet also partially succeeded in deflecting the destructive blood feuds with the concept of *Dar al-Harb*, the external war against unbelievers. To deflect the Arabs from the tendency for tribal pride and particularism, he challenged them to join the super tribe of Muslims and also to remember the international community of believers. For their beliefs in *polydaemonism*, he introduced them to monotheism, but it is noteworthy that many of the Arab tribes were of Christian persuasion.

These concepts that Professor Marmura has summarized in his article were given further elaboration by Professors Philip K. Hitti of Princeton University and Professor Walid Khalidi in the revised edition of Hitti's monumental *History of the Arabs*.[5] One is thus forced to observe that without adequate reference to the Pre-Islamic history of the Arabian Peninsula, one would be at a loss to clarify later problems of revolution and legitimacy in the world of Islam.

Marmura and Hitti were not the only observers of the era before the Prophet Muhammed brought forth his message. It was Islam's first troubled and complex century that sowed the seeds of the following centuries. One may also note the very important article of Eric Wolf, "The Social Organization of Mecca and the Origins of Islam,"[6] where he states, "Our brief historical survey has shown that the tendencies which Muhammad brought to fruition were reaching their peak of development in pre-Islamic times." Wolf indicates that commercial development transformed urban settlements into class groupings that had previously depended on kinship. Centralization of worship of one deity, Allah, further enhanced trade and the disintegration of kinship structures. But often, the weakening of kinship structures led to conflict and the domination by the commercial elite. The religious revolution associated with Muhammad permitted the emergence of a rudimentary state structure and eliminated or weakened kinship ties and blood feuds. In their place emerged the armed forces of the faithful that included believers and nonbelievers. A rudimentary judicial system was started from the pronouncements of the Prophet governing al-Madinah, and both Muslims and non-Muslims were taxed on pre-Islamic models for the new goals. Unfortunately, the wealthy Quraish, especially the Umaiya, took over the state apparatus that Muhammad had created, rather than the armed brotherhood of Medina.

There is no question in the eyes of Muslims that the Prophet Muhammad had overthrown the old ruling elites, the merchant oligarchy of Mecca and Medina. Thus, we may recognize that the founding of Islam is indeed the *First Revolution* in Islam. At the same time, we must acknowledge that almost as soon as the Prophet died in AD 632, the old ruling families and especially the Umaiya family began once again to assert its influence. At first, Abu Bakr (632–634), the close friend of the Prophet, was appointed as the Prophet's successor in the leadership. In fact, the very term in Arabic for successor, *Al-Khalifah* (in English, *Caliph*, was adopted by succeeding leaders of the Islamic community: "The Successor of the Prophet of God." Upon the death of Abu Bakr, another close associate of the Prophet and a valued military leader, 'Umar ibn al-Khattab (634–644), took up the reigns of power. He is often likened to Moses as a distinguished patriarch of Islam.

II. The Rise of Shi'ite Opposition and Umayyad Consolidation

While most of the believers accepted the appointment of the first two caliphs, Abu Bakr and 'Umar, the acclamation of the third caliph, 'Uthman, from the most powerful clan in Mecca, al-'Umaiya, a clan that long had opposed the Prophet and the Muslims, brought forth a strong opposition party led by the Prophet's first cousin, Ali, son of the Prophet's uncle, Abu Talib. Ali was also married to Fatima, the only surviving daughter of the Prophet. Ali, after the death of his father, lived in Madinah with his cousin Muhammad. He was also one of the first to believe in the Prophet's message, as were Abu Bakr and 'Umar. Upon the Prophet's death, when Ali was about forty years old, there formed a political party known as the Party of Ali, or in Arabic, *Shi'at 'Ali*. While all inhabitants living in Mecca were deemed to belong to the Quraish tribe either by blood or by clientship, the Quraishis who followed the Prophet to al-Madinah in AD 622, called the year of the *hijra* or flight, were known as *muhajirun*, the immigrants. The residents of al-Madinah who soon accepted the Prophet's message were known as *al-ansar*, or the supporters.

The Party of Ali's supporters came to be known as Shi'ites (Ar., *Shi'at 'Ali*, the Party of Ali). They believed that only direct descendants of Muhammad's clan, the Hashemites, should lead the Islamic community. They deemed that Muhammad was a charismatic leader in the vein of Max Weber's classification of modes of authority (rational-legal, traditional, and charismatic) and that only members of the Hashemite

6

clan could receive the mantel of hereditary charisma. In other words, the Shi'ites made a case for hereditary succession.[7]

Even before Dr. Takim set forth the position of the Shi'ite ideology, he indicated, quoting Hamid Dabashi, how the Prophet's charismatic authority was dissipated during the era of the so-called rightly guided caliphs of Abu Bakr (632–634), 'Umar (634–644), 'Uthman (644–657), and 'Ali (656–661). Dabashi noted that the Prophet's authority became diffused into various subsections, the political (the caliphate, successors to Muhammad's leadership), the religious (the *ulama,'* Islamic jurists), the spiritual (Sufism, the mystical part of Islam), the legal (the *qadis*, Islamic judges), and the military (*umarā'*, known as amirs [commanders]). Thus, the so-called rightly guided caliphs actually reverted to pre-Islamic norms. Even the successors were limited to members of the Quraishi tribe and, to be sure, to the wealthiest members of that tribe; hence, the Umayyad Dynasty (AD 661–750) took charge of the caliphate.

It is well-known that 'Ali was implicated in the death of 'Uthman in AD 656, and thus, it comes as no surprise that 'Ali was assassinated on the steps of the Kufa mosque by a Kharijite supporter of 'Uthman in 661. This crisis in Islamic leadership was papered over during 'Ali's caliphate, but Mu'awiya, a cousin of 'Uthman and the appointed governor of Syria, took up the cause of 'Uthman's assassination and forced 'Ali into a series of serious military clashes. Mu'awiya not only had the support of the Kalb tribe in Syria, but many of these troops had been trained in the military arts and discipline of the former Byzantine legions. Obviously, the use of trained troops gave to the Ummayad cause a military advantage over the impetuous desert cavalry of 'Ali.

One of the most astute observers of changes in the Islamic polity in Umayyad times was Erich Pritsch.[8] Pritsch points out various important nuances of the Ummayads. When their rulers used the title *Khalifat ar-Rasul-Allah* (successor of God's envoy), it took on a connotation of *Vicarius Dei* (the Vicar of God), possibly reflecting Byzantine influence. The Umayyad rulers introduced hereditary rule, thus giving up the idea of election. An heir was usually designated by the reigning caliph. They considered themselves worldly rulers, *mulūk* (kings), and required an oath of allegiance (*Al-Baya*) to the designated heir.

Dr. Takim goes into much detail to describe how the Prophet's function of prophecy or revelation, a combination of the Quran and the *Sunna* or personal statements of the Prophet, was taken over by the 'ulama' for interpretation under the Umayyads. Thus, during the course of early Islamic history, the so-called Sunnite branch of the Muslims separated into four legitimate schools of law, depending on a conservative or liberal version of a school, known in Arabic as *mathhab, pl., muthahib (schools of law)*. Hence, the term *Sunni* or *Sunnite* was applied to the branch of Islam perpetrated by the Umayyads and the successor dynasty of the 'Abbasids. Initially, the interpretation of the *Sunna* (the sayings of the Prophet other than the Quran) was claimed by the scholars of Medina because most of the Sunna of the Prophet took place in Medina after the Hijra. The spokesman for their rigid interpretations (*mathhab*) was Malik bin Anas in his early treatise on Islamic law, the *Muwatta'*. His school of law was known as the *Maliki Mathhab*.

But the scholars of Kufa held to a variant view of authority. They believed that the authority for determining Islamic law derived from local reasoning rather than local practice. Abu Hanifa, the doyen of the Kufa point of view, believed that authority came from reasoning, that is *ra'y*. He felt that he must use his own powers of interpretation (*ijtihad*). It follows that his school of law was known as the *Hanafi Mathhab* and was deemed the most liberal of the *muthahib*. It was a popular doctrine in the "Ottoman Empire and the Moghul Empire" of India.[9]

Finally, early in 'Abbasid times (750–1220), Muhammad bin al-Idris al-Shafi' (d. 820) differed from the schools of Medina and Kufa. He insisted that other schools of law must show a clear link between reasoning and prophetic practice. They must derive opinion from prophetic Sunna. In short, they must rely on an accredited *Hadith* (eyewitness authenticated actions and conversations of the Prophet). Even the Sufis, in the eleventh century, introduced a new challenge to the de facto acceptance of the 'ulama' and the *faqihs'* as the interpreters of Islamic law. They based religious law on an esoteric interpretation of Islamic revelation deriving from Ibn Al-'Arabi, Al-Andalusi.[10] The Baghdad School of Law was known as the Shafi'i Mathhab and became most prevalent in North Africa.[11] But the most rigid and conservative of all the Sunni Schools of Law (*muthahib*) turned out to be the doctrines of Ahmad ibn Hanbal, a student of Al-Shaf'i in Baghdad, who served as a bulwark against the Mu'tazilites so popular under the rule of the Caliph Ma'mun (813–833). The *Musnad* in six volumes is ascribed to him, in the eighteenth century, by the Sheikh Ibn Al-Wahhab and has been spread by the rich dynasty of the Saudis through their *madrassas* (Islamic prep schools) serving the *Taliban* (lit., students) in Pakistan and Afghanistan.[12] They are known to follow the *Hadith* more strictly than other law schools.

III. The 'Abbasid Revolution

The new al-Shaf'i followers wished to make their doctrine dominant in the 'Abbasid Revolution, established in AD 750, but the Mu'tazilites appear to have dominated 'Abbasid thinking in the first decades. Under the Umayyads, the Islamic Empire had spread eastward through Persia to the Jaxarta (Amu Darya) River in central Asia and across North Africa westward, incorporating Egypt, Libya, Tunisia, Algeria, Morocco, and Al-Andalus or Islamic Spain. This rapid expansion may be followed in any standard text.[13] Even though the Ummayads had greatly refined their administration of such a vast empire by adding *Diwans* or centralized ministries to the system, it was inevitable that centrifugal forces and an archaic financial system could not check the tendency for far-off provinces to break away from central control. The 'Abbasid capital was moved from Damascus to the newly planned city of Baghdad; thus, the imperial traditions of Iran began to make their impression on the ruling elite.[14] Even the secretariat now was composed of many Persians who were trained in *Adab*, the sophisticated mores, tastes, and literature of the Persian elite, much less in the Islamic traditions of *'Ilm*, the knowledge of the holy scriptures, writings of the Arabs and their poetry.[15]

The 'Abbasid rulers no longer felt themselves limited to the worldliness of the Umayyad caliphs who managed the empire but left spiritual authority to the 'ulama'. The 'Abbasid caliphs removed themselves from the daily stress of administration, leaving the details to their *wazirs* and military leaders. They did, however, demand a presence in their capacity as lawgivers and spiritual leaders. They even promulgated or relied on customary laws (*Qanun*) to cover new situations that had arisen with the rapid expansion of territories. But the caliphs, unable to demand absolute obedience from such a far-flung empire, adapted a common expedient in the ninth century. They appointed provincial governors, the *amirs*, to rule in their stead, even giving up, in some cases, the rights of *Sikka wa Khutba*, the privilege of coining money and having themselves blessed in the Friday prayers. The first violation of the unity of the faithful, known as the ummah, occurred in Umayyad Spain, where the Umayyad offshoot declared themselves separate caliphs. Under Persian influence, the office of caliph no longer depended on the will of the people but on God's grace, legitimate only by divine charisma. If the divine charisma were lost, there now crept into the ideology that the caliph could be removed from power. The Kharijites, a group of warriors, had failed to support Caliph 'Ali bin Abi Talib in a fateful battle with Mu'awiya in AD 657 and were henceforth known as those who "had left the field."[16]

According to Shaban, the 'Abbasid Revolution began in Khorasan among the politically and economically exploited Shi'ites and Arab and Persian *mawali* (clients to Arab tribes) who resented being governed by the old Persian elite (the *Dihqans*). The *da'is* or agents among them asserted the legitimacy of the house of Hashim, the Prophet's own family. The Sunnites among the mawali supported Muhammad ibn Ali, the direct descendant of the Prophet's uncle, Al-Abbas, for the caliphate. To be sure, the Shi'ites also recognized the preeminence of the Hashemite clan, but they hoped to place in the caliphate a direct descendant of 'Ali and Fatima, son of the seventh descendant, Imam 'Isma'il. Both factions put their trust in Abu Muslim, the brilliant Khorasani Persian commander, who pushed their claims to the gates of Baghdad. Caliph Marwan II, the last Umayyad caliph, was defeated at the Zab River in AD 750, and the bloodbath of all Umayyads and their supporters began under Caliph Abu l'Abbas, As-Saffah (750–754), the Killer, and continued under his brother, Caliph Al-Mansur (754–775), the Victor, who actually completed the round city of Baghdad. Unfortunately, the

Shi'ite claims to an imamate died with Abu Muslim in AD 755. Al-Mansur moved the capital of the empire to Baghdad in 562.

One may continue to trace the destruction of the de facto unity of the caliphate from the brilliance of the court of Caliph Harun Ar-Rashid (786–809) to the ideological excursions of his son, the Caliph Al-Ma'mun (613–633), who favored the philosophic position of the Mu'tazilites, a movement wishing to introduce more rationality into Islamic law. By and large, the 'Abbasid caliphs generated their problems by remaining remote from daily decisions. Caliph Al-Mu'tasim (833–842), the third son of Harun Ar-Rashid to succeed him, had placed so many unruly and arrogant Turkish troops in his guard regiments that they disturbed the residents of Baghdad. Al-Mu'tasim consequently had to build the separate city of Samarra to house them. Without the street power of the Baghdadis, the caliphs soon became captives of their Turkish guard regiments.

IV. The Persian Amirates
(The Persian Intermezzo)

In the year AD 935, the *'amir al-'umara* (the commander of the armed guard), Muhammad ibn Ra'iq, took control of the administration from the caliph and his wazir. Now only the functions of the spiritual leadership (the imamate) and the symbols of sovereignty were left to the actual Caliph Ar-Radi (934–940). These events ushered in the historic events known as the Era of the Amirates. We have already alluded to this era above. The expanse of the empire was so great, a region equivalent to the borders of France to the heart of India, that no military force could be dispatched quickly enough from Baghdad to protect the borderlands. Thus, the reigning caliph had to assert control indirectly through his appointment of semi-independent provincial governors (the amirs). Not surprising, one begins to hear from Persia and central Asia of the semiautonomous principalities of the Samanids and the Saffarids and from North Africa of the Idrisids, the Aghlabids, and the Tulunids. Closer to Baghdad, the 'Abbasids continued their war with Byzantium, but by the middle of the tenth century, the Buwayhids had taken over the Baghdad administration. Originally, the Buwayhids had come from Daylam in Northern Iran. Ali ibn Buyah and his brothers, Hasan and Ahmad, had initially defeated the caliph's Turkish General Yaqut in 934. Thereafter, they gave lip service to the powers of the 'Abbasid caliphs, but they ran their expanding conquests with their Daylam infantry and Turkish cavalry. To maintain the loyalty of their troops, they allotted tracts of land known as *iqta'* to them as a means of gaining funds for the warriors but also paying a tax to the state. The Buyids (Buwayhids) initially professed Zaydi or Fiver Shi'ism but later chose Twelver Shi'ism in line with many of their subjects. The numbers associated with the belief systems of the Shi'ites correspond to the successors to Ali. The Buwayhids, sometimes identified as Buyids, proved to be quite tolerant of other religious ideologies. Their control gradually diminished, and they were replaced by the Seljuk Turks under Tughrul, who conquered them in AD 1055. Scholars of Arabic literature will remember the story of the clash between the Buwayhid, Saif ad-Dawla, in Aleppo, and the famous poet, Al-Mutanabbi. Because of his insults to the amir, 'Saif ad-Dawla decided to execute the poet. The poet fled Aleppo but was later recognized as he returned from Egypt to Baghdad. His companions said to him, "Weren't you the poet who penned the phrase *'Al-Khaylu, wa'l Leylu wa'l Rimhu ta'rafuni, Wa al-Sayfu, W'al-Qalamu, wa'l Qurtas*?" (The horse, the night, and the spear know me and also the sword, the pen, and the parchment.) And the poet said, "Indeed, I am that poet!" Then his companions said, "Please join with us to fight the amir." So Al-Mutannabi joined the ruffians to defend his poetry and manhood and was killed in 965.[17]

V. Isma'ili Doctrine and the Qarmatian and Fatimid Revolutions

Who were the Isma'ilis, and how did they become such a threat to the 'Abbasid concepts of the unity of Islam? The Isma'ilis, the militant wing of Sevener Shi'ism, had shared in the political goals of Abu Muslim at the time he was executed by the Caliph Mansur in AD 755. Abu Muslim had defeated the Umayyad forces in Khorasan by gaining the support of both the Sunni and Shi'i, who were disgruntled and disenfranchised *Mawali* (clients to Arab tribes). The Sunnis had sought legitimacy to succeed the Umayyads as the 'Abbasids were direct descendants of 'Abbas, the Prophet's Hashemite uncle. The Shi'ites sought the legitimacy to establish an imamate through a direct descendant of 'Ali, who had married the Prophet's daughter, Fatima.[18] They believed that the "Prophetic Spark" lay with Muhammad bin Isma'il, the son of Ja'far al-Sadiq, who would be Al-Mahdi, the savior who would bring justice and prosperity to all believing Muslims. The problem was that Ja'far had four sons: 'Abdallah al-Aftah, Isma'il, Musa al-Kazim, and Muhammad. Each of his sons attracted followers from 'Abdallah al-Aftah. After five generations, there developed the Fatimid caliphate beginning with *Ubaydallah*. From Isma'il, there developed the Isma'ili claim to be the authentic line of the Seventh Imam. From Musa al-Kazim's descendants, there developed the Ithna 'Ashari, the Twelver Shi'ites, the foundation of the beliefs of the Iranians in the sixteenth century.

But the father of Abbas Hamdani, Husayn Hamdani, a contemperaneous scholar, published for the first time a document that has changed the entire interpretation of the origins of the Isma'ilis.[19] In summary, after five generations of bickering about who inherited the "Prophetic Spark," 'Abdallah al-Mahdi married the daughter of Muhammad ibn Ahmad as the only way to solve the two claimants to the true imamate, deriving from the last fully recognized imam, Ja'far al-Sadiq and his two sons, claiming the imamate, Abdallah al-Aftah and Isma'il. Of course, there were many descendants of both lines before 'Abdallah al-Mahdi wrote his tract and married the last of the line, the daughter of Muhammad ibn Ahmad.[20]

As the 'Abbasids began to pry into the affairs of the Isma'ilis, the Isma'ilis took their organization underground only to reappear as a vibrant political movement at the end of the ninth century. The 'Abbasids, in the years 869 through 883, had to face another serious revolt of black slaves who had been drafted to work on irrigation ditches in the soil of the rich soil of the Sawad district near Basra. This was known as the Zanj Revolt. The Zanj developed a fierce fighting force that often struck 'Abbasid troops by night. Taking advantage of this distraction in the empire, an Isma'ili base was set up in Yemen by the da'i (propaganda agent) Ibn Hawshab Mansur al-Yamani (d. 914).[21] In this essay, I often quote from Professor Abbas Hamdani, the doyen of Isma'ili studies, because he has given us a succinct summary of Isma'ili doctrine that is the precursor of the Qarmatian and Fatimid Revolutions. It is to be remembered that Isma'ili doctrine supports the Shi'ite position of the son of Ja'far al-Sadiq, either Isma'il or his brother, Abdallah al-Aftah, as the Seventh Imam, whom Isma'ilis believe is in occultation, that is hidden, but who will return as the *Mahdi*, the savior of all believers. This perception of a "hidden Imam" becomes the standard belief of all Shi'ites whomever imam one chooses to follow. "The imam is in hiding to avoid being killed but will emerge as the Messiah or *Mahdi* to help his followers at the appointed time."

Once the 'Abbasids had gained full power, they had abandoned their messianic doctrines in favor of their military, cultural, and economic prowess, but the Isma'ilis further developed the concept of *Da'wa* (invitation or message) of the coming of the Mahdi, and the *da'is* remain active into Fatimid times. They developed their own theory of creation: the Prophets, Adam, Noah, Abraham, David, Moses, Jesus, and Mohammad were deemed sacred, but Mohammad was considered the "Seal of the Prophets." To quote Professor Hamdani, "Now a new cycle, characteristically Shi'i, is grafted on to the previous development—that of the imamate in the family of Ali and Fatima. This line of imams, father to son, comes down to the end of the Umayyad period with Isma'il, the son of Imam Ja'far al-Sadiq (Ar., al-Sadiq, The Truthful). Through this process runs the divine light (*Nur Ilahi*) as the source of the process of the Creator Himself." Thus, the designated imam is infallible (*Masum*).[22]

Professor Hamdani also deals with the important question of to what extent the Isma'ili doctrines were spread through the guilds or trade organizations. Quoting from the *Rasa'il Ikhwan al-Safa (The Letters of the Brethren of Purity)*, "an early Isma'ili work written between AD 873 and 909," Professor Hamdani directs our attention to two chapters on professions and crafts. From these chapters, he concludes that by the ninth century, professional organizations had developed in the Muslim cities to such an extent that governments became fearful that these groups would become centers of sedition. Hamdani points to the regulations of the *Hisba* (market rules on proper practices) and the market master, the *muhtasib*. The fact that the *Rasa'il* mentions further that the Isma'ilis had agents in the various trades but that they urged tolerance of all doctrines, Proessor Hamdani points to the early stages of this major social movement. It is important to note also that the *Rasa'il* makes a particular appeal to the young guild members. The foregoing notes only serve to emphasize the importance of the Hamdani family in our understanding of Isma'ili doctrines and the Qarmatian and Fatimid Revolutions.

We must here note also the tremendous contribution to Isma'ili studies of Professor Bernard Lewis. He does not refer to his early work on the Isma'ili assassins, *The Origins of Isma'ilism* (Cambridge, 1940), but in his brief essay on "An Interpretation of Fatimid History," Professor Lewis indicates his mastery of Fatimid history and emphasizes the role of missionary work under the chief missionary (the *Da'i 'l Du'at*) and the ultimate failure of the Fatimid mission because the Seljuk Turks reenforced the Sunni position of the 'Abbasid caliphs and other great changes in the struggle for legitimacy in Islam.[23]

The Qarmatian Revolution was a true revolution in the sense that it overthrew elements of the preceding 'Abbasid regime and put in their place an entirely new organization and ideology. The Qarmatians worked from a base in Syria but eventually established a firm footing on the Persian Gulf island of Bahrain. A major peasant uprising took place in the town of Wasit in 890, led by Hamdan Qarmat. His followers did not accept the legitimacy of Ubaydullah's claims to being the Mahdi in North Africa, preferring the hidden Seventh Imam, Muhammad bin Isma'il. And thus, Ubaydullah became the founder of the Fatimid claims.

The Qarmatians once again revolted in A. D. 897 near Kufa, and in 900, in a nearby town, they burned the houses of the inhabitants and killed many occupants. Not unlike the doctrines of the Zanj, they believed that they should inherit the possessions of their victims. Thereafter, they were expected to pool all their possessions in order that their leaders could redistribute all possessions equally. The peasant armies were no match for the trained forces of the 'Abbasids, but some *da'is* among the Bedouin, appealing to their desire for booty and their belief in the supernatural, converted them to Isma'ili doctrine. They occupied Damascus for a time, pillaged Homs, but were defeated by Aleppo townsmen and 'Abbasid forces in 903. To be sure, what stymied the peasant revolts in Syria and Iraq was the inclusion of the Bedouin among the Isma'ilis, as the Bedouin were the enemy of all peasant communities. Realizing that the Isma'ili movement drew upon the resentment of the poorer classes, peasants, artisans, and common laborers, the Turkish generals of the 'Abbasids hesitated to wipe out whole communities because the economy relied on these villagers. The 'Abbasids naturally were alarmed when they learned how widespread the Isma'ili doctrines had grown. The founder of the movement, al-Ahwazi, known as a pious and simple man, had instructed Hamdan Qarmati in his doctrine of justice and equality of all believers. Henceforth, these attributes were imputed to Hamdan Qarmati, and the Qarmatian movement adopted his name. One of the leading principles of the Qarmatians was illustrated by the *Ulfah*. These were villages restructured by Qarmat into peasant communes. This model appealed to the poorer classes, and to some extent, the leadership was able to apply these principles to Bahrain and surrounding communities. The Persian, Abu Sa'id Hasan bin Bahram al-Jannabi, was sent by Qarmat in 866 to Bahrain where he soon won over the entire island to his leadership and made al-Ahsa his capital. Upon his murder in 914, he was succeeded by his son Sa'id. To take care of the poor remained a basic principle of the state. The six sons of al-Jannabi sat on a large *divan* (basically a raised bench upon which one could sit cross-legged), and opposite them on another *divan* sat their six ministers. In this manner, they guided an elemental democracy. There is no doubt, however, that the merchant class was favored by the governing council, and these merchants reputedly controlled the trade routes of southern Iraq.[24]

The Fatimids, a dynasty founded also with the ideology of the Isma'ilis, came into prominence in the history of North Africa and Egypt when a certain Ubayd Allah (909–934) or Ubaydullah claimed that he was the *Mahdi* descending from the Shi'ite line of Ali and Fatima. His claim has received much scrutiny equally by Muslim, European, and American scholars. For sure, his genealogy has remained quite obscure. There is also the question of whom might be the real *Mahdi*, as the second Fatimid caliph, Muhammad Abu l'-Kasim al-Kaim bi-Amr Allah (934–936), had the right characteristics and also may not have been the son of Ubayd Allah! The 'Abbasids, of course, did all in their power to discredit another rival to their legitimacy (not forgetting the Umayyad claims in Al-Andalus). Yet two Sunni historians, al-Makrizi and Ibn Khaldun, accepted the claims of the Fatimids.[25]

The first four Fatimid caliphs, Ubayd Allah, al-Kaim, al-Mansur, and al-Mu'izz, lived in Tunis (Ifrikiya). Only al-Mu'izz (953–975) was able to move to Fustat (Old Cairo) 1 July, 969 when his general, Jawhar of Sicilian or Slav origin, had defeated the surviving Aghlabid forces, the amirs who had controlled Cairo for a generation. In North Africa, the Fatimids had much trouble with Maliki Sunnis and Kharijites and also warring Berber tribes. Jawhar, the general, who commanded mostly Berber troops, was able to bring all Western African Muslims under Fatimid control. Even Mecca and Medina came under Fatimid control, but Syria gave the Fatimids much difficulty.

Professor Sumaiya Hamdani has published a detailed study in her *Between Revolution and State: The Path to Fatimid Statehood Concerning the Works of Qadi Nu'man.* Qadi Nu'man worked closely with the Fatimid caliphs to make the Isma'ili doctrines acceptable to the large Sunni population of North Africa and Egypt. Qadi Nu'man held the important post of *Qadi al-Qudat* (head judge of all Fatimid territories) for the first four caliphs until his death in 974, one year after al-Mu'izz entered Al-Fustat. His ideological contribution was to transform the esoteric (*batini*)doctrines of the Isma'ilis into doctrines of public discourse (*zahiri*) in a manner acceptable to the majority Sunnis.[26]

During Fatimid times, the amirs or caliphs could not neglect their navy because former Aghlabid amirs had controlled the island of Sicily. The Fatimids also had elaborate relations with the Byzantine emperors and a more troubled relationship with their fellow Isma'ilis in Bahrain. In the end, the Fatimid caliphs did not have the strength to deal with the Crusaders from Europe and the rising power of the Seljuk Turks. In the era of Caliph al-Mustansir (1036–1094), the caliph was obliged to melt down his gold and silver household treasures to pay his revolting Turkish troops. In 1070, the Fatimids, to gain Sunni help, were obliged once again to recognize the overlordship of the 'Abbasid caliph in Baghdad. By the later period of Mustansir's reign, he had to recognize a *wazir*, or deputy to the caliph, "the vezier of the pen and the sword." The dynasty came to an end when the Ayyubid Dynasty under Salah ed-Din defeated the last wazir.[27]

The Ayyubids were essentially a Kurdish dynasty that had received its initial appointments from Alp Arslan, the Seljuk ruler in the mid-eleventh century. The Seljuks had conquered Baghdad in 1055. When the Great Seljuks lost control of the central lands of Islam, shortly after the death of Sultan Malikshah (d. 1092), there followed a period in which "*atabegs*" (father amirs) took administrative control of various provinces formerly controlled by the strong Seljuk Sultans. The atabeg

Zanki, the Turkish master of Mosul and Aleppo in 1138, systematically defeated the Kurds and then recruited them into his army, giving them '*iqtas* or land grants to sustain them as a military force. Zanki's son, Nur ed-Din, favored Ayyub and sent him to conquer Egypt. Ayyub died a few weeks later in 1169 but was quickly replaced by his nephew, Salah ed-Din (Saladin in European sources), the actual founder of the dynasty, who defeated the Crusade of the Emperors (1189–1192), led by the three greatest European monarchs of the day: Frederick Barbarossa, Holy Roman emperor (who drowned en route), King Richard I of England, and King Philip II of France. Only King Richard remained to negotiate a truce with Salah ed-Din in 1191, marrying his sister, Joanna, to Salah ed-Din's brother, who then was appointed governor of Jerusalem.[28]

VI. Al-Andalus (Islamic Spain)

Musa ibn Nusayr, Umayyad governor of North Africa, was appointed about A.D. 700 by the Umayyad caliph, 'Abd al-Malik (685–705). He drove the Byzantine remnants out of North Africa from Carthage to the Atlantic Ocean with the exception of Count Julian of Ceuta, who had sided with the Muslims. Musa, though containing many Arabs in his retinue, relied mostly on Berber tribesmen and sent a small expeditionary force toward the Rock of Gibraltar under Tarif, who landed on the peninsula that later bore his name. This successful incursion in July 710 was followed in the spring of AD 711 by a large force of twelve thousand Berbers under the leadership of Tariq ibn Ziyad, a freedman and a lieutenant of Musa. Tariq gave his name to Gibraltar, which was later westernized from the Arabic "*Jabal Tariq*" (Tariq's Mountain [i.e., Gibraltar]). Musa and the Berber army were bent on acquiring booty when they learned, presumably from Count Julian, of the strife in the Visigothic Kingdom in the Iberian Peninsula over the succession to the Visigothic crown. In fact, Ceuta became the staging area for Tariq, and Count Julian, probably under duress, was rumored to have supplied the vessels for the crossing to Gibraltar, being some thirteen miles away. At the mouth of the Barbata River, Tariq met the new Visigothic King Roderick, who had a force of twenty-five thousand. In spite of his large army, Roderick was defeated by the Muslims, owing to the treachery of Witiza's brother, Bishop Opas, because Roderick had removed the son of Witiza, the former king, from his rightful succession. Tariq then led his main force toward Toledo, the capital of Al-Andalus, with detachments capturing Archidona, Elvira, and Cordoba. Seville was initially avoided because it was strongly fortified. Toledo fell to Tariq with the aid of Jewish residents who had been maltreated by the Visigothic government. The city of Ejiha proved to be Tariq's toughest siege.[29]

The unexpected success of Tariq ibn-Ziyad, who now held sway over half of the Iberian Peninsula, surprised Musa ibn-Nusayr and aroused his jealousy. Musa crossed over to Al-Andalus in June 712 with ten thousand Arabs, mostly from Syria. He now conquered cities that Tariq had passed over because of their strong defenses such as Seville, the intellectual center and former capital of the Romans. Merida fell in June of 713. Near Toledo, Musa met Tariq and placed him in chains and whipped him for insubordination. Meanwhile, Musa's force, combined with the Berbers, continued the campaign to Saragossa and into the highlands of Aragon, Leon, Asturias, and Galicia. Now the Caliph Al-Walid (705–715) became upset with Musa, charging him with insubordination, the same charge as with Tariq ibn-Ziyad. These Arab leaders were a jealous lot! The Caliph Al-Walid ordered Musa to return to Damascus, the seat then of Umayyad power. Musa eventually succeeded in buying the caliph's favor with a large retinue of slaves, four hundred Visigothic princes, and tons of booty. Years passed as this retinue proceeded across North Africa, and meanwhile, the Caliph Al-Walid became ill. His brother, Caliph Sulayman, and successor (715–717) wished to delay the entrance of this famous procession until his installation as caliph, but Caliph Al-Walid received the retinue in February 715, in the courtyard of the magnificent Umayyad Mosque. But Caliph Sulayman tortured Musa, confiscated his property, and removed him from all authority. The chronicals describe him as dying as a beggar.[30]

Hitti gives a plausible explanation to the Muslim conquest of the Iberian Peninsula. He contends that the Visigoths had to fight other Germanic tribes to gain the peninsula such as the Suevi and the Vandals, and even when they arrived in the fifth century, they were following the Arian form of Christianity; hence, they did not bond well with the still extant Spanish-Roman population. After they established political dominance, they soon accepted Roman Catholicism, thus blending more easily with the Hispano-Romans, whether their subjects were slaves or freedmen. As most of the Goths had become territorial lords by the end of the sixth century and as the number of serfs and slaves among the Spanish had swollen, as well as the persecuted Jews, who were pressured to become Christians in a law of 612, it is no wonder that the Muslims often put Jews in control of captured cities. King Roderick's usurpation of the throne, mentioned above, had thrown the government into disarray just when Tariq ibn-Ziyad had invaded. With the fall of Saragossa, there remained only the Pyrenees as a barrier for the invasion of France. Once again, the lure of rich booty drew Muslim leaders such as al-Hurr 'Abd ar-Rahman al-Thaqafi to cross the mountains into France about AD 718. His successor, al-Samh ibn Malik al-Thaqafi, learned of the dissension between the Merovingian court and the dukes of Aquitaine and invaded in 720. He set up a large military depot in Narbonne and attacked Aquitaine in the following year only to suffer martyrdom.[31]

It was between Tours and Poitiers in October 732 that 'Abd ur-Rahman ibn 'Abdullah al-Ghafiqi, governor of Al-Andalus, met Charles Martel, mayor of the palace of the French Merovingian court, whom the Duke Eudes of Aquitaine had asked for aid. After seven days, the light cavalry of the Muslims failed against Frankish squares of foot soldiers, and when 'Abd ur-Rahman died, the Muslims retreated to the Pyrenees. Thenceforth, until 'Abd ar-Rahman ibn Mu'awiyah, grandson of Caliph Hisham, the tenth caliph of the Umayyads, escaped the bloodbath of the Umayyads in 750 and appeared in Al-Andalus to take up the factional strife between northern Arabs, the Mudarites, and the southern Arabs, the Yemenites, a struggle that almost destroyed Arab power in Al-Andalus. The Yemenites tended to follow Shi'ite doctrine, while the Mudarites remained strictly orthodox, which is Sunni. To this strife was also added the strife between Berbers and Arabs.[32]

'Abd ar-Rahman of the Umayyads barely escaped with his life in Syria and Palestine when the 'Abbasid Dynasty took control of Damascus, and but for his faithful and savvy freedman, Badr, would have surely perished. They made their way across North Africa with the aid of friendly tribes and ample disguises, reaching Ceuta and Berber relatives of Badr in 755. Badr crossed the straits and negotiated with Syrian troops from Damascus and Qinnasrin, and they welcomed the chance to unite under the banner of a genuine Umayyad. Even the Yamanites buried the hatchet because they despised Yusuf, the current governor of Al-Andalus. As 'Abd ar-Rahman moved northward, he received the allegiance of the fortified towns held, for the most part, by Syrian troops. On 14 May 756, the armies of Andalus Governor Yusuf and 'Abd ar-Rahman of the Banu Umayyad met on the banks of the Guadalquivir River near Cordoba. The Umayyads won the day with a banner of a green turban held on a spear devised by the Yamanite leader of Seville, but the looting of the capital city of Cordoba was only partially averted. Yusuf, the governor, fled northward and continued to foment resistance until the Governor Yusuf was beheaded near Toledo. Toledo did not fall to 'Abd ur-Rahman until 764. The Berbers revolted because they resented the Syrian Arabs taking most of the choice lands for their estates. Even Badr, who had helped 'Abd ur-Rahman escape from the 'Abbasids, lost his property and was banished to a border town. The 'Abbasid caliph, Al-Mansur (754–775), appointed his own governor of Al-Andalus, al-'Ala' ibn-Mughith, but the appointee was soon decapitated, and his head was wrapped in camphor and a black flag, a symbol of revolt, and returned to the caliph.[33]

Before his death in 788, the Amir 'Abd ar-Rahman I also might have faced Charlemagne of France. Evidently, there is evidence that upon Charlemagne's invasion of Al-Andalus in 778, Charlemagne was acting in alliance with the 'Abbasid Caliph Al-Mahdi (775–785) but was locally invited by the Arab governor of Barcelona, who represented a number of Arab leaders opposing 'Abd ur-Rahman. Charlemagne advanced as far as Saragossa but was barred from the city. He then returned to France through the Pyrenees, losing many men and much baggage to the Basques. It was in this retreat that the hero, Roland, lost his life and was eulogized in the famous ballad of French literature, *Chanson de Roland*.[34]

To protect his own interests, 'Abd ur-Rahman I developed a well-trained army of forty thousand Berbers. He discontinued the *khutbah*, the ritual prayer in honor of the 'Abbasid caliph in 757, but much later, 'Abd ur-Rahman III assumed the title of caliph in 929. Until that time, rulers in Spain used the title *amir* (roughly commander or governor). Apart from building his own estate, *Munyat al-Rusafah*, outside Cordoba, 'Abd ur-Rahman I is noted for rebuilding the Great Mosque of Cordoba and bringing an aqueduct to the city. Upon his subjects fell the usual Islamic tax system: the poll tax or *jizya* on Christians and Jews could be heavy and induce them to consider becoming converts to Islam as in other Muslim states; women and children and the infirm were not taxed. The *kharaj* (or land tax) amounted to about 25 % of the harvest and was payable no matter what status the landowner claimed. Many city-dwelling Christians were attracted to Islam, regardless of motive, and they were known as *Muwalladun* to the Arabs and in Spanish, *Muladies*. This complex mixture of peoples, Arab and Syrian, Berbers and Arabs, Christians and new converts to Islam, gave ever-increasing complexity to governing Islamic Spain. It was these complex entities and the new converts that rebelled against the state. The converts to Islam were drawn largely from serfs, slaves, and freedmen, and consequently, the Arabs, as a whole, treated them as inferior even though the poorer classes quickly became the majority in most cities. Eventually, the social strife of Arabs and Berbers and Arabs and *Muwalladun* destroyed Islamic Spain.[35]

During the leadership in Cordoba of the next amir, Hisham I (788–796), as he was pious and scholarly, he passed through a relatively peaceful era, but his successor, Amir Al-Hakam I (796–822), was homosexual and addicted to wine and the chase. His habits and his guard regiment, mainly of blacks who spoke no Arabic, aroused the ire of the neo-Arabs living in the poor district of al-Rabad in Southern Cordoba. These inhabitants came under the leadership of a Berber holy man who fostered a revolt. The amir retaliated by razing the district, impaling many leaders, and driving the rest into Fez in Morocco and into Alexandria, Egypt. Amir Al-Hakam also faced chronic revolts of Christians in Toledo and consequently appointed Amrus ibn-Yusuf, a neo-Arab, to be Toledo's governor in AD 807. On the occasion of the visit to Toledo of the fourteen-year-old crown prince, 'Abd ar-Rahman,

Amrus ibn Yusuf invited the dignitaries of Toledo to a banquet. Most conveniently, a trench had been dug to supply clay for Amrus's new castle. As each guest arrived, he was killed by an executioner, and his body was thrown into the trench. After this slaughter of the trench, Toledo remained quiet for some years. When 'Abd ar-Rahman II (822–852) took over the amirate, he was greatly influenced by his favorite wife, Tarub, and also her favorite eunuch, a Spaniard named Nasr, who became royal chamberlain. Finally, the amir was influenced by a Berber *faqih* (an expert in jurisprudence), Yahya ibn Yahya, and a Persian singer, Ziryab. Yahya ibn Yahya turned out to be the leader of the revolt in al-Rabad in the days of Al-Hakam, the amir's father. Yahya had been a student of the famous Malik ibn-Anas in Baghdad, and as a result, Yahya had introduced Al-Andalus to the Maliki School of Islamic law. Ziryab, the Persian, reputedly knew ten thousand songs but also was well-versed in geography and astronomy. He was the favorite of the amir and also became the leader of good taste in the realm. The native Christians of Cordoba began to adapt Arab ways and speech to such an extent that they came to be known as *Mozarabs*, the popular word for the Arabic *Musta'rib* (he who adopts the Arabic language and customs). Bishop John, bishop of Seville, is said to have made an Arabic translation of the Bible about AD 724 for the sake of Arabized Christians and the Moors of North Africa.[36]

As a means of stopping mass conversions to Islam, a priest named Eulogius started a movement publicly to revile Muslims and the Prophet Muhammad. This movement took place toward the end of 'Abd ur-Rahman II's amirate. As a result of this negative movement, some forty-four martyrs, men and women, were executed. The movement was only stopped when Muhammad (852–886), one of 'Abd ur-Rahman I's forty-five sons, assumed leadership of the amirate. 'Abd ur-Rahman II almost lost his life, owing to the treachery of his wife, Tarub, and the trusted eunuch, Nasr, over the succession of Crown Prince Muhammad, who was borne to a Spanish wife. This type of incident in Islamic history frequently has played out over the rivalry of multiple wives who vie for the designation of their son as heir apparent or crown prince. When Muhammad I became amir, he soon put to death Eulogius, the prime instigator of the movement called the holy death, even after Eulogius had become bishop of Cordoba. But the Amir Muhammad I and his two sons, his successors, al-Munthir (886–888) and 'Abdullah (888–912), faced a number of rebellions by *Muwallatun, Mozarabs*, and Christian kings wishing to drive the Muslims and their followers out of Spain. The amirs of Islamic Spain following 'Abd ur-Rahman I were deeply in need of a strong national leader because the commanders of many major cities were Muslim but often made alliances with Christian kings with little regard for the survival of Islam.[37]

By the accession of 'Abd ur-Rahman III (912–929 amir, 929–961 caliph), the Muslim amirs controlled only Cordoba and its suburbs. Slowly, the new amir took back the lost provinces and cities of Islamic Spain--Ecija (912), Seville (913), and Regio, but only after the death of the Regio bandit/hero ibn Hafsun (917). The city of Toledo (932) capitulated after famine and a heavy siege. External enemies of Al-Andalus included the newly organized Shi'ite Fatimids of Egypt and North Africa and the Christian kings of Leon and Castille in the North. Also, Navarre and Aragon were beginning to form strong rival state systems. Now Islamic Spain was consolidated under a wise autocratic leader. 'Abd ur-Rahman III realized quite soon, even though at his accession in 912 he was only twenty-three years old, that North Africa was so close that its control was necessary. By 917 or 918, Morocco recognized his suzerainty, and he took possession of Ceuta in 931. Improving his navy, he was able to dispute with the Fatimids the control of the Western Mediterranean. His fleet in 956 heavily raided the African coast in retaliation for a previous raid on Islamic Spain by Sicilians directed by the Fatimids. After several raids on Islamic Spain by the kingdoms of Leon and Navarre, 'Abd ur-Rahman did battle with King Ordono II of Leon and Sancho the Great of Navarre in the Val de Junqueras (Valley of Reeds), defeating them decisively, then four years later demolished Pampeluna, the capital of Navarre. After pacifying the lands of his principal enemies, 'Abd ur-Rahman III declared himself caliph on 16 January 929, using the title *al-khalifah al-nasir li-din Allah* (victorious caliph for the religion of Allah) and the time-honored *amir al-mu'minin* (commander of the believers). The caliph felt it was his religious duty to fight the Christian domains to the north, but he became overconfident and was decisively defeated at Alhandega (Arabic *al-Handaq* = the Moat), just south of Salamanca, by Ramiro II of Leon and Queen Tota, regent of Navarre and the widow of Sancho the Great. By a turn of fate, Queen Tota showed up in Cordoba for a royal visit with her grandson, Sancho the Fat, and asked the Jewish court physician, Hasday ben-Shaprut, to cure her son's obesity, which he did over time. Moreover, they sought the caliph's help to restore Sancho the Fat to his kingdom. This happy outcome was accomplished in 960.[38]

Caliph 'Abd ur-Rahman III had created a brilliant court during his almost fifty years in power. Envoys from most rulers—Byzantium, Germany, Italy, and France and others—were represented at court. To extend hospitality to hosts of visitors, the caliph started building a palace in 936 called Zahra', inspired by a slave of the same name. Cordoba had a half million residents, seven hundred mosques, and three hundred public baths. At Zahra', the caliph hired 3,750 Slav troops as bodyguards and to head his army. These troops were actually *Mamluks* (lit., belonging to the sovereign), basically Europeans chosen to reduce the power of the old Arab aristocracy in the military, but for the most part, these Europeans were Arabized (i.e., spoke Arabic). The royal revenue at this time was estimated at 6,245,000 dinars that was divided three ways: $1/_3$ to the military, $1/_3$ for public works, and $1/_3$ to be held in reserve. We can imagine how the sovereign demanded dinars for his privy purse! The caliph died at the age of seventy-three years (961). His successor, al-Hakam II (961–976), and later, the dictatorship of al-Hajib al-Mansur (977–1002) maintained the system and gained international respect.[39]

The government of the Western caliphate functioned like its Eastern counterpart. For a time, however, there existed simultaneously three caliphs: the 'Abbasid caliph in Baghdad, the Fatimid caliph in Cairo, and the caliph in Cordoba. If there was a *hajib* (chamberlain), he functioned above the *vizirs* (commanders). Following the *vizirs* were the *kuttab* (scribes), and with the vizirs, they functioned as an advisory ruling body, known as the *Diwan* (they sat cross-legged on a dias). The important cities received *walis*, or governors. Mostly, the

judiciary was in the hands of *qadis*, or the *Qadi al-Qudah*, the chief
judge in Cordoba. The *Sahib al-Shurtah* heard police cases, and the
Sahib al-Muzalim heard cases against government officials. Finally, the
market master and maintainer of *Hisb*, or proper behavior, fell to the
muhtasib. The city possessed 130,000 homes, 21 suburbs, 70 libraries,
and numerous bookshops, palaces, and mosques, and the streets were
paved and well lit at night. Quite a contrast to the "barbarian" Christian
cities of northern Europe! The state mainly collected import and export
taxes for its income. Industries in tanning, weaving, brass making, and
glassmaking thrived, and they taught other peoples these skills. The
peasantry raised all manner of fruits and vegetables, and pottery and
mining also brought wealth to the state. The *dinar* represented wealth in
gold, and the *dirham* for silver. Moorish gardens took hold as models of
formal gardens. Al-Hakam II established 27 free schools and patronized
richly the arts and scholarship. The University in Cordoba preceded
the Nizamiyya of Baghdad (eleventh century) and Al-Azhar (the tenth
century) in Cairo. The royal library was said to house 400,000 books
and manuscripts. The government also ran a postal service. These years
were the glory days of Islamic Spain. It is also very interesting that
Caliph 'Abd ur-Rahman III and Caliph Al-Hakam II were very much
interested in what was happening intellectually in Baghdad, a Sunni
stronghold, and also Cairo and Qayrawan of the Fatimids.[40]

By 1031, any order and discipline in Islamic Spain began to fall
apart. Thirty major cities now were ruled by independent amirs. In the
same year, a council of ministers, who basically only controlled Cordoba,
voted to abolish the caliphate. This disintegration of Islamic Spain
became known as the era of the "party kings" (Sp., *reyes de taifas*; Ar.,
Muluk at-Tawa'if). The obvious reason for this debacle was particularism,
and even the mountainous landscape encouraged isolation and local
decisions. But digging deeper, the *Saqaliba*, whether Slav or Northern
European, had become important in administration, and al-Mansur,
the warrior amir (fl. 960–1002), had imported large groups of Berbers
who differed from those Berbers of long residence in Islamic Spain. In a
most interesting and thoughtful passage in their study, Professors Watt
and Cachia search for the reasons for the breakdown of Islamic Spain

under Arab leadership. They point out that the wealth accumulated by Islamic Spain in the tenth century, not unlike the wealth accumulated by the 'Abbasids in ninth-century Baghdad, turned both societies into materialistic entities. No longer did the upper classes meld with the lower classes in terms of religious ideology. One could urge the lower classes to make holy war (*jihad*) on the infidels of northern Spain, but if the upper classes and their large slave households remained secure in their estates without fighting, many changes would take place. In 'Abbasid Baghdad, when Arabs became wealthy, the Turkish mercenaries began to dominate. In Islamic Spain, this same dichotomy of rich and poor was evident. But Watt and Cachia also discuss the weakness or absence of a middle class that would support a strong central government. They also point out that the wealthy upper class had lost its religious compass through which they could combine in purpose with the proletariat who fought the wars.[41]

Even under these dire circumstances, the court of the Qadi Muhammad ibn 'Abbad (1013–1042) in Seville and of his son, Mu'tadid (1042–1068), and grandson, Mu'tamid (1068–1091), carried on the old intellectual traditions of Cordoba. But the Christian kingdoms quickly took advantage of the Muslim weakness, especially King Alfonso VI of Leon and Castille (1065–1109). He was able to demand tribute from Badajoz, Toledo, and Saragossa and later from Seville, and in 1085, he annexed Toledo outright. Yet the authors are left with the sense that the Christian Spaniards and the Arabo-Iberian Muslims were part of the same border population in Islamic Spain. There is at least a parallel in Turkish history wherein the borderers in Asia Minor were Turkish speaking, whether Christian on the Byzantine border or Muslim on the Seljuk border. The difference may lie in the powerful Berber kingdom of the Almoravids in North Africa that were called upon to help the Arabo-Spanish *Reyes de Taifas* (party kings) on several occasions. Finally, its leader, Yusuf ibn-Tafshin (fl. 1088–1106), decided to take over Islamic Spain and to fight the infidel kingdoms of the north. The Berbers collectively belonged to the Sanhaja confederation that stretched across the deserts of Morocco, Algeria, and Mauritania as far as the Niger River in present-day Senegal, a name linguistically related to Sanhaja. The modern-day Tuaregs are directly related to the Sanhaja.[42]

The religious influences on the Sanhaja are complex and are unnecessary for our narrative. The important points are that ibn-Yasin became the spiritual leader, but the mystical side of Malikite jurisprudence was introduced to the Sanhaja by Abu Imran al-Fasi, who, in turn, took refuge in a ribat on an island in the Niger River; hence, the Arabic word designating the Almoravids was *Al-Murabitun*. The original meaning of a *ribat* was a fortified border post, but our authors stretch this meaning to "a house of retreat." Abu Bakr ibn-Umar (fl. 1056–1087), after the death of ibn-Yasin in 1058, remained the amir of the Almoravids, and while he expanded his sway in North Africa, he had delegated to his cousin, Yusuf bin-Tashfin, to expand in Islamic Spain. Yusuf also founded Marrakesh as his capital in 1062 and made conquests of Eastern Algeria and Morocco; he also gave allegiance to the 'Abbasids of Baghdad, though they were under attack by their own governors (amirs). Yusuf Bin-Tashfin (fl. 1088–1106) and his generals began to taste the splendor of Al-Andalus when they helped the Muslims for the second time in 1090. But the decisive victory of Yusuf bin-Tashfin over Alfonso VI at Zallaqa in 1086 did nothing to alter the Christian settlements of *Mozarabs* in Northern Spain. When King Alfonso I of Aragon retook Saragossa in 1118, it was the beginning of the end of *Al-Murabitun* power with further excursions by Alfonso in 1125 and 1126. Also, Alfonso VII of Castille had his way in the south of Spain in 1133. The success of Christian resettlement policies proved decisive, but perhaps the Muslims of Spain, the ordinary proletariat, got a wake-up call of the threat to their way of life.

The Almohad or Arabic, *Muwahidun* (1130–1223), was a new group of Berbers mainly from the Atlas Mountains. Ibn Tumart, the founder (fl. 1115–1130), had visited the Arab centers of learning as a young man, typical of many Arab leaders of the past. His philosophy may have been influenced by the Ash'ari movement then receiving prominence in Baghdad. In any case, he emphasized *tawhid*, the unity of Islam, hence *Muwahidun*. Before his death, he proclaimed himself *al-Mahdi*, the savior of all the ills of Islam. He died in a battle, spreading

32

his philosophy in 1130, but he had designated a successor, 'Abd al-Mu'min, who took Marrakesh in 1147, ending the *Murabitun* Dynasty. Eastern Algeria fell to his forces in 1151, and Tunis and Tripolitania soon followed in 1160. The amirs of this Unitarian faith often styled as caliphs entered Al-Andalus only in 1171. Early deaths of the leaders or demands for basic operations in North Africa postponed the marshaling of troops in Al-Andalus until 1189 when *Abu Yusuf Yaqub al-Mansur* (1184–1199) forced the Christian kings into a five-year truce in 1190. In July 1195, the Almohads won a decisive victory over *King Alfonso VIII of Castille* at Alarcos. While the Almohads, under the son of al-Mansur, Muhammad an-Nasir (1199–1213), rested on their laurels, the Christian rulers of Leon, Castille, Navarre, and Aragon combined forces and, in July 1212, defeated the Almohad force so decisively at Las Navas de Tolosa that their power in Al-Andalus was permanently broken.

As one might expect, the preponderance of Christian power on the Iberian Peninsula did not abruptly end the need for understanding the surviving strong roots of Arabs, Berbers, Moriscos, Mudejars, and other political and cultural entities peculiar to Muslims. An Arab whose forebears were Meccan, Muhammad ibn Yusuf ibn Nasr, known as Ibn al-Ahmar (fl. 1231–1273), managed to set up a small kingdom in Granada, about sixteen square miles. One must then study why such a small kingdom was able to survive another two hundred years as a self-conscious Islamic State. Our authors, Watt and Cachia, point to the mountainous and easily defensible terrain, but this would not hinder a determined enemy. Rather Muhammad I became a vassal of Castille, as did other Muslim statelets. As many Muslims resided in Castille, a safety valve of discontents could have kept Granada alive. The closeness of Africa could have been a deterrent because of access to volunteers. The power of Christian states was greatly increased by the marriage of Ferdinand of Aragon and Isabella of Castille in 1459. In 1462, Gibraltar was seized by a duke of King Ferdinand, indicating a rise in Spanish nationalism. But even after the final capitulation of Granada in 1492, the majority of the population in Castille were Muslim. In Valencia, the Christians were only a small group. One must mention that Muslim craftsmen and merchants were essential for most Spanish provinces. Moreover, Muslims could only with difficulty practice their trade elsewhere. Muslims left in place were known as *mudejars* from the Arabic *mudajjan*, "permitted to remain." The Jews of Spain in 1492 were required to be baptized or leave the country. Their departure in many cases strengthened the Ottoman Empire and other Muslim states because they were also craftsmen and merchants. An insurrection in Granada followed the burning of many Muslim philosophical texts by Christian leaders and priests. As punishment, the Granadians also were given the choice of baptism or exile. The Moriscos chose to be baptized, but secretly, they received a dispensation from *qadis* (Muslim judges and administrators) to practice "*taqiyya*," or concealment of one's true religion. As an answer to concealment, the Inquisition in 1478 was placed under the control of Spaniards instead of the pope, making this form of torture often harsher. The Moriscos proved themselves inassimilable in Spain under the Christian regime; hence, a half million moved to North Africa, where they added to the strength of these societies. Spain was now committing itself to the discovery of the Northwest Passage in America and probably also had demands for sailors and settlers. It is not surprising that this intolerant state was conquered by France in the seventeenth century.[43]

When one visits Spain today, a tourist is shown the splendid architecture of Muslim palaces and gardens such as the *Alhambra* in Granada or the Grand Mosque of Cordoba or the elegant jewelry of Toledo, but one passes unaware of the depth of culture the Spanish inherited from Al-Andalus in horsemanship (*al-furusiye*), in architecture (*al-mi'mariya*), in the making of fine jewelry (*al-jewahariya*), philosophy (*al-falsafa*), weaponry (*al-islaha*), medicine (*al-tibbiya*), and other arts and skills.

VII. The First Turkish Revolution: The Great Seljuks

It is no accident that the Turks have dominated the Middle East for a thousand years, from the tenth century to the twentieth century. Until the eleventh century, when their tribes arrived in large numbers in Iran, Iraq, and Asia Minor, the Turks had remained largely under the influence of China. The natural habitat of the Turks was the Eurasian Steppe, stretching from the Caspian Sea to the Great Wall of China. The Chinese, in their long history, often were invaded by the steppe tribal confederations consisting mostly of Mongols and Turks. Even the Great Wall of China, started by the Ch'in Dynasty (BC 221–207), was built by the Han Dynasty (BC 206–AD 220) to keep the steppe nomads from invading Northern China. As an illustration of the peril, the Turkish Hsiung-nu or Huns surrounded the emperor in BC 200. From the Chinese, the Turks learned of shamanism as a means of harmonizing spiritual with political life. They picked up the Chinese zodiac, the complexities of politics and warfare and trading and commerce. In times of peace, the Turks, noted for horse and other livestock breeding, traded fine horses and cavalry mounts for silk, weapons, and comestibles. Some of the Chinese cuisine was introduced by the Turks into the Middle East. Think of the Chinese egg roll and compare it with a Pierogi or the Berek, where the *p* and the *g* are matched by a *b* and a *k*. The Turks also protected the silk caravans of Muslim and Chinese merchants. Offshoots of the Turks founded the Khazar state of the Caucasus (fl. AD 550–1030), and their leaders preserved their culture by adopting

35

Judaism. The Turks also gave rise to the Bulgar state of the upper Volga in the seventh century; later, the Slavs invaded their homeland on the Danube. Likewise, the Turks played a role in the Mongol Liao Dynasty that dominated the steppe and Northern China from AD 935–1125. The remnants of the Liao lived on as the Kara Khitai (the "Cathay" of Marco Polo) in central Asia until destroyed by the Mongols in 1218.[44]

Two events on the steppe may have propelled the Oghuz tribal confederation into the Middle East in 1055. In the first place, a large number of Turks had been converted to Islam in the eighth and ninth centuries, and stories of the wealth of the Muslims doubtless filtered across the steppe. As already noted, thousands of young Turks found ready employment in military slave units and cavalry (as *Mamluks*, juridical slaves, but highly privileged) in various Muslim dynasties. Leadership posts also opened up for politically savvy Turkish officers. Speaking of the Mongol Liao Dynasty, one may also factor in that young Mongols dominated their military regiments. As C. E. Bosworth has indicated in his book *The Ghaznavids*, Turkish Mamluks who had settled in the province of Khorasan in Northeastern Iran served the Sultan Mahmud of Ghazna (d. 1030), but Mahmud's son and successor, Mas'ud, could not resolve the pressures generated by the invading Oghuz Confederation.[45] Sultan Mahmud is noted for his support of the great literary figure Firdousi, writer of the *Shahname*, and Al-Biruni, a noted Arab geographer. I suspect there was also a problem that bedeviled Mas'ud and many caliphs. With such a dependence on Turkish *Mamluks*, there was always the question of ultimate loyalty. Would a Turkish *Mamluk* always be willing to fight against a tribe known or related to him?

The Oghuz tribes essentially split into two major branches. The northern branch, known as Cuman or Kipchak, gave their name, *Desh-i Kipchak*, to the steppelands north of the Black Sea (later, the Ukrainian Steppe). The Russians called them Polovtsy (fair-haired), and eventually, they were responsible for the partial destruction of the Kievan Rus State. As Nicholas Riasanovsky notes, "The Pechenegs replaced the Khazars, and the Polovtsy, but the fighting continued . . . the Mongols came to give the *coup de grâce*."[46] The mass invasion of the Turks into the Arab and Persian heartlands in the South could potentially cause an ideological and religious problem for the Muslims because most Turks in this early period were followers of shamanism. For the first time, whole populations of Muslims might be expected to serve a ruler without the usual trappings of legitimacy. But I have raised the question before that possibly the Seljuk leaders sought the new discipline of Islam to replace the waning discipline of shamanism.[47] The late Fuad Köprülü, renowned scholar and Turkish foreign minister, discussed, in an important article, that many of the beliefs and practices of shamanism reappeared in the Middle East as certain practices of the dervish orders (*Tariqāt*). He also believed that population pressure propelled the Turks into the Middle East.[48]

In the past, Muslim dynasties had claimed descent from the Prophet Muhammad, as did the Umayyads and 'Abbasids. Also, the Shi'ites had claimed that their leaders descended directly from the family of Ali and Fatima, daughter of the Prophet, notably the Buwahids, the Qarmatians, and the Fatimids. The Seljuk leaders seem to have been well aware of the question of legitimacy and immediately took steps to claim legitimacy through elaborate forms of investiture administered by the captive 'Abbasid caliphs. The investiture included presenting robes of honor (*khil'āt*) and a scepter (*'asā*). George Makdisi has indicated in an important article how the wily Seljuk Sultans, on many occasions, arranged marriages with daughters of the caliphs to secure for their progeny a permanent legitimacy. Even Tughril Bey married the daughter of the reigning caliph but died before he could conceive children.[49]

The Seljuks, under the brothers Chagri Bey and Tughril Bey (d. 1063) and later his nephew, Alp Arslan (d. 1072), son of his brother, Chagri, conquered the Ghaznavids and the Buwayhids and then, after the fall of Baghdad in 1055, seized Syria, Palestine, and the Hejaz from the Fatimids. As described above, the Ayyubids, a branch of the Syrian Seljuks, led by Salah ed-Din, defeated the remnants of the Fatimids in Egypt, and foiled the Third Crusade under Richard I of England, known as the Lionhearted. Alp Arslan and his court, 1064–1072, were under Persian influence. He and his son, Malikshah (d. 1092), fortunately had as their vizier Nizam al-Mulk, one of the most

outstanding leaders in medieval Islamic history. Nizam al-Mulk not
only governed the vast empire; he also wrote an important guide of
how to rule, the *Siyasetname*, and also devised the madrassa system (the
Nizamiya), an advanced college to train young men in the fine points
of philosophy and Sunni Islam. He was assassinated in 1091 by his
classmate, Hasan bin Sabbah, head of the Order of Assassins, a terrorist
organization fostered by the Isma'ilis. The story is told that Nizam al-
Mulk, Omar Khayyam, the poet, and Hasan bin Sabbah of the Assassins
were classmates, and they swore they would try to become great leaders.
Each succeeded in his own way!

Alp Arslan decisively defeated the Byzantine army at Manzikert
in AD 1071, a date that marks the beginning of the Turkish takeover
of Asia Minor. Henceforth, apart from his receiving the investiture
of traditional legitimacy, he was accorded the sacred title of *amir al-
mu'minin* (commander of the faithful). His son, Malikshah (1072–
1092), who witnessed the epitome of Great Seljuk power, also moved
the imperial capital from Rey to Isfahan. The same fate of bickering
among heirs to leadership that cursed all far-flung empires caused the
Great Seljuks rapidly to break up into lesser satraps, now called *atabegs*
(father beys) instead of the traditional title of amirs. The Turks often
divided their realms among their children, thus assuring that each
would struggle to eliminate rival brothers. Only the Seljuks of Rum
(1077–1307) in Asia Minor, with their capital in Konya, the Iconium
of classical times, flourished another century and a half until their
power was destroyed by the Mongols, led by Bayju, at the Battle of
Köse Dağ in 1243. By constantly fighting Byzantium, whom they
decisively defeated at the Battle of Myriokephalon in 1176, and by
overcoming the marauding Third Crusade led by Frederick II of the
Holy Roman Empire, they maintained a capable standing army that
was serviced by the *iqta'* system, a land-holding system designed to give
Mamluks financial support. As the Mongols exerted more pressure on
them after Köse Dağ, the Rum Seljuks became a vassal state, collecting
taxes for the Mongols, and when possible, from the dozen or so Turkish
tribal statelets in Asia Minor. The heyday of the Rum Seljuks came
in the twelfth century, especially under Kilic Arslan II when he built

kervansarays (safe merchant hostels and trading posts) and controlled most ports on the Mediterranean and Black Sea. They partook also of the lucrative slave trade by sending Mamluks from the *Desht-i Kipchak* and the Caucasus supplying the Egyptian Mamluk State with fresh recruits from the Polovtsy and the Circassians.[50]

One must assume that each Rum Seljuk Sultan had to announce his accession with rich gifts to the Baghdad caliph and await the proper robes of honor, a scepter, a ceremonial sword, and even a dagger and a suit of armor from the caliph. We have specific references from Osman Turan's account of this procedure in his article on Kay Kavus I (1208–1220), who captured Sinop, made the Byzantine so-called Empire of Trebizond a vassal in 1214, and subjugated Sicilian Armenia in 1218. At this time, a new type of legitimacy began to be claimed by the Rum Seljuks because of the *Ghazawāt*—that is, the meritorious, under God, almost constant warfare against Crusaders and Christian Byzantium; hence, the Rum Seljuks could claim a special legitimacy. This claim became very important for the Ottoman *Gazis*, the heroes of *Ghazawāt*.[51]

VIII. The Mongol/Turk Revolution

The Mongols must be considered spoilers of the fine-tuned game of Islamic legitimacy in the Middle Ages, the seventh and eighth Islamic centuries. Essentially, in the beginning of their conquests, they did not give a whit for Islamic legitimacy. They were soon able to create their own legitimacy, but until Jenghiz Khan instituted the Mongol Empire, the Mongols were more interested in having legitimacy for their confederation bestowed upon them from the Ch'in Dynasty in Northern China. In the early years of the thirteenth century, the Mongol armies were led by Mongols, but they also included thousands of Turks in the ranks. They suddenly conquered the Ch'in Dynasty of Northern China in AD 1215, second, the Khwarezmshahs of Transoxiana (central Asia) and Iran in 1219, and finally, Russia and Eastern Europe in 1240 and 1241. It is important to mention here at the outset of a discussion of the Mongol Empire that the Mongols were always able to muster various ethnic groups to fight under their banners. At first, they were highly organized Mongol troops, but very soon, they were able to conquer neighboring Turkish tribal and Chinese special units. After they conquered much of Russia in the thirteenth century, they also used Russian troops to swell their ranks. This was one of the two purposes of the Mongol census, the *Chislo,* taxation and recruitment.

Quite foolishly, the Khwarezmshah Muhammad II (fl. 1206–1220) had the diplomatic envoys of Jenghiz Khan killed about 1218. This sudden hostile act immediately caused Jenghiz Khan to call a *kuriltay* (a Mongol term designating the calling together for consultation of the Mongol leaders and commanders). The devastating attack on Khwarezm came the following year, a disciplined army of one hundred thousand to one hundred fifty thousand against a feudal army of possibly three hundred thousand. In central Asia, the Mongol forces attacked and destroyed the four main Khwarezm cities of Bukhara, Otrar, Samarqand, and Urgenj, the Khwarezm capital on the Amu Darya (Oxus) River. After his defeat, the Khwarezmshah Muhammad II fled to India with his son Jelal ed-Din. Later, he sickened and died on an island in the Caspian Sea with a Mongol detachment in hot pursuit. The above-noted cities, when they refused to capitulate, had the city walls destroyed and many thousands killed as they were given over to the army for pillage. At the time, pyramids of piled-up heads were reported. Bukhara, in particular, was invested and burned in 1220. At Urgenj, a major dam was destroyed, and consequently, the irrigation system upon which Khwarezm depended for food production was greatly damaged. The two famous generals of Jenghiz Khan, Jebe and Subudey, had been in pursuit of the Khwarezmshah. They proceeded as far as Azerbaijan then gained permission from Jenghiz to strike the Khazars and the Kievan Rus in the years 1221–1223. The army passed through the Caucasus at Derbent and destroyed the Kievan Rus army at Kalka in 1223. The main Mongol army that destroyed Urgenj also met and defeated Jelal ed-Din, son of the Khwarezmshah, in 1221. Jenghiz Khan returned to Mongolia in 1225, having reorganized the Khwarezmshah realm with the expert advice of Mahmud Yalavach, a local merchant trusted by Jenghiz Khan. Now Jenghiz Khan prepared to punish the Tanguts, a Turkish tribe that had refused to join the Western Campaign. During the course of this campaign, the Great Jenghiz Khan was injured when he was unseated from his horse and died. The year was 1227. His youngest son, Tuluy, took charge of the army. The famous *Yasa* or Mongol law code became guiding principles in the Mongol realm. Also, the sayings of Jenghiz Khan, the *Bilik*, were revered for generations, and true to custom, only direct descendants of Jenghiz Khan were considered legitimate rulers in the vast Mongol Empire.[52]

Prior to his death, Jenghiz Khan assigned to each of his four sons the specific *ulus* (the territory) where each would rule. Interestingly,

41

although he had many wives, he only chose the four sons from his first marriage to Borte. Other wives often had been bargaining chips in the expansion of the empire. The youngest son, Tuluy, received the central and western parts of Mongolia. Later, his holdings became the Il Khans[53] of the Middle East. Chagatay inherited the region once controlled by the Kara Khitay, roughly central Asia. Ugedey received the territory of Jungaria then part of the upper Irtish River. Juchi was destined to receive Kazakhstan and eventually Russia and Eastern Europe. As Juchi died before Jenghiz Khan, his realm passed to Juchi's second son, Batu. The great *kuriltay* to select a new leader took place in 1229. As Tuluy withdrew his candidacy, Ugedey was elected unanimously. Ugedey rightly concerned himself initially with China and Iran, where Mongol control was uncertain. The defeat of Jelal ed-Din of Khwarezm caused the dislocation of other Oghuz tribal members. Vernadsky believes that the Ottomans got their start from these troubled times, and the timing is close. Ertogrul, father of Osman, of the Ottomans, was indeed born just after the death of Jenghiz Khan.[54]

Batu, in 1236–1237, became head of a large number of Turkish troops and also of contingents from other uluses, about fifty thousand. Subudey, the Mongol general, who already knew the Russian scene from 1223, led this large western army first of all against the Bulgars on the Volga and the Cumans on the Desht-i Kipchak (Ukraine). In the next four years, most Russian cities were conquered, and wherever the Mongol/Turkish armies met resistance, the cities were destroyed. Only Novgorod was spared because of the approaching spring thaw that was devastating to cavalry in Russia because of the mud. Hungary, Poland, and even Silesia had to deal with Mongol forces, but no permanent garrisons were established. At this juncture, the Livonian and Teutonic knights in 1237 started their crusade against the Russian Orthodox Church that they considered deviant from the true Catholic religion! Ugedey died on December 11, 1241, thus sparing Western Europe from a newly planned attack. The sudden change of plans took place because the numerous Mongol princes serving in the Western Campaign to help Batu now wished to return to Mongolia and take part in electing the new khan.[55]

Another Russian Historian, Dr. Riasanovsky, has assessed the movement of Batu and his troops. He estimated that Batu had under his command about 150,000 cavalry, Mongols and Turks, and siege equipment manned by Chinese. He puts to rest the idea that the Mongols had only superior numbers. Rather, he emphasizes the superior organization, discipline, and command structure that he likened to a modern general staff. He also mentioned, as a means of control, the newly built roads, a courier system (the *Yam*), and a crude census (*Chislo*) to assess taxation and recruitment. They besieged and razed Riazan in 1237, in 1238 the capital, Vladimir of Suzdal, fell that had been the seat until then of the grand prince. Chernigov fell in 1239. The Mongols preferred winter warfare when the ground, lakes, and rivers were frozen. Kiev, Galicia, and Volynia and also Hungary and Poland saw defeat from the Mongol attacks and destruction in 1239–1242. Batu set up his headquarters and eventually his capital in Old Saray on the lower Volga River. This division of the Mongol Empire was known as the Golden Horde by Russians (*Zolotoi Ordu*) possibly because of golden tiles in the tent of the khan.[56] As ties between the central Mongol government and the ulus of the Golden Horde weakened, a state revenue collector, known as the *Daruga*, was set up to manage taxation of the Russian states. At first, the various Russian princes were expected each year to deliver the tax to Saray and receive legitimacy from the khan for their continued princely role. Later, the Moscow grand prince became the tax collector for all of Russia, and he alone had to journey to Saray to deliver the tax, prostrate himself, and receive his new investiture. The collections of the *Daruga* were certified by the tsar then checked by central boards or ministries (*divans*). The secretaries of the divans were called *Bitikchi*. As the Golden Horde came under Shariah Islamic law with Khan Berke and, later, when other Khans became converts to Islam, the courts came under the supervision of a *qadi*. In the older Mongol system, the district judge was known as a *yarguchi*, and the chief judge was known as the *amir yargu*. Vernadsky believes that because merchants were so important to the khans as sources of prosperity and even for their loans to the government, they were protected in all Mongol lands and undoubtedly organized themselves in guilds. The position of the peasants is not clear, but Vernadsky believes that they were burdened with taxation and may have faired better on the estates as serfs of officials. The Mongol administration was basically for two purposes: to collect taxes and to draft recruits for the cavalry. The Mongol census (*Chislo*) served both purposes. Saray and other cities contained mostly craftsmen, government officials, and the military units. As the Turks, after the conquest dominated the cities, the *lingua franca* became Chagatay or Northern Turkish. For other details of Mongol administration, one should further consult Vernadsky.[57]

It is not our place to give the full history of the Mongol-Turkish occupancy and control of Russia. Vernadsky has done this. For our survey, it is important to remember that the Mongols interrupted the medieval legitimacy of Muslim rulers and substituted their own brand of legitimacy that was closely linked to the Mongol/Turkish taxation system and their recruitment of troops. Troop recruitment and taxation also greatly weakened the Russian principalities. As for the rise of Moscow to prominence, its role as chief tax collector for the Mongols was very important, but Moscow also was a hub of inland waterways between the upper Volga and the upper Oka and soon became the seat of the Russian Orthodox Church. In earlier crises of the Golden Horde, the great khan could act as a mediator. This was no longer true at the end of fourteenth century when Timur (Tamerlane) appeared in central Asia. Before Timur's[58] arrival on the scene in central Asia, two new centers had formed in central Asia to oppose the government in Saray: one was located at Sygnak in Kazakhstan on the lower Syr Darya River, and the other, in Samarqand near the Amu Darya River. In Saray, a Mongol general, Mamay, held the power and backed various Batu'ids as legitimate descendants of Jenghiz Khan. In Sygnak, a brother of Batu, Orda, had a son, Urus, who took control about 1360. Shortly thereafter, Timur overthrew the ruler, Husein, in Samarqand. In this period, Timur was wounded in the leg and henceforth was known as Timur, the Lame. In a strategic move, Timur made himself the vassal of the first Ming emperor in China. Here he was following a steppe tradition that Jenghiz Khan had used with the Chi'n. At the point when Urus Khan took control of Saray in 1373, Toktamish, one of his best generals and a descendant of Tuka-Timur, a brother of Batu, joined Timur. Eventually, another general, Edigey, deserted Timur. At the end of this major internal strife, Toktamish occupied Saray, while Mamay was suffering a Russian defeat at Kilukovo Pole in 1380 from Dmitri, grand prince of Moscow. Toktamish defeated Mamay in 1381, who then fled to Kaffa and was killed by the Genoese for his treasure. Toktamish now had to deal with the Russian rebellion. In 1382, he surrounded Moscow and talked the Muscovites into opening their gates, promising safe passage. A slaughter ensued, and the wealth of Moscow was sacked. Now once again, all the Russian principalities were required to renew their taxes. Only four years later, Toktamish began to take on airs that annoyed Timur, his overlord. Toktamish laid claim to Khorezm and also Azerbaijan and began raiding these provinces. Russian troops were already present in Toktamish's army in 1388. The final clash came on the Middle Volga in June 1391. Timur had even altered the tactics of Jenghiz. He dug trenches, provided a regiment of sappers, and also used Alan infantry from the Caucasus. Toktamish was completely routed. Timur-Kutlugh and Edegey were left in charge, but Toktamish regrouped with loyal Russian princes. A second clash in 1395 completely smashed the army of Toktamish, and Timur then turned to the conquest of India. Timur had destroyed the major centers of commerce—Urgenj, Astrakhan, Saray, and Azov; hence, the economy of the Golden Horde suffered for many years. A clash between Vitovt, prince of Lithuania, who had joined Toktamish against Edigey, proved futile. Now Timur in 1405 planned to attack China and hence accepted Toktamish's obeisance as a check on Edigey in Saray. Fortunately, for China and the Golden Horde, both men died.

Vernadsky now turns to the interconnections between what happens with the great khan in Mongolia and Northern China and the expansion of the empire under the Il Khans of the Middle East. Batu died about AD 1255 and was succeeded by his son, Sartak, who became a Nestorian Christian. His short reign and the reign of Ulagchi, another son, only lasted three years to 1258 when Khan Berke (fl. 1258–1266), Batu's brother, came to power. Berke became a convert to Islam, and events therefore changed appreciably in his relations with the

Middle East. After the death of the Great Khan Ugedey in 1242, there had been an interregnum in Mongolia to 1246. Tuluy's son, Mongka, a friend of Batu, wished to be chosen at the *kuriltay*, but Guyuk (fl. 1246–1249), son of Ugedey, had the inner track with the support of his mother, Khatun Tarakina. Bad blood had risen between Batu and Guyuk because Batu had not attended the *kuriltay* of 1246. It would seem that Guyuk died or was poisoned just before a military clash with Batu. At the *kuriltay* of 1250, a serious split took place among the four branches of the empire. Batu and Tuluy and their descendants squared off against the descendants of Chagatay and Ugedey. This latter group refused to attend the *kuriltay*. Therefore, the following year in 1251, the Batu-Tuluy faction held a separate *kuriltay* and elected Tuluy's son Mongka (fl. 1251–1259) as the great khan. This change at the top also prompted a change in *ulus* policy. Mongka's brother, Kubilay, continued successfully to conquer Southern China to such an extent that Mongka became jealous and recalled his brother, Kubilay, in 1257. Mongka took charge of the Chinese front, but an epidemic of dysentery struck the army, and even Mongka died from dysentery in 1259.[59]

Another Mongol army under Baiju-Noyan had defeated the Rum Seljuks at Köse Dag in 1243 but then failed to set up local institutions. With Mongka as great khan, he assured Batu that he would continue his control of his *ulus* in Russia and Eastern Europe and then placed his own brother, Hulagu, as the leader who recently had conquered the Khwarezmshahs, in charge of Iran and the Rum Seljuks. In 1256, Hulagu took up his charge and crossed the Amu Darya River. He then directed his troops to destroy the Order of the Assassins, as noted above, an active wing of Isma'ili doctrine. Some one hundred fortresses were destroyed, including Alamut, the headquarters in Northern Iran. In 1258, Hulagu stormed and looted Baghdad and had the last 'Abbasid ruler, Caliph Musta'sim, killed. This act indicates the Mongol utter disregard for Islamic legitimacy. When Hulagu learned of Mongka's death, true to custom, he postponed the invasion of Syria to attend the *kuriltay*, taking his best troops with him. After facing a rebellion by Arik-Buka, Mongka's youngest brother, Kubilay, was proclaimed great khan in 1260 in Peking. Kubilay made *Khan-Balyk* (Peking) the official seat of power in 1271 and called his dynasty Yuan. It was under Kubilay that the Mongols of the Far East came strongly under Chinese influence. Kubilay became a Buddhist. The Sung Dynasty of South China continued to resist Mongol rule until 1279. Marco Polo, who became an official in the court of Kubilay Khan, noted the many reforms of Kubilay, who also revised the law of succession and made peace with Tibet and Burma. Kubilay died about age seventy in 1294. The Yuan Dynasty came to an end after much internal bickering and strife in 1369. It was replaced by the Ming Dynasty.[60]

It is in this era that we see how the great khan in China and the Mongol appendages, especially the Golden Horde and the Il Khans of Persia and Asia Minor, become deeply involved in Byzantine, Seljuk, and Mamluk Egyptian politics and economies. By the time the Ottoman Turks become powerful, only the Mamluks and Byzantium could play a decisive role. In his absence attending- the *kuriltay* of 1251, Hulagu faced two setbacks. Khan Berke from the Golden Horde had sent a contingent of troops to Hulagu when he fought the assassins and the Baghdad caliphate. Now Berke laid claim to Azerbaijan, whose rich pasturage attracted both leaders. Berke seriously defeated Hulagu's troops in 1263–1264. By his absence at the *kuriltay*, Hulagu's general, Kit-Buka, with a small troop of Kipchak Turks, faced Sultan Baybars (1260–1277) and the Egyptian Mamluk Turks at 'Ayn Jalut in Palestine in 1260 and was soundly defeated. This defeat placed a damper on further Mongol expansion in the Middle East. Interestingly, the troops on both sides were Kipchak Turks! Meanwhile, the interests of Berke's successor, Mangu-Temir, in the Golden Horde continued to spill over into relations with Baybars. These two rulers wished to keep trade lines open between them, especially to transport Mamluk recruits, and also they wanted their diplomats to freely move through Constantinople. The spoiler turned out to be Emperor Michael VIII Palaeologus (1260–1282), who was allied to the Il Khans in Asia Minor and initially blocked freedom of trade through the Bosphorus. Khan Mangu-Temir of the Golden Horde was a sky worshipper, like Jenghiz Khan, and hence had no Muslim tie with Egypt. He thus concluded a treaty with Khan Abaga, son of Hulagu, and the new head of the Il Khans of Iran and Asia Minor in 1269–1270. This treaty was unfavorable to Baybars, but Nogay (fl. 1265–1300), an important general of Mangu-Temir and also a direct descendant of Jenghiz Khan, forced Emperor Michael to make peace in 1273 and open the Byzantine Straits, a treaty that was sealed by Michael's illegitimate daughter being married to Nogay. Nogay, at this time, was virtually coruler with Mangu-Temir, and when the latter died in 1279, Nogay named himself khan of the Golden Horde. Essentially, none of the succeeding khans of the Golden Horde could act independently until Nogay lost his command of the army. Thus, Khan Tuda Mangu (1280–1288) and other successors had to concern themselves not only with Russian affairs but also with rebellion within their own armed forces. Khan Uzbeg (fl. 1313–1341) became a Sufi under the influence of the Great Konya Mystic (Jelal ed-Din Rumi) and, for a time, lost interest in ruling.[61]

The last chapter of the Golden Horde came in 1480 when Tsar Ivan III (1462–1505), known as the Great, announced Russia's emancipation from the "Tatar Yoke." In 1443, Prince Kasim of the Golden Horde had placed his region and his followers under the control of Moscow. Haji Giray started his dynasty in the Crimea in 1449. Soon the Batu'ids of the Saray remnant established Kazan and Astrakhan as successor principalities. These khanates were eliminated by Tsar Ivan IV (1533–1584), known as the Terrible (Rus., Grozni), in 1550 and 1552. Not surprising, the khanate of Crimea and parts of the Caucasus, under Ottoman tutelage and protection, survived until 1783.[62]

There remains to summarize the last century of Ilkhan intervention in the Middle East. Four centers of power interrupted Ilkhan policy: Byzantium and the Crusades, the sudden and overwhelming power of Timur (Tamerlane), and the rising power of the Ottomans. As with the Golden Horde, the Il Khans set up a system of taxation and recruitment in Persia and Asia Minor. Michael VIII of Byzantium once again began to curry favor with the Il Khans as he had with the Golden Horde; he married Maria, a second illegitimate daughter, to Khan Abaga of the Ilkhans. There is very little information about Abaga's sons, Argun and Jaihatu. Argun did send a letter to the French king in 1289, asking for assistance against the Mamluks of Egypt. The era of Gazan Khan (1295–1304) was important for showing tolerance to Nestorian Christians, as had Kubilay in China, as we know from the account of Marco Polo (fl. in China, 1275–1292). Gazan has also been memorialized in Rashid ed-Din's history. Rashid ed-Din, Gazan Khan's vezier and historian, was a convert from Judaism to Islam. During the reign of Gazan Khan, the Great Khan Timur (fl. 1294–1307) and successor to Kubilay, had all the Mongol *uluses* agree to a pan-Mongol peace in 1303. He also intervened in Ilkhan affairs to elect Oljaitu (1304–1316) as khan of the Ilkhans. As the successor to Oljaitu, Khan Abu Said was to demonstrate, by occupying the Terek Valley in the Northern Caucasus in 1318–1319, that the old feud between the Golden Horde and the Il Khans had persisted. But at this stage, the powerful Uzbeg Khan (d. 1341) of the Golden Horde drove him back to Azerbaijan. The power of the great khan reached its apogee under Kubilay Khan and Timur Khan. Thereafter, the power of the Great Khans and of the Il Khans rapidly disintegrated. The Il Khans proved no match for the ties between Mamluk Egypt and the Golden Horde. Very soon also, the Ottomans proved to be a major rising power in Asia Minor and the Balkans.[63]

It seems only appropriate that we draw on the excellent work of Marshall Hodgson to understand what the net effect of Mongol conquest served on the central lands of Islam. In Hodgson's words, "Finally, we may guess at the relation between the intersection of agrarian weakness and pastoral strength in the Late Mid-Islamic Period." Hodgson's point is that "from the Nile to the Oxus and in the Maghrib, many areas now good only for grazing once were rich farmlands. And also, accordingly, in the arid areas, agricultural productivity, once begun, depends more than elsewhere on a continuity of well-balanced human initiative." Hodgson has realized, more than most historians, that the Mongol era in the Middle East served to emphasize a grazing economy and that the Mongols understood only superficially the need for constant attention to an agricultural economy based on irrigation or dry farming techniques. Hodgson also marks the decline of attention to the essential details of agriculture not only of the Mongols but also to the decline of caliphal power under the repeated scourge of warfare.[64]

IX. The Ayyubids and Mamluks Eliminate the Crusaders

The weakness of the 'Abbasid Empire had a number of immediate consequences. The pressure on the Byzantine Empire ceased, and in the Eastern caliphate, the so-called Persian Intermezzo ruled a number of amirates until the Seljuk Turks swept away the amirates in the eleventh century. In the Western caliphate, the Qarmatians of Syria and Bahrain and Fatimid Egypt with Ifriqiya (Tunisia) spread the Ismai'li Shi'ite doctrines of the Seventh Imam. The Fatimids had replaced the short-lived Turkish amirates of the Aghlabids of Qayrawan (800–909), the Tulunids (868–905) of Fustat, and the Ikshidids (935–969), also of al-Fustat. As we have noted above, the Umayyads of Spain also stretched their hands to Morocco, Algeria, and Tunis from time to time, with the aid of various Berber dynasties.

When one traces the decline of the 'Abbasid Empire, one must also recall certain positive features: the influence on *belles lettres* of Persian traditions and also the importance of *Hellenism* and the translation of many Greek classics into Arabic. In AD 830, the Caliph Al-Ma'mun (813–833) established his famous *Bayt al-Hikmah* (House of Wisdom). Until this time, the translation of Greek classics had been haphazard. Because of the power of Persia on literature, the literary classics of the Greeks remained without translation. The Nestorian Christians in Baghdad became the expert translators of Greek scientific and medical texts. Many famous texts including Galen, Hippocrates, Ptolemy, and Euclid were first translated into Aramaic, the language of the Nestorians, and then rendered into Arabic. The most famous of 'Abbasid translators was Hunayn ibn-Ishak from al-Hirah (809–873). Caliph Al-Amin appointed Hunayn as head of the Dar-Al-Hikmah in 836 where he could supervise the translation of many works.

Of the works for which the Arabs and Persians are noted, we must mention Al-Razi (865–925), the greatest of the Muslim physicians. He completed, for example, a ten-volume compendium of medical knowledge, *Kitab al-Tibb al-Mansuri* (the book of medicine dedicated to Mansur), and also gave the first clinical account of small pox and measles. His most important work was *Al-Hawi* (an encyclopedia of medical knowledge). He was followed in medical knowledge by Ibn-Sina, a Persian (980–1037), known as Avicenna in Europe. He prepared the *Al-Qanun fi al-Tibb* (the law in medicine), a final codification of Greco-Arabic medical teaching that became a manual in European medical schools to the end of the seventeenth century. 'Ali ibn-Isa (fl. 1025–1050), the most famous oculist (*kahhal*) wrote the *Tadhkirat al-Kahhalin* (notes of the oculists) describing 130 eye diseases. Abu al-Hasan 'Ali ibn al-Nafis (d. 1288) charted the exchange of oxygen between the heart and lungs and also suspected that there was a relationship between the veins and arteries some three hundred years before Servetius and Harvey explained capillaries in the seventeenth century.[65]

As the Seljuk Turks overran Persia, Iraq, Syria, and Asia Minor, defeating Byzantium at the Battle of Manzikert in 1071, Emperor Alexius Comnenus of Byzantium made a plea for military support from Pope Urban II, who then answered the emperor's call to free the Holy Land in a speech delivered in Clermont, France, on 26 November 1095. In the spring of 1097, some 150,000 noblemen, commoners, and rabble assembled near Constantinople and then besieged Nicaea and Dorylaeum, winning from the Seljuk Sultan Qilich Arslan (1092–1107) both cities. If a warrior took part in a Crusade, the papacy offered a Christian reward in the form of *indulgences,* a privilege for a believer or his relatives to pass more quickly through purgatory and achieve the rewards of heaven. Also, materialism played a major role. A nobleman could attain a kingdom, while a commoner could take advantage of pillaging or murder to increase his material wealth in this world. The cities of Pisa, Venice, and Genoa had interests in establishing trade relations. The first Crusade created four states: the county of Edessa, the principality of Antioch, the county of Tripoli, and the kingdom of Jerusalem. En route, the armies massacred thousands of Jews, Orthodox Christians, and Muslims. The Crusaders also wrecked the seaports they passed through. The slaughter of Jews and Muslims in Jerusalem was never forgotten. As often is the case without contingency planning, the Muslims were caught unawares as they were fighting their own internecine battles.[66]

Here we are not called upon to review the history of the Crusades in detail, but we must examine the Ayyubid and Mamluk response to the proximity of Christian forces. At the time of the Second Crusade (1147–1149), the Crusader states had to deal with 'Imad ad-Din Zangi (1127–1146), the son of a Seljuk slave, who had carved out a principality for himself and his heirs in Aleppo, Harran, and Mosul. Zangi had besieged Ruha' in the county of Edessa because it lay close to Baghdad, and Edessa had been seized in the First Crusade. Its conquest in 1146 by Zangi signaled to Europe the need for a Second Crusade. Pope Eugenius IV dutifully asked crusaders to regain the lost territory, and his sermon was seconded by the monk Bernard of Clairvaux. Two kings, King Louis of France and the Holy Roman Emperor Conrad III, made the journey, but their armies were defeated by the Seljuks because they disagreed on strategy. Zangi had been succeeded by Nur ed-Din, his son, and his lieutenant, Shirkuh, had become the Egyptian amir in 1169, with the approval of the Fatimid Caliph al-'Adid. There was a problem, however; Al-Adid (1160–1171), the last Fatimid ruler, only reluctantly gave up power. When Shirkuh died, he was succeeded by his brother Ayyub's son, Salah ad-Din, of Takrit on the Tigris River. The Ayyubid lines were Kurdish by origin. Salah ad-Din was better known in the West as Saladin (1138–1193). Saladin had sworn to reestablish Sunni Islam in Egypt and also to wage holy war against the Crusaders. The Fatimids, as they were of Isma'ili origins, it is not surprising that on two occasions, the Isma'ili terrorist wing, known as the Assassins, tried to kill Saladin; thus, he vowed to eliminate that threat in 1186 by besieging their headquarters in Masyad and succeeded in exacting a pledge from Rashid ed-Din Sinan, called the Old Man of the Mountain, to take Saladin off the list slated for murder. After making peace with the Order of Assassins, Saladin now could attack the Christians, and Saladin awakened the Third Crusade by conquering Jerusalem in 1187. This Crusade, known as the Crusade of Kings, brought three rulers to the Holy Land: Frederick Barbarossa, the Holy Roman Emperor, King Philip Augustus of France, and King Richard of England. Barbarossa drowned in Silesia, King Philip returned to France, and only King Richard remained to fight and lose to Saladin. King Richard, known in the West as the Lionhearted, struggled three years against Saladin, but in his defeat, he finally made a lasting truce with Saladin. The Crusaders still controlled a coastal strip of Palestine and Syria, but Jerusalem was lost.[67]

Saladin (Salah ed-Din) died in 1193 and was succeeded by his brother Al-'Adil (d. 1218) and his grandson, Al-Kamil Muhammad (1218–1238). Al-'Adil had taken advantage of quarreling among his relatives and gained control of Egypt and most of Syria. The Egyptian branch remained the most important, and the Crusaders began to recognize this fact. As the various branches of the Ayyub line squabbled among themselves, the Crusaders were able to take back such conquests of Saladin as Beirut, Safad, Tiberius, 'Asqalan, and Jerusalem (1229). Under Al-Kamil, clashes with the Franks once again became serious. The Franks even occupied Damietta in Egypt. The problem of the Franks, apart from needing European foot soldiers, was their bickering: Venice vs. Genoa or Knights of the Templars vs. the Hospitallers. The Italians wanted their ships to reach the Red Sea and share in the wealth of the Indies, hence the siege of Damietta. In a conflict lasting two years, 1219–1221, Al-Kamil forced the Franks out of Damietta but gave them free passage for trade. Al-Kamil had conceded Jerusalem to Frederick II, Holy Roman Emperor, in 1229, but it was soon restored to Islam by Khwarizm Turkish Mamluks in 1244, invited by a Kamil successor, Al-Salih, Najm al-Din (1240–1249). King Louis IX of France, leader of the Sixth Crusade, once again took Damietta in 1149, but his army was cut to pieces in the Egyptian canal system, and he died shortly thereafter in Tunisia. This marked the end of the Ayyubids and the rise of the Mamluks.[68]

The origins of the Mamluks, virtually a slave dynasty, are as bizarre as their accomplishments, ending the incursions of Crusaders, defeating the Mongols of Hulagu in 1260 and rebuffing Timur and his troops about 1400. A female slave, Shajar-ad-Durr, formerly in the harem of Caliph Musta'sim (1242–1258), ended up in the harem of the Ayyubid Al-Salih (d. 1249) and was freed or manumitted by him after she gave birth to a son. When she was widowed in 1249, Shajar assumed all power in Egypt for eighty days, having coins minted in her name (*Sikkah*) and having a blessing upon her in the Friday prayers (*khutbah*). These privileges of *Sikkah Wa Khutbah* were traditionally reserved for sultans or caliphs. When her consort and military commander, 'Izz ed-Din Aybak (1250–1257), was chosen as the Sultan, she arranged to marry him and share in the rule of Egypt, but when he planned to take on a second wife, she saw to his murder. Shajar also suffered the same fate. She was murdered by retainers of Aybak's first wife. Aybak had been the first Mamluk Sultan. The Mamluks are rather artificially divided into two groups, the Bahri Mamluks and the Burji Mamluks. The *Bahri* (from the sea) Mamluks initially were housed on the island of Rhoda (Ar., Rawdah) in the Nile river and were mostly Kipchak Turks from the Desht-i Kipchak, modern-day Ukraine, at the time held by the Mongol Empire. They held the sultanate from 1250 to 1390. They were replaced in the sultanate by the *Burji* (Ar., Burj = tower) Mamluks, who were housed in the tower of the Citadel, built by Saladin. They mostly were Circassians from the Northern Caucasus, and they occupied the sultanate from 1390 to 1517, the year Egypt fell to the Ottoman Turks. As noted by a number of historians, these Turks and Circassians received their training as bodyguards, first of all, with the Ayyubids and then with the Mamluk Sultans. When they attained high rank in their regiments, they were in a position to contend for the Mamluk Sultanate. This feature of the Mamluks would then account for the relatively short-lived reigns of most sultans.[69]

Aybak spent most of his sultanate consolidating Egypt, Palestine, and Syria that he had inherited from the Ayyubids. He was followed by Sultan Al-Muzzafar Sayf ed-Din Qutuz (1259–1260), who usurped the throne from Aybak's young son. A year later, Qutuz was killed by Baybars, who had expected to receive Aleppo as a fief after his unit's defeat of Qitbugha, the commander of Hulagu's forces at the Battle of 'Ayn Jalut (1260). Because of his victory over the Mongol advance to Syria and Egypt, Sultan Baybars (1260–1277), known as a crossbowman (note: the author Khowaiter uses the alternate spelling of Baibars), has become one of the most celebrated Muslim leaders in history and the most distinguished of the Mamluks. His fame also rests on his defeat of the Crusaders, and he is also credited with breaking the power of the Assassins. In the realm of foreign relations, he had good relations with the Golden Horde and the Byzantine emperor, Michael VIII Palaeologus, but he developed a rivalry with the Il Khans of Persia and Syria that lasted into the reign of Qalawun until the Il Khans became Muslim under Ghazan Khan. Khowaiter gives us specific references to Baybar's relations with the Golden Horde of Russia: "It is recorded . . . that Mangu Timur was a sky worshipper and not a Muslim like his predecessor. This was not to the advantage of Baibars in inciting Bereke against the Il Khans."[70]

Baybars also was noted for his many good works: he established a famous hospital in Cairo (1284), improved the canals for irrigation, reorganized the army and navy, built the Great Mosque (1269), and organized the *mahmil* (an elaborate chamber on a camel symbolizing a powerful leader) to Mecca and Medinah during the pilgrimage. Baybars began using the powerless 'Abbasid caliphs to authorize the legitimacy of the Mamluk sultans.[71]

Baybars was soon followed by Sultan Qalawun (1279–1290), who replaced the young sons of Baybars. He assumed office about the time when the Mongol Il Khans in Persia began attacking Syria. Qalawun is noted for eliminating certain Mediterranean Crusader states. He also further weakened the remaining Crusader states and banned Christians from government offices. The scourge of the Burji Mamluks proved to be Timurlane, who claimed Mongol ancestry. Timur captured the Ottoman Sultan, Bayazid I, at the Battle of Ankara in 1402, and kept him imprisoned to his death. Timur died on his way to defeat China in 1405. Even Ibn-Khaldun (1332–1406), the famous Arab historian, then a judge in Cairo, helped the Mamluks negotiate a treaty with Timur in 1401. A major blow to the prosperity of Egypt was the navigation of the Portuguese Vasco da Gama around the Cape of Good Hope in 1498. Soon the spice trade that had crossed Egypt now moved around Africa to Europe. The fleet of Sultan Al-Ghawri (1500–1516) often battled the Portuguese, but *triremes* were no match for the ocean-trained fleets and cannons of the Europeans. The Ottomans feared a Mamluk alliance with Shah Isma'il I (1501–1524), the founder of Safavid Persia; hence, they occupied Tabriz in 1515 and then struck the Egyptians at Marj Dabiq, north of Aleppo in 1517. Qansu died on the battlefield, and his slave Tuman Bey, the new sultan, was defeated by the Ottoman artillery and firearms in Egypt, and his body was hung on one of Cairo's gates. The Mamluks had disdained firearms partly because of the expense of new firearms and an empty treasury; consequently, the Ottomans chewed them up with artillery. Sultan Selim I (1512–1520) promptly attempted the legitimizing tactic of the Mamluks and carried the remaining 'Abbasid caliph, Al-Mutawakkil II, to Istanbul, but the Ottoman sultans claimed the right to be caliphs, not simply by the investiture of the 'Abbasids, but through their political prowess leading the *gaza* or holy war against Christians and as keepers of the holy cities of Mecca and Madinah (*Al-Hadim al-Haramayn*).[72]

X. The Second Turkish Revolution
The Ottoman Turks

The origins of the Ottoman Empire do not begin in Asia Minor but in the Balkans and the movement of the Slavic tribes. By the seventh century, the Balkan Slavs had coalesced into four groups: the Slovenes at the top of the Adriatic, the Croatians between the Drava River and the Adriatic, the Serbs in the Central Balkans between the Adriatic and the Danube, and the Slavs from the Middle Danube to the Black Sea, who took the name Bulgaria from their Turkic occupiers. The Slovenes and Croatians soon came under the influence of Rome and Roman Catholicism, while the Serbs and Bulgars looked to Greek Orthodox Constantinople for acculturation. Apart from the Slavs, the Vlachs coalesced in the mountains, who were the descendants of the Roman province of Dacia. The Albanians, descendants of the Illyrians, also kept their identity in the Southern Balkans close to the Adriatic. The Bosnians looked to the Muslims of the Ottoman Empire.

There were medieval Bulgarian heroes, such as King Simeon (fl. 893–927), who saw his education in Constantinople but failed to unite the South Slavs because of his misguided attempts to conquer Constantinople. As long as Byzantium maintained its superior military power, it could dominate the Bulgars and Serbs. There were also a number of Bulgarian leaders who came into prominence in the ninth century. One may call attention to Khan Boris (852–889), who accepted Christianity from Byzantium after Constantinople recognized his conquests. The Greeks sent the missionaries Cyril and Methodius, who gave the Bulgars an alphabet and translated the scriptures into Bulgarian. By the end of the twelfth century, Stephen Nemanja had united the Serbs, and he was known by the title *the Great Zhupan*. This title indicated that nominally, he was still a vassal of the emperor in Constantinople and derived his legitimacy therefrom. During the weakness of an eventual takeover of Byzantium by the Venetians in 1204, the Bulgarians once again revolted in 1185. Now joining with the Cuman Turks and the Vlachs, Kaloyan (1197–1207) and his successor, John Asen II, made Bulgaria the leading state in the Balkans. But the Serbs defeated this crescendo of power in 1330. Now one year later, the greatest of the medieval Serbian leaders, Stephan Dushan (1331–1355), took power. He was known as a military strategist and a lawgiver. He assumed the title of Tsar of the Serbs and Autocrat of the Greeks. But very much like his predecessors, he died en route in an attempt to defeat Byzantium. With the death of Stephan Dushan, a power vacuum was left in the Balkans that was soon filled by the Ottoman Turks. As Stavrianos so aptly noted, the Byzantine Empire or East Rome had gradually lost its economic power in part because of one-sided treaty concessions in 1082 to Venice as payback for the use of its navy against the Norman attacks on Durazzo in the late eleventh century. The Seljuk Turks had also defeated Byzantium at Manzikert in 1071. Henceforth, the Turks gradually settled into Asia Minor, depriving the empire of the rich farmlands of Asia Minor and also the sturdy army recruits that had made the Byzantine forces so formidable. The final blow to Constantinople came with the Fourth Crusade in 1204. The Fourth Crusade was instigated by Pope Innocent III (1198–1216), who had been voted into office to restore the grandeur of the papacy. Among other impressive acts, he insisted on a crusade to attack the infidel Muslims and also to reunite the Roman and Orthodox Christians. Consequently, a Latin kingdom was established in Constantinople controlled by Venice until the Byzantine restoration of Emperor Michael Palaeologus in 1261.[73]

Stavrianos indicates his deep understanding of the future Ottoman rise to power by discussing the underlying ideologies of Western Europe and the imperialistic tendencies of Eastern Europe and the Middle East.

He notes the medieval feudalism and the loosely organized monarchies of Western Europe as contrasted with the development of absolute monarchy and a highly centralized imperial bureaucracy in the East. He believes that Byzantine Rum lent this tradition to the Ottomans. But the Ottoman tradition derived exclusively not only from East Rome but also from Imperial Persia, the 'Abbasid Empire, the Mongols, and China.[74]

Halil Inalcik, the doyen of Ottoman history, has indicated in his monumental study what he considers the major phases of Ottoman history until 1600. The first phase entails the early foundation of the Ottoman State from the defeat of a Byzantine force at the battle of Bapheon of 1301 until the defeat of Sultan Beyazid I (1389–1402) by the world conqueror Tamerlane. Clearly, the Ottomans made their surprising advances against Byzantine territory because their small territory was located near Bursa, close to the then newly restored borders of Byzantium. The system of conquest in place at the time was one the Seljuks of Rum had used to increase their own legitimacy as a Muslim state, namely the *gazā* or holy war. This advantage of the Rum Seljuks ceased to be advantageous as the Mongol Il Khans took direct control of the Rum Seljuk state after 1271. For this reason, settlers gathered in border principalities to avoid Mongol control. As Inalcik emphasizes, the border culture was a contrast to the formal culture of the court of Konya and the courts of the provincial governors. These courts even used Persian as the official language. The border principalities, by contrast, practiced heretical religious beliefs led by dervishes and also followed customary law and lauded epic literature and practiced assimilation with all religious creeds. The border language, because of the great number of Turks, became Turkish. The border fighters were known as *Gazis*, but they often made common cause with the Greek borderers known as *Akritai*. After the initial brutal attacks of the Gazis upon the Greek countryside, the followers of Osman, the Osmanli, made it a hallowed duty of the fledgling state to protect the peasantry for two obvious reasons: they depended on the peasantry for the food they produced and also because the Greek peasantry were subject to the poll tax, the *kharaj*, the traditional Islamic tax levied on non-Muslims. Tolerance of foreign elements derived naturally from this economic necessity. It was this attitude that eventually served to unite the Christian Balkan principalities with the Gazi Muslim principalities of Asia Minor. As the Osmanli eliminated some of their rival Gazi states in Asia Minor, they established their first capital in Bursa in 1326. Osman's son, Sultan Orhan (1326–1362), with the help of his sons, Suleyman and Murad, supported a rival claimant, John Cantecuzenos, to the Byzantine throne in 1346 that was sealed with Orhan's marriage to one of John's daughters. Now his troops supported him against Bulgarian and Serbian rivals. In this manner, Orhan and his sons managed to secure passage across the Dardanelles and to establish themselves in Thrace in 1352. The happenstance of an earthquake on 1 March 1354 destroyed the walls of Gallipoli, the main fortress in the peninsula, and Suleyman's troops quickly occupied the city. Shortly thereafter, Suleyman died, and Orhan groomed Murad to succeed him. Thereupon, Sultan Murad I (1362–1389) began expanding the Osmanli hold over a number of remaining Turkish principalities in Asia Minor. One after another, the principalities of Germiyan, Hamidili, and Karaman came under Ottoman sway. Often the Ottomans claimed that these states, by resisting, were against the righteous Ottoman holy war (the *gazā*) against Byzantium. Sultan Murad I also did not hesitate to use contingents of Balkan Christian-conquered states against recalcitrant Turkish leaders. Murad's preoccupation with conquering Turkish principalities left him vulnerable to attacks in the Balkans because of the great distances and also the Ottoman vulnerability of crossing the Dardanelles without a navy. One such coalition was of Serbian and Bosnian forces Murad defeated in 1389 on the Kosovo Plain. But this battle cost Murad his life, a signal for a revolt of Turkish princes in Asia Minor. Murad's son, Sultan Bayezid I (1389–1402), known as Yildirim (lightning bolt), annexed most of the Turkish principalities and appointed trusted slaves to their governance.[75]

In one final bold move to end Turkish Empire building in the Balkans, a crusade was organized with Venice and Hungary secretly behind the scenes, urging the Bulgarians, the Albanians, and Mircea of Wallachia and even Byzantium to help destroy the Ottomans. But

Bayezid and his forces, including his new standing force of *Yeniçeris* (Janissaries), a standing slave corps consisting of young converts to Islam, were too skilled and rapidly deployed for the Christian forces, and they were soundly defeated on separate attacks or in the defeat of the Crusade of Nicopolis of 1396. Unfortunately for Bayezid, he became overconfident of his prowess and his troops at a time when Timur (Tamerlane) (1336–1405) was at the height of his power, having crushed the Golden Horde in 1395, taken control of central Asia and Iran, and now laid claim to the sovereign rights of the Il Khans in Asia Minor. Meanwhile, all the disgruntled former Turkish rulers had gathered at Timur's capital of Tabriz. Bayezid, relying too much on his auxiliary troops from the defeated Balkan states, challenged Timur at the Battle of Ankara in 1402. Bayezid was defeated and captured, and it was said that he was paraded in a cage before he was executed. Timur left to Bayezid's sons the remnants of the fledgling empire upon their swearing allegiance to him. Upon the death of Timur in 1405, the sons fought each other to regain their inheritance.[76]

As Professor Inalcik aptly notes, how did the Ottomans recover so rapidly after the major defeat and dismemberment by Tamerlane? The Turkish principalities of Asia Minor were basically restored by Tamerlane to previous regimes in exchange for their allegiance. Likewise, Byzantium, Serbia, Wallachia, and Albania regained some of their former territories and began to act independently. Bayezid's youngest son, Chelebi Mehmet, reestablished the dynasty in Asia Minor but was checked by the Venetians when his small naval force tried to break the blockade to defeat all contenders in *Rumeli* (Ottoman term for the "Balkans"). Mehmet died in 1421. The Byzantines now released another son of Bayezid, Mustafa, when he ceded Gallipoli to them. Murad II, who had succeeded Chelebi Mehmet, now defeated Mustafa and then faced a threat from John Hunyadi, the Hungarian hero. Murad attempted to unseat the Hungarians from Belgrade in 1440 but failed. Facing rebellion in Karaman in Asia Minor, Murad signed a peace with Hungary at Edirne in 1444. Murad then abdicated and placed his twelve-year-old son, Mehmet II, on the throne, but his son was not recognized in the Balkans. The king of Hungary and Poland, Vladislav

I (1440–1444), urged on by Pope Eugenius IV (1431–1447), prepared for war. Also, George Kastriota, known as Skanderbeg, revolted in Northern Albania. These events forced Murad II back into the foray. When these enemies converged on Edirne, the Ottoman capital, Murad II passed, with difficulty, the Venetian blockade of the Dardanelles to engage the Balkan forces of Hungary and Albania, led by Hunyadi, at Varna on 10 November, 1444. Murad's victory sealed once and for all Ottoman dominance up to the Danube River. In his last years, he defeated Skanderbeg in 1450 and Hunyadi at Kosovo in 1448. The two Balkan heroes, Hunyadi of Hungary and Skanderbeg of Albania, eventually died fighting Sultan Mehmet II, Hunyadi at Belgrade in 1456, and Skanderbeg in 1467, but their fame is still celebrated in their respective countries up to the present day. Hunyadi's son, Mathias Corvinus, was elected king of Hungary (1458–1490). Murad II took full command in 1446 because the advisers of Mehmet II had disagreed about an attack on Constantinople. The grand vezir, Çandarli Halil, fearing an overcommitment, opposed the attack and created a Janissary revolt to bring Murad II back into action, but Mehmet's tudors (*lale*), Zaganos and Şihabeddin, constituted a war party, and when Murad died in 1451, they urged Mehmet II to conquer the Byzantine's ruler and also other Ottomans who had been used by Byzantium as pawns to weaken Ottoman warfare.[77]

Sultan Mehmed II (1451–1481) proved to be a formidable leader. The drama of his defeat of Byzantium is still worthy of note. He ordered the building of the fortress of Rumeli Hisar facing his father's fortress of Anadolu Hisar in the Straits of the Bosphorus. Henceforth, the fortresses controlled all vessels on the Bosphorus. In 1453, the Byzantines had placed a massive chain at the mouth of the Golden Horn to block vessels from attacking the seawalls of Constantinople. To divide the forces of Emperor Constantine XIII, Mehmet II caused a number of small vessels to be dragged from Beshiktash over the hill and down into the Golden Horn. He also employed massive cannons to blast the land walls, and a breach opened at the Romanos Gate through which the Ottoman troops poured. After three days of pillaging, Mehmet II made peace with the Greek Orthodox patriarch, Gennadius, and gave him jurisdiction over his flock throughout the empire. Eventually, these privileges were extended to the Catholicos of the Armenians under decrees governing the millet system.[78]

At this point in our chronology, we must mention the *Eyup Camisi* or the Mosque of Jacob at the head of the Golden Horn in Istanbul. Mehmet II ordered the building of this mosque, the first mosque in the conquered city, in the years 1458–1459. The reason for this gesture was that Eyup or Jacob was reputedly a companian of the Prophet Muhammad and that he died from an arrow fired by the Byzantines when an Arab army first tried to conquer Constantinople. His burial sight was believed to have been later discovered, making the *turbe* or dome of the mosque over his grave sacred to the Ottomans. Although we could not find the actual date when all Sultans were required to hold this ritual, once they were chosen as the new Sultan, they were required, with their retinues, to make a royal excursion up the Golden Horn to receive the girding of the sword at the Eyup Mosque. Prior to the journey up the Golden Horn, Professor Inalcik informs us also that the *Bi'at*, the sacred oath that all high officials had to take, was combined with the duty of the griding of the sword. The high officials swore their loyalty and allegiance to the new sultan. This act was necessary because when a sultan died, all office holders had virtually lost their positions until they swore allegiance to the new sovereign. The girding of the sword took place within the Eyup Mosque and was probably performed by the Sheikh ul-Islam, the highest Islamic official and the chief qadi. These two ceremonies must be considered essential parts of the sultan's legitimacy to rule. The girding of the sword was followed by the ritual slaughtering of sheep and the distribution to the poor. One may surmise that the girding of the sword was a new ceremony after the building of the mosque and was first followed by Fatih Mehmet II's successor, Sultan Beyazid II (1484–1512). The *Bi'at* was an ancient practice.[79]

After the fall of Constantinople, Mehmet II pursued relentlessly his claim to inheriting the lands of the East Roman Empire. He also understood the importance of controlling the Dardanelles and building controlling fortresses there. He built up his fleet from thirty former vessels up to ninety-two by the 1470s. His fleets secured the shores of the Black Sea and also permitted no power to establish bases south of the Danube. Only an alliance of Hungary and Wallachia threatened the Ottomans in the Balkans because they could rely on the Venetian fleet. In 1463, the threat to the Ottomans became serious when the Venetians opened negotiations with Uzun Hasan (1453–1478) of the Akkoyunlu confederation in Iran and a part of Asia Minor. Uzun Hasan had defeated Abu Said, the last of the Timurid Dynasty, in 1469 and became the de facto ruler of Armenia, Kurdistan, Azerbaijan, and Iran. This plot was foiled when Venice failed to land cannon for Uzun Hasan in Alanya. The lack of cannon and firearms assured the Ottoman victory over Uzun Hasan, leagued with the Turkish amirate of the Karamanids, in the Battle of Başkent in 1473. Now Mehmet II directly attacked Venice with a siege of Scutari in Albania, 1474–1479. His admiral, Gedik Ahmet, seized a bridgehead at Otranto in 1480, and Mehmet II planned an attack on Italy in 1481, but he died en route shortly after leaving Istanbul. The constant pressure of Mehmet II on the Balkans and Asia Minor assured to the Ottomans a solid base from which they could make important territorial, economic, and political gains under Sultan Beyazid II and Sultan Selim I.[80]

Inalcik informs us of the great turmoil that followed the death of Mehmet II. He had pursued relentlessly his dreams of expansion, but the standing army, the Janissary Corps, bore the brunt and rebelled. Also, Mehmet II, to pay for the costly campaigns, had turned a number of freehold peasant farms into *timars* (tracts awarded for military service), debased the silver coinage, and raised customs dues. Those Ottomans, disgruntled by these policies, rallied around the party of Beyazid, the designated successor. This movement upon the death of Sultan Mehmet II (d. 1481) forced the brother of Beyazid, Cem (Jem), also a contender to succeed Mehmet II, to ally himself with Mamluk Egypt and later the Knights of Rhodes. To pacify his troops, Beyazid II led an attack on Moldavia in 1484, an easy victory but an affront to Poland, and also reestablished a number of peasant holdings. There remained the Mamluks in Syria and Egypt, who were looked upon in the Islamic world as the most legitimate and respected of all Muslim rulers. They laid claim to Akkoyunlu lands in Eastern Asia Minor and Persia and also Karaman and Dulkadir, Turkoman principalities, in which the Ottomans held claims. As the great Gazi state, converting Christians to Islam, the Ottomans claimed legitimacy over other Islamic countries. But by 1491, after six brutal campaigns between the Mamluks and Ottomans, these two powers made an antebellum truce. This truce gave to Beyazid II a chance to strengthen his army by equipping a great number with firearms and cannon. Meanwhile the Knights of Rhodes and later the Papacy joined the Cem party. The Ottoman's Cem (pronounced "Jem") Sultan was at first a captive of the Papacy and the Ottomans paid forty thousand ducats annually to keep him in a gilded arrest to avoid a civil war. Upon Cem's death in 1495, Beyazid felt that his navy was strong enough to challenge Venetian seaports in the Morea (the Peloponnesus), a war that endured 1499–1502. On the eastern front of this new empire, the mildness of Beyazid's policies had made possible a great defection of Turkoman tribes in Asia Minor. These tribes were influenced by the preaching of dervishes under the influence of the teachings of the Sheikh Safi of Ardabil (fl. 1252–1334) and his successors.[81]

XI. The Safavid Persian Interlude

Before we continue to deal with the Ottoman Revolution, we should examine briefly the Safavid Revolution because, for a century, it was a major challenge in the Islamic world to Ottoman pretentions of being the leading Muslim power. Safavid prominence in the eras of Bayazid II and Selim I depended on the charisma of Shah Isma'il. He defeated the White Sheep Dynasty in 1501 to whom his wife was closely related. He also had been chosen as the sheikh of the Safavid Mystical Order of Ardabil. By laying claim to being a descendant of Ali bin Abi Talib, first cousin and son-in-law of the Prophet, and also claiming kinship to the ancient kings of Persia, Shah Isma'il strengthened his legitimacy in the eyes of his Turkoman followers. Early in his reign, Shah Isma'il had declared his state would follow the Imami Shi'ism of the Twelfth Imam, whose followers believed the imam to be in hiding and return in due course to bring peace and justice to his followers. Iran, at the time, was basically Sunni. This policy disrupted internal Iranian affairs for many years. The Turkomans were known as *Qizilbash* (Turk., redheads) because they wore a red bonnet of twelve folds symbolizing the Twelfth Imam. They believed in a more fanatical Shi'ism and the two versions, Sunni and Shi'i Islam troubled the belief system of Iran until the era of Shah 'Abbas (1588–1629). As Shah Isma'il claimed to be the representative of the hidden Imam, thus usurping the official senior Shi'i clerics, the *Mujtahids*, he also caused problems. The population of Iran in the sixteenth and later centuries included as much as one-third tribal entities: Iranian, Turkish, Kurdish, Arab, and Baluchi tribes, but the Turkomans played the major role in the sixteenth century. As a standing army, Isma'il I chose the best warriors from each Turkoman tribe and placed them in a unit of about three thousand, known as *qurchis* (Mongol, quiver bearers). Generally speaking, the Turkomans served as warriors and leaders of the various provinces, but the *Tajiks* (native Persians) were universally recognized as the best administrators. This division or specialization also caused friction in Iran.[82]

At the end of the sultanate of Ottoman Bayazid II, the Turkoman tribal problem had gotten out of hand. In 1511, the Turkomans marched on Bursa, the first Ottoman capital, and were led by disgruntled Ottoman *sipahis* (mounted cavalry from each province) who had lost their *timars* (similar to *iqtas*, as payment tracts for military service). Prince Selim, who had advocated a strong policy against the Turkomans, gained the support of the Janissaries and forced his ailing father to abdicate in 1512. Because Sultan Bayezid had brought much stability and prosperity to the empire and also modernized the army and navy with firearms and cannon, he had laid the groundwork for the future expansion in the sultanates of Selim I (1512–1520) and of Suleyman I (1520–1566), known as the Lawgiver. Sultan Selim's prowess as a leader was soon apparent. He followed Shah Isma'il's army to the mountains near the border of Georgia on the plain of Chaldiran. Selim I decisively defeated the Persian/Turkoman army at Chaldiran on 23 August 1514 using cannon and firearms to great advantage. Soon thereafter, the mountainous region from Erzurum to Diyarbekir came over to Ottoman allegiance. Any Turkoman tribes that had not escaped to Iran were driven out of Eastern Asia Minor or slaughtered. Very soon, Sultan Selim invaded Dulkadir because the Egyptian Mamluks laid claim to this principality on the border of Syria. This move in 1515 against the province of Dulkadir was a virtual declaration of war against Mamluk Egypt. Moreover, there was, at this time, another spoiler disrupting trade patterns in the Indian Ocean. The Portuguese had circumnavigated Africa in 1497 and were attacking the Indian trade of Egypt, of the Red Sea, and of the Persian Gulf. Only the Ottomans had naval capabilities to challenge Portugal. The sherif of Mecca, a descendant of the Prophet Muhammad, complained directly to Sultan

Selim in 1516. Sultan Al-Ghawri, then leader of the Mamluks, stung by the Ottoman move against Dulkadir, refused joint consultations about the Portuguese. Sultan Selim occupied Aleppo in 1516 with the cooperation of local Arabs and then defeated Al-Ghawri's Mamluks at Marj Dabik. Sultan Al-Ghawri died in the battle. Sultan Selim in the Great Mosque of Aleppo now received from the last surviving 'Abbasid caliph, Al-Mutawakkil II, the sought-after crowning legitimacy for the Ottomans, the title *khadim al-haramayn* (servitor of the two sacred cities, Mecca and Medina). The Ottomans overcame the remaining resistance of the Mamluks and defeated the new Sultan Tuman Bay at Reydaniyya near Cairo on 22 January 1517. On this campaign, Sultan Selim had annexed Syria, Egypt, and the Arabian Peninsula. On his return to Istanbul, Sultan Selim also had the family of the last 'Abbasid caliph accompany him. As Professor Inalcik noted, "The Empire was no longer a frontier state but an Islamic Caliphate . . . protectors not only of the frontiers but of the entire Muslim World." Shah Isma'il after Chaldiran had turned to the Portuguese for help against the Ottomans, but no special relationship developed. In fact, until his death, the Safavids were basically on the defensive because they did not possess firearms and cannon. Professor Blow points out that after Isma'il's death, nine years of civil war broke out among the Turkomans for dominance. Only in Khorasan had Shah Isma'il been able to drive out the Uzbeks, Sunni allies of the Ottomans. In the era of Sultan Suleyman (1520–1566), we observe a concerted effort of Shah Tahmasp (1524–1576) to build up a force of arquebusiers and cannoneers. During the era of Sultan Suleyman, three wars took place between the Ottomans and Safavids, and although Tahmasp was considered a weak ruler, Professor Savory points out that he and the Ottomans negotiated the Peace of Amasya in 1555, basically a settlement of the territories each army occupied, and the Ottomans expected two hundred *yüks* of silk as tribute each year (a yük is estimated by Inalcik as 154 kilograms, a small camel load). Shah Tahmasp meanwhile built up his specialized forces using captives from neighboring regions: Georgia, Armenia, and Circassia. These were known as Slaves of the Royal Household. To ensure their loyalty, they were forced to become converts to Twelver

Shi'ism. Tahmasp also trained a special troop of Turkomans in firearms known as *Shahi-Sevenler* (Lovers of the Shah). Professor Blow points out that Shah Tahmasp became deeply worried about the legitimacy of his regime in Shi'ite circles and invited a number of Twelver Shi'ite *mujtahids* (leaders in the interpretation of Islamic law) from Lebanon to instruct his religious leaders.[83]

The greatest challenge to Ottoman dominance took place during the reign of Shah 'Abbas (1588–1629). It is because of famous leaders like Shah Isma'il, Shah Tahmasp, and Shah 'Abbas that we have accredited the Safavids as the *the eleventh Islamic revolution*. After the death of Shah Tahmasp, ethnic intrigues of the Shah's wives determined the succession. Prince Haydar, a known leader and half Georgian, was killed by the Daghestan rivals, and Shah Isma'il II, a Turkoman candidate, was crowned for a year and attempted to reinstate Sunnism. He was also killed by the Turkomans.[84] Finally, the half-blind Shah Khodabanda, son of a Turkoman wife of Tahmasp, gained the throne (1578–1588). It was in the Ottoman interest to keep Iran weak, but to start a war just because the leadership was in disarray caused equal problems for the Ottomans. Ottoman leadership also was approaching a period of disarray that eventually involved also a set of *harem* intrigues and ethnic politics. The basic problem was that the Ottomans exhausted themselves fighting in the difficult terrain of the Caucasus for mixed goals, including control of silk production against Persian regular forces that often used guerrilla tactics. They made a peace treaty with the new Shah 'Abbas in 1588, but only five years later, they started a war with Austria 1593–1608. The seasoned Ottoman viziers opposed the war, fearing a two-front war with Iran and Austria. Shah 'Abbas bode his time, preparing to take back a number of provinces that the Ottomans had occupied in the Caucasus. In 1603, Shah 'Abbas made his move driving the Ottomans out of the Central Caucasus. The Ottomans managed to hold on to the Georgian western provinces bordering the Black Sea as they were protected by the Ottoman Navy. Shah 'Abbas, faced with almost continual rebellion among the Georgian provinces of Kartli and Kakheti, began wholesale deportations of young Georgian men and women, inducting the men, upon their conversion, into his armed forces, and the famed Caucasus beauties were forced into the harems of leading government officials. This policy in the long run changed the ethnic composition of the Iranian upper class. The bitter fighting between the Ottomans and Safavids only ended with the death of Shah 'Abbas in 1629 and the rise of Sultan Murad IV (1623–1640), who overcame his youthful exploits and sobered up enough to lead his forces against Iranian forces in Iraq to regain Baghdad and its border areas before his death in 1640. The Safavids, for the most part, showed no signs of the active leadership so typical of Shah 'Abbas, and their dynasty was replaced in the eighteenth century.[85]

XII. Continuation of Ottoman Analysis to World War I

After introducing the important Safavid Revolution, it is imperative that we survey the reign of Sultan Suleyman the Lawgiver (1520–1566). This period in Ottoman history is considered the era par excellence of the Ottoman Empire, but as with all histories of empires, one may also note certain weaknesses of Suleyman's administration. In the era of Sultan Suleyman, the Ottomans became deeply involved with the affairs of France and the Holy Roman Empire, the latter a loose entity that encompassed much of Spain, the low countries of Belgium and the Netherlands, parts of Germany, Italy, and Austria. The meeting of the electors of the Holy Roman Empire chose Emperor Charles V (1519–1556) of the house of Habsburg of Austria and Spain to head up this empire. By choosing Charles, the electors had basically snubbed King Francis I (1515–1547) of France. Both rulers had pledged to fight the growing power of the Ottomans. As a consequence of the election, France and the empire fought wars against each other in the next decade, and Francis I was captured in 1525 and was forced to give up claims to Italian cities and the province of Burgundy.[86]

Meanwhile, both France and the empire had to deal with the rise of the Reformation instituted in 1517 when the Bible scholar and monk Martin Luther (1483–1546) tacked up his ninety-five theses on the door of Wittenberg Cathedral in Germany, criticizing Catholic religious practice as counter to the Bible. He particularly objected to the misuse of indulgences and the purchase of absolutions from sin.

Soon however, Luther enlarged his concepts to "the priesthood of all believers," virtually rendering unnecessary a priesthood that served as an intermediary between the individual Christian and God. There seems no doubt that the strife between France and the Holy Roman Empire made possible the rapid spread of the Protestant faith. It is also of interest that the Ottomans soon took sides with France as they feared the concentration of power of the Habsburgs. But the Ottomans also noted that the Protestant faith resembled Islam in the fundamental issue of a direct relationship between God and the worshipper.[87]

Hungary became a major concern of Sultan Suleyman. On 29 August of 1521, when Charles V was putting pressure on France, Suleyman saw his opportunity to take the fortress of Belgrade, called the key to Hungary, and also the island of Rhodes, then in the hands of the Knights of St. John, a major player in the Eastern Mediterranean and an Ottoman enemy. As further aid to Francis I, Suleyman, with a large army, defeated the Hungarians on the plain of Mohacs on 28 August 1526. After the Ottomans departed from Buda, the Hungarians elected John Zapolya as king. Meanwhile, the partisans of the Habsburgs elected Archduke Ferdinand, the brother of Charles V, as king, and he occupied Hungary. Sultan Suleyman again invaded Hungary in 1529, placed Zapolya once again on the throne, and besieged Vienna, the Habsburg capital, for three weeks. This game of musical chairs with Ferdinand continued in 1531 and 1532. Finally, the Ottomans, after John Zapolya's death in 1541, occupied Hungary outright, making it a *beylerbeylik* (that is, a province). Zapolya's widow and son were sent to Transylvania, an Ottoman vassal province of Hungarians and Vlachs. Ferdinand, controlling the northern sliver of Hungary, made a play for Transylvania in 1550. The Ottoman response was to set up a new *beylerbeylik* in Temesvar in Southern Transylvania.[88]

With Ottoman support for the Reformers, the Habsburgs finally recognized Lutheranism as a formal religion in the Peace of Augsburg in 1555. In 1536, a formal treaty was concluded between France and the Ottomans. This treaty also entailed trade agreements and naval support at a time when the great Turkish Admiral Hayreddin Barbarossa was named *kapudan-i derya* (that is, Grand Admiral). He defeated the Habsburg Admiral Andrea Doria in 1538, leaving the Ottomans masters of the Mediterranean Sea.[89]

By the middle of the sixteenth century, one may observe the emergence of a pattern of alignments. We have spoken of the alliance between France and the Ottomans. To this alliance, Poland-Lithuania of the Jagellon Dynasty adhered, but only precariously. As a Catholic power, but opposed to papal mandates and the coziness of the Papacy and the Habsburgs, most of the Polish nobility cooperated with the Ottomans and France because the Ottomans protected their southern flank during its incessant warfare with Orthodox Russia. When the Jagellon Dynasty died out in 1569, King Henri de Valois of France was elected briefly as King of Poland in 1573, before he occupied the French throne. The Ottomans under Sultan Suleyman had established a buffer zone in Eastern Europe by controlling Transylvania, Wallachia, Moldavia, and the Crimean Tatars. By encouraging an attack on Podolia and earlier having occupied Moldavia, the Ottomans had overstepped good relations with Poland. Hence, the Polish nobility elected King Stephan Bathory (1575–1586) to the kingship of Poland in 1575. He had married Anna, the last surviving Jagellon. He was fortunately also favored by the Ottomans because of his former service to the Ottoman state. We should note that good relations with Poland often became precarious because of the raids of the Crimean Tatars on Polish territory and, likewise, the raids of the Zaporozhian Cossacks on Ottoman settlements. Sweden often found itself in the Ottoman camp because of Moscow's desire for Swedish territory. Finally, the English, because of favorable trade agreements and the animosity of the Spanish Habsburgs, also cooperated with the Ottomans.[90]

Before we complete our discussion of the complex sixteenth century, we must mention again the all-important relations of the Ottomans to the rise of Safavid Persia. The Ottomans, ever mindful of the distance to their western frontier with the Habsburgs and their eastern frontier with Safavid Iran, at all costs, tried to avoid a two-front war. Hence, in 1534, Sultan Suleyman signed a truce with Crown Prince Ferdinand in Hungary then led his army to Tabriz and Baghdad and annexed Azerbaijan and Iraq. Other border states who were nominally in the

Safavid orbit acquiesced in Ottoman control, and Basra became another base of the Ottoman navy. But the Persians counterattacked when the Ottomans opened a new front in Hungary. After a long, intermittent war, the two parties agreed to the Treaty of Amasya on 29 May 1555. The Ottomans retained Baghdad, and Shah Tahmasp (1524–1576) agreed not to permit the cursing of the first three caliphs—Abu Bakir, 'Umar, and 'Uthman—and to pay two hundred yüks of silk each year as tribute, which was mentioned earlier.

At about the same time as the Treaty of Amasya, a little noticed event took place on the Volga River that basically altered the relationship between the Ottoman Empire and the upstart state of Muscovy. In the recent past, partly because of the devastation wrought by Tamerlane upon the Golden Horde in 1393 and 1395, the Ottomans no longer had a reliable buffer on the Ukrainian steppe to counter Muscovy. The Golden Horde gradually broke up into three separate khanates: Kazan, Astrakhan, and the Crimea. In the tsardom of Ivan IV (1533–1584), both Kazan (1552) and Astrakhan (1554) fell to Muscovy. The Ottomans had protected the Crimean khanate since 1475 and often used the khan's cavalry in Eastern Europe and the Caucusus. By taking full control of the Volga River down to the Caspian Sea, Muscovy now had access to trade with Iran across the Caspian Sea and also blocked Ottoman access to the amirates of central Asia and Ottoman alliance with the Uzbeks. Meanwhile, many landless serfs and other disgruntled or persecuted elements of the Polish and Russian monarchies had begun to settle on the Dnieper, Don, and Volga Rivers and in the Northern Caucasus. These were known as Cossack settlements from the Turkish word *kazak*, meaning free-living marauders.

These conquests by Muscovy limited Ottoman steppe relations to such an extent that in 1569, the Ottomans mounted a major expedition to connect the Don and Volga Rivers with a canal. Such a canal would have made it easier for the Ottomans to attack Astrakhan with naval support. The enterprise failed for a complex of reasons but made possible, in future years, for lively trade and political cooperation between Russia and Iran through the Caspian Sea.[91]

In this brief description of the Ottoman Revolution and its struggle for Islamic legitimacy, we still are challenged to account for the gradual decline of the empire and its tenacity to survive into the twentieth century. Professor Inalcik, in his study of Ottoman history from 1300 to 1600, has provided a great amount of detail about how administrative decisions, and the technological advances of European and Asian adversaries already greatly weakened the empire by the year 1600. If we look to the challenges to the Ottoman naval forces, we are struck by the rapid advance of European navies building great galleons, equipped with cannon, while the Ottomans still maintained fleets of galleys often rowed by slaves. Consequently, the Ottomans lost their former dominance of the high seas. This factor meant that they lost the support of the North African Emirates, and they were hard-pressed to support Egypt, Syria, Lebanon, and various islands by losing control of coastal sea-lanes. They also lost control of the coastal trade of the Indian Ocean at first to Portugal and then, after 1580, to Spain and finally to the powerful Dutch and English fleets. As we also have noted in the Safavid Revolution, Shah 'Abbas (1588–1629) tried to limit the overland export of silk through Ottoman territory, one of the outstanding reasons for Ottoman attacks on Iran.[92]

Inalcik emphasizes, however, that changing circumstances such as a 40 percent increase in population in the sixteenth century in the Ottoman territories and new realities brought added strain to old systems. The *Ulema*, responsible for law enforcement in every province, the medresse training system, and administration of *awqāf* or pious foundations, became weakened by bribery and nepotism. Inalcik basically recognized three centers of power in a province, the *Beylerbeyi* or governor, together with the *Sipahiyan* or land-based cavalry represented the sultan's authority. The *qadis* or district judges formed the backbone of Ottoman administration, making sure that the laws were enforced. The *hazine defterdari*, in the province, represented the interests of the central treasury. The local *defterdar*, like the *qadi* and the governor, could report directly to the capital and could report abuses. The *timar* system, whereby outstanding warriors and their families were traditionally awarded land tracts and villages, became gradually obsolete. In the past, in exchange for their supervision and the income of the *timar*, they were required to serve as cavalry in times of war, but by 1600, they were losing their tracts to courtiers or to *awqāf* (pious endowments) and were not equipped with modern firearms. To offset this drain on active warriors, the Ottoman government began increasing the size of the Janissary Corps, who then were equipped with firearms and cannon. But the Janissaries required payment in cash, thus placing a great strain on the sultan's treasury (*hazine-i has*) and the central treasurer (*defterdar*). Moreover, after Suleyman the Lawgiver, or even beginning with him, the influence of courtiers and harem factions began to affect the quality also of the sultans. The heirs to the throne were no longer trusted with governing provinces with mature tutors (*lale*) out of fear that they might revolt. Consequently, they were placed in their quarters in Topkapi Palace in what was appropriately called the *Kafes* (the Cage). In addition, as the *devshirme* system, the draft of youths from non-Muslim families, ceased to function in traditional fashion, many landless peasant youths or youths from newly conquered territiories, such as Circassia, Abkhasia, or even Arabs, joined the Janissaries. Unfortunately, they also often led local rebellions.[93]

To account for the longevity of the empire, in spite of the handicaps aforementioned, one must look to fresh analyses. Chaim Gerber, in his seminal book *The Social Origins of the Modern Middle East*, initially gives credit to Barrington Moore's paradigm as an inspiration for producing his study. Moore had written a book entitled *The Social Origins of Dictatorship and Democracy* in which he discussed a paradigm as follows: Moore looked at the special forms of political regimes such as the peasantry, the aristocracy (i.e., the landed upper class), and the urban bourgeoisie. He particularly looked at the landed upper class and their alliance with other groups. "Moore assumed that an aristocratic government is not compatible with parliamentary democracy because tight control of the peasantry necessitates a strong repressive apparatus." A form of parliamentary democracy should appear if a capitalist economy is in place and there is a large middle class. Such a society does not need a strong repressive apparatus. For example, the British monarchy was weak because to pay for an army or a bureaucracy, the parliament would have to vote appropriations. But as parliament was controlled by the landed aristocracy, they traditionally could not be taxed, and only in emergencies were funds available. According to Professor Theda Skocpol, a Moore critic, "Moore posited three routes to the modern world—'bourgeois revolution' (England, France, and the United States), 'revolution from above' (Japan and Germany), and 'peasant revolution' (China, Russia)." Moore's controlling factor seemed to be the strength of the impulse toward modernization that both Gerber and Skocpol find a weak part of Moore's analysis.[94]

Yet Gerber still regards Moore's analysis as key to his own. He agrees most thoroughly with Halil Inalcik in calling attention to the basic conservativeness of Ottoman laws relating to land holdings. There seems to have been awareness in the sultan's bureaucracy, as born out by *qadi* records (that is, court records), that the Ottoman regime should guard against the formation of a powerful landed aristocracy. In theory, all grain-producing land was *miri* (that is, owned by the state). Land defined as *mulk* was land owned by the village collectively, including orchards and pasturage. There were also strict laws forbidding the transfer of *miri* land into *waqf* (a pious foundation for fountains, mosques, schools, etc.). The Islamic judges (*qadis*), as the state's local administrators, always gained more power and wealth if land was turned into *waqf*. We may then conclude that the tenure of a peasant's holding for him and his family was basically permanent as long as the land was regularly tilled. This observation is very important for the longevity of the empire. Most peasant holdings remained in the hands of peasants until the twentieth century, and by and large, the state did not have to maintain a repressive organization in the countryside. We may also gain an idea of the size of the *çift*, a basic holding used also in taxation. The *çift* or the land a pair of oxen could till in a season was considered enough to sustain a peasant family. This measure amounted to 60 to 150 dönüms (as an old measure, about 1000 square meters; today, 1 hectar or about 2.5 acres). As for taxation, Gerber notes that there were two kinds: the *'ushur* or basically 10 percent on the produce and the *çift resmi*, a land tax with varying rates. The government frowned on a peasant dividing up his *çift* to give land to his offspring, but Gerber cites a sixteenth-century study of Michael Cook that indicated how often peasant holdings were divided among their offspring.[95]

The other counterpart of the countryside regime was the *timar* system, the traditional Ottoman system of rewarding brave warriors with tracts of land or villages for income only, not control. The *sipahis*, the rural mounted Ottoman cavalry, collected the land tax from the villagers to sustain their needs and to provide mounted cavalry whenever the sultan demanded calvary. The cavalryman, if he tried to circumvent the laws, had to answer to the provincial governor and the district *qadi*. As the peasants usually paid in kind, the *sipahis* had to deal with grain sales or storage. In the seventeenth and later centuries, *mültezims* (tax farmers) began replacing the *timar* holders and had to pay taxes in cash to the government to offset the high cost of the standing army, the Janissaries. If we read the seventeenth-century findings of Gerber, we also note that as many as 25 percent of the population around Bursa apparently had no access to cultivated lands but earned large profits by sheepherding or cultivating orchards. Even today on the hills of Bursa, one finds rich stands of olive and fruit trees. Also around Bursa, Gerber found a considerable number of large estates, *çiftliks*. One must consider the rich volcanic soils around Bursa, the natural hot springs, and an attractive mild climate that still attracts upper-class Turkish society.[96]

Gerber's analysis in the nineteenth century still finds that land transactions were very conservative. The state apparatus still tended to protect the actual tiller of the soil in spite of the abuses of the sultan's favorites who were given land grants called *temlik*. Without a truly coercive apparatus in the hands of absentee landlords, both Moore and Gerber agree that such a country has the possibility of adopting a parliamentary system. The new spoiler in the nineteenth century is the Industrial Revolution. The Ottomans realized that they were at a disadvantage in modern technology in the seventeenth and eighteenth centuries, but they only gradually adopted new methodologies, mostly in applications to military science. There were even theoreticians among the conservative *Ulema* that believed the sultans need only rejuvenate the institutions so victorious under Sultan Suleyman the Lawgiver in the sixteenth century. These theories were known even in the eighteenth century as *As-Sulafa'* (the predecessor regimes) and are reminiscent of the movement *Al-Salifiya* founded in Egypt by Mohammed 'Abduh (1849–1905).[97] This belief is still followed by the Muslim Brotherhood and reputedly by the new coalition of Iraq and Syria, known as ISIS (the Islamic State of Iraq and Syria).

The Industrial Revolution, above all, challenged Ottoman legitimacy. Gerber, citing a study by Dominique Sourdel, notes that Ottoman handicrafts continued to contribute seriously to the Ottoman budget until the 1820s when European goods began to enter the Ottoman market through the increased use of steamships. Steamships drastically lowered the costs of transportation and European goods. But to bring produce to seaports also presented serious costs. Studies by Orhan Kurmuş and others probably greatly weaken Immanuel Wallerstein's modern world system, which holds that after the sixteenth-century capitalism dominated, the world and was divided into core countries (Britain and other Western European states), semiperipheral and peripheral countries (such as Asian countries and the Ottoman Empire). The theory held that core countries did all the manufacturing, and the peripheral countries supplied the raw materials. Gerber, by indicating even at the beginning of the twentieth century how much local manufacturing survived, calls into question Wallerstein's system as it applied particularly to Anatolia, the Ottoman core. Closer studies of the Balkan area by Bruce McGowan confirmed that, given easy access to shore communities or navigable rivers, such as the Danube, commercial agriculture played a significant role.[98]

Gerber and Inalcik account for the longevity of the Ottoman system because of conservative land laws. Professor Suraiya Faroqui, when surveying the sixteenth and seventeenth centuries, has made some interesting observations about Ottoman legitimacy in a chapter entitled "Symbols of Power and Legitimation." Faroqui, apart from the Ottoman protection of Mecca and Medina, has added the sultan's protection of the annual pilgrimage to Jerusalem, Mecca, and Medina, the *hajj*. Also, we may note Ottoman festivities. Faroqui calls attention to the circumcision of a prince as one of the most important festivals rather than the date of birth of a prince. We have a prime example of the circumcision of Prince Mehemmed on 29 May 1582 in the middle of a war with Iran. The birth of the Prophet Muhammad, the celebration at the end of Ramadan, and the commemoration of the conquest of Istanbul of 1453 are examples of other important festivals. Palaces, fountains, and elaborate tombs of the Ottoman Dynasty also add to the prestige of the Ottomans. All rulers drew upon the prestige of beautiful or monumental architecture. The image of a warrior sultan or regular attendance at the Friday noon prayers, as did Sultan 'Abd al-Hamid II (1876–1909), enhanced the power of the dynasty.[99]

Gerber makes one final observation about Ottoman consistency in land law. The very important law of 1858 actually undercut the previous laws in that it provided deeds (*tapu*). This land law made possible the acquisition of large land tracts (*çiftlik*), basically for the elites or tribal leaders if the land was completely void of tillers. Then the land became virtually private property (*mulk*). The abuse of this system is apparent. If a tribal sheikh placed his name on the deed, what formerly had been a collective ownership now was possessed by the sheikh's family. Gerber discusses the growing power of the *'ayan* or Ottoman provincial notables. Gerber, like McGowan, observes that these notables grow powerful in the provinces whenever the central government is weak such as at the beginning of the nineteenth century.[100]

Bruce McGowan, in his contribution to the collective work on the Ottoman Empire, from 1600 to 1914, is particularly interested in "The Age of the Ayans, 1699–1812." Of special interest in this study is McGowan's covering much of the same history dealt with by Gerber. McGowan, specializing on the Balkans and looking closely at European history, gives us further insights. He notes that the Ottomans still maintained the myth of its military and social prowess through much of the eighteenth century in spite of the loss of Hungary in 1699 to the Austrian Habsburgs and, even later, the loss of Belgrade, only to regain it with strong French diplomatic support in 1739. But the Russians under Tsar Peter the Great (1689–1725) had serious exposure to European technology that was put to the test under Tsarina Catherine the Great (1762–1798) when the Ottomans faced a series of serious defeats under the withering fire of Suvorov's artillery. McGowan points out that the population of Russia doubled in the eighteenth century. He also notes that the Ottomans managed some new technologies in the production of soap, glass, sugar, gunpowder, and paper but gained insufficient knowledge of the role ballistics and other weapons played in strategic warfare. He also relates that the Ottomans spent much time and treasure building fortifications, libraries, schools, and bathhouses, but few grand mosques. Most strikingly, he seems to give more credence to Wallerstein's theory that the Ottomans became suppliers of raw materials, and notably cotton, in the eighteenth century. There was a definite tendency toward complacency. One is reminded of the Tulip Era in the days of Sultan Ahmed III (1703–1730) when the Ottoman elite vied with each other for rare tulip bulbs. The Janissary Corps now married into Istanbul families and, still carrying their tax exempt status, became less a military force and more a militia, a faction revolting against reform measures if the grand vezier was weak. McGowan sees, along with others, the problem of dual citizenship, the danger of Ottoman minorities serving as commercial partners with powerful European firms. Ottomans were basically proponents of free trade, but merchants able to circumvent Ottoman custom duties produced the dangers of a colonial pattern of trade, a partial alienation of minority merchants and investment in trade rather than industry. The Ottoman bureaucracy could not match the efficiency of the Europeans, nor could neither the *Ulema* nor the bureaucracy amass the wealth needed to pass on wealth to descendants; hence, there was no experimentation in new technologies. In the "Age of the Ayans," McGowan gives much insight into the power of local dignitaries (i.e., Ayans) in the provinces, as noted by Gerber, whenever the sultans or the veziers could not assert power from the center. Finally, late in the century systematic military reform was undertaken by Sultan Selim III (1789–1807) in his *Nizam-i Jedid* (the New Reform), but who was overwhelmed by the reactionary Ayans, Janissaries, and *Ulema* and executed in 1808. Only when his nephew, Sultan Mahmud II (1809–1839), eliminated the Janissaries in 1826 could real reform begin. In the nineteenth century, this took the form of American frigate building in the 1830s and 1840s, general English military and naval support, and German military advisers in the 1830s and the 1880s and the 1890s. The great British foreign minister and prime minister Lord Palmerston (fl. 1807–1865), the tireless supporter of liberal ideas, realized that British troops could not police the Middle East after the Crimean War (1853–1856) and the Sepoy Rebellion in India in 1857–1858, and Palmerston threw his support behind the modernization of the Ottoman armed forces as Russia relentlessly took more Ottoman territory and promoted rebellion among the religiously Orthodox states in the Balkans.[101]

It is not necessary for us here to rewrite Ottoman history. It is, of course, important to report the overthrow of Sultan ʿAbd ul-Hamid II (1876–1909) by the Young Turk Revolution of 1909, shortly after the sultan reinstated the Constitution that he had instituted in 1876 but had abrogated in 1877. The Constitution was enacted by Midhat Pasha (1822–1884), the liberal grand vezier, who was soon dismissed and accused of the murder of the previous Sultan ʿAbd ul-ʿAziz (1861–1876). He was sentenced to death but actually was murdered in exile. Sultan ʿAbd ul-Hamid II was the last ruling sultan, praised for his devotion to Pan-Islam and his building of the Hijaz Railroad, but condemned for his reign using an elaborate spy system on his own subjects and his closing of the First Parliament. One should note the many changes that took place in this period that heralded constitutions and parliaments among many Middle East governments in the twentieth century.[102]

XIII. Imperial Powers in the Middle East Prior to World War I

At the close of World War II in 1945, the imperial European powers had experienced the devastation of six or seven years of warfare on their homelands and on their imperial holdings in the Middle East and worldwide. This reality forced upon the European governments a retrenchment or an outright divestment of their overseas possessions. In many cases, they asked the United States to assume some of their former responsibilities. Here we propose to survey the experience of key European powers that gained in the nineteenth century a great deal of power over the Ottoman Empire, whose strength and finances to defend its own imperial borders had greatly diminished.

For many years, historians have sought to simplify the complex history of the nineteenth-century Middle East by the term *the Eastern Question*. This term was used to express the question of when the Ottoman Empire would collapse. And one may ask, why was the Ottoman Empire so important? Even before the fall of Constantinople and the Byzantine Empire in 1453, the Ottomans had become the foremost Muslim power in the Middle East. Its armies and fleets would take control of the Balkan Peninsula up to the walls of Vienna, conquer all lands in the Middle East and North Africa including Algeria, and challenged even the Safavid Persian Empire. The Ottoman ruling elites, some conservative, some liberal, were aware, because of a century of lost wars and lost control over market forces that drastic changes were called for if the empire were to survive.[103] Diplomatic affairs were somewhat complicated because the Ottoman Empire was predominately Muslim, while the encircling European powers were basically Christian. There were other nuances complicating European intervention. The British and the Germans were considered Protestant Christian, while France, Austro-Hungary, and Italy professed Catholic Christianity. Russia was the predominant Orthodox Christian power and claimed a protective role over Orthodox lands in the Balkans: Greece, Roumania, Montenegro, Serbia, and Macedonia.

The two principal ideological forces, nationalism and liberalism, shook the foundations of all multinational states in the nineteenth century, including the Ottoman Empire, the Russian Empire, and Austro-Hungary. The British, French, and Dutch Empires managed to maintain some semblance of their old empires until the end of World War II. Nationalism, the glorification of one's country (*la patrie*) and of ethnic or blood ties, took its inspiration from the exploits and conquests of Napoleon, but liberalism also took its inspiration from the French and American Revolutions and Napoleon's issuance of the Rights of Man in 1801. Nationalism attained its expression by advocating patriotic parades, strong investment in one's armed forces, honoring the flag and limiting popular control of business by controlling trade unions. Liberalism was very much tied to the concepts of written constitutions that spelled out one's rights. Liberalism also called for rapid change or a revolution against the reactionary forces of the old regimes: religious or state censorship, forced military service, and other forms of legal, religious, and governmental coercion. It also sought to protect minorities, to provide safety nets for the poor and aged, and to encourage free and open markets. Liberalism was marked by the rise of a strong middle class secured by business activity and the rise of Protestant Christianity. In governmental terms, liberalism expected a separation of powers, the formation of political parties, the security of a constitution, and a parliament of contending ideas passing rational laws. It also gave access to secular beliefs free from former religious restrictions, freedom of choice in training and employment, and a belief in progress. Intellectuals, writers, and artists, under a liberal government, expected freedom of expression, the right of free assembly, and freedom from racial discrimination.

It is easy to see why governments and demagogues found it easier to emphasize nationalism rather than liberalism. One could deliver nationalism with rhetoric, flags, military parades, a compliant police force, and company-sponsored trade unions. If a government wished to give lip service to liberal institutions, it often sponsored strictly controlled political parties and a parliament with upper class or property rights for membership. Religious organizations continued to retain their flocks by controlling access to sacraments and a priesthood promising eternal life.

Another nineteenth-century expression to describe the rivalry between the Russian and British Empires was the term *the Great Game in Asia*. If we leave aside the various attempts of Russia and Austria-Hungary to foment local pro-Christian rebellions in the Balkans as Ottoman power receded from Europe, the first stage of the Great Game may well have been the British diplomatic support to Iran after Russia, in 1800, formally annexed Georgia, a former protectorate of Safavid Iran. Soon thereafter, the Russian Army pushed deeply into Azerbaijan, forcing Iran to sign the Treaty of Turkmenchay in 1828. This treaty defined the border of Russia in Azerbaijan, the Aras River until the breakup of the Soviet Union in 1991 when the modern states of Azerbaijan, Armenia, and Georgia were founded.

The Crimean War of 1853 to 1855 grew into a conflagration of much greater consequence in Russian-British rivalry. Britain and France continued to support the Palmerston system, helping the Ottoman Empire with troop commitments against Russia. As a result of the war, Russia was forced to give up its claim to protecting Orthodox Christians in the Balkan Peninsula, a controversial clause written into the Treaty of Kuchuk Kaynarji of 1774. Russia continued to counter Britain in Asia by annexing three Muslim states in central Asia (Kazakhstan, Uzbekistan, and Tajikistan) between 1868 and 1890. The British fought three Afghan Wars to stabilize the Afghan frontier in order to protect Afghan approaches to India. Eventually, the "Great Game" led their rivalry to the Russo-Japanese War of 1904–1905 that ended in a Japanese victory, in part because the British spy, Sidney Reilly, gave the Japanese fleet the location of Russian mines placed in the harbor of Vladivostok.[104]

Adding to the details of this rivalry, there is probably no better summation of Britain's approach to the Middle East in the nineteenth century than to refer to the Palmerston system. Viscount J. T. Palmerston was British foreign minister 1830–1834, 1836–1841 and, later, prime minister, 1855–1858 and 1859–1865. He recognized that Britain need fear only one rival, the Russian Empire, and also Britain was required to protect British communications with India and her influence over the weakened Ottoman Empire. But Palmerston, ever mindful of British worldwide commitments, knew that Britain did not have the manpower or financial resources to match Russia or to garrison the Middle East. He thus advocated the incredibly wise policy of supporting the modernization of the Ottoman army and navy in order for them to defend their own lands and indirectly British interests. Apparently, he did not oppose the German military mission to the Ottomans led by Captain Helmut von Moltke from 1834 to 1839. Nor did he object to the American naval mission of Commodore David Porter to Sultan Mahmud II in 1831.[105] One should also not forget that the British support of the Ottoman Empire was richly rewarded by trade treaties such as the one signed on the Bosphorus at Balta Liman Harbor 1838 that permitted British merchants to trade in the empire for a mere 3 percent ad valorem. Britain, with its occupation of Egypt in 1882, had basically abandoned the Palmerston system, by which time Sultan 'Abd ul-Hamid II (1876–1909) had turned to imperial Germany to continue the modernization of his army.[106]

XIV. Churchill at Gallipoli and the Five Promises to Save the Empire

Britain and France held the greatest sway in the Middle East prior to World War I (1914–1918). France, to maintain its imperial structures in North Africa, notably Morocco, Algeria, and Tunisia, claimed that her imperial structures were a part of metropolitan France, backed up by the French Foreign Legion and many French settlers. To maintain its hold over Middle East routes of communication with India such as the Suez Canal and to maintain other strategic positions in the Middle East, including access to Iraqi and Persian oil, Britain was forced, after the first year of its debacle at Gallipoli, to undertake desperate diplomatic measures to hold together its coalition of European powers. Upon the outbreak of war between the Central Powers of Germany, Austria-Hungary, and the Ottoman Empire and the Entente Powers of Britain, France and Russia, Britain, hoping to separate the weak Ottoman Empire from the Central Powers, followed the policy of Winston Churchill, the young head of the admiralty (the British Navy), by making a naval attack on the Straits of the Dardanelles and a land assault on Gallipoli, the peninsula overlooking the Dardanelles. Three unforeseen events upset this otherwise brilliant plan:

1) German officers joined the Turkish armed forces to bolster their defenses; modern German weapons, including modern machine guns and heavy, modern siege artillery, had been supplied to the Turks prior to the war.

2) Modern siege artillery was emplaced on the Dardanelles and succeeded in sinking twenty-five major war vessels before the attack was called off in 1915.

3) Finally, the Australian and New Zealand forces of the British Empire were landed at night on the steepest part of the Gallipoli shore only to face the withering fire of Turkish machine guns and artillery commanded by a young major, Mustafa Kemal (later Ataturk, president of the Republic of Turkey).

As a consequence of the great British disaster on the Gallipoli Peninsula, the British had to make diplomatic concessions to the leading Entente Powers to hold together the Western Alliance.

1. Constantinople and the Straits of the Bosphorus and Dardanelles Promised to Russia

The mentality of the "Great Game" persisted in Britain, and also, due to the rivalry of German naval expansion before the war, Britain wished to suck France into an anti-Russian position should postwar events deteriorate in the Middle East, and Russia moved southward from the Caucasus. Russia already had received the promise of the political plum of Constantinople from Britain. According to Fromkin, Russia had urged Kitchener and Churchill to attack the Turks through the Dardanelles. Yet the Russians, fearing a British victory against the Turks, had second thoughts. Sergei Sazanov, Russian foreign minister, telegraphed both London and Paris on 4 March 1915, asking, in the name of Tsar Nicholas II, that Constantinople and its environs be turned over to Russia in exchange for Russia's cooperation with other allied plans for the postwar Middle East. France demurred, viewing Russia as a future rival of France in the Middle East, but Sir Edward Grey, British foreign minister, as early as 1908, had told Russia of his favoring their takeover of Constantinople and the straits. He argued that the "Great Game" competition with Russia across Asia no longer applied. Fearing that Russia might make a separate peace with the

Central Powers, the British Cabinet, on 12 March 1915, acceded to the Russian postwar takeover of Constantinople and the straits. France reluctantly signed the secret agreement on 10 April 1915.[107]

2.   The Promises to France – The Sykes-Picot Agreement

After its losses in the Dardanelles and Gallipoli campaigns, Britain, realizing that the Arabs could not be turned against their Turkish overlords without a new offensive, had to settle for slower ground operations against the Turks, requiring a heavy commitment of troops. A front was opened through the Persian Gulf and Iraq, using commonwealth troops from India, many of whom were Muslim. Before starting a second front in the Sinai desert, led by General Allenby, the British needed French approval to move British units out of France. This diplomatic move required that Britain shore up not only Russian resolve but also France, with important new concessions. Germany had launched its counteroffensive at Verdun in early 1916, ushering in the bloodiest phase of the war. France refused Britain's desire to move troops to the Sinai. Percy Sykes, well-known in Britain for his travel books, was viewed by the British foreign ministry as the mouthpiece of General Kitchener. Sykes arrived in London in December 1915, saying that it was most important to win over Sherif Hussein of Mecca; otherwise, the Arabs would fear breaking with the Ottoman Turks. Thus, Sykes, though new to diplomacy, was called upon to negotiate with his French counterpart at the French embassy in London concerning the borders of the postwar Middle East. He seemed ideal for Britain. Sykes was pro-French, Catholic, and also was French-speaking; he would be most acceptable to the French with regard to their interests in Lebanon.

Having long-term family ties with colonial ambitions of France, Georges Picot became the ideal French negotiator. He was also closely associated with France's "mission historique" with regard to the "Syrian Party" in the French parliament. Of course, both England and France were deluded in thinking that the Sunnis of Greater Syria preferred the rule of either great power. Picot, French consul general in Beirut at the beginning of the war, planned to hold out in negotiations for a Syria stretching as far as Mosul, a region believed to contain oil. Unknown to Picot, the British wished to extend French interests also to Mosul, a region touching on territory into which Russia might later expand. The real problem was that Sykes had not comprehended what the Arabs were expecting, that they would receive control of the Arabian Peninsula and most of Syria and Iraq with possibly the exception of the Christian parts of Lebanon. The Sykes-Picot negotiations were completed in January of 1916 and accepted by the British and French cabinets in early February and by Russia in April. The territory of Palestine was left vague except that France, Britain and Hussein, Sherif of Mecca, would retain an interest. Sykes agreed to French interests in Lebanon and also accepted vaguely their claims to Syria extending as far as Mosul. Sykes was unaware of a secret agreement that Russia would support France's claim to Palestine. Though Sykes had heard of Jewish interests in Palestine and had consulted Herbert Samuel, Secretary of the Home Office, he failed to mention Zionist interests to Sazanov, Russia's foreign minister, and to Picot, out of fear that they would not honor their respective agreements.

The British, other than Sykes, looked upon the Sykes-Picot Agreement as a betrayal of British interests. General Gilbert Clayton, chief political officer of General Allenby, had been a protégé of General Allenby in the Sudan and, later, of Reginald Wingate, and Clayton was also considered an expert on the Sudan and the Middle East. When Herbert Henry Asquith, the British prime minister when World War I began, appointed field marshal Horatio Herbert Kitchener to head the War Ministry, Clayton became head of all intelligence in Egypt, and it was largely his opinions that prevailed in London until Wyndham Deedes, a real Ottoman specialist, showed up in Cairo in 1916 and discovered that the Cairo police force was riddled with Turkish spies! Ronald Storrs, another Kitchener favorite, had joined the staff of General Allenby and was later appointed the first governor of Palestine. He and the British establishment did not trust French interests in the Middle East because they believed the French, as in North Africa, were annexationists. The French believed that the British way, as in Egypt, was to remain in one's own clubs and compounds, only emerging to administer the government in Egypt, otherwise leaving the natives to their own devices!

Storrs promoted the idea that Syria and Palestine should become a part of Greater Egypt. It was also Storrs's idea, as oriental secretary to Kitchener, that Egypt should not be an outright annexation, as the Asquith cabinet proposed, but a protectorate of the British Empire, and this designation prevailed.[108]

3. Promises to the Arabs: The Sharif Hussein-McMahon Letters

Kitchener, when the war started in 1914, was British High Commissioner in Egypt. He was, by far, the most respected of British Middle East specialists because of his long years of service in the Sudan and Egypt. Kitchener thought of Hussein bin Ali, the Ottoman-appointed Sharif of Mecca, as a spiritual leader, and Hussein had told Kitchener in correspondence in late 1914 that he wished to remain neutral regarding his relations with Britain. Meanwhile, in January of 1915, Sharif Hussein had learned that the Ottomans planned to dismiss him at war's end. In mid-1915, the new British high commissioner in Cairo, Henry McMahon, received a letter from Sharif Hussein asking that virtually all of Arab Asia be turned over to him as his kingdom after the war. McMahon politely suggested that a discussion of borders should be postponed until the war's end. The British had thought of making him the caliph, a spiritual head, without political implications. Faisal, son of Hussein, had journeyed to Damascus and Constantinople, testing the waters. Upon his return to Damascus on 23 May 1915, Jamal Pasha, the Ottoman military governor of Syria, had discovered the extent of Arab officers plotting against the Ottoman government on the basis of secret French records that Jamal Pasha had seized in Beirut after the French had closed their consular offices. Thus, before Faisal had returned from Istanbul, Jamal had arrested a number of Arab officers who had been in direct contact with the French. Jamal Pasha also sent a number of the junior Arab officers, probably suspected of being members of the anti-Ottoman Arab secret societies, to fight against the British on the Gallipoli Peninsula. One such young Arab officer from Mosul, Lieutenant Muhammad Sharif al-Faruqi, had been sent from Damascus to Gallipoli. He deserted the Ottomans in the fall of 1915 and got through to the British lines. He immediately told his captors that he had important information for the British in Egypt; consequently, he was transported to Cairo for interrogation by British intelligence, headed by Kitchener protégé, Gilbert Clayton. Al-Faruqi claimed to be a member of the *Al-Ahd* secret Arab organization and repeated the claims of the "Damascus Protocol" that had been drawn up by the Arabs to gain British support for the Arabs. As the protocol was similar to what Sharif Hussein of Mecca had sent to Sir Henry McMahon, the British high commisioner in Egypt, Clayton accepted al-Faruqi's claim that he represented the al-Ahd organization and, later, that he spoke for Sharif Hussein. As Fromkin sharply notes, Clayton was duped on both misrepresentations. Faisal, son of Sharif Hussein, even stated that he did not know al-Faruqi.[109] Evidently, Sharif Hussein, seconded by al-Faruqi, had given up his initial claim that Arabs should also have the coastal areas of Lebanon, Syria, and Palestine. Clayton knew that France would claim Lebanon and the coastal areas of Syria and Palestine. However, the line of the French-built railroad through Syria, the Aleppo-Homs–Hama-Damascus provinces, according to the "Damacus Protocol," should remain in Arab hands. This designation also seemed to favor the inclusion of Palestine in Arab territory. Fromkin makes another keen observation: these provinces were the part of Syria wedged between the mountains and the open desert, Syria's most fertile region. From Damascus, the railroad connected to the Hejaz Railroad, extending to Madina, within the jurisdiction of Sharif Hussein. Mark Sykes, when he came through Cairo in November 1915, was, for the first time, alerted to the possibility by Clayton and Storrs that an Arab revolt was feasible and, indeed, would greatly help the British cause in Gallipoli and elsewhere.[110]

With the arrival of Sykes in London in December, Kitchener, the chief government expert on the Middle East, urged McMahon strongly that he should respond more favorably to Sharif Hussein. Before this new approach, McMahon had only stated to Sharif Hussein that, in keeping their concern for French interests, the coastal regions of Lebanon and Syria would not be granted to Arab rule. By June of 1916, in a secretly published note in the British *Arab Bulletin*, Britain had only promised the promotion of Arab independence where Arabic was spoken but gave no hard promises about how these regions might be governed. Gray, the British Foreign Secretary, spoke of the McMahon letters as contingent on an Arab revolt that would never materialize; hence, "the whole thing was a castle in the air." But there was hot air on both sides. The Arabs had no army, and al-Faruqi and Sharif Hussein stated clearly that there would be no Arab revolt without the British first landing troops in Syria and Palestine. 'Aziz al-Masri, an Egyptian general and founder of al-Ahd, also saw through the façade and stated that the Arabs would not support British dominance or a protectorate. Wyndam Deedes, the Ottoman expert in Cairo, noted that there were three Arab positions:

1. The attitude of the Syrians who despised the prospect of a French protectorate;
2. Sharif Hussein wanted to be named King of the Arabs;
3. Finally, the Arabs of Iraq expected independence, but the government of India, at the time, talked of annexing Iraq.

Hence, Deedes was skeptical of any rational settlement with the Arabs.[111]

4. A Promise to the Jews: the Balfour Declaration

As we have noted, during the course of the first two years of the war, the British cabinet, ever mindful of holding the wartime coalition together, had made three solemn but poorly conceived promises to Russia, France, and the Arabs: Constantinople and the Straits to Russia, Lebanon, Syria and part of Palestine to the French and extremely vague promises to Sharif Hussein. There remained two contenders for British favors: Central European Jews and the Italian monarchy. Italy had, early in the war, been induced to join the Entente coalition. The Jewish nationalists, known as Zionists, had petitioned King Wilhelm II of Germany to establish a Jewish national home in Palestine. But Percy Sykes and Lloyd George, the future prime minister, held successful negotiations with Chaim Weizmann and Nahum Sokolow. They were mindful of Weizmann's contribution to Britain's war effort because Weizmann, as a chemist, had extracted cordite, an explosive, from ordinary corn. Arthur James Balfour, Britain's Foreign Secretary, relied on Sykes to sort out the Zionist aims. The American Zionists led by Justice Brandeis of the U.S. Supreme Court also stood close to U.S. president Woodrow Wilson, who was on the verge of committing U.S. troops to the Western front when Sykes had made contact with Weizmann. Out of these meetings and correspondence with Justice Brandeis, Britain issued to Lord Rothschild, considered the titular head of the Zionists, the so-called Balfour Declaration on 2 November 1917:[112]

> His Majesty's Government view with favour the establishment in Palestine of a national home for the Jewish people, and will use their best endeavors to facilitate the achievement of this object, it being clearly understood that nothing shall be done which may prejudice the civil and religious rights of existing non-Jewish communities in Palestine, or the rights and political status enjoyed by Jews in any other country.

Before the issuance of the Balfour Declaration, there had been a number of stumbling blocks, largely from British Jews. Edwin Montagu, in the Lloyd George government, held the very important post of Secretary of State for India. He and a large proportion of the British Jewish community felt that they had finally been accepted by Britain as full members of British society. They believed that a Jewish national movement would jeopardize the trust that Jews had gained in every country. As Montagu lamented, "I have been striving all my life to escape from the ghetto." Moreover, in 1913, hardly more than one percent of world Jewry supported the Zionist aims, but this figure changed during the war. Montagu also received strong support for his position within the government, which was led by Lord Curzon (George Nathaniel Curzon), former viceroy of India. Even President Wilson suspected the motives of Britain and asked for a delay or the declaration until mid-October of 1917. His closest foreign affairs adviser, Colonel Edward Mandell House, saw the move as Britain assuring a lifeline to India and a continuation of the empire. House opposed the declaration as he had the Sykes-Picot Agreement. In a very real sense, Justice Louis Brandeis, a prominent Boston lawyer and a leading figure in Wilson's Progressive Movement, became the adviser to Wilson on Jewish matters. Brandeis had assumed the leadership of the Zionist movement in the United States in 1914 when the membership was about twelve thousand. By 1919, under the Brandeis leadership, it had soared to 175,000. The British Foreign Office persisted in the belief that the support of the Zionists would help defeat Germany. This theme later was picked up by Adolf Hitler in his book *Mein Kampf,* known as the "Stab in the Back" of German Jews when actually many of them died fighting for Germany. Indeed the Balfour Declaration strengthened Jewish support for American war efforts. Weizmann was at once more blunt and more practical. He pointed out that a Jewish Palestine would help Britain offset the rise of Arab nationalism.[113]

5. Italy and Greece

The Italians and Greeks fared poorly in the wartime promises. When the leaders of the Entente Powers assembled in the Palace of Versailles near Paris, France, in 1918–1919, Lloyd George of Britain had the intent of letting the Americans under President Wilson deal with the French, Armenian, and Italian issues, while the British carved up the Arab Middle East. But when Woodrow Wilson lost control of the U.S. Congress in the election of 1918, it became clear that the Americans would assume their old position of isolation from European affairs. Yet President Wilson, wishing to fulfill his role of personal participation in the peace deliberations, returned to Paris. Lloyd George, realizing that he had to seek French support on British plans for the Middle East, played the trump card by giving control of Syria to the French so long as Georges Clemenceau, Prime Minister of France, gave up French claims, stemming from the Sykes-Picot Agreement, to Mosul and Palestine.[114]

Meanwhile, Italy had previously invaded Libya in 1911 and expected territory in Asia Minor on the basis of Agreement of St. Jean de Maurienne, concluded with France, Russia, and Britain in mid-1917. Hence, Italy began occupying Antalya, in southern Turkey, in mid-March of 1919, ostensibly to keep the peace, but her temporary occupation began to take on permanency. Emanuele Orlando, Italian prime minister, realized he was going against President Wilson's principle of "self-determination" (i.e., the native people should decide who governs them), but he had to answer to the rising tide of Italian nationalism. Wilson shamed him at the conference by speaking of Italy's "imperialist ambitions," but Lloyd George, much more the diplomat, appealed to the Italian sense of nobility. Lloyd George knew that he was charting the downfall of Orlando's government. Wilson had fallen into one of Lloyd George's traps.

To offset the danger that Britain feared of Italy advancing deeply into Asia Minor before the delegates had dealt with the Ottoman remnant, Lloyd George convinced President Wilson that they should invite Greece, long waiting in the wings of the conference for a role in the war effort, to invade Asia Minor at Izmir, thus blocking Italian ambitions. The Greeks and the British emphasized to President Wilson that Izmir (Smyrna) was already half Greek and that the coast of Asia Minor had been Greek since antiquity. This position, of course, convinced President Wilson of the fulfillment of his principle of "self-determination." Eleutherios Venizelos, prime minister of Greece, used his well-recognized charm and diplomacy to win over President Wilson and Lloyd George, appealing to the long-standing Greek-British friendship. The Greeks landed their troops on 15 May 1919, using in some cases British vessels, but the "peacemakers" were unaware of the storm of Turkish nationalism that such an invasion of the Turkish heartland would create. It was this invasion that forced General Mustafa Kemal (Ataturk) to take charge of the Turkish national movement, to lead the newly formed Turkish National Army, and to drive the Greeks back across Asia Minor to Izmir and a humiliating defeat.[115]

XV. The Shaping of the Interwar Years

Under the mandate system of the League of Nations, established in the Treaty of Versailles in 1919, Britain and France initially held the responsiblity of "tutoring" certain Arab regions of the defeated Ottoman Empire until they were "mature enough" to manage their own affairs and to enter the League of Nations. Also set up in the Treaty of Versailles, Britain was awarded Palestine, Transjordan, and Iraq as mandates, while France was allotted Lebanon and Syria. Britain had already been in occupation of Egypt since 1882 and continued to manipulate Egyptian politics even after World War II until the Nasser Revolution of 1952 and the Treaty between Britain and Egypt of 1954. France had occupied Algeria in 1830 and Tunisia in 1881 and had held a protectorate over Morocco since 1912. After the Iraqi revolt of 1920, ruthlessly suppressed by Britain, Winston Churchill, newly appointed Colonial Secretary by Lloyd George, decided to hold a conference in Cairo to settle outstanding Middle East problems. The conference convened on 12 March 1921 and ended on March 22. Churchill undertook to settle four problems at the conference:

1) The political leadership in Iraq;
2) Quelling the rebellion in Transjordan that opposed plans for a Jewish national home in Palestine;
3) Answering French concerns over latent rebellions in Lebanon and Syria;

4) Answering the opposition of Ibn Saud concerning the elevation of the Hashemites, his rivals, to kingships.

Sir Percy Cox, British high commissioner in Iraq, was directed to ease the Iraqis into the acceptance of Prince Faisal ibn Hussein as King of Iraq. His brother, Abdullah ibn Hussein, was temporarily invited to represent Britain in both Palestine and Jordan because the British did not have enough manpower to quell the opposition to the Balfour Declaration. The French were sent assurances that Abdullah's appointment staved off his desire to attack the French in Syria (Faisal's troops had first occupied Damascus and had been unseated by the French.) To ease Saudi objections, Churchill increased their British subsidy to one hundred thousand British pounds per month to the Saudis. Faisal was able to consolidate his position in Iraq by obtaining the cooperation of a number of Iraqi generals and notably Ja'far Al-Askari, who was an outstanding Iraqi general. The British also promised full independence to Iraq as soon as they were admitted to the League of Nations. Iraq thus became nominally independent in 1931 with the usual British provisos regarding alignment with British interests, control of oil resources, and the placement of military bases. Churchill and his minions came to the conclusion that British air bases should be held by them across the Middle East as a means of maintaining domestic order.[116]

Churchill faced a formidable challenge in getting Palestinian Arabs to accept a Jewish national home. The House of Lords had voted sixty to twenty-nine that Britain should renege on its promise to the Jews. But Churchill, long in sympathy with the plight of the Polish and Russian Jews, came before the House of Commons on 4 July 1922 to defend his position. In the Commons, through an extraordinary defense of his policies, he gained support 292 to 35, and consequently, on July 22, the League of Nations accepted the revised Palestinian mandate as proposed by Churchill. Churchill had conceded that the Balfour Declaration would apply only to Palestine west of the Jordan River. The remaining portion of Palestine would be known as Transjordan, also under British Mandate, but with the nominal kingship of Sharif Hussein's second son, Abdullah. Fromkin makes no bones about the fraudulent nature of the Balfour Declaration and the subsequent arrangements particularly because a number of the Palestinian ruling class happily sold land rights to Zionists at exorbitant prices.[117]

Churchill and his supporters tended to point out the great economic advantages accruing to the Arabs from Jewish settlement. Churchill chose to overlook relevant factors. Jewish settlement by Europeans would alter forever the way of life of the Arabs. Moreover, if an Arab landowner sold out his estate, the Arab laborers who had toiled his fields for generations would likely be replaced by Jews, whether they professed Labor Socialism or not. Churchill was prone also to harp on the ancient right of the Jews to Palestine, overlooking that Arabs had occupied Palestine since the Jewish Diaspora, and many Arabs were most certainly Jewish converts to Islam or Christianity in the past. When Arab delegations spoke of the insupportability of Palestine for further settlement, Churchill accepted Arab complaints as if they were purely economic issues, and the British government thus supported a number of commissions to examine the effect that Jewish immigration would have on Palestine.[118]

In 1930, after a series of clashes between Arabs and Jews had occurred all over Palestine in 1929, the British began the commissions assuring the Arabs that they had nothing to fear because Jewish immigration would be on a small scale. The Shaw Commission of 1930 and the Simpson Report of the same year failed to allay Arab suspicions. With the sudden increase of Jewish immigration in 1933 and subsequent years, upon the rise of Adolf Hitler to power in Germany, the Arabs, by 1936, had declared a general strike against Britain. William Yale points out that between 1933 and 1935, 135,000 Jews had entered Palestine. The new immigrants were often specialized in their professions and were generously backed financially. To manage such an influx attests to the skill and hard work of the new and older Jewish immigrants, but this did not solve the problem for the Arabs. Seeking a peaceful solution to this impasse, Britain sent a new royal commission in 1935, the Peel Commission, which concluded that the mandate terms, given the Zionists' desire for rapid immigration and the Arab desire to limit immigration to a trickle, were unattainable and recommended the dissolution of the mandate and a partition of Palestine into Jewish and Arab entities. The British cabinet in 1937 sent Sir John Woodhead at the head of a partition commission; however, in light of the Zionist and Arab pressures, the cabinet gave up the idea.[119]

As a European crisis and possibly a new world war threatened Britain just as the Arabs broke into open rebellion, the British were forced to put down the revolt with military force. While Jews were brought into the defense forces and allowed to bear arms, the Arabs, by contrast, could be imprisoned or shot for bearing arms. The Arabs had failed to calculate this negative effect of rebelling against the British government. Britain once again attempted in London to negotiate with the Arabs and Jews, but failure led to the promulgation of the "White Paper of 1939." A white paper in British parlance was a statement of British policy. It made clear that now the British intended to appease the Arabs, given their vast numbers in the Middle East. Otherwise, Britain faced pro-Axis propaganda that would turn all Arabs against the British cause. It was stated, for example, that it was not British policy "that Palestine should become a Jewish state." It further limited Jewish immigration into Palestine to seventy-five thousand over the next five years; thereafter, immigration of Jews would be left to the acquiescence of the Palestinian Arabs. In addition, land transfers after 1940 could be stopped altogether by the High Commissioner. Eventually, the White Paper was accepted by the Arab leadership but adamantly opposed by all Jewish parties. The Zionists, however, realizing that Jewish interests were predicated on Britain winning the war, agreed to support Britain to the end of the war. This was called the Biltmore Program because it was thrashed out at the Biltmore Hotel in New York City in 1942.[120]

At the time of the Cairo conference in 1921, General Allenby held the post of British High Commissioner in Egypt. He had decided that Britain should not go against Arab nationalism but support it. This meant that he took a position quite the opposite of Churchill, who made his Cairo moves to thwart Arab nationalism by supporting Sharif Hussein's sons as Arab leaders, believing that they would support British interests. By contrast, Allenby wanted to end the Arab protectorate over Egypt and give the Egyptians a measure of independence. Under threat of resignation, Allenby prevailed with a unilateral declaration of Egyptian independence on 28 February 1922. To be sure, as in all such British unilateral declarations, there were reservations dealing with foreign policy, government advisers, and the use of military bases. The issue of Egypt's status came into serious focus after World War II when Egyptian Army officers, led by Gamal Abd an-Nasir, Anwar Sadat, Zakariyah Muhiyeddin, Salah Salem, and Ali Sabri forced Britain to give Egypt full independence in 1954.[121]

XVI. The "New Legitimacy" after World War II and the Undermining of the Halpern Thesis

But the constitutions and parliaments did not placate the growing number of liberals in the Middle East. Manfred Halpern, a Professor at Princeton University, realized that most constitutions were violated by conservative elites or by rulers placed on their thrones by Western Powers such as King Faisal in Iraq. Moreover, the parliaments largely contained members of the upper class. Fortunately, there remained one outlet for poor and exploited citizens of Middle Eastern countries. In the late nineteenth century, in the Ottoman Empire and after World War I (1914–1918) in other Middle Eastern countries, either occupying Western powers or local elites began to train lower-middle-class young men in the armed forces of various countries. These young men, often with a combination of influential relatives or pure brilliance, had passed the entrance exams for their respective military academies and began to occupy the lower ranks of the officer corps of their military establishments. This new middle class, such as Mustafa Kemal Ataturk and his coterie of officers, served the Ottoman government in World War I (1914–1918), overthrew the remaining sultan's government, fought the War of Independence, and formed the Turkish Republic in 1923. Soon thereafter, the Ataturk government abolished the Sultanate (1923) and the Caliphate (1924). Reza Shah in Iran, head of the royal cavalry, crowned himself Shah in 1925 and soon brought secular

ran. These processes recognized by Halpern was the "New
cy" introduced by the "New Middle Class."

fter World War II, the Arab lands, released from the stranglehold
the mandate system or other colonial powers, began to topple the
governments controlled by corrupt parliaments, the old military class,
and colonial leadership. This pattern accounts for Nasser and the
Young Officers' Association that overthrew King Farouk in 1952. The
remaining years of the twentieth century are witness to this repeating
pattern in Iraq, in Tunisia, in Libya, in Syria, and in other Middle
Eastern states. Only those kingdoms such as Jordan and Morocco,
led by dynasties that could trace their ancestry back to the Prophet
Muhammad, have so far survived the overthrow by army colonels. The
one exception is the Kingdom of Saudi Arabia, which now derives its
legitimacy by protecting the annual pilgrimage (*the hajj*) and is keeper
of the holy cities of Mecca and Medina (*Khādim al-Haramayn*).[122]

To gain a flavor of Halpern's insights, we include in these chapter
notes from Halpern's chapter 4, "The New Middle Class as the Principal
Revolutionary and Stabilizing Force." Halpern indicates that the
traditional Middle Eastern elite, the sultans, the kings, the landowners,
and the bourgeoisie have, for the most part, yielded their places to the
new middle class. He notes that the new class is salaried by the state,
giving this class more economic stability, including the army, skilled
modern bureaucrats, and modern professionals. His analysis "focuses
on men interested in ideas, actions, and careers . . . that will fashion
opportunities and institutions providing careers to all who have modern
skills . . . The older merchants, propertied elite, and middlemen cannot
compete with the New Middle Class who can mobilize the power and
capital of an entire state." In fact, Halpern notes that there are very few
important jobs for individuals outside large government institutions.
The intelligentsia are viewed as the most important of the new class
because they can expose "the weakness or irrelevance of tradition."
Quoting Le Tourneau's observation, "young men from the hinterland
now form the essential backbone of the middle class."[123]

Halpern cites Nasser as a perfect illustration: "The son of a
postmaster, he graduated in 1938 from the first class of the Egyptian

Military Academy that admitted students other than the upper classes." Such young men took advantage of new avenues to expertise and status. Landowners, the bourgeoisie in commerce and tradition-bound artisans, and peasants do not make up the classes in transition to the modern age. The new middle class could act as a separate force because (1) they were free of traditional bonds and knew how to manipulate armies and voluntary organizations once in control of a modernizing state; (2) it possessed a power base superior to any other class; (3) within the modern sector, the new middle class was numerically the largest; (4) they are more cohesive and better trained; (5) they make decisions about social change and the position of other classes; (6) this class is also capable of gaining mass popular support. Such a new middle class thwarts any social and political vacuum. Also, this class may minimize antagonism by associating its objectives with the stated mission of the entire nation. Halpern also issues a word of caution. There is also within the new middle class a certain tension because only a limited number can gain the security of being salaried. The remaining members cannot find work suitable to their modern skills and values and are caught in status quo regimes.[124]

While at the time taking the Turkish, the Egyptian, and possibly the Tunisian examples as the best examples of the new middle class in action, Halpern turns to the example of Iran as a state, under Reza Shah, not permitting the new middle class to emerge. Iran, he notes, could absorb most educated persons in the 1920s and 1930s. The chief cause of frustration was that status depended on traditional rank rather than merit. Top posts went to those of prominent families who had studied abroad and were loyal to the ruling regime. By the 1940s, the overflow of young Iranians in government jobs was apparent all over. At this point, the great number of students graduating from Iranian universities overwhelmed the job market. Now the older government officials were faced with the challenge of a latent middle class seeking significant employment. Under such circumstances, the youth became more radical and blamed the ruling elite. The rulers become more autocratic and dictatorial and held on to their positions for life, thus not letting the new classes take on the new challenges.[125]

Halpern reminds us that there were other Middle East leaders in the nineteenth century that had realized the need to modernize the army, the bureaucracy, and the foreign trade in order to survive as separate states. This note had been true of Muhammad Ali of Egypt (1805–1848) and Sultan Mahmud II (1808–1839) of Ottoman Turkey and their successors. In the mid-twentieth century, it was the new middle class that had to have the vision to develop roles for a new kind of world. It is hoped that the heirs to the new middle class will dominate these new societies and give the ongoing drama "a moderate orientation." Many sons of the traditional elite joined the upper echelons of the new middle class because they were trained as military officers. They had the advantage, as did Nasser and Sadat of the lesser bourgeoisie, to master modern technology and administration. Another challenge to the new middle class is to give relevant education to members of the lower middle class who are trained in jobs no longer needed. Halpern gives the example of many lawyers trained in Shari'ah law or non-useful archaic languages.[126]

Halpern delineates what he sees as the three overlapping tasks of the new middle class: (1) the battle between the new middle class and the traditional ruling class; (2) the drive by the successful new middle class to supply cadre for all five groups that compose the elite in modern society (political leaders, government administrators, economic directors, leaders of masses, and military leaders); (3) the struggles among strata within the new middle class for predominance, especially in the light of uprooted peasants and workers. There is no doubt that their leaders would push for revolutionary action. They dare not perpetuate the traditional norms and laws of their society. From the youngest supporters, one may expect the growth of extremism. The absence of violence is noteworthy in the changes involving the new middle class, but herein lays the challenge: to establish modern integrating institutions "that will mobilize the spirit and resources of the entire nation."[127]

In the case of Colonel Qasim's overthrow of the Nuri as-Said government, the British government took seriously Qasim's threat to occupy Kuwait and sent in troops, unlike the response of the U.S.

government in 1990, which gave Saddam Hussein a mixed message.[128] One is seriously left to speculate what went wrong in the waning years of the twentieth century, which made Manfred Halpern's rather optimistic conclusions about leadership in the Middle East, 1950–1970, turn so negative from that time until our own days. The paradigm of Gamal 'Abd an-Nasir serves here as a study of Halpern's thesis—namely that young salaried leaders after World War II took over leadership in various Middle Eastern states. These young men represented the new legitimacy, even though they rise from the petite bourgeoisie, because they are, for the first time, admitted into military academies; they obtained strategic positions in newly forming political parties, or they acquired modern technical skills, such men as Nasser of Egypt, Bourguiba of Tunisia, Boumedienne and Ben Bella of Algeria, and Hafez al-Asad of Syria. The elder statesmen and the first to match these criteria were Ataturk of Turkey (d. 1938) and Ja'far Al-Askari (assassinated in 1936) and Nuri as-Said (killed in 1958), the latter individuals, though trained in the Ottoman staff college at Harbiye in Istanbul, had risen to power in their respective countries. On 14 July 1958, General 'Abd al-Karim Qasim, of mixed Sunni and Shi'i origins, led a military coup that resulted in the assassination of most of the royal family and cooperating government officials. But in many ways, his background supported the criteria of Manfred Halpern. He was in power for less than five years. As a virtual dictator, he made many reforms in land holding benefitting the peasantry and also stopped British influence in Iraq, previously favored by the monarchy, and also nationalized untapped oil concessions that had been previously leased to the British Iraq Petroleum Company. He fell afoul of a Kurdish War for autonomy, angered Iran over claims to Khuzistan, and was overthrown in February 1963 by the Ba'ath Party when he turned to the Iraqi Communist Party and the Soviet Union to thwart the popularity of Nasser's Pan Arabism. Not unlike the overthrow of Mossadegh in Iran in 1953, there were rumors also that the CIA and MI6 had a hand in the overthrow of General Qasim.[129]

Perhaps the first individual to alter seriously the background picture of leaders like Gamal 'Abd an-Nasir, identified in the Western Press as "Nasser," was Miles Copeland, a CIA agent, who, on occasion, posed as a member of the State Department. His important book, *The Game of Nations*, used the example of Nasser as a paradigm of how the United States might have dealt with African and Asian leaders who were trying to improve their societies in spite of dire social and economic problems that their countries faced, such as a high birthrate, lack of financial resources, and grinding poverty. Copeland completed his study in 1969, one year before the death of Nasser, but he has fortunately given us an inside picture of how the CIA sized up Nasser in a difficult era. In short, Copeland's study illustrates the behind-the-scenes events that made Halpern's paradigm prove important.[130]

Copeland was born in Alabama in 1916 and became a first-class trumpeter and played in, among others, the orchestra of Glenn Miller. At the beginning of World War II, he gained a job in army intelligence and was sent to London. He eventually married a coworker, Lorraine Adie, from Scotland. He stayed with the Office of Strategic Services (OSS), headed by William J. Donovan, until it evolved into the Central Intelligence Agency in 1947. In an early posting, he served in Damascus and possibly studied Arabic. In 1953 found him in Iran working closely with Kermit Roosevelt, Donald Wilber, and Britain's MI6 to overthrow Mohammed Mossadegh, prime minister of Iran. His overthrow was, in part, because Mossadegh had nationalized the Anglo-Persian Oil Company in 1951 and forced the Shah, Mohammed Reza, to sign the decree. The British and the International Oil Consortium immediately placed a ban on the sale of Iranian oil. As for the Truman government, it had been initially more concerned with the technicalities of oil contracts, but when the Eisenhower government took office in January of 1953, the United States feared that Mossadegh was turning to the Communist Bloc for support of his position. Consequently, Mossadegh was overthrown in August 1953 by the CIA and the British MI6.[131]

Copeland left the CIA in 1953 to work as a consultant for Booz, Allen, and Hamilton, a strategy and technology consulting firm to the U.S. government, but he still worked, under cover, for the CIA and was sent to meet Nasser in Cairo after he and his officer associates had overthrown King Farouk.[132] The United States had relied on Britain in the past to manage the relations of Middle East countries with the West.

But in 1947, a bankrupt Britain from expenditures during WWII facing revolt in Palestine and India, was unable to cope with Soviet threats to the status quo in Greece and Turkey.[133]

From this crisis, the United States was forced to define its policies in regard to Soviet incursions, the birth of Israel, and petroleum politics. In 1955, Copeland officially returned to the CIA. When Israel in February had made a retaliatory raid on Gaza, they killed a number of police officers because of Palestinian border raids. Nasser believed that Egypt should have defensive weapons, and when the United States refused to help him, Nasser concluded an arms deal with the Soviet bloc. Nasser's opposition to the Baghdad Pact in 1955 came about in the same year as his arms deal with Czechoslovakia. In the same year, under pressure from Egypt, Glubb Pasha, a long-serving English general, was removed from the head of Jordan's Arab Legion. Stemming from Nasser's deal for arms from the Soviet bloc, Secretary of State John Foster Dulles advised President Eisenhower to refuse support in July 1956 for Egypt's high-dam project. But one must consult Mohammed Heikal's more detailed background to recommendations of Secretary Dulles to President Eisenhower for refusing the U.S. support for the high dam. Nasser had revised the arms list of King Farouk. Basically, Farouk had requested weapons for internal security; Nasser wanted heavy weapons to thwart Israeli attacks. On the request list of October 1952, Nasser wanted an armored division and three squadrons of jet fighters. This became a political football in the U.S. government. Nasser essentially had to reach President Eisenhower through two brothers: John Foster Dulles, secretary of state, and Allen Dulles, the head of the CIA. The Truman government was replaced by President Eisenhower in January of 1953. The high dam, which the Soviets eventually supported, had been proposed by Nasser to enhance Egypt's manufacturing base with cheap electricity and to stabilize the Nile flow for irrigation of Lower Egypt. Eisenhower, on Dulles's advice, refused his support.[134]

This ill-timed move by the United States fomented the Suez Crisis. Nasser immediately nationalized the Suez Canal Company, promising, inter alia, to repay the stockholders. Nevertheless, the nationalization of the Suez Canal prompted the invasion of Britain and France into

Egypt's delta and Israel into the Sinai up to the Suez Canal. President Eisenhower took the position of Nasser and condemned the invasion partly because the British and French had lied to Robert Murphy, our envoy to Britain, about having no plans for an invasion. Also, Khrushchev and Bulganin had threatened to bomb London and Paris. Ironically, this coincided with the Hungarian Crisis of 1956. This diplomatic move placed the United States on the side of the hard-pressed governments of emerging nations. This bold move of Nasser also made him immensely popular among the poor and hard-pressed people of Egypt and throughout the Middle East. Copeland, in 1961, retired from the CIA soon after he opposed President Kennedy's "Bay of Pigs" invasion of Cuba. He died in 1991 at the age of seventy-five.[135]

Just after President Eisenhower had orchestrated the overthrow of Prime Minister Mossadegh in 1953, Moshe Sharett, in early 1954, replaced Ben-Gurion as prime minister of Israel. Moshe Sharett was sincerely interested in working for peace with Arab countries. Working against these good intentions were Pinchas Lavon, Israeli defense minister, and Moshe Dayan, Israeli chief of staff, with, of course, Ben-Gurion supporting them in the shadows. To thwart any peace negotiations of Sharett, the military continued to make border raids into Egypt and Jordan, in this time frame, to humiliate Arab neighbors. These raids were in keeping with the doctrine of "massive retaliation" for the slightest Arab provocation. At the end of June 1954, the *Modiin*, the Israeli military intelligence organization, gave orders to begin sabotage against Egyptian, American, and British targets in Egypt. The weapon of choice were firebombs, and agents firebombed the Alexandria post office, the American U.S. information libraries in Alexandria and Cairo, and a British-owned theater. Eventually, the Egyptian police rounded up eleven spies but the two leaders, Abraham Dar (alias John Darling) and Avraham Seidenwerg (alias Avri El-Ad, alias Paul Frank) escaped. As noted, if the desire was to blame the Egyptians for the firebombings, the intent failed, to the embarrassment of Israel. But if the intent was to drive Pinchas Sharett out of the prime ministry to stop his peace initiatives and to replace him with Ben-Gurion, the intent succeeded. For years, Lavon contended that Ben-Gurion had given the order to attack the Egyptian targets! Stephen Green, who describes these events, contends that the Eisenhower administration missed an important opportunity to make peace between Israel and her neighbors.[136]

Returning briefly to Copeland's observations, Copeland highlights in his study, *The Game of Nations*, how the U.S. government in February 1948 started a "center of peace" games wherein various experts in the U.S. government played the roles of various world leaders to ascertain what these leaders might do in crises. This group met periodically and depended for its sources on the latest dispatches from the State Department, the CIA, and other relevant government bureaus. There were only three rules of the game: (1) moral judgments were only relevant if they applied to the country under study; (2) the participants assumed, unless proved otherwise, that a national leader's first priority was to stay in power; (3) also the participants assumed that a national leader would act in the best interests, as he saw it, of his own country. The goal of this exercise was to give our own U.S. leaders "decision information." This group hoped for about 85 percent accuracy in European countries, but their predictions in Afro-Asian and South American countries were much less accurate or predictable. Miles Copeland often played the role of Nasser because of his experience, and he became the CIA agent closest to Nasser.[137]

As noted previously by Copeland, the U.S. commitment to Middle Eastern affairs started with the stark position of Britain in early 1947 at a time when the Soviet Union was pressuring Turkey and Greece to give up territory and also challenged the right of Turkey to control the straits (the Bosphorus and the Dardanelles) under the Montreux Convention of 1936. He also notes that this crisis period initiated the organization of the CIA and the need to recruit staff that could deal with the current Middle East. George Kennan's dictum of "containment," when he headed the State Department Planning Board in 1947, became the leading policy for dealing with the Soviet Union. The CIA set forth its initial goals in the Middle East: (1) to prevent regional struggles, (2) to promote strong governments so they could deal with the threat of international Communism, (3) to urge a climate of investment for U.S. firms. They also concentrated on supporting the rise of the "right kind of leaders," publicly idealistic but secretly Machiavellian, also known as crypto-diplomacy. Copeland also details the U.S. government's failure, in which he was involved, when it engineered the coup d'état of General Husni Za'im of 30 March 1949 in Syria, which led to a series of military coups, in short, how not to involve the United States in the affairs of another country![138]

The clandestine services of the United States had supposedly learned their lessons in Syria, as indicated in Kim Roosevelt's report to Dean Acheson, Truman's secretary of state, two months before Nasser's coup. Roosevelt had spoken with officers close to Nasser, but never Nasser himself. He noted the following:

1) A "popular revolution" that the Communists, the Muslim Brotherhood, and the U.S. State Department expected would not happen.
2) The army would be involved, contrary to American fears after the Syrian debacle.
3) The officers would have only modest aims.
4) The U.S. government could expect the removal of King Farouk and possibly the monarchy.
5) The United States should basically keep a hands-off policy about calling for democratic institutions.
6) It would be an Egyptian coup d'état that would be against the interests of the Egyptian upper class and the British, not Israel.

Egyptians were tired of the British humiliating them with the concurrence of their own upper class, and they needed a charismatic leader, a "Muslim Billy Graham," as had previously been discussed. Roosevelt also left the inference that the U.S. government would cooperate with the Egyptian officers. The coup took place on 23 July 1952 (in some references, July 22 is the date given). Copeland reveals how General Steve Meade, an Arabic-speaking paratrooper, who had participated in many coups, was sent by Secretary of State Dulles in 1953 to size up the "free officers." Meade concluded that (1) Nasser had recruited good organization men among the officers; (2) Nasser, the coup leader, was of the same social class as his followers; (3) the coup must be constructed to operate on a military hierarchy, not personal loyalty; (4) the coup would initially depend on the army and its acceptance by the people. In addition, we are able to see the background consultation work of James Eichelberger, a political scientist; Ambassador Caffery; Mohammed Hasanein Heykel, newspaper reporter of *Al-Ahram*, the leading newspaper; his boss, Mustafa Amin; and Nasser's most thoughtful and reasonable deputy, Zakaria Mohieddin.[139]

Copeland then continues to analyze how Nasser nurtured his "repressive base" with the help of Professor Eichelberger: Nasser noted, "But to be a good leader, you must influence the mob to aspire to what is really best for it." But why did Nasser lead his poor country into such adventures as the threat to Lebanese independence in 1958, the UAR experiment of controlling Syria, 1958–1961, the coup of Colonel Sellal in Yemen and the overthrow of the Nuri as-Said government in Iraq in 1958? The briefest answer to this question is that Nasser believed he could unite all Arabs in one country, a doctrine known as Pan-Arabism. Nasser's ultimate mistake was failing to count on Israel making a preemptive strike when he removed the UN buffer in the Sinai Peninsula in 1967. Also, he might have realized that no international naval force could deploy rapidly enough when he blocked the use by Israel of the Straits of Tiran, a concession that had been supported by the Eisenhower government in 1956.

Copeland provides another answer. The Command Council decrees (in place of legislation), the cleansing of the police force, the organization of the Egyptian intelligence service, and the removal from the army of dissident officers all conspired to shield Nasser from the outside world, in short, from reality. Nasser, in the end, had surrounded himself with "yes men" like so many political leaders. It is surprising, of course, that even the complete destruction of the Egyptian Air Force by Israel did not break the popular support for Nasser by the vast majority of Egyptians. Only death in 1970 removed this remarkable and popular leader from power.[140]

Before leaving Copeland's analysis of Nasser, it is important to view Nasser's interest in promoting the Egyptian "constructive base" and to understand Nasser's leverage on the United States and the Soviet Union. Nasser was quoted as saying, "The first task of a leader is to be the leader; only after you have ensured that you are the leader can you start thinking about becoming a good leader." Nasser envisioned three phases: (1) since Egyptians were basically quiescent, Nasser wanted to control any popular revolt that would pull the Egyptian ruling class off its pedestal; (2) the second phase was to discredit the old order, the privileged classes of Egypt, the subservience to the landlords, the monopolistic merchants and members of the former regime; (3) only then could Nasser introduce the single party, the Arab Socialist Union, his ideal of big government wherein he promised a job for every college graduate and produced his own myth, as revealed in his book, *Egypt's Liberation: The Philosophy of the Revolution*, reputedly in part written by Heikal. In his book, he complains of being an actor without a role, noting Pirandello's comments on theater, "He opened the breach, but the people did not follow him." He proposed three circles of activity for his followers, the Arab Circle, enhanced by electricity from the high dam, the Muslim Circle, and the African Circle, "a battle in which the colored man is sure to triumph in the end" over the European.[141]

It is interesting to note the various aims of Western leaders as they tried to convince Nasser of their good intentions. Prime Minister Anthony Eden of Britain and John Foster Dulles, U.S. Secretary of State, met with President Eisenhower in 1953 to discuss organizing a Middle East Defense Organization. Eisenhower and Dulles were interested in a Middle East defense against the Soviet Union. Eden was not quite on the same wave length. Britain was more interested in retaining its bases in Suez, on Cyprus, and in the Gulf. This same anti-Soviet aim prompted the United States to participate in the Baghdad Pact in 1955 fostered by the same intentions against the Soviet bloc. Nasser opposed such organizations and took an active role in forcing the British to sign the Anglo-Egyptian Treaty of October 1954, which removed the British bases from Egyptian soil. One month later, Copeland was present at a meeting of American colonels Albert Gerhardt and W. Bill Eveland, sent by the U.S. Pentagon to inquire about supplying the above-mentioned arms to Egypt for internal use. Nasser and his chief of staff, Abdel

Hakim 'Amer, were present. Gerhardt explained the reasons for the formation of NATO as an alliance against a Soviet attack. He then urged on the Egyptians the importance of a regional defense against the Soviets. As Nasser listened to the arguments, he concluded, "The Arabs will say you are trying to get them to fight your enemy, the Soviet Union, while Arab military planners will say that Israel is our enemy!"[142]

In a chapter termed Nasser's "Positive Neutralism," Copeland deals with the problem created when Secretary of State Dulles failed to support Egypt's high-dam project in 1956, a project that the Soviet Union partially funded then, and Nasser had planned that his nationalization of the Suez Canal would pay for the High Dam. Also, in spite of the arms mission of the two colonels noted above, the Eisenhower government failed to provide defensive weapons for Egypt and, hence, forced Nasser to deal with the Soviet bloc in 1955. In spite of these setbacks to American policies, official Washington was basically friendly to Nasser's Egypt until the 1958 Lebanon crisis and the overthrow of the Iraqi kingdom by Colonel Qasim. These events had caused the American business community to turn against Nasser. Radio Cairo, as explained by Copeland, also had urged the overthrow of the Iraqi monarchy.[143] It is clear that the Lebanon crisis would threaten Israel, and the change in Iraq might threaten oil supplies. It also soon turned into an expansion of Soviet influence. While President Kennedy (1959–1961) had more understanding of the revolutionary spirit of Nasser because of his ties to Ireland, President Johnson (1961–1969) soon saw his role as clipping Nasser's wings. He supplied to Israel the aircraft and financial support that made possible Israel's preemptive strike in 1967.

Mohamed Heikal (note Heikal's variant spelling of Muhammed) also gives a great deal of inside information on Sir Anthony Eden, British foreign secretary and deputy prime minister to Prime Minister Winston Churchill. Eden's encounter with Colonel Nasser on 26 February 1955 was not a pleasant occasion, as Heikal describes the scene at the British embassy in Cairo:

> Every aspect of each man was completely opposite of the other's. Heritage, upbringing, appearance, dress,

experience, outlook, loyalties and ambition, everything
conflicted. The dinner was not a social occasion, it was
a confrontation between the ultimate representatives of
two inimical ways of life, a confrontation that was both
personal and national and that ended in tragedy.

Nasser was, of course, pleased that Britain had agreed to the
evacuation of the Canal Zone, but Nasser wanted to foster good relations
with Britain. Nasser was taken aback because Eden spoke fluent Arabic
and wanted to talk about Arabic poetry. Nasser brought up the question
of why Egypt was opposed to the Baghdad Pact. Surprisingly, Dulles
had carefully listened to Nasser's point of view, but Anthony Eden was
bored with the conversation stating, "I am acquainted with all those
arguments . . . Why attack Nuri Es-Said and the Hashemites?" Nasser
drove home his point: the Baghdad Pact would drive a wedge between
the Arabs, and Egypt would be left alone to defeat Israel. Meanwhile,
Humphrey Trevelyan, British ambassador to Egypt, had learned that
King Hussein of Jordan had fired Glubb Pasha, and the Americans were
upset with Nasser for giving diplomatic recognition to China. Thus,
when both Dulles and Selwyn Lloyd, special British envoy to Nasser,
withdrew the U.S. and British support for the high dam on Friday, 20
July 1956, Nasser nationalized the Suez Canal.[144] In the introduction
to Heikal's book, Edward R. F. Sheehan noted that two prominent
Egyptian professors attacked the Nasser program in different ways.
Dr. Louis Awad stated that Heikal was Nasser's alter ego, and Awad
attacked the structure of the educational system. Tawfiq al-Hakim, a
prominent author, attacked the Arab Socialist Union (ASU) as a "market
of donkeys." But we must remember, as Sheehan points out, Heikal is
silent on what happened in the 1967 War. Later, Heikal blamed the
whole social system. As we know, Sadat removed Heikal from power.[145]
The analyses of both Heikal and Copeland are important to gain
a fuller knowledge of the complexities of Nasser's thinking on a host
of problems. Nasser very soon realized that, as a nation with very few
resources to nurture a burgeoning population, he would gain much
more aid from the Soviet bloc and also from non-Communist countries,

including the United States, if he joined the nonaligned countries such as Yugoslavia and Indonesia while threatening to join one bloc or another. According to Copeland's calculation, Nasser was able, with this approach, to raise more than one billion pounds in aid benefits.[146]

At this point, we believe that anyone interested in legitimacy problems in Arab politics, in the twentieth and twenty-first centuries, should read chapter One of Michael Hudson's important study, *Arab Politics: The Search for Legitimacy*, wherein he reviews the important writings on this subject of many key political scientists and sociologists, including Max Weber, David Easton, Ted Robert Gurr, Dankwart Rustow, Karl Deutsch, Hisham Sharabi, Manfred Halpern, Clifford Geertz, Iliya Harik, Daniel Lerner, Seymour Martin Lipset, and many others.[147] Max Weber, the doyen of such studies, writes, "Without legitimacy . . . a system is hard-pressed to attain . . . long-run stability and good government."

Ted Gurr suggests, "Regimes are legitimate 'to the extent that their citizens regard them as proper and deserving support.'" Hudson notes, "Every (modern) Arab politician of consequence has felt compelled to endorse . . . Arabism, democracy and social justice." But Arabs are "caught between ideology and political-administrative realities . . . (their skepticisms) appear to be rationally derived from unhappy prior experience." Dankwart Rustow notes three prerequisites for political modernity: "authority, identity, and equality." To these thoughts, Hudson adds, "The legitimate order requires a distinct sense of corporate selfhood: the people within a territory must feel a sense of political community which does not conflict with other subnational or supranational communal identifications." "Social Mobilization as Karl Deutsch has called his observations, has profound effects on the politics of new states, effects that are both functional and dysfunctional for building political legitimacy." Clovis Maksoud, a Lebanese spokesman, has called attention to the "all-Arab" core concerns. And Hudson considers the occupation by Israel of Palestine as an "all-Arab" core concern. Not only did Nasser have pan-Arab concerns, "pan-Arab commitments such as the Ba'ath Party and the Palestinian national movement are now quite institutionalized without having forsaken

their goal of All-Arab solidarity." Also, Hudson wishes us to consider
"Legitimacy and Change: Three Perspectives"—the transformationist
model, the mosaic model, and the social mobilization model. The
transformationist model sees the "complete displacement of traditional
by rational sociopolitical systems" by a revolution induced by changes
in the social structure. The mosaic model "emphasizes the persistence
of primordial and parochial loyalties even during rapid modernization"
that require "reconciliation, bargaining and conflict management." The
social mobilization model believes that modernization comes with "an
educated, tolerant 'civic' polity." Hudson chooses Hisham Sharabi to
illustrate the transformationist model. Hisham Sharabi bluntly states,
"Revolutionary leadership is 'rational,' choosing specific means to
achieve specific ends, whereas patriarchal leadership is 'traditional,'
accepting inherited values and goals and employing customary means
to achieve them." Hudson looks skeptically at Manfred Halpern's rather
optimistic "assertion that a new professional middle class is building a
new, pragmatic science- and technology-based legitimacy formula . . .
but appreciates his insight into the profundity of the social changes" of
the new middle class.[148]

Here we must interject another brilliant observer of the Egyptian
scene. P. J. Vatakiotis had been born in Jerusalem in 1928 of Greek
parentage. After attending Greek preparatory schools in Palestine and
learning Arabic, he took his BA degree at the American University of
Cairo and his PhD in Middle East history at Johns Hopkins University.
He had held a number of university positions in the United States,
where he was a citizen, and died at the age of sixty-eight while a
professor emeritus of Middle East history at the School of Oriental and
African Studies of the University of London. Professor Vatikiotis wrote
a number of books about the history of Egypt. In this treatise, I follow
the insights of Vatikiotis in his *Nasser and His Generation.*[149]

Nasser became an Arab nationalist after the Egyptian army became
involved with the Israeli armed forces in 1947 and 1948. Nasser had also
trained Palestinians and volunteers from the Muslim Brotherhood who
were willing to fight for Palestine. He also knew that it was necessary
for an Egyptian leader to guard the eastern frontier, as had Muhammad

Ali and his son, Ibrahim, who had conquered Syria and Palestine in the nineteenth century, only to be thwarted by the great powers and a British occupation from 1882 to 1954. A former friend of Nasser, Ahmad Abu al-Fath, wrote in 1962 that Nasser did not respect the Arabs, but they had control of petrol, money, and population that Egypt could exploit.[150] Only Egypt could lead the Arabs with her experience, social and cultural achievements, human resources, and skills. Nasser firmly believed that the imperial powers had forced a division between Arab countries. Nasser aimed, with Egyptian leadership, to bring Arab countries back into the fold.[151]

After the Suez Crisis in which President Eisenhower had helped Egypt, Nasser, on the verge of accepting the union with Syria in February of 1958, attacked the Saudis on the grounds that they had attempted to bribe Colonel 'Abd el-Hamid Serraj, head of Syrian intelligence. This coup was followed by the fall of the Hashemite kingdom in Iraq and the Sunni favoring of Nasser in Lebanon. This latter incident had prompted the Eisenhower Doctrine and the landing of the Marines in Lebanon. Nasser had been reacting against the Baghdad Pact of the conservative regimes and the United States. By 1963, Nasser had already accepted arms from Czechoslovakia and became deeply involved in Yemen. Brigadier Qassem, the leader in Iraq, had disappointed Nasser by building up the Ba'ath Party instead of joining the UAR, the union of Egypt and Syria. Vakiotis discloses that, after the Egyptian Air Force was destroyed by Israel in the 1967 War, Nasser suffered great disillusionment with other Arab countries before his death in 1970.[152]

Vatikiotis contends that Nasser had a poor understanding of Israel's ability to harm Egypt. When he closed the Straits of Tiran to Israeli traffic, he fully expected that President Johnson or a coalition of European nations would send a fleet to the straits. 'Amer, head of the Egyptian Air Force, had evidently not considered a preemptive attack. Nasser counted on the United States to restrain Israel if the Soviets protected him. As Vatakiotis notes, "The crushing defeat of Egyptian armed forces in Sinai in the Six-Day War constituted a defeat for Nasserism in the Arab world." But the rejection of Nasser's envoy of Mohammed Fawzi by Israel was not as Vatikiotis claims because

Jews did not belong in an "Arab milieu" but because of Zionism's expansive policies. American deception in Washington, DC, and the rapidity of Israel's strike rendered a counterstrike by the Soviets as useless. One positive result of Egypt's defeat was the rapid ending of the war in Yemen. In addition, Israel's continuation of air attacks inside of Egypt caused elements of the officer corps to seek revenge, but Nasser refused to commit to a "people's war." Now he sought to recover Sinai with the UN Resolution 242. By his policy of "No war, no peace," he believed that he might wear down the Israelis. Meanwhile, the Soviets, awakened to Egyptian desperation, began manning the SAM missile defense system, and even Russian pilots flew MIGS over Egypt.[153]

Nasser, because he was from the people, not like the previous Westernized rulers, captured the heart of ordinary Egyptians. He also ate the standard Egyptian diet of *ful, ta'miyya, and mulokhiyya*. But Nasser also had grassroots observers that later expressed their views. Vatikiotis voices some of these opinions. For example, he notes that Tawfiq al-Hakim tends to praise Nasser uncritically, while Louis Awad, another prominent writer, is more critical. Nasserism to Awad is a negative force, "the ending of colonialism." Nasser preferred state capitalism over Socialism in 1960 after Americans were slow to invest in Egypt. The 1962 charter promised "freedom, Socialism, unity," very vague concepts according to Awad. Industrialization only began after 1962, but nationalization of foreign assets came in 1956–1960. Later, Egyptian companies became subject to the dragnet. Vatikiotis concludes with Dr. Awad that some of Egypt's finest traditions from many years of contact with the West were subsumed to Arab nationalism "from the Atlantic Ocean to the gulf," including "democratic rights and freedoms, the separation of state and religion, the supremacy of law, the freedom of political thought, expression and organization, work and choice."[154]

Raymond A. Hinnebusch Jr., in his study of *Egyptian Politics under Sadat*,[155] makes important observations of the Nasser regime as an introduction to Sadat's Egypt. Nasir, as Hinnebusch prefers to spell his name (closer to the original Arabic), together with his fellow officers, imposed, "An etatist-populist revolution" on Egypt and challenged "Western control of the Middle East."[156] Nasir evidently wished to reintegrate Egypt into "the Western market and state system," but as his popularity and charisma expanded, this gave rise to the old Arab dream of uniting all Arabs under one banner, a policy known as Pan-Arabism. As noted above, the very expansion of Egyptian influence ran into both inner Arab political and economic roadblocks and also international and former colonial interests of the great powers. Nasir (Nasser) and his fellow ideologues attempted to balance the former dominent bourgeoisie with the interests of the working class. This attempt ultimately failed in the eyes of Hinnebusch because a private sector was permitted to survive, rather than using a Socialist idea with the backing of the working class to break the power of the bourgeoisie. The very power of the bureaucratic elite, their corruption, and high consumption undermined the state's ability to accumulate capital for socially beneficial investment in state enterprises. The loopholes and high consumption instead permitted private accumulation. Hinnebusch notes the major dichotomy between this developing reality and the "populist course favored by the leader and his mass constituency." Nasir was undone by the Egyptian bourgeoisie, world forces, notably President Johnson, the disastrous attack by Israel in 1967, the impotence of the Soviet Union, and petrocapitalism. And indeed, Nasir and the Egyptian military grossly miscalculated their own strength, not expecting a covert attack from Israel.[157] Hinnebusch calls into question the so-called functional approach to Egypt for two reasons: (a) the Egyptians were "susceptible to infection by its traditional political culture," and (b) "as modernization proceeded, they were unable to absorb the participatory demands of new social forces." Halpern and others, for example, praised the rise of the new salaried middle class. These political scientists seem to be keeping alive the Turkish example of Mustafa Kemal Ataturk (d. 1938).

The "functionalist" political scientists of the 1970s and 1980s could watch Egyptian society evolve after Nasir and came to the conclusion that the resurgence of traditional Arab culture produced authoritarianism, clientalism, and patrimonialism. And they blamed the Nasir era for failing to build sound political institutions that would have checked these forces.[158]

Nasir was indeed a charismatic leader in the vein of Max Weber's theories, but such a leader must continue to pull rabbits out of the hat. In 1967, Nasir once more relied on the international community to save his move to shut the Straits of Tiran to Israel, but President Johnson had strengthened Israel's air force to such a level that Israel could act quickly with a preemptive strike before Egypt's representative and former foreign minister, Mahmud Fawzi, could complete his flight to Washington, DC. Until 1967, the Soviet Union had made enormous advances in its influence with Middle East governments, but the implied failure of Soviet arms in the 1967 War had its effect, even though the strike on the Egyptian airfields happened so fast that a Soviet response would have been futile. The Soviet lack of response, however, caused a new acclaim for the conservative bourgeoisie in Egypt and the conservative Arab regimes, notably the kingdom of Saudi Arabia. The occupation by Israel of the Sinai Peninsula also deprived Egypt of revenue from Sinai oil fields, the Suez Canal, and tourism.[159] The Saudis received consequently much praise for funding the reequipping of Arab armies, but no longer could Egypt challenge the Saudis in Yemen and elsewhere. In short, the foreign adventures of Egypt came to a sudden halt. But as James Surowiecki notes in his article, there had been a flaw in the state planning of all Middle Eastern governments. Each government, by keeping alive major investment in state capital projects, had killed off the entrepreneurial skills of their young people, who often could not receive bank loans for their projects. In Egypt, feeding an already bloated bourgeoisie with government favoritism may be considered the real *coup de grâce* of Halpern's very astute early observations.[160]

After the death of Nasir (Nasser), a power struggled followed. Nasser had not groomed a successor, but Ali Sabri, a newly appointed vice president, assumed the position of leader of the soon-discredited left-wing officers who held many of the senior government posts. Anwar Sadat, the senior vice president, had been confirmed as president by the Arab Socialist Union's (ASU) executive and a plebiscite because he held "superior legal legitimacy," but the Sabri ASU group envisaged a collective leadership in which Sadat's decisions would be controlled by the senior officers favoring heavy industrialization, state Socialism, the party superior to the army and cabinet, and a foreign policy of "militancy toward Israel and a close alliance with the USSR." Sadat was known to oppose many of these policies.[161]

Sadat's first move was to appoint Mahmud Fawzi, a seasoned diplomat, as prime minister. It seemed that Sabri might have the upper hand because his faction controlled the coercive and communications apparatuses, but Sadat "forged alliances with the second-ranking officials in these institutions." The control of the army was vital. Sadat fought the high command of the military and finally defeated them with a vote from the Egyptian parliament. Sabri, by scapegoating the army for the 1967 defeat, aroused deep resentment particularly because *important weapon systems were late in delivery from the USSR*. Sadat then fired Sabri from the vice presidency. His party weakly struck back with a mass resignation and the attempt to organize a mass movement under the auspices of the Arab Socialist Union (ASU). Its failure indicated how weak the party structure had been. Sadat, with his authority, was able even to lock up some of his enemies. He also helped the bourgeoisie by making it possible for them to regain properties that had been sequestered under Nasir. Sadat also had served as speaker of the parliament, and thus, he had won over parliament through former alliances he had made with the conservative members and who also nurtured a resentment of the police methods of the Sabri group.[162]

Next, Sadat had to devise some method for regaining Egyptian possession of the Sinai. At first, Sadat tried to interest the Americans in a diplomatic solution. The Nixon presidency, at first, tried the Governor Scranton mission advocating an "evenhanded" approach in 1968. Nixon disavowed the approach when his national security adviser, Henry Kissinger, and Israel objected. William Rogers, Nixon's first secretary of state, also put out a plan that failed because of the disapproval of Kissinger and Golda Meir, the Israeli prime minister. David Rothkopf reminds us that Nixon wanted foreign affairs to be controlled in the White House, and he and Kissinger, the national security adviser, did just that. Rogers resigned under duress in August 1973 and was replaced by Kissinger.[163] When the gesture to the United States failed, only then did Sadat turn to a military option in 1973. By slowly moving up to the Suez Canal the antiaircraft weapons in frequent army exercises and also increasing the army's capabilities in laying pontoon bridges, the army struck in September (Yom Kippur / Ramadan War) with tanks, fire hoses, and frogmen. The frogmen were used to incapacitate Israeli gas mains shooting flames into the water's edge. The fire hoses dissolved the sand barriers of the Israeli Bar Lev line, and the tanks rolled in, catching the Israelis completely by surprise. Only with the U.S. massive reequipping of Israel from U.S. Army supplies in Germany could Israel stabilize her Sinai front. Israel had lost five hundred tanks and forty-nine aircraft.[164]

The details here mentioned have flushed out some of the difficulties facing the early optimism of Manfred Halpern and like-minded observers. They were right in depicting the charismatic hold that Nasser held over Egyptians and other Middle East countries that brought him wide legitimacy in many of his political moves. Sadat, however, optimistically indicated, in his struggle for power, that if the middle class is allowed to flourish, then legitimacy can be routinized because they will create the wealth for a modernizing country. Only then could Egypt overcome the disadvantages of its high birthrate and few natural resources.[165]

Sadat, after the Yom Kippur / Ramadan War continued to place his own men in key positions. The army chief of staff, Saad ad-Din Shazli, who was very popular because he had masterminded the war, was dismissed in December 1973 because he objected to turning the negotiations on the Sinai over to Kissinger in the United States. He preferred the option to fight Israel and rely on the Arab oil boycott. Meanwhile, Muhammad Hassanein Heykal (also spelled Heikal), a close confidant of Nasser, now editor of *Al-Ahram*, Egypt's most influential newspaper, also questioned the policy of relying on the Americans and was dismissed from his post. (Kissinger, in his capacity as secretary of state, national security adviser to President Nixon, and head of the National Security Council, had, in the height of the war, declared, virtually unchecked by other U.S. institutions, a "national emergency" to mobilize U.S. forces, thus confronting the Soviet Union's plans to aid its beleaguered allies.)

Saad ad-Din Shazli, one of the senior members of Nasser's "free officers," was replaced by Hosni Mubarak, commander of the air force, in April 1975. Mubarak was destined to lead Egypt after Sadat was assassinated. Also, Sadat's cabinet in 1974 was formed under the leadership of 'Abd al-'Aziz Higazi, who had excellent ties with international business. Sadat placed his confidant, Sayyid Marei, as speaker of the parliament, where Sadat meant that he should nurture his ties with the bourgeoisie. The Arab term *infitah*, or "openness," was the regime's symbol of liberalizing measures . . . "liberalization of trade, an end to punitive taxation of high incomes and to limits on land ownership, permission for foreign banks to come into Egypt, and a reduction of the public sector in favor of private enterprise." Hinnebusch notes further how remarkable it was that there was little mass protest with the dismantling of Nasser's programs for the poor Egyptians, the overwhelming mass of Egyptians who adored Nasser. Sadat was clearly favoring the haves over the have-nots, but Egyptians were willing to try new ways after the humiliation of the 1967 War. Agriculture, the traditional occupation of most Egyptians, virtually received no investment, while Osman Ahmad Osman, minister of reconstruction, was given virtually a *carte blanche* in his widespread enterprises, including permission to build on scarce farmland in the Nile Valley.[166] Hinnebusch had these observations about *infitah*: "Nasirism had its costs, so did Sadat's policies." The political struggle elevated the interests of the bourgeoisie, the upper middle class. "Unrestricted infitah resulted in damage to national industry, hemorrhages of capital and skilled labor, the dissipation of much of the new wealth in conspicuous consumption, and the channeling of private investment into speculative activities. Reliance on foreign financing translated into mounting debt and dependency." The foreign policy of Sadat and his successor, Hosni Mubarak, gained peace for Egypt and a return of the Sinai Peninsula, but the ensuing fragmentation of the Arab world enhanced American penetration and increased Israeli power to dominate her neighbors. One should also consult once again the important observations of James Surowiecki in footnote 145. I should like also to acknowledge the paper of a brilliant graduate student, Judith Kohn, for a paper she wrote, "The

Muslim Brotherhood and Militant Islam in Postrevolutionary Egypt."
In this paper, Ms. Kohn acknowledges that Sadat basically tried to get
along with the Muslim Brotherhood and thus differed from the policies
of Nasser. She also mentioned that *Al-Ahram*, on 17 January 1977,
noted that a militant underground movement, known as At-Takfir
wal-Hijra, was discovered in Mansoura, inspired by Sayed Qutb, the
author of *Social Justice in Islam*. A member of this same organization
killed Sadat four years later.[167]

Many young officers in the Egyptian military were not happy with
Sadat's negotiations with Kissinger, Carter, and Israel over the Sinai
Treaty in 1978 that gave to Israel complete dominance over Egypt and
the ignoring of the Palestinian occupation by Israel. Sadat received
ample warning. He had symbolically changed the name of the Arab
Socialist Union and disbanded its leaders for the new party, the National
Democratic Party, with new leadership in 1978. His newly appointed
cabinet of 1978 resigned after the treaty was signed at Camp David.
Also, the bread riots of June 1977 must have shocked the regime. The
treaty sparked underground organizations such as the Egyptian Islamic
Jihad and the Gama'at al-Islamiyah, which planned to overthrow the
government, take charge of army headquarters, state security, television,
and radio, and foment a general uprising. Getting wind of these plans
in February of 1981, the Sadat government arrested some 1,500
key personnel of Islamic jihad, but they missed the cell of Lt. Khalil
Islambouli, who had recognized the *fatwah* (religious decree) of the
blind imam, Omar 'Abd ur-Rahman, permitting him to kill Sadat.
Sadat was killed on 6 October 1981 while watching the annual parade
commemorating the Egyptian Army's crossing of the Suez Canal in
1973.[168]

In the new government of Hosni Mubarak, at first, very little
changed. The legacies of Sadat continued: "a consumption infitah,
massive dependency on the United States, and the reliance of the
regime on the bourgeoisie." Import-driven consumption and expensive
American arms at high interest rates meant large and costly food
imports, while Egyptian food production dropped below 50 percent.
Soon the national debt soared to a point where it could no longer be

serviced by national income. This state of affairs and a serious rise in coercive measures by the military and the repressive services led to the dictatorship of Mubarak and the Arab Spring revolt in Tahrir Square of 2011. Mubarak was forced to resign after the needless killing of thousands of unarmed civilians. For a close analysis of the troubles that the Mubarak government faced in the 1990s and the first decade of the twenty-first century, one must consult the article by Andrew Heiss, "The Failed Management of a Dying Regime: Hosni Mubarak, Egypt's National Democratic Party, and the January 25 Revolution." Heiss indicates how influential the writings of Sheikh Omar Abdur-Rahman and Ayman al-Zawahiri became to their respective parties of Gama'at al-Islamiya and Islamic jihad. These groups made violent attacks on government officials and their agents, killing over 1,200 Egyptians, and fifty-eight German tourists were killed at Luxor in November 1997. There were also economic upheavals because the Egyptian government tried to follow demands of the World Bank and the International Monetary Fund. Many state-owned enterprises were sold to Mubarak-favored cronies, and state subsidies to the poor were greatly cut back. No longer were opposition parties such as the Muslim Brotherhood and the Wafd permitted to maintain representatives in parliament. In short, Mubarak, through increased repression of dissidents and a complete breaking of ties with the vast majority of poor Egyptians, hastened the subsequent confrontation of January 25, 2011, in Tahrir Square and the collapse of the regime.[169]

Only on 24 June 2012 have we learned that Mohammed Morsi, the Muslim Brotherhood candidate for the presidency, had won. It remains clear the Egyptian Army will not bow out of politics. The military high command has written into the constitution the power to block legislation and limit the choices of the presidency, but in the short run, it appeared that the power of the Islamic brotherhood, since its creation in 1928, would trump the power of the Egyptian armed forces. President Morsi dismissed most officers in the Egyptian high command posts. But Morsi soon brought non-Brotherhood Egyptians back into the streets of Cairo when Morsi forced upon the Egyptians a new constitution without any feedback from opposition parties, and also many of the hard-fought women's rights wrested from the Mubarak regime were not reinstated. Consequently, the Morsi regime was removed from office by the military, and they were supported by at least half of the Egyptian population, who do not wish to be placed in a religious straitjacket of the Muslim Brotherhood nor wish for a dictatorship reminiscent of the Mubarak era. As Carrie Rosefsky Wickham, a specialist on the Muslim Brotherhood from Emory University, has noted in her *New York Times* article of 28 July 2013, "Egypt's Missed Opportunity," the Egyptians had wished for "a truly democratic order," but the old guard of the Muslim Brotherhood took over the agenda for the new regime and paid no attention to the narrow margin of victory of the Muslim Brotherhood and the desires of its liberal wing. President Morsi and his cabinet then enacted virtually their own constitution without judicial review by other parties and ran roughshod over the Coptic Christian problem and the hard-fought political and social gains of the women.[170]

True to the rapid change in Egyptian politics, President Morsi replaced Mohammed Hussein Tantawi, as head of the Egyptian Armed Forces, with General El-Sisi. El-Sisi assumed also the posts of minister of defense and military production at the same time. He had graduated from the Egyptian Military College in 1977 and married his sweetheart Entissar 'Amer, with whom he has had four children. General El-Sisi has had a great deal of exposure to training in other countries. He served in the Joint Command and staff college in the United Kingdom in 1992 and in the war course, U.S. War College, in 2006. Presumably, he served in the First Gulf War under General Schwarzkopf in 1993. Later he studied at the basic infantry course of the U.S. Army. In Egypt, he served principally in mechanized infantry divisions or in military intelligence.

Initially, he was accepted and well-liked by the President Morsi appointees. As noted above, President Morsi had irritated the non-Muslim Brotherhood populus with irregularities in confirming the new constitution, and as a result, responding to the Tamarod Movement, on 30 June 2013, demonstrations took place in Tahrir Square and other key cities. At this point, the Egyptian Army intervened and asked the various parties to resolve their differences by July 3. On July 2, President Morsi declared the legitimacy of his elected presidency and objected to the army's deadline of forty-eight hours. Consequently, on July 3, President Morsi was removed from office, and many prominent members of his supporters were arrested. General El-Sisi declared on national television that President Morsi "has failed to meet the demands of the Egyptian people." Also, Adly Mansour was appointed as interim head of state. In August, the Muslim Brotherhood organized protest camps, but the army disbanded them with some loss of life. El-Sisi believed strongly that the army and the Egyptian people were acting together. Now a movement began to draft El-Sisi for the presidency. Leading Egyptians declared for El-Sisi. The U.S. government of President Obama initially received much criticism for not supporting the "voice of the Egyptian people." Yet the U.S. secretary of defense, Mr. Hagel, was in Egypt on 24 April 2013, and Secretary of State John Kerry met with General El-Sisi on March 3, 2013, and again on November 3, 2013. On 24 July 2013, General El-Sisi spoke at a military parade, saying there should be mass demonstrations in support of the army and police to legitimize a crackdown on terrorists. Non-supporters believed that this gesture would be to cover up a military coup and disguise it as "popular will." Later, the military and the police disbanded sit-ins in various parks that were sponsored by the Muslim Brotherhood. Unfortunately, there were deaths and damage to public property. In an interview to the *Washington Post* on August 3, El-Sisi criticized the U.S. government for not supporting "the will of the people." Thereafter, press write-ups improved, and El-Sisi became enormously popular, even being claimed as the Person of the Year by the 6 December 2013 issue of *Time* magazine. Convinced that he could win an election, El-Sisi stood for the presidency and was elected by twenty-two million Egyptians on 26, 27, and 28 May 2014. President El-Sisi is a complex person. He first moved to improve the economy and then urged the police to crack down on the molestation of women. In a move that surprised many in the international community, the Egyptian El-Sisi government sided with Israel in its current attacks on the Gaza Strip when the Morsi government had been so friendly to the Hamas leadership of Gaza.[171]

For better or worse, we are left with the El-Sisi government in Egypt for the near future. I do not need to remind our readers that Egypt is the most populous of the Arab countries and that its religious institutions, filmmaking capabilities, and literary output shine bright in the Arab world, even though once again, the military dominates in political and economic terms. If the poor and petite bourgeoisie are left out of Egypt's present, we can count on a new explosion of these elements in the near future. On that occasion, the United States will be called upon once again to have its ducks in a row.

XVII. The American Presidents and the Middle East

Following World War II (1945), when the Allied powers had defeated Imperial Japan and Nazi (national Socialist) Germany, the same Allied powers (notably, the United States, Britain, France, the Netherlands, Belgium, and Portugal) were forced to give up their colonies in the Middle East, Asia, and Africa. Many subject peoples struck out on their own to form viable, independent countries. Some of these countries became involved in the post–World War II international division of states. Prodemocracy states joined the U.S.-led bloc, while pro-Socialist or Communist states either joined or were forced to join the bloc led by the Soviet Union. A third bloc existed precariously and was termed the nonaligned bloc. This bloc tried to keep itself free from the other two blocs and was typified by such countries as India, Jugoslavia, Indonesia, and Egypt. Also, the era after World War II became known as the Cold War in popular parlance because the United States and the USSR tried to gain advantages for their respective blocs at the expense of the rival bloc.

There was also another factor that played an important role in the configuration of postwar states and economies. This factor depended on where the respective armed forces defeating Nazi Germany ended their onslaughts. The Soviet Union, thanks to a great deal of lend-lease matériel, sent by rail through Iran and a heavy commitment of troops, moved westward from its own territory to occupy Poland, Hungary, and East Germany. The Western allies, starting from the British Isles, made troop landings in North Africa, Italy, Greece, and Normandy, pushing their forces northward and eastward to join the Russians south of Berlin. Eventually, these troop movements led to the neutralization of Austria, Greece, and Yugoslavia, but the Soviets forced Poland, Hungary, and East Germany into their own restrictive system.

This writer has often applied the term *the New Mongols* to the American presidents after World War II. At war's end in 1945, the United States, the foremost power, gradually forfeited the strength to conduct diplomacy or to the use of its armed forces because it was indeed very easy to bribe presidential candidates and members of Congress by donations to their respective election campaigns. Also, the Supreme Court, theoretically free from party politics because of their lifetime appointments, became involved in the financing of political parties by the Citizens United decision of 2012. This decision made possible the unlimited donations of corporations and foreign governments to campaign committees without disclosing the origins of the donations. Consequently, the U.S. presidents and their administrations have strayed ever further from the interests of Middle Eastern peoples.

Here we might recall the Mongols in the era of Jenghiz Khan (d. 1227) because the medieval Mongols did not concern themselves about the legitimacy of their rule over millions of Muslims. The first wave of Mongol armies was indeed very destructive of Muslim cities and more interested in legitimacy for their rule in the eyes of the emperor of China. While Manfred Halpern and many like-minded political scientists held high hopes for the new emerging elites in the Middle East, who, like Kemal Ataturk of Turkey, Reza Shah of Iran, and Gamal 'Abd an-Nasser of Egypt, had absorbed a high respect for professionalism in the military and government institutions and for improving the lot of the exploited classes in their societies, their interests and intentions were greatly weakened or destroyed by nonproductive ideologies and inept politicians. We have reviewed the example of Nasser, who followed the dream of Pan-Arabism. Sadat, his successor, albeit saddled with an Israeli occupation of the Sinai Peninsula, put faith in his business class, the bourgeoisie, to bring Egypt into the international system. Both systems failed, and Egypt became totally dependent on the United States, which, in turn, followed Israeli policies and caused Egypt to block its border with the Gaza enclave of Palestine. In short, Egyptian leaders, devoid of natural resources, except the Nile, and facing a major growth in population, had to face the undermining of their good intentions.

Elsewhere, as in Egypt, traditional forces, cronyism, paternalism, tribalism, sectarianism, and sexism, encouraged by the great powers, became entrenched. These negative forces, rather than democratic principles or the idealism of new leaders, helped the great powers gain access to natural resources and notable oil. The late political scientist, George Lenczowski, has produced an important study, *American Presidents and the Middle East*,[172] that details how successive American presidents and their subordinates overwhelmed Middle East leaders through their disastrous policies. Also, Lenczowski shows how Israel, though a second-class player in the great-power games, gradually gained a veto over American foreign policy, as noted above, because it became so easy for Americans and foreigners to bribe U.S. senators and congressmen for their pet policies. To catch the ear of a senator or congressman, one simply made a generous donation to his or her election campaign, regardless of whether or not the policy was in the best interests of the United States or one's constituents. We have also seen that it has become overt Israeli policy to control Middle Eastern countries by fostering sectarianism, through influence on U.S. policy or Israeli military action. This policy came to light in the important article by Oded Yinon, published in Tel Aviv in Hebrew, "A Strategy for Israel in the 1980s."[173] We have subsequently observed this policy in a number of Middle East crises.

Lenczowski starts his analysis by noting six basic facts of the Middle East:

1) The Mideast is close to the borders of the Soviet Union.
2) Oil from the Middle East plays a vital strategic role.
3) Islam is the dominant faith in most countries.
4) Nationalism is the main ideology of these countries.
5) In these economies, there is a general state of underdevelopment.

133

6) In many countries, there is a need for foreign aid and technical assistance.

1. The Presidency of Harry S. Truman (April 1945 to January 1953)

President Harry Truman, during his administration, was involved with four Middle East crises: (1) withdrawal of the Soviets from Iran, (2) Soviet threats to Greece and Turkey, (3) the recognition of the state of Israel, and (4) the Egyptian Revolution of the Free Officers Association, led by Gamal 'Abd an-Nasser, (5) he was also saddled with the Korean War, trapped between making war or peace on China.[174] The Soviets and Britain had occupied Northern and Southern Iran, respectively, at the outbreak of World War II (1939) in keeping with a treaty of 1907. After the war, they were required to remove their troops. Britain complied; the Soviets did not. Instead, the Soviets set up two puppet states: the Republic of Azerbaijan and the Kurdish Republic of Mahabad. Truman supported the Shah's military action, and the Soviets withdrew.[175]

Meanwhile, Britain signaled the United States in February 1947 that it could no longer sustain its commitments to protect the Northern Tier countries of Greece, Turkey, and Iran from saber-rattling from the Soviet Union. In Turkey, the Soviets laid claim to the eastern provinces of Kars and Ardahan and proposed international control over the Bosphorus. In Greece, the Soviets promoted guerrilla warfare from Macedonia and Bulgaria. In keeping with the Truman Doctrine, sizable financial aid was given to both countries, and military advisers helped their armed forces.[176] This move was a tremendous boost to American prestige in the target countries.

Truman's recognition of the state of Israel shortly after its Declaration of Independence on 14 May 1948 had the opposite effect in the Arab countries. He backed Israel in spite of the objections of most of his advisers ("the boys in stripped pants") and the expected alienation of the Arab countries. Truman was sympathetic to the plight of Jewish refugees, but his support boiled down to his desire to strengthen his Democratic Party in an election year! Truman stated, "I do not have hundreds and thousands of Arabs as my constituents."[177] Truman did attempt to alleviate Arab hostility by his Point Four Program announced at his second inauguration in January 1949. The idea was to issue low-cost loans to foster technical assistance to Third World countries to improve agriculture and health. This writer visited a medical clinic in 'Amman, Jordan, in 1967 that had been started by Point Four funds. This clinic indeed left a good impression on local inhabitants. But Henry Hazlitt, the famous publicist and editor, had written a book, *The Illusion of Point Four*, as early as 1950, indicating that the United States already provided technical assistance through the Export-Import Bank and the International Bank for Reconstruction and Development. He objected to making taxpayers foot the losses of loans to Third World countries when he believed that the losses should be absorbed by private investment. The Point Four Program was eventually funded by other programs.[178]

The Truman administration gave very little attention to the overthrow of King Farouk of Egypt on 23 July 1952 by a group of military officers led by a Colonel Nasser. But the CIA agent, Miles Copeland, was assigned to follow Egypt and, eventually, Nasser very closely, a story that has been detailed above. It is clear that the Truman administration was preoccupied by events in the Northern Tier of the Middle East and how the Soviet Union was making inroads. Only after General Naguib was discovered to be a front man for the revolution, not the prime mover, and with the Anglo-Egyptian Treaty of 1954 did the State Department and the CIA begin to take serious notice. Only in the Eisenhower administration did Nasser loom large, particularly after John Foster Dulles, the Secretary of State, advised President Eisenhower not to support Egypt's high-dam plans, and Nasser, in retaliation, nationalized the Suez Canal Company in 1956. Only then did all U.S. government officials clamor for copies of Nasser's *Egypt's Liberation: The Philosophy of the Revolution*, which was initially translated by the Egyptian embassy in 1954. In this small book, Nasser set forth his goal of Egypt operating in three circles: the Arab Circle, the African Circle, and the Islamic Circle. As we shall learn in the following presidency, President Eisenhower initially won great praise and trust from the Arab nations when he called for Britain, France, and Israel to withdraw their troops from Egyptian soil after they had colluded together to remove Nasser from power, but President Eisenhower, somewhat later, also gave his support to the rise of the Muslim Brotherhood.[179]

2. The Presidency of Dwight Eisenhower (January 1953 to January 1961)

Truman's successor was General Dwight Eisenhower. President Eisenhower had to deal with six Mideast crises:

1. The Mossadegh oil crisis—1953
2. The Nasser purchase of Czech arms—1955
3. The Suez Crisis—1956
4. Issuance of the Eisenhower Doctrine (March 9, 1957)
5. The Lebanon Civil War and American intervention
6. Secret support to the Muslim Brotherhood

Mohammed Mossadegh, the prime minister of Iran, had nationalized the Anglo-Iranian Oil Company in 1951. The West wanted Iranian oil; hence, the American CIA and the British MI6 overthrew the Mossadegh government in 1953, excusing it to the public as the fear of a Communist takeover. Soon a consortium was formed to distribute Iranian oil by large international oil companies. For the best description of who Mossadegh was and why he was so important to Iran, one must consult James Bill.[180] Bill takes the position that the United States acted with Britain in the interests of the oil companies. Yet Bill makes it clear that U.S. officials believed that the Anglo-Iranian Oil Company (AIOC) was acting against its own best interests and virtually caused the crisis leading to Mossadegh's nationalization of its oil holdings. The United States had accepted in 1950 a fifty-fifty split with Saudi Arabia in the profits from the oil fields of ARAMCO (the

Arabian American Oil Company). This move had followed the fifty-fifty split of oil profits with Venezuela. The Iranian government had asked the AIOC management to consider four points: (1) a price for Iranians of oil at the lowest price that was given to other customers; (2) a program of Iranization, more Iranians in top positions; (3) a check on the Anglo-Iranian bookkeeping to control profits; (4) and possibly a change in percentage because Iran was gaining only about 20 percent. George Mcghee, a seasoned diplomat and undersecretary of state to Dean Acheson and the Truman government, pleaded with the Anglo-Iranian leadership and the incoming Conservative British leadership of 1951, particularly with Anthony Eden, foreign secretary, to take a more liberal view of the Mossadegh government demands. The United States also stated that it would recognize the right of a state to nationalize with proper compensation. This position obviously changed under the Eisenhower administration. Bill holds that the Eisenhower government did not fully understand Mossadegh, and the American press only emphasized Mossadegh's holding of conferences and interviews in his pajamas. At the time, he was sixty-seven years old and in bad health when the CIA and the British MI6 removed him from power.[181]

After Israel reacted to Palestinian border attacks by killing a number of officers in a Gaza police station in February 1955, Nasser asked the United States and Britain for serious defensive weapons. When the weapons were not forthcoming, Nasser bought Czech arms. John Foster Dulles, secretary of state, then advised President Eisenhower not to support Nasser's high-dam project in 1956, a project to boost Egyptian power generation. To gain the funds, Nasser nationalized the Suez Canal. This move prompted an invasion of Egypt by Britain, France, and Israel. Eisenhower, not being informed of the attack beforehand, soon forced their withdrawal, which regained briefly for the United States an aura of impartiality. As Robert Dallin astutely reminds us in a chapter called "Cold War Orthodoxy: Eisenhower and Dulles," when the president and Dulles removed Mossadegh from power, they believed that any Asian country that acted in its own interest was anti-American and would soon become Communist. This same mentality was applied to Nasser. Dulles and Eisenhower naively believed that if they supported the High Dam, Egypt's principal economic priority, then Nasser would forego his arms deal with the Soviet bloc, but Congress virtually vetoed this course of action because it seemed to appease Nasser's nationalization of the Suez Canal, threatened the cotton trade in southern states, and was hostile to Israel. Thus, when Nasser recognized Communist China in May 1956, Dulles and Eisenhower pulled the plug on support for the High Dam.

In addition, even though Eisenhower had moved against the invasion of Egypt, popular reaction was further dissipated when the Eisenhower government issued the Eisenhower Doctrine in January 1957 because the popularity of Nasser had created popular movements in many Arab countries. Nasser's popularity in Lebanon, deemed by Dulles as a threat from international Communism, coincided in 1958 with President Camille Chamoun's desire to extend his presidency illegally; hence, a civil war began in May 1958. Many individuals in Lebanon supported Nasser's pan-Arab movement and wished to join the UAR, as had Syria. Meanwhile, Colonel Qassem had overthrown the monarchy in Iraq, and the United States in July then landed marines in Lebanon basically because Nasser supposedly filled the bill as a Communist in terms of Eisenhower's doctrine. These two events affected deeply the relations between the United States and the Middle East.[182]

To add insult to injury, the Eisenhower government secretly began to support the Muslim Brotherhood through the efforts of Said Ramadan. Said Ramadan had married Wafa al-Banna, the daughter of Hasan al-Banna, the founder of the Muslim Brotherhood in 1928. Ramadan had met Eisenhower briefly in September 1953 in a group of Islamic scholars who had previously attended a colloquium at Princeton University, organized by the State Department and Dr. Philip Hitti, resident scholar at Princeton. Ramadan, an Egyptian by birth, had graduated from the law faculty of Cairo University in 1945 and early became the secretary and chief propagandist for his father-in-law. Ramadan opened cells of the brotherhood all over the Middle East and Pakistan. He had been invited to the colloquium in September 1953 at the recommendation of Jefferson Caffery, ambassador to Egypt at the time. Later, Ramadan settled in Switzerland and, from this vantage point, served as an American and British agent to foster the rise once more of the Muslim Brotherhood in Egypt and Saudi Arabia that had been banned in 1950. The idea of fostering the Muslim Brotherhood was deemed the answer to the threat of the Soviet Union making inroads in Middle Eastern countries. Clearly, with Eisenhower, Middle East problems were no longer limited to the Northern Tier states. President Eisenhower set a pattern of wariness of the Middle East that most presidents followed after him.[183]

3. The Presidency of John F. Kennedy (January 1961 to November 1963)

President John F. Kennedy (20 January 1961–22 November 1963), in his attention to the Middle East, was friendly to Nasser's Pan-Arabism because of his familiarity with Irish nationalism. Kennedy, therefore, did not agree with the confrontation ideas of John Foster Dulles, former Secretary of State. Nasser's neutrality did not worry Kennedy. He gave his support for Egyptian reforms and modernization. While Khrushchev of the Soviet Union held similar views, he always saw events in terms of the "class struggle." In the Cuban Missile Crisis, Kennedy got the Soviet rockets out of Cuba by removing U.S. rockets from Turkey and Iran. But the gravity of the Missile Crisis of October 1962 was indeed the most serious that Kennedy and McGeorge Bundy, his national security adviser, faced.[184]

When Britain made the important policy change of relinquishing its colonies "East of Suez" in 1961, Kuwait was declared independent, yet President Qassem in Iraq laid claims to Kuwait on the grounds of its having been a part of the province of Basra in the Ottoman Empire. Kennedy also accepted the overthrow of the Qassem government by the Ba'ath Party in 1963, but in the long run, the overthrow of Qassem gave to the party hack, Saddam Hussein, the opening later to take control of Iraq. Walt Rostow's ideas of "the takeoff into self-sustaining growth" impressed Kennedy, and he personally advocated rapid economic development for Arab countries. For the Palestinian issue, he recommended to Israel either repatriation or compensation, but in George Lenczowski's view, Kennedy failed to understand the refugee problem and, consequently, the frustrated Palestinian nationalism. Basically, Middle East questions in the Kennedy White House were dealt with by Robert Komer and Meyer Feldman. Fortunately, for Kennedy, his ambassador in Cairo was John Badeau, who could explain the intricacies of U.S. policies to Nasser and Arab politics to Kennedy.[185]

The Kennedy government wished to support progressive states, but the Yemen move by Nasser in 1962 to support the overthrow of the king and religious leader, Imam Muhammad al-Badr, strained even the Kennedy White House. The Saudis and Jordan, both Arab monarchies, supported King Badr and the Yemeni tribes, while Nasser backed the overthrow of the king by Abdallah al-Sallal, an army colonel. Nasser, in the previous year of 1961, had lost Syria from the UAR (United Arab Republic) because of his heavy-handed policies and the incapability of joining together two so different economic systems. Both the Saudis and the Egyptians bombed their opponents. Finally, the United States recognized the new government of Al-Sallah on December 19, 1962. This type of foreign adventurism eventually undid Nasser's reforms because of the cost of waging war. A new study by the Israeli scholar, Jesse Ferris, follows this general argument, as announced in the new Princeton University Press Catalogue of 2012, but as the subtitle claims, it is a serious stretch to say *How Intervention in Yemen Caused the Six-Day War and the Decline of Egyptian Power.* Israel knew beforehand that Nasser was not planning a strike on Israel, but the Israelis made a preemptive strike on Egypt, while Egypt was sending a deputy to Washington to negotiate peace.[186]

4. The Presidency of Lyndon Johnson (November 22, 1963, to January 20, 1969)

President Kennedy was assassinated on November 22, 1963, and his vice president, Lyndon Baines Johnson, succeeded him. Johnson was poorly suited for his foreign policy decisions, and Johnson had shared the ticket with Kennedy as a master of congressional affairs. President Johnson resented the Eastern establishment of the Kennedy crowd and chose as his secretary of state Dean Rusk from Georgia, who was well-versed in Far Eastern affairs. Johnson, often reluctantly, also consulted George Ball and McGeorge Bundy. As a master of congress, Johnson tended to link foreign policy decisions to domestic affairs. While dedicated to his concerns about the Great Society, his presidency had to deal with the growing Vietnam War. We must consider very positive the great strides made by President Johnson in recognizing the voting rights and affirming the constitutional rights of African Americans, but as Melissa Harris-Perry has emphasized, the marches of the blacks in the Deep South, the pressure of the labor movement, the assassination of Martin Luther King, and the ridicule of the United States by the Soviet Union because Southern police officers led attack dogs on children, helped place pressure on President Johnson and the Congress to pass the Great Society legislation.[187]

To McNamara, Johnson's secretary of defense, Johnson left many crucial decisions on Vietnam. But even the Kennedy government deeply involved the United States in Vietnam by hastening the collapse of the government of Ngo Dinh Diem in South Vietnam. Nevertheless, it was McGeorge Bundy's open-style model service to Kennedy that saved Kennedy and the nation from many hardships.[188]

McGeorge Bundy attempted to mitigate Johnson's harsh response to the Gulf of Tonkin incident that led to the Vietnam War. Some North Korean PT boats had attacked the destroyer USS *Maddox* in the Gulf of Tonkin off the North Vietnam coast after the United States had bombed North Vietnam. President Johnson wished to make a strong response but appear to make a "measured" response in an election year in which he would run against Barry Goldwater, who was deemed "trigger-happy." President Johnson completely overruled Bundy's urging caution; consequently, Johnson got Congress to back him, making war inevitable. Henceforth, Bundy felt that he was no longer an adviser but an errand boy. It is important also to read Undersecretary of State George Ball's predictions. He predicted to the cabinet that if we involved ourselves more deeply in the defense of South Vietnam, we would lose the war and the support of the American public. But President Johnson's cabinet decided to send in one hundred thousand troops in 1965 and more again in 1966, in keeping with the requests of General William Westmoreland.[189]

President Johnson, in the beginning of his presidency, understood very little about the intricacies of our Middle East policies. In fact, Johnson basically neglected the Middle East while concentrating on Vietnam. He had dealt with the domestic repercussions of foreign policy in the Senate, as we shall note. The London-Zurich Accord on Cyprus was negotiated in 1959. The island of Cyprus contained about 15 percent Turks and 85 percent Greeks. Archbishop Makarios was president of Cyprus and preferred dealing with the Soviets or the nonaligned nations, and under his watch, the Turkish villages were under constant military attack. Ismet Inonu, the prime minister of Turkey, issued an ultimatum to the Greeks on January 28, 1964, to stop attacks on Turkish villages. Undersecretary Ball wanted a NATO force to protect the Turks, but Makarios wanted a UN force because he knew there would be a long delay in setting up such a force. It was also known that Johnson's wife, "Lady Bird," was of Greek origin. Johnson was burned in effigy in Ankara as the tensions increased. Unfortunately, a grossly undiplomatic note, ordered by President Johnson, was then composed by Secretary Rusk, Harlan Cleveland, and Joseph Sisco of the State Department Middle East desk. This harsh note was sent to Prime Minister Ismet Inonu without consulting George Ball, stating that no NATO arms could be used by the Turks to attack Greeks on Cyprus. The Turks were shocked by this insult to their government, because Prime Minister Inonu stood only second to Ataturk in the respect of the Turks for leaders of the revolution. General Lemnitzer was hastily sent to Turkey on the eve of a Turkish air attack on Cyprus, bringing U.S. apologies and a request for postponement. Prime Minister Inonu reluctantly agreed to call off his attack in a response of June 13, 1964.

A military coup in Greece in April 1967 eased the cry for enosis or union with the Greek mainland, and John Brademas, in the U.S. Congress, also of Greek origin, maneuvered his colleagues into further insulting the Turks with an arms embargo. The issue of Turkish villagers on Cyprus being continuously under attack was finally settled with a Turkish invasion of the northern part of Cyprus in 1974, under the leadership of Turkish prime minister Mustafa Bulent Ecevit.[190]

As Lenczowski so succinctly put it, under Presidents Eisenhower and Kennedy, the United States was trusted as a power seeking to balance various interests of Israel, Iran, and Arab countries. With the handling of the 1967 crisis over the Straits of Tiran and the Six-Day War by President Johnson, the United States reached a turning point, never to be trusted in Middle East negotiations again. With his open support for Israel, one should not accept the idea that President Johnson did not know how to quiet the Jewish lobby. Michael Beschloss, who published the secret tapes of President Johnson, reveals a tape of February 20, 1965, in which Abe Feinberg, a strong supporter of the Democratic Party and of Israeli causes, objected to the United States equipping Jordan with some types of the latest military equipment. Johnson told Feinberg, chairman of the Kayser-Roth Corporation, that if we do not send a few weapons to Jordan, Jordan will become a client of the Soviet Union like Nasser and that also this blocking of aid to Jordan may also lead to the blocking of aid for Israel![191]

Abba Eban, Israel's foreign minister at the time of the Six-Day War, has recorded in his memoir details of President Johnson's statements regarding the pending negotiations about Nasser's closing of the Straits of Tiran. President Eisenhower had already assured Israel in 1956 that the Straits of Tiran would be open to Israeli shipping. Eban had received a warning from President Charles de Gaulle in France to Israel: "Ne tirez pas la premiere balle." (Don't fire the first shot.) From Prime Minister Wilson in Britain, he was assured that Britain would support the ending of the blockade. An important note Abba Eban mentioned in his memoir: he was surprised by "Nasser's ignorance of Israeli mentality" regarding the Straits of Tiran. One can only surmise that Nasser expected President Johnson to lift the blockade of the Straits of Tiran.[192]

Johnson met Eban at the White House on Friday afternoon (May 26, 1967) on the Memorial weekend when most members of Congress were absent from Washington. Johnson, apart from worrying about baseball tickets, had paid a courtesy visit to Canada, while Eban, on Friday morning, met with Secretary of Defense Robert McNamara and General Earle Wheeler, head of the Joint Chiefs of Staff, at the Pentagon. The United States believed that the Egyptian armed forces were much weaker than the Israelis, but this appraisal differed greatly from the Israeli assessment produced by Eban. The U.S. military also confirmed that Israel would win any engagement regardless of who took the air initiative. Also, the U.S. military noted logistic confusion in the Egyptian armed forces. Johnson, in the presence of Walt and Eugene Rostow, Secretary of Defense McNamara, General Wheeler, and George Christian, the president's press secretary, assured Eban that "he would use any and all measures in his power to get the Gulf of Aqaba open to all shipping, including that of Israel." Johnson also added, "Israel will not be alone unless it decides to go it alone." To St. John, the Eban biographer, the four days of meetings in the United States meant that Eban wanted to win international understanding if Israel made the first move. In this, Eban succeeded.[193]

It was also clear that the Soviets would block any UN action, and this was confirmed by Arthur Goldberg, the U.S. ambassador of the United States to the UN, when he met with Eban in New York City. Goldberg also cautioned that the president would not move without Senate approval, a further delay. Nasser made matters worse by a fiery speech of May 26 that Eban read on his way from Orly Airport in Paris to Lod Airport in Tel Aviv, arriving at 10:00 p.m. on Saturday, May 27. Nasser had stated that Egypt's basic objective was to destroy Israel. Eban addressed a cabinet meeting that was divided between those who wanted an immediate attack and those willing to play for time. Eban asked the cabinet for a forty-eight-hour delay before a final vote. Dean Rusk, the U.S. secretary of state, sent a wire to Levi Eshkol, the Israeli prime minister, that the British navy was joining with other nations to form a naval escort plan. Eshkol chose to inform Israel about recent events but was so rattled by the Israeli military that his voice lacked the assurance that Israelis expected. Hence, there were calls for his resignation or his giving up his defense tasks to Yigal Allon, the Israeli army chief of staff. On the Arab side, it did not help the crisis when King Hussein of Jordan flew to Cairo on May 30 to sign a mutual defense pact with Nasser. Eshkol, on the same day, drafted a letter to President Johnson, with Eban's help, stating that "the continuation of this position [of waiting] for any considerable time is out of the question." The Rafi Party, newly formed by Ben-Gurion, sharply criticized Eshkol, calling for his resignation once again. This time, the Labor Party met, and Eshkol, while remaining prime minister, gave the Defense Ministry to Allon and the post of chief of staff to Moshe Dayan. On May 31, a few Kuwaiti and Iraqi units arrived in Cairo, and Nasser resumed diplomatic relations with Syria. Also, General Aref, head of the Egyptian Air Force, broadcast to his pilots that he would see them in Tel Aviv and Haifa. Meanwhile, no American official of stature had urged caution on Israel for the last forty-eight hours before the Israeli June 5 attack on Cairo, and no move by President Johnson for a U.S. naval response was forthcoming. Only Ambassador Hermann Eilts in Saudi Arabia and David Newsom, the new ambassador to Libya, recommended sending naval vessels to the Straits of Tiran. Eban met with the cabinet on June 4, where all eighteen members voted for a military strike.[194]

In short, President Johnson had initially prepared Israel for a preemptive strike in 1967 by giving the Israeli Air Force a number of spare parts for their aircraft, and France had generously supplied Mystere jets. President Johnson had befriended Prime Minister Eshkol on his visit to Washington in 1964 and gave to Israel a number of offensive weapons and promised F-4 Phantom jets in the next three years. President Johnson also increased yearly grants to Israel of 90 million dollars from the previous fifteen million. However much President Johnson's current biographer may laud him for his domestic policies, the most important neglect of his presidential duties came in the manner in which he dealt with the direct attack of the Israeli Air Force and Navy on the U.S. Navy electronic listening vessel, the USS *Liberty*, on 8 June 1967. Thirty-four naval men lost their lives, and 171 men were wounded, largely as a result of Israeli aircraft napalming and machine-gunning the crew. When some officers received Medals of Honor for distinguished service and bravery in action, their medals were awarded in an obscure Washington gymnasium, and the entire crew was warned never to mention the incident. President Johnson, being openly pro-Israeli and wishing to give Nasser's deemed arrogance a lesson, secretly urged the Israelis to attack Egypt. When most news media praised Israel for its "brave" attack, Johnson chose to hide the attack on the USS *Liberty* by Israel's Air Force and Navy.[195] The Israelis later claimed that the attack was an accident, but since that time, the Hebrew conversations of the Israeli pilots and the Israeli naval vessels have been exposed by James Bamford, confirming that Israel knew they were attacking an essentially unarmed American naval vessel.[196] A plausible rationale for this attack was, doubtless, the Israeli desire not to be known to have made a preemptive strike on Egypt. It was also important to the Israeli cabinet that Israel postpone the cease-fire of the UN and to seize the West Bank of Jordan territory and Quneitra and the Golan Heights from Syria. The USS *Liberty* could have monitored the radio traffic. Finally, Israel apparently wished to hide military atrocities such as the execution of one thousand Egyptian POWs. Meanwhile, Abba Eban and Levi Eshkol told President Johnson that Israel's attacks were purely defensive. It is rather surprising that Johnson covered up the attack on the USS *Liberty* because Johnson had served as an officer in the U.S. Navy![197]

When all the evidence on the Six-Day War is considered, it is clear how incautious President Johnson proved to be. Essentially, apart from Dean Rusk and George Ball, his leading advisers were very pro-Israeli, including Arthur Goldberg at the United Nations; Walter Rostow, national security adviser; his brother, Eugene Rostow, assistant secretary in the State Department; and many others. It may have disturbed Israel's leaders very much because the Eisenhower and Kennedy presidencies appeared "evenhanded" with Muslim states. In fact, in some circles, there is the mention that the Israeli Mossad may have had a hand in the assassination of President Kennedy. Other sources blame President Johnson.[198]

Lenczowski summarized the damage to American foreign affairs of President Johnson's favoritism:

Six Arab states broke diplomatic relations.

Eban admitted, "We involved them very deeply."

A serious escalation of Soviet influence followed.

It hastened the process of anti-American radicalization
in the Middle East.

It caused a massive Palestinian exodus from the Left Bank.

It aided the progress of the Palestinian Liberation
Organization under Arafat.

At the UN, Arthur Goldberg abstained from the former
U.S. position on Jerusalem (as a neutral city).[199]

Some of Johnson's biases regarding advisers have been previously
discussed. Lenczowski listed the most important other factors:
Johnson wanted the Jewish vote and Jewish money for the Democrats;
Johnson was irritated by Nasser's tactics; he was pleased by the Israeli
military performance, and some members of Congress now saw Israel
as a strategic asset in a hostile Middle East. This viewpoint mirrors
Weizmann's initial rationale for the Balfour Declaration to the
British prime minister Balfour in 1917 that when Arab nationalism
became stronger, a Jewish entity in Palestine would serve as a British
friend in the Middle East. As regards the economic revolutions in
the three key states of Egypt, Syria, and Iraq, a deep analysis of these
countries was done by Roger Owen of Oxford University in the book
on Middle East revolutions, edited by P. J. Vatakiotis. Owen deals
with these key countries indicating that their leaders of necessity had
to manage scarce resources through planning. Once they adapted
five-year plans, they were led to Socialist solutions but, in the end,
gained little reward from the state capitalism they adapted. Either
population growth wiped out the financial gains as in Egypt, or the
Syrian and Iraqi regimes failed to apply their norms with adequate
discipline.[200]

5. The Presidency of Richard Nixon (January 1969 to May 1974)

Robert Dallek has written a masterful study of the Nixon and Kissinger years. Anyone wishing a day-by-day description of the peacemaking of President Nixon and his chief adviser, Henry Kissinger, must read the Dallek story. Nixon and Kissinger knew that the buildup of American armed forces in Vietnam, approaching five hundred thousand, had ruined the Johnson presidency. To make peace in Vietnam, Nixon and Kissinger tried the bombing of Phnom Penh, Haiphong, and troop sactuaries in Cambodia, but Nixon and Kissinger also pursued summits in the Soviet Union and in China because these countries were supplying arms and moral support to North Vietnam. What seems most interesting about Dallek's book was the psychological hang-ups and rivalries of both men in their quest to be favored as the "real" peacemakers in the eyes of the American and worldwide observers.[201]

We have already discussed some problems that President Sadat experienced with President Nixon and his national security adviser, Henry Kissinger. The Nixon presidency, January 1969 until the Watergate scandal, forced Nixon's resignation in May 1974, inherited a "burdensome legacy from Johnson" in the Middle East. Nixon gave mixed signals on Palestine, claiming their legitimate rights but concluding that Israel should always remain militarily dominant. Nixon wished to make Iran under the Shah, Mohammed Reza, the surrogate for the United States in the Middle East, promising the Iranians the latest aircraft and encouraging Kurdish attacks on Iraq. Actually, Nixon and Kissinger were chiefly concerned about winding down the Vietnam War and weakening the Soviet Union through gestures to China. This attitude gave rise to the so-called Nixon Doctrine: the United States will keep its treaty obligations but will expect Asian nations to defend themselves with U.S. military aid and technical assistance.

Only after Sadat destroyed the Bar Lev line in 1973 did Kissinger start his step-by-step diplomacy that regained the Sinai for Egypt but also made Israel the dominant Middle Eastern power. When Nixon came into the presidency in January 1969, the burning issue still remained: how to make peace between Israel and Egypt after Israel's stunning defeat of three Arab armies. In June 1967, Israel, pure and simple, had made a sneak attack on Egypt and destroyed the Egyptian Air Force while Egypt was expecting a negotiated peace in Washington, DC. Kissinger summarized the situation by noting that Nasser let the Soviet Union negotiate the Arab position while Kissinger stated that the United States was the only power that could deliver concessions from Israel. Israel's military strength, the Jewish lobby in the United States, and Israeli intransigence, foiled any chance for an early settlement. In effect, however, as Nasser's foreign minister noted, "Kissinger negotiated for Israel." Thus, no progress was made for Arab-Israeli peace until Sadat made his dramatic moves in October, 1973. American presidents are notoriously handicapped before the November elections.[202]

Kissinger states that he did not take Sadat or his peace gestures seriously. Only after Sadat expelled the bulk of fifteen thousand Soviet troops did Kissinger take notice. But Sadat, by moving up his SAM missiles to shoot down Israeli aircraft and also successfully practicing pontoon bridging to cross the Suez Canal, proved that Egypt could match the Israeli military. Sadat's armed forces then made their surprise attack, crossing the Suez Canal and demolishing the Bar-Lev massive sand dunes with fire hoses on October 6, 1973. The Yom Kippur / Ramadan War had begun with Sadat taking the lead with the Egyptian Army. Kissinger, on August 22, 1973 (Lenczowski notes the appointment as September 22), was appointed secretary of state when President Nixon asked William Rogers to resign. To his new post, Kissinger brought his top aides: Winston Lord, Helmut Sonnenfeldt, Lawrence Eagleburger, and assistant secretary of state for political affairs Joseph Sisco as his top Middle East official. Brent Scowcroft, an air force general, though deputy to the NSC, ran the NSC for Kissinger. On Ocober 6, 1973, Joe Sisco called Kissinger at the Waldorf Towers in New York, describing Egypt's attack. Before Kissinger could get back to Washington, Scowcroft had convened the Special Actions Group twice. Attending from the government in the absence of Kissinger were CIA director William Colby, Secretary of Defense James Schlesinger, chairman of the Joint Chiefs Admiral Thomas Moorer, and others. Also attending were Attorney General John Mitchell, deputy assistant secretary of state, Alfred Atherton, and General Al Haig, chief of staff, who had replaced H. R. (Bob) Haldeman.[203] "By day three, Israel had lost about one thousand men, forty-nine planes, and one-third of its tank force (five hundred tanks)." During Egypt's 1973 attack, Defense Secretary James Schlesinger objected to a resupply of Israel on the grounds that Arab states would react unfavorably. But meanwhile, Israel was in such dire straits that it had put on alert its Jericho nuclear defense system; hence, Kissinger pushed for the resupply on the dubious grounds that then Israel would, consequently, be more interested in a peace agreement. On the fourth day of the war, President Nixon ordered Secretary Schlesinger to start the resupply of Israel from stockpiles in Germany. Thirty C-130s brought one thousand tons per day: forty F-4 Phantom jets, thirty-eight A-4 Skyhawks, twelve C-130 transport aircraft, twenty tanks, spare parts, and ammunition. The airlift of the resupply began on October 12. To secure the resolution of the cease-fire agreement with the UN Resolution 242 and the Kilometer 101 Agreement, Kissinger, as newly appointed secretary of state and national security adviser, flew to Moscow for urgent talks with Soviet leader Leonid Brezhnev. Nixon also told Kissinger to work out a comprehensive peace with the Soviets. Kissinger ignored this request because he wished to cut the Soviets out of any peace negotiations. As Kissinger evinced an emotional tie to Golda Meir and to Israel, he acceded to whatever Israel requested. General George S. Brown, chief of staff, reported to this author, in a personal interview in the Pentagon in 1974, that he faced not only the Jewish lobby but also the born-again Christian supporters of Israel. Nixon was chiefly concerned with the Watergate scandal, leaving a completely free hand to Kissinger. When Kissinger authorized a 2.5-billion-dollar credit to Israel, the Arab oil producers started their boycott of many Western countries, notably the Netherlands and the United States, that they considered hostile to Arab interests, and the ban on oil shipments lasted until April 1974. When the Soviets moved to resupply its clients and to share with the Americans the peacekeeping,

Kissinger put our nuclear forces on alert, a move that Rothkopf deemed a bad precedent.[204]

In the Nixon presidency, Henry Kissinger also instituted a policy of far-reaching consequences that Robert Kaplan introduced in his book *The Arabists*. Kaplan's book detailed the biographies of the men and women who served in our Middle East embassies and consulates for most of the twentieth century. Kaplan indicated that many of the ambassadorial ranks of our embassies in the Middle East had incumbents deriving from nineteenth-century missionaries who had suffered great hardships and even death to bring Christianity to Muslim lands. The second generation of these hardy individuals discovered that Muslims and native Christians living in the Middle East were interested in Western schools and medical clinics. Thus, many children and grandchildren of earlier missionaries, who had grown up speaking Arabic, often qualified to serve in the U.S. schools, hospitals, and the U.S. Foreign Service in the Middle East. By 1860, some thirty-three Christian schools had opened in Greater Syria, and this prompted the formation by Daniel Bliss of the Syrian Protestant College in 1866 in Beirut, Lebanon. In the twentieth century, the college was renamed the American University of Beirut and became renowned for its liberal arts and medical school. At the turn of the twentieth century, Beirut became a center for the promotion of Arab literature and sovereignty, but Arab interests after World War I (1914–1918) were rivaled by interests of Zionists laying claim to Palestine, prompted by the British Mandate. The French Mandate over Lebanon and Syria was essentially against Sunni Arab nationalism and was supported strongly by the Maronite Christian Church and French Catholic structures. Kissinger or his assistant and deputy undersecretary of state and head of the NSC, Joseph Sisco, removed from the State Department many Arabic-speaking American personnel because "they did not understand the Israeli point of view" and, hence, left the Arab countries without the insights that the Arabists could have given. The major exception was Hermann Eilts, a refugee from Nazi Germany, like Kissinger, but an Arabist, who often stood against Kissinger and took an unpopular Arab position and yet was admired by Kissinger. Kaplan's subtitle notes that the missionaries cum ambassadors, who supported Arab nationalism, were "the romance of an American elite." In this writer's opinion, it was no "romance" to note that the dominant populations in the central lands of the Middle East were Sunni Arabs and that they deserved a serious voice in any peace process. Israel, population-wise, was less than 1/20 of the Arab population.[205]

After the Nixon Presidency and the profound influence of Henry Kissinger, Lenczowski summarized the results of U.S. policies under Nixon and Kissinger:

- After the Six-Day War, the closing of Arab embassies to U.S. personnel permitted Kissinger to retire many Arabic-speaking foreign service officers.
- The paramount U.S. policy with the Soviet Union was "containment," and securing oil for the West.
- Excessive partiality for Zionist/Israeli aspirations brought Soviet advances in the Middle East.
- Three Arab-Israeli Wars 1956, 1967, and 1973 affected national security and the economy of the "free world."
- Intervention was counter to the U.S. policy of "nonintervention" in Third World revolutions, unless fomented by foreign aggression (Eisenhower Doctrine) or a new state involves itself in foreign aggression (Nixon Doctrine).

King Idris of Libya was a staunch friend of the West and a source of oil but was removed from power by Colonel Muammar al-Qaddafi in September 1969. The American Wheelus Air Base was closed by June 11, 1970, and thereafter, the United States followed a policy of appeasement of the Qaddafi regime, hoping that oil interests would continue. Qaddafi, however, defied Western interests with arms from the Soviet bloc, and he followed a radical Muslim agenda. His own countrymen rebelled against him in the Arab Spring of 2011.

Both Nixon and Kissinger touted Israel as a "national asset" against Arab and Soviet problems, but most of the U.S. military, at the time, believed that Israel was a national liability. This fact becomes most apparent in the Iraq and Afghan Wars.[206]

6. The Gerald Ford Presidency (May 1974 to January 1977)

President Ford held a basic premise, as schooled by Kissinger, whom Ford kept on as his secretary of state, that Israel, supplied with economic and military aid, would contribute to the peace process by facilitating the return of the Sinai to Egypt. But President Ford expected a *quid pro quo* from Israel in the U.S. national interest. Prime Minister Rabin, early in Ford's presidency, gave the United States a shopping list for strategic weapons. When Israel appeared to be stalling on the peace process, Ford sent a telegram to Rabin stating that he was reconsidering an arms deal and also cut the subsidized appropriations. No new arms were extended to Israel from March 1975 to September. Only then as Israel moved its troops beyond the Mitla Pass did Israel receive oil and F-16 aircraft, ostensively making it the third-most-powerful air force in the world. AIPAC (American Israeli Political Action Committee) managed to have seventy-five senators sign a petition to lift the ban, indicating how easy it was to sway senatorial votes. Isma'il Fahmy, foreign secretary of Egypt, objected to the agreement as too high a price to pay for a small withdrawal, stating that Kissinger was "Israel's envoy," as previously noted. In the rhetoric running up to the next presidential election, Carter had taken a cheap shot at Ford, stating that Kissinger was the "unelected president." President Ford was considered by Kissinger and William Quandt to be a weak president, but one must give Ford credit for policy changes more favorable to U.S. national interests. He held up arms and refused to pay subsidies unless Israel complied with fairness. It was clear that the Israelis wished to keep control of the Egyptian oil fields in the Sinai and also the Mitla and Giddi Passes, but Kissinger and Ford had noted that the Rabin-Peres-Allon government pulled in various directions but nevertheless wanted Sadat to give up his state of beligerancy toward Israel. As noted, Ford got his way by talking tough to President Rabin.[207]

Ford also had to deal with a new Cyprus crisis. The new president of Cyprus, Nikos Sampson, who had overthrown Archbishop Makarios on July 15, 1974, opted for E*nosis*, the joining of Cyprus to the Greek mainland. As noted previously, attacks still continued on Turkish villages and their economic interests; consequently, Bulent Ecevit, Turkey's prime minister, ordered an invasion of the island that eventually occupied about 40 percent of the north side of the island from Lefkos to Famagusta. The military junta in Athens collapsed, and the democratic government of Constantine Karamanlis came to power. U.S. military aid to Turkey was suspended on February 5, 1975, with the intervention of the congressional Greek lobby. Turkey retaliated by closing all twenty-six U.S. bases in Turkey to American use except Incirlik, a NATO base. This invasion by Congress of President Ford's prerogatives on foreign policy was deeply resented by President Ford and Kissinger. The Turks stated that they would seek other sources for arms and soon improved relations with the Soviet Union. Also, the Turks restricted the use of ports and overflight privileges of the United States and refused any U.S. temporary subsidies. Only under President Carter was the issue of Turkish bases settled and the arms embargo lifted.

7. The Presidency of Jimmy Carter (January 1977 to January 1981)

President Carter had served in the U.S. Navy as an officer and was very patriotic. As Lenczowski noted, President Carter held high principles, but under pressure, he tended to cave in. He was chiefly interested in the Middle East and dealt with the Arab-Israeli peace, the crisis in Iran, and the Soviet occupation of Afghanistan. Carter had visited Israel but knew few Arabs; hence, President Carter believed that the Arab oil boycott was "blackmail," not an Arab weapon to gain their recognition and their rights. He encouraged the passage of antiboycott legislation for Israel and negotiated with the Soviets to allow more

Jewish immigration. In the universities, we were urged and indeed helped Carter's efforts by making public lectures supporting the Soviet exit visas for Jews. Carter wanted to bring about a comprehensive peace in Palestine based on the UN Resolution 242. He sought a Palestinian homeland, but President Carter ran afoul of Kissinger's earlier promise to Israel of no negotiations with the Palestinian Liberation Organization (the PLO). Cyrus Vance, secretary of state, later noted that Israel had been given a veto over American foreign policy by Kissinger in exchange for a minor piece of land in the Sinai. Carter had indicated his interest in obtaining human rights for the Palestinians. Zbigniew Brzezinski was Carter's national security adviser; Ed Muskie, initially, then Cyrus Vance served as secretaries of state. Andrew Young served as the U.S. ambassador to the United Nations. Carter already observed in August of 1977 that the United States financed Israeli wars and land grabs, but Israel simply defied our best interests. It is important to observe that most of Carter's team was chosen from the Trilateral Commission after Brzezinski had introduced Carter as governor of Georgia to the commission in 1973. This story is aptly documented by Rothkopf in his insightful study.[208]

In May 1977, Menachem Begin was elected prime minister of Israel. This former leader of an Israeli terrorist operation, the Lehi, proved to be very intransigent in negotiations with the Carter team. Gromyko, foreign minister of the Soviet Union, had visited Washington, DC, on 1 October 1977, and had proposed a very reasonable peace plan that entailed (a) Israeli withdrawal from occupied territories, (b) legal rights for Palestinians, (c) peaceful relations between the warring states, (d) mutual respect for sovereignty, (e) secure borders under UN supervision, (f) Americans and Soviets to ensure the peace.

These proposals were "violently" opposed by U.S. Jews and Israelis; thus, the United States retreated from this proposal under pressure from AIPAC (American Israeli Political Action Committee), the Jewish lobby. During future negotiations, Sadat and Carter became good friends. Carter was viewed as weak compared to Eisenhower, and Sadat seemed weak in comparison to Nasser. The legal work at Camp David, 4–17 September 1978, by the Egyptians and Americans was viewed as disorganized as compared to Israel's. Lenczowski believed that Begin made concessions on the Sinai because he had expansionist plans in regard to Samaria and Judea (that is, Palestine's West Bank of the Jordan River). For example, the settler issue was not on the agenda. Only after much hand-wringing and concessions on all sides, Carter was able to get Begin and Sadat to sign the Egyptian-Israeli Peace Treaty on 26 March 1979. Our family in 1979 was on sabbatical leave in Egypt, and one day, in the spring of 1979, we were having coffee in the Cairo bazaar of Khan Khalili when Moshe Dayan and his entourage walked through the main square of the bazaar. The details of the Camp David Summit are given in much detail by William Quandt. Carter went into the negotiations wishing to emphasize three points: (1) withdrawal from occupied territory in accordance with the UN Resolution 242, applying it to the Palestinian West Bank and Egypt's Sinai Peninsula; (2) the problem of Israeli settlements in the Sinai and West Bank; (3) the need to make room in the negotiations for the claims of Jordan and the Palestinians. Sadat would not negotiate on Egyptian land and sovereignty but was flexible otherwise. Begin wanted to separate the most powerful Arab state, Egypt, from other Arab states; hence, he was flexible on the Sinai, but in the end, Begin only gave Carter a moratorium of three months for further Jewish settlements on the West Bank, thus refusing his commitment to Resolution 242. Both Carter and Sadat, in the end, buckled on their desire to help the Palestinians, Jordan, and even Hafiz al-Asad of Syria. Quandt also indicates how difficult it was for Carter to have a running fight with Begin in the American election year of 1980. Begin basically stated that he would never permit the Arabs to have a veto on where Jews could live in Palestine![209]

Quandt does mention the Carter administration's further attempts to break through Begin's intransigence. He indicates that Begin would not meet Sadat halfway by allowing Egypt to have a say in Gaza or in the West Bank (Judea and Samaria, in Begin's references). In the end, Carter had to acquiesce to three billion dollars for Israeli costs with eight hundred million in outright grants, while Egypt only received one billion and a half for its large population, roughly ten times that of Israel. Also, the United States and Egypt had to guarantee oil supplies to Israel after the Khomeini Revolution in Iran had cut off Israeli supplies that the Shah's government had supplied. Finally, the exchange of ambassadors between Israel and Egypt would depend on the rapidity of the withdrawal of the Israeli armed forces from the Sinai. By signing a separate agreement with Sadat and guarantees from the United States, Begin had removed the threat of Egyptian war-making power but left Jordan, Syria, and the Palestinians to fend for themselves. As Quandt observed, American presidents appear to have a lot of power, but that power is checked by domestic politics, and in this case, the power of the Jewish lobby and the favoritism that Congress showers on Israel through the donations of Jews in campaign financing.[210]

President Carter also had to deal with the Islamic Revolution in Iran. In Washington, the Shah, Mohammed Reza, was viewed as a staunch friend. Past U.S. governments had showered the Shah with strategic weapons and went along with his desire to be the policeman of the Persian Gulf and neighboring areas. The Shah also had made a strong case for the legitimacy of his throne and ancient Persian kings, but Carter's emphasis on worldwide human rights brought confusion to the corrupt and corrosive regime. Also, in the case of Khomeini, as Yitzhak Nakash relates in his study of the Shi'ites, President Carter and his advisers could not have known the dominant role that Qum played as a training ground for Shi'ite leaders like Khomeini. These factors leading up to the revolution were dealt with exhaustively by Kurzman and Nakash when they considered political, religious, organizational, cultural, economic, and military factors in the revolution, but they conclude that it is ultimately disorganization, the actual unthinkability of a Khomeini Revolution, that produced incredible change for Iran.[211]

While President Carter, on a brief visit to Iran in December of 1977, deemed Iran "an island of stability," the Shah was already suffering from an unknown ailment, and Iranian students in the United States had led serious protests in Washington, DC, that caught the Carter government by surprise. The greatest threat to the Shah was now brewing in Qum and Najaf where the popular religious leader Ayatollah Ruhollah Khomeini, though in exile, had a profound influence. Khomeini not only criticized the Shah's government; he wrote religious tracts indicating that true leadership of Iran should rest with the supreme religious leaders, the ayatollahs (literally, those marked by God [i.e., serious Islamic scholars]). At first, Khomeini was exiled to Iraq, but later, with his entourage, he took up residence in Paris. Altogether, Khomeini was in exile eighteen years. Meanwhile, within the U.S. government, there were two factions that confused decisions. Brzezinski believed that the Shah's government should be preserved out of fear that the Soviet Union would take advantage of a weak Iran. Cyrus Vance, George Ball, and Ambassador to Iran, William Sullivan, sided with the Khomeini faction, believing they saw a democratic tendency in Khomeini. Before the Shah was admitted to the United States in 1979, President Carter tried to help the new prime minister, Shapour Bakhtiar, and Carter sent General Robert Huyser to give Bakhtiar legitimacy in the eyes of Iran's military. Lenczowski believed that this policy failed because Iran's military held only allegiance to the Shah. Huyser was credited with convincing the generals not to foster a coup. Meanwhile, Ambassador Sullivan helped thirty-five thousand Americans residing in Iran to leave the country. The Shah left Iran on 16 January 1979, and Ayatollah Khomeini entered Iran, with considerable fanfare, on 1 February 1979. When Khomeini arrived as the supreme religious leader, he appointed Mehdi Bazargan as prime minister. Contrary to American estimates, the religious leaders assumed leadership positions throughout the country, prompting secular leaders and many business leaders to leave. Thereafter, the Supreme Religious Council approved the confiscation of private property and the disciplining of any female wearing Western dress. Soon a host of repressive measures, backed by the Revolutionary Guards (*pasdaran*) and youth volunteers (*basij*), ravaged the population, and the universities and schools were Islamized. Meanwhile, many of Carter's foreign policy decisions ignored the natural allies of the Democratic Party, the Jews, the Hispanics, the blacks, the labor unions, and the poor. Paul Volcker, head of the New York Federal Reserve, introduced conservative policies into the Fed that also hurt the poorer constituents. Volcker recognized that inflation was getting out of hand, especially after Ayatollah Khomeini, in 1979, took over the Iranian government, suddenly reducing the supply of oil coming out of Iran.

This made the consumer pay more for gasoline. Essentially, by cutting the money supply, Paul Volcker, head of the Federal Reserve, made a great political expense for Jimmy Carter, who was running for reelection, by inducing a recession in the spring of 1980. This move came in the same time frame as the attempt to rescue the U.S. embassy hostages. Although through the courageous act of the Carter administration and Fed chairman Volcker, the economy was righted for the ensuing Reagan administration, Reagan poked fun at his rival in campaign speeches: "A recession is when your neighbor loses his job. A depression is when you lose yours, and a recovery is when Jimmy Carter loses his!"[212]

Apart from Carter's quest to extend his presidency into a second term, there were disastrous decisions made by Carter in 1979 that affected deeply his presidency leading to his failure in November 1980 to defeat Ronald Reagan. Already in 1978, it was learned that the Shah suffered from cancer about the same time as the U.S. government had expected the Shah to quell rioting in the streets of Teheran. Also, official Washington was surprised by the rioting of Iranian students in New York and Washington, DC. As we have noted above, the Khomeini Revolution had proceeded to such an extent that President Carter had sent General Robert Huyser to Teheran to give support to the newly elected government of Shapour Bakhtiar. There is no Iranian expert, however, who has explained the two factions affecting the Carter administration in such clear terms as James A. Bill.[213] Bill devotes chapter 9 of his book to "Pahlavism in America: The Informal Politics of Foreign Policy-Making." He reports that John D. Rockefeller III, Nelson Rockefeller, and David Rockefeller made frequent visits to Iran. Nelson, one might recall, was governor of New York and also vice president under Gerald Ford. He had been a candidate for the U.S. presidency when he suddenly died in 1979. He had hired Henry Kissinger as his chief adviser in the 1950s when Kissinger was a Harvard professor, long before Kissinger became national security adviser to President Nixon and then to President Ford. Nelson's brother, David, the head of the Chase Manhattan Bank, was the Shah's chief contact in his dealings with Wall Street, and Chase Manhattan Bank received massive deposits from the Iranian government as much as three hundred to five hundred million dollars per week even in 1979. By and large, the power of the pro-Shah group showed its hand in the question of admitting the Shah to the United States to be treated for cancer in 1979.[214]

After the death of Nelson Rockefeller, Kissinger had to deal directly with his brother, David, to muster every support possible for the Shah's entry into the United States. By and large, official Washington and U.S. ambassadors in the Middle East opposed the admission of the Shah. At this time, after many years of suppression of the vast majority of the Iranian people by the Shah and his secret police, the SAVAK, the Shah, Mohammed Reza, was almost universally hated by Iranians. Moreover, because Britain and the United States had been deeply involved with the overthrow of the Mossadiq government in 1953, if the Shah were admitted to the United States, the Iranians suspected that the United States would once again promote a coup d'état. When Cyrus Vance, secretary of state, directly contacted Bruce Laingen, chargé d'affaires in Teheran, on July 28, September 2, and September 30, 1979, Laingen and other U.S. resident officials responded that the admission of the Shah to the United States would "seriously prejudice our interests and the security of Americans in Iran."[215]

Indeed, what Laingen had predicted took place a few days after the Shah was admitted to the United States on October 22, 1979. The hostage crisis in Iran developed when a number of students and street ruffians took control of the American embassy in Teheran. At first, peaceful relations developed with the Khomeini government, but when the Shah was admitted to the United States for advanced cancer treatment in October 1979, the old suspicion arose that the United States was plotting the overthrow of Khomeini and that the embassy was occupied. In the embassy, sixty-six persons were taken prisoner. Later, the guards released the women and the blacks, making a political message to U.S. oppressed classes. Each time negotiations reached a turning point, Khomeini sided with the radical point of view. Khomeini's intransigence finally drove the Carter team to devise a military plan to release the hostages between 24 and 26 April 1980. Unfortunately, the plan had to be aborted when one of the helicopters crashed and killed a number of U.S. servicemen. Apart from the immediate humiliation of

President Carter and the United States, this failure might have cost him the election. As Carter was up for reelection, the Republican Party did all in its power to inform the Khomeini government not to release the hostages before the November 1980 election. Secretary Vance's policy of restraint might have led to the release of the hostages on 20 January 1981, but Carter also considered asking Congress for a declaration of war. To add insult to injury, Khomeini released the prisoners to the new government of Ronald Reagan at noon on 20 January 1981, the day that Carter relinquished the presidency. Lenczowski believes that the hostage crisis revealed a serious weakness of democratic governments when dealing with terrorist attacks. James Bill also reveals another element in the pro-Shah movement in the United States, the funds that the Shah had showered on the leading universities and gifts to members of the mass media. In fact, Bill delineates five circles of pro-Pahlavi supporters rotating around the Shah. The first circle is the Rockefeller-Kissinger group. The second group denotes the lawyers who always facilitated the Shah's affairs. The third group consisted of the leading businessmen with heavy commitments and contracts in Iran. The fourth circle included most Senators and Congressmen whom the Shah befriended and to whom he often showered with gifts. The fifth circle included individuals drawn from academia and the press corps who obtained direct grants to their universities or organizations.[216]

The most troubling aspect of Carter's Presidency came about with the Soviet invasion of Afghanistan in 1979. Events in Afghanistan took a turn for the worse with the overthrow of the Afghan monarchy in 1973 by Daoud Khan. His idea of an Afghan republic was to play off the Soviet Union and the United States for what he could gain. He sent Afghans to be trained in the Soviet Union while taking from the U.S. technical and economic assistance. A Communist regime led by Mohammed Taraki put an end to Daoud Khan's rule in 1978. Under Taraki and then his successor, Hafizullah Amin, three thousand Soviet "experts" eliminated or drove out the remaining ruling class by the usual totalitarian methods used in Eastern Europe. With the invasion of Soviet troops, Babrak Karmal became the nominal Communist leader, and Amin was killed.[217]

The Carter government did not put much stock in reports from the Shah's secret police, the Savak, until the U.S. embassy was attacked in February 1979, and the ambassador Adolph Dubs was killed. This incident and many others prompted President Carter to issue in his State of the Union Address of January 23, 1980. During his State of the Union Address, President Carter stated what was later termed as the Carter Doctrine: "An attempt by any outside force to gain control of the Persian Gulf region will be regarded as an assault on the vital interests of the United States. It will be repelled by any means necessary, including military force." While the Afghan invasion was most troubling, the Iranian Revolution had shaken Washington to its core. The United States immediately placed sanctions on the export of U.S. technology and grain shipments to the Soviets. The United States also formed a Rapid Defense Force but ran into difficulties for basing rights in the Middle East because of the close ties of the United States to Israel. Finally, Carter began the support of Afghan tribal opposition to the Soviets and managed also to gain better relations with Pakistan at the time controlled by General Zia al-Haq and the Pakistani military. Lenczowski opens up for discussion how events might have been different if Carter had shored up the Shah's regime and avoided the rise of Khomeini. Had he not vacillated with the Iranian Revolution, Lenczowski doubts that the Soviets would have made such a bold move in occupying Afghanistan.[218]

8. The Presidency of Ronald Reagan (January 1981 to January 1989)

The Reagan years were extremely complex, in part, because of great confusion in the National Security Council and the State Department and, in part, because there were many unique challenges to American hegemony. In his first year, President Reagan had to deal with a number of festering problems: (a) the consolidation of Khomeini's Islamic government in Iran; (b) the occupation of Afghanistan by the Soviet Union in 1979; (c) warfare between Iraq and Iran, 1980–1988; (d) the cross-border raids of Israeli and Palestinian forces in Lebanon, 1980–1982, and their aftermath with the occupation by Israel of Southern Lebanon. Furthermore, the marked rise of terrorism added a new dimension, especially because many states, including Israel, Libya, and Iran, appeared to sponsor it. Syria also nurtured hard-line Palestinian leadership rather than Chairman Yasir Arafat's more moderate course of the Palestinian Liberation Organization (the PLO). Lenczowski rightly attributed to this stance because the Camp David Peace left Israel in occupation of Quneitra and the Golan Heights.[219]

General Alexander Haig, Reagan's first secretary of state, had not learned from previous U.S. presidencies that there could be no "strategic consensus" between Israel and moderate Arab regimes because Arabs looked upon Israel as their chief concern, not the Soviet Union. Likewise, Israel believed that Arab governments posed their greatest threat. Jordan sought serious defense weapons from the United States but turned to the Soviet Union when rebuffed. Israel also pushed new settlements in the West Bank after seizing the territory from Jordan in 1967. In recognition of the strategic importance of Saudi and Iraqi oil, the United States placed an umbrella of protection over Saudi territory and also favored Iraq in a war with Iran that lasted from 1980 to 1988.[220]

Particularly noteworthy is the confusion of the Reagan government in Lebanon. While Lebanon, at the time, was billed as a democracy because of regular elections and a constitution, it basically was run by hereditary chieftains (zu'ama'), to whom primary loyalty of the clan was expected, not to a national Lebanese state. From World War I to 1946, Lebanon was controlled by France under the auspices of a League of Nations mandate. France, in a census of 1932, declared the Maronite Christians to be in the majority even though France had moved the Lebanese boundaries toward Syria, incorporating many Sunnis and Shi'ites into the general population. Henceforth, the presidency was reserved for a Maronite, the prime minister was reserved for a Sunni Muslim, the speaker of the parliament would be a Shi'i Muslim, and the minister of defense would be a Druze. The National Pact, an unwritten document, recognized this division of power, further requiring the

Christians to renounce allegiance to France and the Muslims not to make common cause with surrounding Arab states. This arrangement held until the late 1950s when Nasser's popularity began to influence Lebanon. The popularity of Nasser sparked the landing of U.S. Marines in 1958 in the Eisenhower presidency at a time when President Camille Chamoun wished illegally to extend his presidency and General Qasim had staged a coup in Iraq. This crisis ended when General Chehab filled the presidency. Shortly thereafter, the Palestinians attempted a coup d'état in Jordan in 1970 but were forced out of Jordan into Lebanon. Their presence in Lebanon and their raids into Israel, with subsequent retaliation, placed hardship on the Shi'ites in South Lebanon and led to the occupation of the Biqa' Valley by the Syrian army in 1976. Israel planned an attack on Lebanon in 1978 but was dissuaded by the United States and the UN. Finally, Philip Habib of the U.S. State Department, an Arabic-speaking expert on the region, as special envoy of President Reagan, brokered a peace on July 24, 1981, between Israel, Asad of Syria, and the Palestinian guerrillas. The cease-fire was honored by the Palestinians, but on June 6, 1982, the Israelis launched a major invasion of Lebanon named at first Operation Big Pines but changed it to Operation Peace for Galilee for propaganda purposes but, citing also the assassination attempt on the Israeli ambassador, Shlomo Argov, in London perpetrated by the Abu Nidal group, a rival faction to the PLO. The Defense Minister of Israel, Ariel Sharon, with full support from Prime Minister Menachem Begin and chief of staff Rafael Eitan, pushed the attack on Lebanon at a time when world leaders were distracted by Britain and Argentina's fight over the Falkland Islands.[221]

As Lenczowski noted, the object of the Israeli attack was twofold: (1) first to destroy the military formations of the PLO and (2) to set up a Maronite-dominated state that would league closely with Israel and possibly cede to Israel the territory south of the Litani River. He might have added the Palestinian refugee camps in Tyre and Sidon and elsewhere were also targets as they were subjected to sustained bombardment by the Israeli Air Force. Patrick Seale notes that the Palestinians should have resisted by guerrilla tactics, not by conventional forces that Israel easily outnumbered and outgunned. On Sunday, June

6, Israel "committed to battle a total of seventy-six thousand men, 1,250 tanks, and 1,500 armored personnel carriers, supported by their air force and navy. In opposition were regular Syrian and PLO forces under Major General Sa'd Bayraqdar of about twenty-five thousand men, three hundred tanks, and three hundred armored personnel carriers, together with some fifteen thousand PLO fighters." Israel, according to its foreign minister Yitzhak Shamir, also wished to have the Palestinians set up their own weakened state in Jordan where it could be dominated by Israel. Israel had assured Washington that the IDF (Israeli Defense Forces) would only move forty kilometers north of the border, but Sharon urged his army into the heart of Beirut, causing thousands of casualties; moreover, the Israeli forces subjected West Beirut to nine weeks of bombardment. Israel also took the occasion of the invasion to strike a heavy blow to Syrian forces in the Biqa' Valley and to destroy eighty Syrian aircraft. Contrary to general knowledge about the invasion, General Haig, secretary of state, was well-informed that Israel would attack Lebanon in early June 1982. Although the United States was well-informed about the invasion through the massing of troops and tanks at Israel's northern border, very few cautionary words were forthcoming out of Washington. This was taken in Tel Aviv as a green light. Even a U.N. cease-fire was vetoed by Reagan on General Haig's advice. Haig was concerned that Israel would receive full blame for the attack and receive sanctions! Answering objections that Israel had used cluster bombs on civilians in Lebanon, the State Department issued a weak memorandum to Congress that the Arms Export Control Act "may" have been violated. Finally, a cease-fire was worked out between the United States and Lebanon on August 18, 1982, that entailed the removal of the PLO fighters from Lebanon to various Arab countries. There is no doubt; Israel was delighted with this arrangement. A multinational force including eight hundred U.S. Marines were called in to facilitate this transfer. Surprisingly, President Reagan and Secretary Haig started referring to this arrangement as a "new opportunity" for peace. Since when does an "opportunity for peace" derive from a much stronger neighbor, Israel, destroying half of a weak neighbor's country? Even George Shultz, the newly appointed secretary of state, recruited from Bechtel Engineering, was content with this rationale. The reasons for the Palestinian, Syrian, and Israeli presence in Lebanon were completely ignored, but not for long![222]

President Reagan, on the advice of General Haig, pulled the marines out of Lebanon because they were attracting hostile fire and receiving casualties. Obviously, the United States forgot their pledge to protect the unarmed Palestinian refugee camps of Sabra and Shatila. After the Israeli invasion, Bashir Jemayel, head of the Phalange forces (Kataib) of the Maronites, was elected president of Lebanon (August 23, 1982). He had the idea to bond with Israel to strengthen the Maronite Christians against the rising influence of Muslims, both Sunni and Shi'i, in Lebanon. He was, of course, deeply surprised when he met with Begin and Sharon in Northern Israel on September 1, learning that Israel wished to turn Lebanon into an Israeli puppet state and have Bashir appoint Major Haddad, a Maronite Israeli puppet operating in South Lebanon, as Bashir Jemayel's minister of defense. Shocked to learn of Israel's intentions, he had very little time to react before Bashir was soon assassinated by a faction supporting Syria. His brother, Amin Jemayel, who held more respect for Syrian forces in the Biqa' Valley, replaced his brother in the presidency on September 21. Unfortunately, for the basically unarmed Palestinians in the Sabra and Shatila Camps, the Israeli forces in control of West Beirut permitted the Phalange forces of the Maronites to kill thousands of the refugees and bury them with bulldozers.[223]

At the time of Israel's invasion of Lebanon in 1982, according to Patrick Seale, Hafiz al-Asad, president of Syria, not only qualified as a legitimate ruler in the vein of Halpern's other post–World War II leaders but also had thought through his role as a key player. He wished to shield Lebanon from an Israeli attack and consequently moved Syrian forces into the Biqa' Valley. This strategy was only partially successful because Israel attacked Lebanon in 1982 to remove the Palestinian fighters from Lebanon and also to deal a blow to Syrian rocket defenses. The Reagan government moved marines into Lebanon to help remove the Palestinians. General Haig advised President Reagan then to put the marines back on their war vessels. Later, after the Sabra and Shatila massacre, Reagan ordered the marines back into Lebanon. This time, the Americans made a serious strategic mistake. They were initially "peacemakers." The second time around, they took sides with the weak Lebanese government. The Israelis had initially occupied the Shouf Mountains to the east of Beirut, and the marine positions lay near the Beirut airport on the Mediterranean shore. In their exposed position in the Shouf Mountains, the Israelis had suffered a number of casualties and, therefore, moved south to more defensible positions. The Shouf Mountains were once again occupied by the Druze and other Shi'ite forces. The marines were now caught in cross fire between the *Kata'ib* (Phalange Christian forces) and the Shi 'ites in the Shouf Mountains. Mistakenly, the marines asked the offshore American battle fleet to open fire on the Shouf Mountains, but the Druze and Shi'ites believed the marines were taking sides. Retaliation was soon to follow. The American embassy was blown up on April 18, 1983, killing many diplomatic personnel and a major CIA unit, including the valuable leader Ames. The marine base was soon to follow on October 23, 1983, killing 265 marines. As a footnote to this episode, the Reagan administration, under the influence of General Haig, had greatly weakened the National Security Council, according to Rothkopf, thus eliminating an influential consultative body that might have avoided the disaster.[224]

Other events also crowded the picture in the 1980s in the Middle East at a time when Americans had virtually no firsthand intelligence; consequently, they permitted Israeli intelligence services to guide a number of their moves. Hafiz Al-Asad also had to maneuver Syria through troubled times. He did not welcome Saddam Hussein's war with Iran, 1980–1988. In 1981 and 1982, Asad had to fight a virtual civil war within his own borders. Events took a serious turn already on 16 June 1979 when the Muslim Brotherhood perpetrated the so-called Aleppo Massacre. As many as fifty-six young Alawi artillery cadets were locked in a room and maimed or murdered on the day of their graduation. Elsewhere, the Muslim Brotherhood had infiltrated and proselytized a large number of Sunni Muslims, who slowly realized how much the armed forces leadership and the clandestine secret police had been taken over by the Alawite Shi'ite faction of northern Syria, a minority comprising about 15 percent of the Syrian population. Hafiz al-Asad, though he had attained leadership as head of the Syrian Air Force, was also an Alawite. He also was elected head of the Ba'ath Party, a secular party founded by Michael 'Aflak and Salah ad-Din Bitar about 1941. The Muslim Brotherhood had, in particular, concentrated their guerrilla forces in Hama, about 130 miles from Damascus. As the brotherhood managed to pull off a number of assassinations of the Syrian leadership and also commanded the streets of Hama, Hafiz Al-Asad, in 1981, brutally suppressed the uprising in Hama using the full force of heavy weapons, tanks, and aircraft to turn Hama into rubble. Estimates say the death toll topped ten thousand individuals. It is no wonder that Asad's son, Bashar al-Asad, is today attempting, in every city, to use similar tactics to crush a major revolt against his rule. Although Patrick Seale is mildly critical of Asad's methods, one wonders, even as today, that there might have been a more peaceful way of settling Syria's deep structural problems. Obviously, Hafiz Al-Asad greatly tarnished his record as a legitimate modern leader by killing his own opposition.[225]

Patrick Seale effectively redeems Asad by showing how well he sized up the power politics of the Middle East. There were only a few major players: Turkey, Israel, Egypt, Iraq, and Iran. Turkey was essentially neutralized as a member of NATO in a contest with Greece over Cyprus. Asad believed he had an ally in Egypt until Sadat and President Carter signed the Camp David Agreement in 1978 with Menachem Begin of Israel, under the tutelage of Henry Kissinger and Cyrus Vance. Syria was not even mentioned in the agreement, but the treaty made Israel stronger and took Egypt out of confrontation. Asad then tried to persuade King Hussein of Jordan, the Palestinians, and the Lebanese leaders not to make separate deals with Israel, indicating that united, they could negotiate from strength. However, this move failed with Israel's attack on Lebanon in 1982. President Carter had not chosen to stand up to Israel, and President Reagan, by dismantling the National Security Council, as an instrument for foreign policy, made possible the utterly foolish calls of his secretary of state, General Haig. Asad also, for a short time, tried to play his card with the other

Ba'athist state, Iraq. But Saddam Hussein had another plan: he thought that Khomeini's triumph over the Shah in 1979 would make Iran ripe for plucking of its Arabic-speaking province of Khuzistan. Only then did Asad reach out to ally Syria with Khomeini's Iran. Asad believed in maintaining a power parity with Israel. The Israeli leadership knew Asad's plans and did all they could to thwart his coziness with Soviet leaders, the Shi'ites in Lebanon and Iran. After all, if the United States helped Iraq to maintain a stalemate in its war with Iran, the Israelis had long since helped the Shah "with agricultural expertise . . . weapons and training for the armed services and for SAVAK, the Shah's secret police, in exchange for oil." In fact, Seale makes a strong point of Israel's feeding information to Saddam Hussein from various sources, emphasizing the weakness of Iran and the squabbles between various armed factions upon the arrival of Khomeini. Israel urged on a war between Iraq and Iran because these states would weaken each other and could do no harm to Israel.[226]

It is important that we summarize the popularity of Ayatollah Khomeini because his initial aims were largely misunderstood or distorted in Western and Sunni media. The most important reason, however, for understanding the Khomeini regime is the naive involvement of the Reagan administration in what became known as the Irangate Scandal. As Ervand Abrahamian lucidly describes in his important study, "Khomeini broke sharply with Shi'i traditions, borrowed radical rhetoric from foreign sources, including Marxism, and presented a bold appeal to the public based not on theological themes but on real economic, social, and political issues . . . The final product had more in common with Third World populism—especially that of Latin America—than with conventional Shi'ism." Abrahamian also noted how Khomeini remained committed to middle-class property, noting in his writings that Islam considered property, the bazaar merchant class, and the laboring masses as sacrosanct. The Khomeinists also distorted modern and medieval history to show that the clerical class had always sided with the "downtrodden masses" against the Iranian monarchy, the wealthy urban elite, and the intruding foreign powers. As an example of a major distortion, the secular role of Mossadegh's reforms between 1951 and

1953 are attributed to the ayatollahs, especially Ayatollah Kashani, who actually failed like Khomeini, to give his support to the nationalization of the Anglo-Iranian oil company. Finally, Abrahamian's study indicates the paranoia throughout the Iranian system of government wherein most political actors were considered "puppets," manipulated from behind the scenes (*post-e perde*) by plots, spies, servants, dependents, traitors, and fifth columnists, hence the ever increasing need for internal and external vigilance. The war with Iraq, 1980–1988, solidified the control of the clerics over the Iranian political system. The clerical classes in Iran also enriched themselves with the estates of the wealthy Iranians who fled abroad.[227] The rosy picture that Khomeini projected before he came to power began to unravel as Khomeini arrived in Teheran on 1 February 1979. There soon developed two basic viewpoints: the viewpoint of those who had either studied abroad or went into exile to escape the Shah's regime and the viewpoint of those who had stayed in Iran and weathered the storm. The clerics, the bazaaris, and the bulk of the ordinary working class sided with Khomeini. Prominent among those who had resided abroad was the new president Bani-Sadr, who had lived in France and joined Khomeini's Islamic Revolutionary Council when Khomeini was exiled to France. President Bani-Sadr and his predecessor, Mehdi Bazargan, were basically Khomeini's straw men who became the symbols of those expecting that Khomeini would live up to a moderate program of freedom of speech and a regime respecting all liberal civil rights. While Bani-Sadr had the backing of a number of splinter parties, he could not match the strength of the IRP (the Islamic Revolutionary Party) and the majlis, the Iranian Parliament, that backed Khomeini. The IRP described the seizure of the American embassy on 4 November 1979 as the Second Revolution after Khomeini's initial revolution. The ouster of Bani-Sadr, a trained economist who understood the "poor shape of the Iranian economy," came about on 21 June 1981 and was described as the Third Revolution! Khomeini had already given his seventeen lectures in early 1970 known as the *Velayat-e Faqih: Hokumat-e Islami* ("The Jurist's Guardianship: Islamic Government"), which outlined his basic position of the *Ulema*, taking control of the executive, legislative, and judicial branches of government. Thus, there remained no halfway house for Iran to become a free society as millions who supported Khomeini had expected. This meant that only those among the *Ulema* who were liberal-minded could cushion Iran from a government inspired by Khomeini's Islamic government based on the rule of the *Ulema* and a strict interpretation of the Shari'a and the Quran. Unfortunately, the revolutionary party, the *Mujahedin-e Khalq*, which was supported in strength by the educated young people, were suspected of setting a thirty-kilogram dynamite bomb adjacent to a meeting of the high command of the IRP. The explosion killed the bulk of the moderate IRP leadership. The Ayatollah Beheshti, a popular moderate who was on good terms with all parties, was addressing the IRP when he was killed along with seventy-three other mostly moderate party leaders on 28 June 1981. He had been fluent in English, German, and Arabic in addition to his native Persian. Khomeini was absent from the meeting but shocked by the explosion and, fearing a wider attack, had the Revolutionary Guards surround the army barracks in Teheran. With the explosion died "the idea of a broad-based anti-imperialist ruling front."[228]

There were other assassinations and deaths of key individuals after Khomeini's return to Iran. Ayatollah Motahhari was killed in May of 1979, who had been the moderate chairman of the Islamic Revolutionary Council. He might have brought the *Mujahedin-e Khalq* into the party. In September, Ayatollah Taleghani died. He was viewed as a bridge between the Persian majority and the non-Persian minorities. While he lived, there was a confrontation between the secular left and the conservative Islamic right. After his death, the Islamic left faced the Islamic right wing. The Ayatollah Shariatmadari, an Azeri of the liberal school, believed that the *Ulema* should not involve itself in the day-to-day political administration. Khomeini was an interventionist who used the weight of the Iranian state to overcome his rivals. With the elimination of Bani-Sadr, Khomeini controlled the majlis (the parliament), the judiciary, all revolutionary military organizations, and the media. One of the anomalies of the early Khomeini state was that the *Mujahedin-e Khalq* and the Islamic Revolutionary Party drew members from similar bases: traders, merchants, artisans, the young

Ulema, and the Persian-speaking heartlands. They generally followed Ali Shariati's dialectical approach, emphasizing the spirit of Islam, not the Islamic corpus of the Quran and Islamic law that served as absolute rules for the Khomeinists. The watchword to follow of the Khomeinists became "neither East nor West." The revolution destroyed quickly the old power structures of the Shah, the aristocracy, the Westernized upper and middle class, the feudal lords, and the urban rich and was largely class-based. The military drew most of its members from the lower middle class, as in many Western and Muslim countries, and a large part of the *Ulema* originated in the petty bourgeoisie also, and they were, in turn, closely related to the traders and shopkeepers. Hence, the revolution seemed closest to the bazaaris, the *Ulema*, and the mosque. It is not then surprising that Khomeini protected these supporters and made a strong pitch for property rights. Also, Khomeini favored the poor and lower classes when the war with Iraq forced upon Iran the rationing of many items. Many of Khomeini's loyal followers considered him a divine figure, an aide to the Twelfth Imam, at the heart of their Shi'ite beliefs. Many critics, of course, objected to the lack of a future orientation; rather, the Khomeinists held to a seventh-century ideal that the Quran and the Shari'a provided a model for all Islamic society.[229]

Here we have in a brief summary the nature of the Khomeini government that was beginning to be locked in a serious struggle with Saddam Hussein's Iraq. We have seen how Israel and even the United States in the Reagan presidency supported different aspects of the war that lasted from 1980 to 1988. Even though Iran was about five times more populous than Iraq, about seventy-five million to fifteen million, and possessed about twice as many tanks and four times the number of combat aircraft, Iraq largely drew upon the military and financial resources of the gulf states, the United States, and Europe, while much of Iran's military equipment lacked spare parts and other essentials. Iran thus used its close relationship to Lebanese Shi'ites to take American hostages. Iran also used Israeli expertise, as under the Shah, to train Kurdish guerrillas and various other technical services in exchange for oil. Whenever the Iraqi forces were overwhelmed by Iran, as in the south in the struggle over Faw Island or in the north when a Kurdish intrusion took place, Iraq would resort to the use of poison gas. Meanwhile, as Rothkopf informs us, there was deep rivalry in the Reagan presidency between George Shultz of the State Department and Caspar Weinberger of the Defense Department over the reduction in atomic weapons between the Soviet Union and the United States. Fortunately, for President Reagan and his negotiators, Mikhail Gorbachev became the new prime minister of the Soviet Union in March 1985. Robert McFarlane as well, who replaced hard-liner William Clark as national security adviser, together with Paul Nitze, arms control specialist for George Shultz, applied Weinberger and Richard Perle's formula for a reduction in intermediate-range missiles and succeeded in the INF Treaty (Intermediate Range Nuclear Forces Treaty) of 1987. The SDI, or Strategic Defense Initiative, that President Reagan had proposed was held in abeyance. As for the Reaganite claims to have overthrown the Soviet Union in 1990, one perceptive person quipped that "this was like a rooster claiming responsibility for the sunrise."[230]

After Reagan's reelection in November 1984, apart from strategic arms, the question of how to fund the contras in Nicaragua arose after Congress had cut off U.S. funding. No one on the NSC seemed to consider that the Sandinistas did not pose a threat of the Communists taking over Central America! George Shultz had preferred a compromise settlement. The question of coupling Nicaragua with ongoing problems of Khomeini's Iran arose when two members of the NSC, Howard Teicher and Donald Fortier, wrote a draft proposal in 1985, a so-called NSDD (National Security Decision Directive), suggesting there should be a check on Soviet influence in Iran, a consultation with friendly governments and "to discreetly communicate our desire for correct relations to potentially receptive Iranian leaders."[231] This note sparked the sending of Michael Ledeen in May to speak with Israeli leaders and Prime Minister Shimon Peres. Then in July 1985, McFarlane met with David Kimche when Kimche showed up in Washington. David Kimche, director general of the Israeli foreign ministry, also had strong Mossad connections. As very few records survived, later, McFarlane was able to deny to Shultz that Ledeen was sent by the NSC. Meanwhile, American hostages had been seized by the Hezbollah in Lebanon. Shortly after the president had stated publicly that the United States would not deal with terrorists, McFarlane met with an Israeli arms dealer. The president was then briefed about an arms-for-hostages swap. It was at this time that Lt. Col. Oliver North, an NSC staffer, was assigned to work with the Iranians on the release of hostages. Both Shultz and Weinberger were opposed to this arrangement, but the president was frustrated because of the hostage crisis and the lingering problem of Nicaragua. Before McFarlane turned over his post as national security adviser in December 1985 to Admiral John Poindexter, he is alleged to have said, "One of the things I should have taken care of is to get Ollie North out of the NSC. He is a loose cannon."[232] But the Walsh report investigating Irangate found that McFarlane and North in 1996 frequently discussed Nicaragua and Iran. Moreover, McFarlane met secretly in London the Iranian arms dealer, Manucher Ghorbanifar, who proposed that the United States provide more advanced weaponry in exchange for releasing the hostages. McFarlane reported that the meeting was difficult and recommended that the program be discontinued. In spite of Shultz and Weinberger advising against it, Poindexter drafted a "presidential finding" in January 1986 that President Reagan signed, approving arms for hostages. Ledeen kept up the contacts with the Israeli arms dealers. Soon, an arrangement was made for Israel to transfer a number of its own TOE antitank missiles to Iran, and the United States would then legally resupply Israel. Reverend Benjamin Weir, a hostage, was soon thereafter released. Surprisingly, Poindexter gave more latitude to Colonel North in the NSC to act on his own to continue arms sales. North also controlled the bank account into which the Iranians deposited cash. This cash was then transferred to Nicaragua to fund the contras, the right wing, supported by Reagan to unseat the Nicaraguan Sandinista government. McFarlane, still acting behind the scenes, agreed to head up a mission to Iran in May 1986 including North and a number of persons from the CIA to meet top-level Iranians and to discuss the release of hostages. The mission failed to meet top-level Iranians, and no hostages were released. However, on July 26, Father Lawrence Jenco, a second hostage, was released in Beirut. Later, David Jenkenson was released on November 2. North and Poindexter thus received encouragement to continue. But when the Sandinistas shot down a plane on 5 October 1986 that was carrying military supplies to the contras, the cat was out of the bag. The pilot confessed that he worked for the CIA. North now closed down his operation and destroyed the documents revealing payments to the contras. Both North and Poindexter destroyed records and attempted to rewrite the record. North also, in a private meeting with Ledeen, attempted to control what Ledeen might say to the Tower Commission concerning the transfer of the Hawk missiles to Iran. President Reagan had appointed the Tower Commission in December 1986 to investigate Irangate. Poindexter and North, who had virtually been in charge of American foreign policy, were both fired, and the NSC was criticized for taking steps to implement its own policies. President Reagan was reminded that the NSC was an ad hoc advisory body without statutory controls and must be watched closely. The Reagan administration received a black eye from the "loose cannons." Other hostages had to wait for other means for their release. Altogether, four arms deals were completed in 1986; the downsides of this arrangement were clear. The United States had encouraged its own blackmail by Iran; the more the weapons needed, the more the hostages taken. The deliveries ceased when, on November 3, a Beirut magazine, *Al-Shar'iya* (Legitimacy), published a detailed account of the American arms deals. Iran had gained important weapons, Israel had renewed its own weapons, and the United States greatly hurt its standing in the gulf states and the European countries. By our strengthening Iran, the gulf states worried about their own sizable Shi'i populations. As the whole deal had been cooked in Israel, it redowned to their interest more than to the United States. But President Reagan was particularly motivated by the hostage crisis. This point is clear in his November 13, 1986, speech dealing with the reasons for the Iranian exchange: (1) to renew ties with Iran, (2) to end the Iraq-Iran war, (3) to eliminate state terrorism, and (4) "to effect the safe return of all hostages."[233]

Technically, Iraq had started the war but under much provocation. At the end of 1981, Saddam Hussein indicated that Iraq wished to negotiate an end to the war, but the ayatollahs wanted to punish the Iraqis. One must read into this position that Iran wished to activate the

Shi'ite majority of Iraq against its Sunni rulers. Also, Iran believed that because of its enormous population and military equipment, it would soon overwhelm Iraq. This idea began to wear thin by 1986 when Iran involved itself in the aforementioned hostages for weapons affair. Also, Iran began attacking the oil shipments of Kuwait, the Emirates, and Saudi Arabia in the gulf. By 1987, the United States was able to aid the gulf states a great deal by protecting the oil shipments of friendly states through flagging their vessels as U.S. shipments. Iran had also placed a number of mines in the gulf, but the United States soon remedied its shortage of minesweepers after the frigate *Samuel B. Roberts* was struck by a mine in mid-April 1988. The United States immediately knocked out the important Iranian oil terminals, Sirri and Sassan, in the southeastern gulf and destroyed half of the small Iranian navy. By mid-1988, Iran was ready to make peace because it had lost many lives in the Iraqi minefields and by poison gas, and its economy was in shambles. Moreover, the United States rationalized that if the United States did not secure the Persian Gulf, the Soviet Union might. After all, the Carter Doctrine had been issued in 1979 when the Soviets occupied Afghanistan out of the fear that the Soviets were then in strategic range of the gulf.[234]

President Reagan laid down the lines incorporating Israel into the U.S. foreign policy system when he welcomed Prime Minister Begin to Washington in September 1981: "You may rest assured that the security of Israel is a principal objective of this administration and that we regard Israel as an ally in our search for regional peace and stability." In an additional note to Begin in 1982, he declared the need to keep Israel militarily superior to all Middle East countries: "Dear Menahem, I am determined to see that Israel's qualitative edge is maintained . . . Any decision on future sales to Jordan or any other country in the region will be made in the context of my Administration's firm commitment to Israel's security and the need to bring peace to the region." Already in the Johnson and Nixon administrations, there had been a major increase in grants and loans to Israel. This trend continued and reached extremely high levels under Reagan, greater than three billion per year. Also, Reagan, very early in his administration, in spite of the Fourth

Geneva Convention that was against changing the demography of occupied territory, mentioned that the new Israeli settlements in the West Bank "were not illegal." In spite of this fawning for Israel's favor, there were issues between the two countries that were deemed not in the U.S. national interest: (a) Israel's development of atomic weapons and the attack on Iraq's Osirak reactor, (b) the AWACS controversy and Saudi Arabia, (c) a Strategic Cooperation Agreement, (d) annexation of Syria's Golan Heights, (e) the Reagan peace plan, (f) retaliatory attacks by Israel, (g) the Shultz peace plan, (h) the PLO sudden change recognizing Israel.[235] It is obvious that none of the policies of the United States or Israel during the administration of President Reagan had any thought of consulting Muslims about their future. Legitimacy had become a one-way street. In fact, many of the positions of the Reagan administration were contradictions of settled U.S. policy.

On 7 June 1981, Israel bombed the Osirak site of a nuclear reactor in Iraq that was not even complete. Before the House Foreign Affairs Committee, Undersecretary of State Walter J. Stoessel Jr. condemned the attack because the Iraqis made the points that (a) they had the right to pursue peaceful uses of atomic energy, (b) Iraq had signed the nonproliferation treaty that Israel had not signed, (c) Osirak had received an official inspection by the International Atomic Energy Agency in January 1981. Israel was also in violation of its agreement of 23 July 1952 with the United States not to use American weapons, including F-15 and F-16 aircraft, to take aggressive action. The international community also learned from an Israeli atomic worker visiting England in 1986, Mordechai Vanunu, that Israel had developed a number of atomic weapons in the subbasements of its "peaceful" reactor at Dimona. While initially showing displeasure and blocking arms sales for a week, President Reagan and his staff, as in all relations with Israel, did whatever Israel requested.[236]

When Saudi Arabia in 1980 expressed an interest in having AWACS and F-15 aircraft, sixty-four senators, in a letter, had discouraged President Carter from doing anything. When President Reagan's staff broached the subject again in 1981, the usual Israeli pressure began to mount. This time, President Reagan dug in his heals and fought for the sale. Indeed there were restrictions placed on the AWACS (Airborne Warning and Control Systems), a radar surveillance plane that could track aircraft deep into enemy territory, and the F-15s were to have smaller fuel tanks, but Reagan's personal intervention saved the sales to the Saudis. In 1986, given the Khomeini Revolution, Saudi Arabia negotiated for more U.S. weapons. When AIPAC used its influence on the U.S. Senate to block additional sales, the Saudis made a major arms agreement with Britain estimated to be worth thirty-six billion to sixty-eight billion dollars. It was a big loss for U.S. business, and labor estimated at 750,000 jobs. As a Saudi official stated, "We would prefer to buy weapons from the United States. American technology is generally superior. But we are not going to pay billions of dollars to be insulted."[237]

On 30 November 1981, the United States and Israel completed a Strategic Cooperation Agreement. The purpose of this agreement was (a) to form a committee to plan joint military exercises and the use of Israeli ports for the U.S. Sixth Fleet; (b) also Israel agreed to stockpile supplies for the U.S. Rapid Deployment Force; (c) to resume delivery of American cluster bombs; (d) Israel to build and the United States partially to fund the Lavi for the Israeli arms market (much objected to by American aircraft companies), U.S. military aid to increase by 425 million dollars; (e) Israeli preferential treatment for imports and exports. This agreement meant that, because there was no complementary agreement with an Arab country, the United States could not be an honest broker. This agreement was reconfirmed on 21 April 1988. To add insult to injury, Israel formally annexed the Golan Heights on 14 December 1981 after settling the area with Israelis and driving out the remaining Syrians. In spite of the objections of European countries and a negative vote of the UN Security Council, the United States, after a temporary suspension of the Cooperation Agreement, reinstated the agreement on 29 November 1983.[238]

The so-called Reagan Peace Plan of September 1, 1982, registered by George Shultz after replacing Alexander Haig as secretary of state, dealt with Israel and the Palestinians shortly after the Israeli invasion of Lebanon. The president noted the U.S. involvement in deporting the Palestinian fighters, and he also complimented Premier Begin and President Mubarak for Israel's withdrawal from the Sinai on 25 April 1982. The plan included a five-year transition to see if Gaza and the West Bank could run their own affairs and not disturb Israel. The measure militated against settlements, and Israel should not occupy the West Bank or Gaza. The conflict should be settled on the basis of land for peace according to UN Resolution 242. Jerusalem should remain undivided, and final status should be negotiated. Also, any proposal that threatens Israeli security is nonnegotiable. This plan and several other peace plans were proposed. On August 7, Crown Prince Fahd of Saudi Arabia proposed a "just settlement" of eight points. Nine days after the Reagan Plan, on 9 September 1982, the Arab League of twenty nations meeting in Fez, Morocco, put forth a nine-point plan called the Fez Plan. Basically, Israel's hard-liners, Menachem Begin, Yitzhak Shamir, and Ariel Sharon, objected to all the peace plans, especially the idea that Israel would give up land for peace. Israel had its eyes on settling the occupied territories and driving out the Palestinians. At a later date, because of the Arab West Bank and Gaza uprising or Intifada in December 1987, Secretary Schulz recorded one more peace plan in January 1988. With the Intifada of December 1987, Israel simply shot rock-throwing youths. Later, they resorted to beating the youths with steel rods to break vital bones. Finally, they started using rubber bullets that killed the youths or maimed them at close range. In his letter to Premier Shamir of Israel, Schultz called for negotiations with all parties to achieve "a comprehensive peace providing for the security of all the states in the region and for the legitimate rights of the Palestinian people." In his mid-March visit to Washington, Shamir put forth Israel's old shibboleth. By returning the Sinai to Egypt, Israel had fulfilled the UN Resolution 242; hence, there was no obligation to vacate the West Bank and Gaza. The United States soon delivered seventy-five F-16 fighter jets to Israel and extended the Strategic Cooperation Agreement for five years, thus forcing its acceptance on the next presidential government. So much for U.S. peace plans without teeth. About this time, Arafat's aide, Bassam Abu Sharif, wrote in London's *Arab Mirror*, mentioning a two-state solution and implying that the Palestinians would accept the UN Resolutions of 242 and 338, dealing with the return of Israel's occupation of Palestinian territories.[239]

One of the final events of U.S. Middle East policies of Reagan originated with the Justice Department's closing of the PLO office in Washington and the move to close the Palestinian Observer Mission to the UN in New York on grounds that the PLO was a terrorist organization. Israel's ambassador to the UN, Bibi Netanyahu, nowadays prime minister, also supported this move with a *New York Times* article. The UN General Assembly, including all the Third World states, objected and had the World Court rule in favor of the Palestinians. Shortly thereafter, Secretary Arafat of the PLO decided to address the UN General Assembly and describe the recent acceptance of the 450-member Palestinian Parliament that they agreed to the Resolutions 242 and 338 and that they recognized Israel's right to exist in peace and security. The Palestinian parliament in exile also proclaimed an independent Palestinian state based on UN Resolution 181 from 1947. Surprisingly, the wrench in the gears became George Schultz, secretary of state, who refused to issue a visa to Arafat, as head of an organization deemed terrorist, to speak at the United Nations. In refusing a visa, he overruled the advice of most of his Middle East team, Richard Murphy and Michael Armacost, seasoned diplomats and Schultz's undersecretaries, Colin Powell, national security adviser, and defense secretary Frank Carlucci. As a result, the general assembly held its December plenary session in mid-December in Geneva, Switzerland, after a vote of 154 to 2, the holdouts, the United States and Israel. And in Geneva, Arafat made his "olive branch" peace speech. This policy move indicates to what lengths some members of the Reagan government would go to support Israel at a time when the PLO was making serious gestures for peace with Israel. The Reagan government, however it is remembered today, was a government that bungled every aspect of its Middle East policies.[240]

As Lenczowski concluded his important study of American Presidents and the Middle East, he notes three recurring themes: the Soviet challenge, the Arab-Israeli problems, and the importance of maintaining oil supplies. We have seen that experience in foreign affairs of Eisenhower, Kennedy, and Nixon, and their respective appointments to cabinet and other government positions gave them support on crucial occasions. John Foster Dulles, Eisenhower's secretary of state, however, failed to support Nasser's high-dam proposal, giving the Soviets a strong position in Arab countries. It was also clear that Johnson, in particular, but Nixon, Carter, and Reagan also succumbed to domestic pressures. It was a difficult lesson for all presidents to learn and understand that Israel, as an expanding military state, was much more a threat to Middle Eastern governments than was the Soviet Union, yet American pressure on Middle East governments persisted. In spite of the great popularity of Ayatollah Khomeini with his Shiʻite leadership of Iran in the 1980s, the Arab states could not neglect the steady occupation of Palestine by Israel. Already in the presidency of Ronald Reagan, the potential for a Shiʻite coalition of Lebanon, Syria, Iraq, and Iran became apparent, but the poor quality of presidential advisers in the twenty-first century completely ignored this factor so apparent now in the Middle East. Meanwhile, the presidential negotiators for peace in Palestine, notably Dennis Ross and others, clearly favored Israel and the settlement movement and, hence, made matters worse. After the assassination of Yitzhak Rabin (November 1995) and the death of Ariel Sharon, after eight years in a coma (d. January 2014), no Israeli of stature could override the settler/neo-Judaic coalition that wished to seize all of Palestine from the Palestinians, a doctrine that Sharon adhered to until his coma. For an excellent analysis of the Nixon's, Reagan's, and the Elder George Bush's attitudes toward Israel, one should consult Avi Shlaim's account of these presidential policies and also his sharp criticism of Golda Meir's launching of the Six-Day War in 1967. Shlaim details the problem of having Dennis Ross as the chief negotiator of Arab-Israeli affairs by both the presidency of of the Elder George Bush and the two-term presidency of William Clinton. After the Six-Day War, the continued support of the United States for Israel's colonization of the conquered territories became the sticking point of all subsequent peace negotiations.[241]

9. The Presidency of George H. W. Bush (January 1989 to January 1993)

David Rothkopf was quite impressed by the orderliness of George Herbert Walker Bush's presidency and efficiency in contrast to the hodgepodge of the Reagan presidency. What made the difference was the wide-ranging experience of Bush Senior and his closeness to his appointees. He had served as an active pilot in World War II. Later, he would serve in Congress and then spend time as head of the CIA. Bush also managed a stint as envoy to China. Because of his expertise in foreign affairs, Bush Senior was said to be underutilized as vice president to President Reagan. His long service in Washington, DC, had brought him in contact with many persons whom he appointed to responsible positions in his administration. Experience mattered in his administration. As an exception, he chose Dan Quayle as his vice president and running mate. Dan Quayle, the young senator from Indiana, was only thirty-three when he won his Republican Senate seat. He had defeated Senator Birch Bayh, scion of a leading Democratic Indiana family, whose father had served in Congress, but Quayle was a member of the Pullian family, who owned the *Indianapolis Star*, the leading Indiana newspaper. In 1986, Quayle was reelected to the Senate. As a rising Republican star, he was chosen as Bush Senior's running mate to gain young voters but may have been Bush's weakest appointment. Unfortunately, Quayle's law training was inadequate for speaking on foreign and domestic topics. He was known for his inept public speeches.[242] If Quayle turned out to be odd man out in the administration, most of Bush's cabinet and other appointments were former associates. For secretary of state, he chose his old friend, James Baker, from Houston, Texas. They were both natives of Houston. Baker, in turn, chose Larry Eagleburger as his deputy, who had worked for Kissinger. It is thus not surprising that Robert Kaplan cited James Baker as another secretary of state that eliminated Arabists from the foreign service in large numbers and used Dennis Ross," who traveled in pro-Israeli, Neoconservative circles."[243]So Baker and Ross fulfilled a Jewish lobbyist's dream, even if the Jewish lobby was never grateful to them for it: they emasculated the Arabists by running Arab-Israeli affairs directly through the policy planning staff—which Ross headed—rather than through NEA (Near Eastern Affairs).[244]

Baker also knew Cheney as a fishing buddy. As national security adviser, President Bush chose general of the U.S. Air Force Brent Scowcroft, whom he knew from his own service in the U.S. Air Force, and he had served as national security adviser for President Ford when Bush was head of the CIA. Scowcroft had also worked for Kissinger Associates. There were rarely differences between Scowcroft and Baker since Baker was the exterior spokesman while Scowcroft worked behind the scenes. Cheney was appointed secretary of defense, and Robert Gates became his deputy. John Sununu from New Hampshire was appointed Bush's chief of staff, and William Webster, head of the CIA. General Colin Powell was elected chief of staff for the armed forces. Finally, Dennis Ross, a Soviet specialist, became the chief Middle East negotiator for the Bush and Clinton administrations. In hindsight, Dennis Ross basically favored Israeli political and economic solutions to U.S. policies and, hence, was viewed as the wrong negotiator for Mideast peace. Apart from Ross and Quayle, here were a solid series of appointments that worked together like a well-oiled machine.[245]

When Iraq occupied Kuwait on 1 August 1990, President Bush and his secretary of state, James Baker, knew that they had to build a broad coalition to attack an Arab country. This coalition building was in stark contrast to the hell-bent-for-leather attitude of George W. Bush and Dick Cheney eleven years later. The father of George W. Bush and his subordinates built a coalition of seven Arab nations before attacking Iraq in February of 1991. The United States also had planned landing rights with various gulf states before our troops were flown in. General Gus Pagonis, Desert Shield logistics chief, had put together an amazing number of troops, equipment, and aircraft. On 19 December 1990, General Powell and Dick Cheney arrived in Riyadh to inspect the readiness of the coalition forces to face Saddam Hussein. Powell, after this tour of inspection, had to report back to the president. As Powell noted in his memoir:

> The President was leaning on me: "When are we going to be ready? When can we go?" Dealing with Norm (General Schwarzkopf, head of Desert Shield) was like holding a hand grenade with the pin pulled. Dealing with the President was like playing Shehrezade, trying to keep the king calm for a thousand and one nights.[246]

An early problem was Scud missiles landing in Israel. If the Israelis deployed paratroops to destroy missile launching sites in Iraq, the Arab coalition would fall apart. Cheney and Powell had General Norman Schwarzkopf, whose command was in charge of the attack on Iraq, to deflect some aircraft to hunt down missile sites. This move placated the Israelis, who were then governed by the Likud Bloc, with Yitzhak Shamir as prime minister. Meanwhile, the returning pilots were talking about a "turkey shoot" on the road leading north from Kuwait to Basra. Only later did one learn from a detailed British film that pilots were gunning down civilian vehicles fleeing from Kuwait that were mixed in with the fleeing military vehicles. It was after Schwarzkopf had been ordered to stop firing on these mixed columns that Seymour Hersh, in a story in the May 1991 *New Yorker*, revealed that General Barry McCaffrey ordered his troops to attack retreating columns of civilians and military in spite of the cease-fire. Meanwhile, the Arab troops were not eager to see a large American force of over two hundred thousand troops occupying an Arab country. In particular, the Egyptians and Saudis did not want to empower the latent majority of Shi'ites in Iraq. It follows that George Bush Senior and his appointees were aware of this problem and, hence, made a separate peace with Saddam Hussein and his generals. But a moral dilemma remained. By permitting many units of the Republican Guard, Saddam's best-equipped troops, to survive, these troops were used to suppress Shi'ites revolting in southern Iraq and the Kurds revolting in the north. We must not forget, however, that the Bush Senior presidency had encouraged internal revolt and never instituted a no-fly zone until much later. Phebe Marr, in her article, "Iraq's Future," appearing in the collection just after "Desert Storm" by Ibrahim Ibrahim, the editor of *The Gulf Crisis*, confronts the crisis in

Iraq with positive and negative predictions. She notes that if Saddam Hussein still follows the path of Iraqi regional grandeur instead of repairing his infrastructure, Iraq is slated for even tougher times.[247]

There remains the question of Iraq's weapons of mass destruction. Richard A. Clarke, as Deputy Assistant Secretary of State, set up a U.S.-UK working group to focus on Iraq's advances in nuclear technology. The group was known as the UN Special Commission for the Disarmament of Iraq, abbreviated as UNSCOM. Hence, UNSCOM was shown tons of chemical weapons and some missiles, but the UN Commission wished to learn also about Iraqi developments in atomic weapons, and Robert Gallucci, deputy executive chairman of UNSCOM, was in charge. Israel had reported a concerted effort by Iraq to build nuclear weapons but gave no proof. UNSCOM learned that the atomic weapons program records were hidden in the Agricultural Ministry. By feigning an inspection of another site, UNSCOM broke into the Agricultural Ministry and found the records before the Iraqis knew what was happening. Soon UNSCOM agents were surrounded by Iraqi troops and ordered to give up the documents. Indeed the inspectors discovered that the Iraqis were less than a year away from exploding a small bomb. Cell phones could not be used with a fax machine, and digital cameras were not yet perfected. How could these vital documents see the light of day? Finally, it was discovered that Beverley Roundtree, a State Department secretary, could take down shorthand rapidly, so Bob Gallucci, in charge of the operation on the ground, read the incriminating documents over his cell phone, and Beverly took down shorthand of the contents of the documents in her State Department office—a remarkable feat! After the defeat of Iraq, Israel would have preferred the destruction of the Iraqi army and the removal of Saddam Hussein, but the Senior Bush government did not want a U.S. occupation of Iraq. Would that the presidency of Bush's son had avoided that trap! This choice emphasizes the insights of the Bush team. The opposite became true of the younger Bush presidency. His presidency was controlled by the Neocons from January 20, 2001 to January 20, 2009, who operated as a fifth column for the Israeli desire to destroy Iraq. The Senior Bush's government did not want to link the

Palestine problem of Jewish settlement to the war in Iraq. But the very fact of an Arab coalition supporting a war on Iraq meant that some progress would be required in the Palestinian peace process. Also with the Cold War ending with the collapse of the Soviet Union in 1991, the United States became the sole target for everything going wrong in the Middle East. The rationale for Bin Laden to organize Al-Qaeda was that the United States had stationed a great number of American troops in Saudi Arabia because Saddam Hussein and his army had not been destroyed. In short, once again, a Great Power had ignored the necessity of considering what was and what was not "legitimate" in the eyes of most Muslims.[248]

Bush Senior, as noted, had appointed James A. Baker III as his Secretary of State. Baker was known for his skills in making deals. Before the Gulf War, Baker and Bush had managed to bring Yitzhak Shamir to accept negotiations with a Jordan delegation with a few nonresident Palestinians as part of the team. Also, they had cajoled Hafiz al-Asad, President of Syria, into attending a peace conference, but they had misread Saddam Hussein's intensions when he invaded Kuwait on August 1, 1990. The Middle East team, including Deputy Secretary of State Larry Eagleburger, Dennis Ross, and Richard Haass, began to think in terms of a new beginning to the Arab-Israeli impasse after the Gulf War. Baker had already spoken to the AIPAC convention on 22 May 1989, in which he had noted that the Bush government supported a "territorial withdrawal" based on UN Resolution 242. Thus, the Shamir government got wind of how the Bush government would proceed. On 30 October 1991, under the joint chairmanship of Bush and Gorbachev, the peace conference got started in Madrid, Spain. In attendance were delegates from Israel, Syria, Lebanon, a joint Palestinian-Jordanian delegation, a UN representative, and Bandar bin Sultan, Washington's ambassador for Saudi Arabia. The United States, true to previous arrangements, would not intervene on the Arabs' behalf to force an Israeli position. The Shamir government had, however, asked for a loan of ten billion dollars, which was delayed by the Bush government until after the Israeli elections of 23 June 1992, when the less intransigent Labor government of Yitzhak Rabin came to power.

Even then, the Bush government reserved the right to hold back any funds earmarked for colonial activity in the West Bank. Unfortunately, for the Madrid conference, the President Elder Bush lost his election to President Clinton on 3 November 1992, and the peace process had to be revived under a new team, with the appointments of President Clinton.[249]

10. The Presidency of Bill Clinton (January 20, 1993 to January 20, 2001)

The George H. W. Bush White House had not viewed terrorism as a threat to the United States and, hence, had no directives anticipating government terrorism. The only incident of terrorism had been the bombing of Pan Am Flight 103 over Lockerbie, Scotland. This incident was dealt with by diplomacy. Tony Lake, the Clinton National Security Adviser, had provided some continuity by asking Richard Clarke to continue at the White House to monitor global issues, but terrorism was placed far down the list of issues he was monitoring. Apart from Lake, Al Gore had been nominated as Clinton's Vice President. To Secretary of State, Clinton appointed Warren Christopher, who had headed Clinton's transition team and had served as Carter's undersecretary of state. Lake had served on Kissinger's team and as Secretary Vance's planning chief. It had not been forgotten that Lake parted company with Kissinger after his decision to invade Cambodia under Nixon. Sandy Berger served as deputy to Anthony Lake and had previously served with Lake on the Policy Planning staff of the State Department. Madeleine Albright, a former NSC staffer under Carter, represented Clinton in the United Nations and later as Secretary of State. Lake headed the NSC, and his deputy, Leon Fuerth, held two hats: Al Gore's chief of staff and deputy to Lake; this made him head of the NSC deputies committee. Clinton chose an old friend, Mack McLarty, as chief of staff and R. James Woolsey to head the CIA. Richard Holbrooke, soon named as ambassador to Germany, had had Lake as a roommate in graduate school at Princeton, and both had grown up in the State Department, but they differed sharply on what the United States should do in Bosnia. The Clinton transition team admired the smooth running of the Senior Bush White House, and hence, they wished to perpetuate the National Security Council structure of "the principals" and "the deputies." The principals were the appointed secretaries of the government, and each had a deputy. But the Clinton transition also instituted a new entity, the NEC, or National Economic Council, to be headed by Robert Rubin, then head of Goldman Sachs. Thus, Clinton looked to the NSC for advice on foreign affairs and to the NEC for economic policy. Robert Reich served as Clinton's Secretary of Labor, and Lloyd Bentsen as Secretary of the Treasury. Bentson fulfilled Clinton's need of a prominent Southerner. He had been the running mate of Michael Dukakis and later headed the Senate Finance Committee that had worked on NAFTA (the North American Free Trade Agreement) under Bush, which soon became law under Clinton. Congressman Lee Aspin of Wisconsin was chosen to head the Department of Defense. Ron Brown, incoming Secretary of Commerce, was noted for his probusiness stance and had been head of the National Democratic Committee during the campaign. Leon Panetta, head of the House Budget Committee for years, was viewed as a centrist and became head of the OMB (Office of the Management of the Budget). This excellent team soon found out that the rhetoric of the campaign did not mesh well with the realities of governing, as noted by George Stephanopoulos, the young adviser to Clinton who often served as Clinton's spokesman.[250]

Brent Scowcroft, National Security Adviser for George Bush Senior, had been brought back from retirement to clean up the mess Colonel North and Admiral Poindexter had left with their Irangate affair. Tony Lake had just taken over his job at NSC in late January only to be confronted with the killing of three persons at the entrance to the CIA by a Pakistani named Mir Amal Kansi, who flew out of the country and escaped without a trace of his motives. The first bombing of the World Trade Center soon followed and was initially blamed on Serbia. Secretary of State Baker in the Bush administration did not like to share his role with the NSC, hence the initial diminished role of Richard Clarke. The bombers of the Trade Center turned out to be Palestinians who had shown up at JFK Airport without proper documents one year previous. One Palestinian, Ahmed Ajaj, had "*How-to-Make-Bombs*" manuals in his luggage and was detained; the other was Ramzi Yousef, whom the FBI later figured out was the leader. He got out of the country after the attack but was traced through his rental truck. In fact, his buddy Muhammad Salahmeh was arrested at the Ryder truck rental office when he attempted to pick up his deposit on March 4, 1993. The other cell members were eventually picked up, and Ramzi Yousef finally turned up in the Philippines. CIA and the FBI had not linked Salahmeh or Yousef to Al-Qaeda because Bin Laden had only formed his group three years previously. Soon the blind sheikh from Egypt, 'Abd ar-Rahman, was discovered in Brooklyn and recognized as the spiritual leader of radical Egyptians. Through his contacts, another cell was discovered with plans to blow up the Manhattan tunnels and the UN building. Later, El Sayyid Nosair, who had assassinated Rabbi Meir Kahane in 1992, was linked to Bin Laden. Kahane had been head of the Jewish Defense League, also operating as a terrorist group in the United States against prominent U.S. Arabs. It turned out that Khalid Sheikh Mohammed had been Bin Laden's paymaster for the cell of Ramzi Yousef, and Ramzi Yousef was Sheikh Mohammed's nephew. Later Sheikh Khalid was pinpointed as the mastermind of the second attack on the World Trade Center on September 11, 2001. Ramzi Yousef also had a second life as a terrorist. He had planned to blow up a number of U.S. aircraft operating in the Far East. A timely grounding of all American passenger aircraft operating in the Far East saved this new threat. In January 1995, Ramzi Yousef was arrested for the last time.[251]

On a Sunday, in April 1993, Richard Clarke had received a translation of a London Arabic newspaper that claimed Kuwaiti police had foiled a plot to kill former President Bush on his visit to Kuwait. By contacting Ryan Crocker, the American Kuwaiti ambassador, Clarke found out that Saddam Hussein's intelligence unit had planned to kill Bush, the Elder, and the Kuwaiti Amir. An alert policeman had discovered the bomb-laden vehicle. Lake heard the news from Clarke, and soon there was a retaliation planned with Les Aspin at the Defense Department, Warren Christopher at the State Department, and Anthony Lake. On the evening of Saturday, June 6, missiles fired from vessels wiped out the Iraqi Intelligence building in Baghdad. The President and Vice President Gore wanted immediate proof, which would not be forthcoming until satellite photos would come in at dawn. Thus, President Clinton called up CNN. Their man was not in Baghdad, but the CNN contact called a cousin living near the building and confirmed it had been obliterated. That was enough for President Clinton! Later, President George W. Bush was to claim that one reason he wanted to attack Iraq was because Saddam Hussein had tried to kill his father. Yet when the Israeli Mossad had also planned to kill George Bush Senior in Madrid on 30 October 1991, George W. Bush had forgotten or never knew about it.[252]

At the end of President Bush's administration in January 1993, there was a huge problem developing in Somalia. Bush had sent troops into Somalia to protect food supplies because seven hundred thousand Somalis were on the verge of starvation. Many relief organizations had sent in food and clothing, but these were being confiscated by armed gangs and sold to the highest bidder. When Clarke, on the NSC, brought this to the attention of Lake, Lake mistakenly believed that our troops were no longer needed because the Bush people had believed that the United Nations troops, under Secretary General Boutros Boutros-Ghali, would be sufficient, but the UN forces were slow in forming units and Boutros-Ghali suggested that there be a joint operation under the command of an American. "Lake persuaded Scowcroft's deputy, Admiral Jonathan Howe, to take the job." In June, Farah Aidid's group, the leading gang in Somalia, killed two dozen Pakistanis in the UN units. Admiral Howe decided that Aidid should be arrested and his militia eliminated. He asked for the Delta Force and the use of AC-130 aerial gunships. The Pentagon at first refused the Delta Force and permitted only a short-time use of the gunships, but Aidid's military was still active, and some of his warehouses that were full of weapons were intact. When three American troops were killed in September, the Pentagon sent the Delta Force, but Aidid was now in hiding, and the Delta Force, used to night operations, came into Mogadishu in helicopters in broad daylight. On October 3, 1993, in the Black Hawk Down incident, two helicopters were brought down by rocket-propelled grenades, killing eighteen Americans, some of whose bodies were dragged through the streets. Clinton was furious and took control of the operation. He sent in as many aircraft and tanks as needed, delivered food to the needy, and put the UN on a six-month limit for use of U.S. forces. No more troops were killed, and the United States pulled out in six months. But there were deeper problems in the Clinton administration. On October 11, soon after the Black Hawk Down debacle, the USS *Harlan County* was sent to Port-au-Prince, Haiti, with lightly armed U.S. and Canadian troops to seat the government of President Aristide in place of the military junta. Soon the U.S. naval vessel was driven away by a jeering mob. In Washington, the Clinton team was viewed as a group of weak sisters. Les Aspin, Secretary of Defense, in particular, was singled out for replacement. By December, Aspin was out, and by February 2004, his deputy William Perry held the post and gave the president the leadership he needed. Also, General Colin Powell was replaced as head of the Joint Chiefs by General John Shalikashvili, a tough immigrant who had risen to the top, because he did not hesitate to use military force if needed. During this shake-up at the top, Clinton also replaced Mack McLarty with Leon Panetta as chief of staff. Clinton needed the structure that Panetta envisioned. Warren Christopher at the State Department believed in compartmentalizing specific countries. Thus, Strobe Talbott was Clinton's go-to person on Russia, just as Dennis Ross became the chief Middle East negotiator and Richard Holbrooke was assigned to the Balkan problems.[253]

What disturbed Clarke was the lack of CIA intelligence on the ground in all the above operations. Later, it was learned that Al-Qaeda had a hand in the killing of the Americans in Somalia. Moreover, according to Clarke, Al-Qaeda got the wrong message from Bin Laden's ousting of the Russians from Afghanistan in 1989 and the American failure to capture Aidid in Somalia—namely, that even Great Powers can be defeated through well-planned operations of small groups. This was the seed that developed into the second attack on the World Trade Center on 11 September 2001.[254]

Once again, terrorism struck the Clinton administration, this time from Oklahoma City in March 1995. At first, it was rumored that the attack was from the Middle East and that the usual Muslim Americans were under suspicion, but it was soon discovered that the bombings were done by Timothy McVeigh, an American who was unhappy over the U.S. attack of the FBI and federal marshals on the Waco, Texas, compound, where the Branch Davidians had taken refuge. McVeigh was later executed for bombing the federal building in Oklahoma City with a high casualty figure for men, women, and children. This terrorist attack and others caused Clarke, head of the antiterrorist group, and President Clinton to seek a large increase in the funds earmarked for counterterror. The budget increased from $5.7 billion in 1995 to $11.1 billion in the year 2000. The President also, in January 1995, issued the executive order making it a felony to raise or transfer funds to designated terror groups. But this executive order caused the House Republicans to agree with the National Rifle Association that "restrictions on bomb making infringed on the right to bear arms!"[255]

Tony Lake aptly rephrased Brent Scowcroft's "New World Order" into "Other dogs continue to bark." This proved to be the case with the suppression and the mass killings of Muslims in Bosnia and Herzegovina by the Serbian army of Slobodan Milosevic. Milosevic, born 20 August 1941 in Yugoslavia, graduated in law from the University of Belgrade in 1966. He moved quickly through the ranks of the Yugoslav Communist Party on the coattails of Ivan Stambolic, whose uncle, Petar Stambolic, had been Prime Minister of the Serbian state and, later, including the eight Republics of Yugoslavia. By 1978, Milosevic became head of Beobanka, one of Yugoslavia's largest banks. He became virtual prime minister of the Serbian Republic in 1986. In 1987, he became popular with his Serbian constituency all over Yugoslavia when Milosevic took sides with the small Serbian population (about 10 percent) living in the Kosovo autonomous province, peopled mostly by ethnic Albanians. The Serbs had sizable minorities in Bosnia-Herzegovina, Croatia, and Macedonia and the Serbian army remained dominant over all provinces. The Jugoslav Republics of Montenegro and Voivodina were counted as Serbian, while Slovenia eventually was permitted to detach itself from Yugoslavia. Basically, in 1987, Milosevic adapted a Serbian nationalist agenda by forbidding the cessation of Croatia, Bosnia, and Kosovo.

The Milosevic policy continued by removing large non-Serb ethnic groups from their home bases and giving the territory to Serbs. With this policy, ethnic cleansing by Serbs began. Some of Milosevic's critics felt that he was trying to be a second Tito, a successful Croatian leader of Jugoslavia following World War II. Milosevic is said to have followed the policies of Alexandar Rankovich, who became popular with the Serbs because he perpetrated harsh police methods against ethnic Albanians and Muslim Slavs. By 1988, Milosevic was advocating that Serbians and Montenegrins "take to the streets," and their watchword became "Give us arms" and "Long live Serbia—death to Albanians." Yet Milosevic still claimed that he was not a Serbian nationalist. As the Communist Party of Yugoslavia collapsed in 1990, the Yugoslav People's Army began supplying arms to Croatian Serbs. This move fostered the beginning of ethnic cleansing throughout the Yugoslav provinces. The Serbian state–run newspaper *Politika* began urging attacks on Croatia and Bosnia-Herzegovina.[256]

It has remained a mystery until recently why the presidents George H. W. Bush and William Clinton held such a hands-off view as the former state of Yugoslavia began to break apart under the leadership of Slobodan Milosevic. But once we have learned the extremely important role of Lawrence Eagleburger in the halls of presidential power in Washington, we have at least a partial answer to this mystery. Eagleburger began his life in Milwaukee, Wisconsin, 1 August 1930, where his father practiced medicine and his mother served as an elementary schoolteacher. He received his BA and MA degrees from the University of Wisconsin in Madison. If he studied Turkish history there, he possibly studied under Professor Kemal Karpat, graduating with a degree in political science. Upon graduation, Eagleburger served two years in the U.S. Army, 1952–1954, obtaining the rank of first lieutenant. Eagleburger joined the staff of the State Department in 1957. He had divorced his first wife with one child in 1966 and married Marlene Heinemann, with whom he spent his life until her death in 2010. They had two additional sons and were members of the Lutheran church. From 1961 to 1965, he served on the staff of the U.S. Embassy in Belgrade, a post that defined much of his future career as he became the State Department individual to seek out on policy for the Balkan Peninsula. From 1969 to 1971 in the Nixon administration, he became an assistant to National Security Adviser Henry Kissinger. After a stint in Brussels as an adviser to NATO and other posts and on the basis of his former service in Belgrade, President Carter appointed Eagleburger as ambassador to Yugoslavia, 1977–1980. President Reagan appointed him to the number 3 post in the State Department, undersecretary for political affairs, which Eagleburger held for a number of years before resigning from the State Department to serve as president of Kissinger Associates, thus avoiding the scandal of the Contra Affair. In 1989, when Yugoslavia started breaking up with a civil war, President Bush appointed Eagleburger Deputy Secretary of State and then Secretary of State when James Baker resigned to run Bush's reelection campaign. Eagleburger's advice on Yugoslav affairs from 1989 to 1992 became quite controversial because he strongly favored the position of the Serbs and turned a blind eye to the atrocities of Serbian units in Croatia and Bosnia-Herzegovina. The European press dubbed Eagleburger "Lawrence of Serbia." His views must also have had a serious effect on the Clinton presidency because Clinton permitted the weak views of the British and French to prevail at the beginning of his administration. President Clinton, in his memoir, never mentions Eagleburger but quotes Richard Holbrooke's book, *To End a War*, on five failures in Bosnia: (1) a misreading of Balkan history claiming that positions were too ancient and ingrained, (2) the apparent loss of Yugoslavia's strategic importance with the end of the Cold War, (3) the triumph of nationalism over democracy as the dominant ideology, (4) the reluctance of the Bush administration to follow the Gulf War with another, (5) turning the issue over to a weak Europe rather than NATO, and Clinton added another item; some Europeans wanted no Muslim states in the Balkans.[257]

While Russia tried to keep a lid on the *jihad* (Muslim holy war) of al-Qaeda in Chechnya, Bosnia-Herzegovina and its suppression and ethnic cleansing by the Serbs became front-page news for years. As Richard Clarke points out, gradually, the hand of Al-Qaeda and Bin Laden became apparent when a number of Arabs volunteered to serve in Bosnia and became known as the *Muj* (abbreviated for Mujahideen).

The Bosnian President, Alija Izetbegovic, would like to have avoided ties with Iran and the Arab Mujahideen, but the United States and its European allies in NATO contributed only pretty speeches instead of military action against the Serbs. The United States initially hoped to make the Yugoslav problem a European problem to be dealt with by European forces. Meanwhile, Iran sent weapons and troops, and the Arabs sent well-trained fighters who had fought Russia in Afghanistan. Muslim charities in a number of countries also sent contributions to support the front line fighters. Many well-known members of Al-Qaeda showed up in the Bosnian War but were not recognized as al-Qaeda until later. To end the war in Bosnia became a high priority for President Clinton, Tony Lake, Madeleine Albright, Tony Berger, Ambassador Richard Holbrooke, and General Wesley Clark, head of NATO forces. To his credit, Anthony Lake supported the Iranian intervention in Bosnia. Thus, the Dayton Accord was hammered out at the U.S. Wright-Patterson Air Force Base in Dayton, Ohio, on 21 November 1995 and signed in Paris on 14 December 1995 in the presence of Jacques Chirac of France, Bill Clinton of the United States, John Major of Britain, Helmut Kohl for Germany, and Viktor Chernomyrdin for Russia. Milosevic had to witness air strikes on Belgrade to bring him to the Dayton negotiations. The settlement that Ambassador Holbrooke worked out was partially guided by what the various warring factions held at the time of the armistice. The Bosnian Serbs occupied 46 percent of Bosnia-Herzegovina, but the Bosnians were allotted 53 percent of the former territory; 41 percent was allotted to Croatia, and 6 percent to Serbia. Because of the corridor allotted to Serbia and territory allotted to Croatia, Bosnia-Herzegovina was left in a weakened position.[258]

Clinton brought in a new team in his second term. The deputy to Tony Lake in the first term, Sandy Berger, was now appointed national security adviser. Clinton chose Madeleine Albright, who had done well at the United Nations, for the State Department. Finally, he chose a Republican to head the Defense Department, William Cohen, formerly the Senator from Maine, because Clinton needed bipartisan support. His appointment of Cohen was only partially successful because Cohen often reflected the military's skepticism about involvement in military action in the Balkans.[259]

The Clinton administration did not extricate itself yet from the Middle East. Al-Qaeda now engineered the bombings of U.S. embassies in East Africa, and Iran's Revolutionary Guards, Quds Force, had created Hezbollah groups in Bahrain, Kuwait, and Saudi Arabia. The U.S. Air Force had been given a bloc of apartments near the town of Khobar, Saudi Arabia, close to the concentration of Shi'ite Saudis in the Persian Gulf region. On 25 June 1996, a car bomb in Khobar, Saudi Arabia, killed nineteen Americans. Clarke wanted a separate investigation, but the Saudis refused cooperation. They were skeptical that the United States would launch a major attack on Iran. Clinton's response was to send in an aircraft carrier to the Gulf for a few weeks.[260]

While Bin Laden had directed much of his operations in the Balkans from his base in the Sudan, he then moved back to Afghanistan in 1996. The policies of Milosevic in Bosnia and Croatia were now repeated in the province of Kosovo, possessing a population 90 percent Albanian. The autonomy of Kosovo had been lifted by Milosevic ten years previously. Clinton's response to Bin Laden and President Turabi in Sudan was to bomb Al-Qaeda bases in Afghanistan and also an alleged bomb factory in the Sudan. The latter turned out to be a pharmaceutical company. The bombing of Afghanistan's bases was termed Operation Desert Fox and lasted four days, 16–19 December 1998. In March 1999, General Wesley Clark, at the time Supreme Allied Commander of NATO, and General Klaus Naumann, chairman of the NATO military council, were convinced with President Clinton that Milosevic would only give up the ethnic cleansing of Kosovo as a result of strategic bombing of Yugoslav targets. The NATO bombing of targets in and around Belgrade resulted in a Serbian request to the UN for peace. Thus, under the Security Council Resolution 1244, the bombing ended on 10 June 1999. Very soon thereafter, Milosevic and the commander of the Bosnian Serbs, General Radovan Karadzic, were indicted for war crimes, and Milosevic was released by his Serbian successor to the International Court of Justice in Den Hague, Netherlands. General Karadzic evaded capture by NATO troops but has recently been apprehended. Holbrooke once again was brought into the negotiations on Kosovo. Meanwhile, Serbian tanks continued to destroy Kosovo villages in spite of the bombing of Belgrade and the destruction of many tanks in Kosovo around Prishtina. Later the Clinton government was accused of promoting the Kosovo crisis at a time when Congress was in the process of the impeachment proceedings of President Clinton. Actually, Sandy Berger later removed documents that would have shown light on this claim, and Berger hence was reprimanded and lost his security clearance.[261]

Clinton also had noted in his State of the Union address in January 1998 that Saddam Hussein may still be pursuing nuclear weapons. This statement prompted the President to weaken Saddam's power by signing HR 4655 into law on 31 October 1998, instituting a policy of "regime change." Thereafter, Clinton started a four-day bombing of various Iraqi military sites, 16–19 December 1998, and routinely thereafter, the U.S. Air Force attacked hostile antiaircraft facilities throughout Iraq.[262]

The Oslo accords between Israeli and Palestinian representatives of 2000 gave to President Clinton the incentive to broker a peace between the two contending parties. Clinton invited Israeli Prime Minister Ehud Barak and Palestinian Authority Chairman Yasser Arafat to Camp David. But the negotiations failed when Clinton placed his final status negotiations to the principals on 23 December 2000. What actually happened was not the way Benny Morris, the erstwhile exposer of Israeli myths, described the new myth. Barak had made a proposal in July 2000 that Arafat rejected, but Arafat basically accepted Clinton's proposals in December: notably, an independent Palestinian state over the whole of Gaza, 94 to 96 percent of the West Bank, Palestinian sovereignty over the Arab parts of Jerusalem, and a solution to the Palestinian refugee problem. Also, Morris neglected the progress in Taba in the last week of January 2001. But by this time, Clinton and Barak were passing out of power, and George W. Bush and Ariel Sharon were replacing the two leaders. The root of the problem, according to Morris, was the Palestinian failure to recognize the existence of Israel, a policy that had been accepted earlier by all Palestinian parties. But the Palestinians could not accept understandably Israel's continual occupation of the Palestinian territories occupied in 1967 and the insistence of the right-wing parties to unlimited settlements. Arafat had turned down the proposals of President Clinton on the basis of "the right of return" of all Palestinians. We should also note that in the troubled administration of President Clinton, to have Dennis Ross and Martin Indyk as the two principal U.S. negotiators, it is no wonder, given their solid pro-Israeli credentials and the "Israeli First" doctrine they preached, that Arafat never clinched a peace deal with Ehud Barak and President Clinton. But even Arafat's own delegation found Arafat unreasonable.[263]

There is no doubt that Naomi Klein has actually revealed what really happened to peace negotiations between Israel and Palestinian leaders. She notes that Israelis tend to blame suicide bombings or the assassination of Yitzhak Rabin in 1995 for their own intransigence. Klein's perspective derives from her book *Disaster Capitalism*, which is partially a critique of the Chicago School of Economics doctrines of Milton Friedman (d. November 2006) that affected negatively every country in which these doctrines were applied. The new state of Russia, after the demise of the Soviet Union, began the drastic measures of the Chicago School under Yeltsin in 1993: tax cuts, free trade, privatized services, cuts in social spending, and deregulation. This meant, among other factors, the impoverishment of most Russians who could not buy state enterprises. Also, these measures affected many of Russia's Jewish population in the professional classes at a time when the Elder Bush and Clinton governments were pressuring Russia to permit Jewish immigration to Israel. As Klein points out, eventually, a million Jews immigrated to Israel, more than 18 percent of Israel's new population. Until this influx, some 150,000 Palestinians had left their homes every day from Gaza and the West Bank to work in Israel. Meanwhile, Arab farms in the West Bank supplied Israel with tons of farm produce. But with the influx of Soviet Jews, the Arab workforce was gradually replaced. Also, during the Oslo period, there were frantic settlement projects in the West Bank to change "facts on the ground" during Barak's premiership. Klein further indicates what was fueling the Israel manufacturing sector: "Years before the U.S. and European companies grasped the potential of the global security boom, Israeli technology firms were busily pioneering the homeland security industry, and they continue to dominate the sector today. The Israeli Export Institute estimates that Israel has 350 corporations dedicated to selling homeland security products." In short, Israel enjoys great prosperity but continues to make war against its neighbors and escalates the brutality against the occupied territories. Klein calls this present condition in Israel the guns-and-caviar economy. Naomi Klein also echoes the analysis of Avi Shlaim, "If I were a Palestinian, I would have rejected Camp David as well." Although the Clinton administration dealt with many Middle East problems, it basically failed the test of legitimacy and simply kicked the Israeli-Palestinian problem down the road, but there was one last ditch operation of the intelligence team, the Millennium Terrorist Alert detailed by Richard Clarke.[264]

The Millennium Terrorist Alert developed out of a hunch raised by Cofer Black, a deputy to George Tenet of the CIA and head of the CIA's Counterterrorism Center, that al-Qaeda would attack the United States at the turn of the millennium. He learned of the Jordan cell discovered in Amman, Jordan, that had amassed tons of explosives, and he felt that it was grounds enough to call a principals' meeting and alert our embassies in every country. Sandy Berger then, as National Security Adviser was head of the Principals Committee. Clarke informs us that the FBI had poor communications with its various branches, unlike the CIA, the NSA, and the State Department that flooded Clarke's office with e-mails every day. Only the New York Office of the FBI was aware of terrorist threats to the United States. All during the year of 2000, drone technology was improving to the point of arming the predator drones to be used against Bin Laden in Afghanistan. But rightly so, President Clinton had placed his hopes on an agreement between Israel and the Palestinians that would change the entire equation between the United States and the Muslim world. These hopes, discussed above, were ended on 24 December 2000. Meanwhile, the USS *Cole* had been attacked in Aden in October, killing seventeen U.S. sailors. Mentioned above, Clinton was even criticized by his Republican opposition for bombing al-Qaeda targets in Afghanistan supposedly as a cover-up for the misdeeds of his personal life. Hence, the incoming

Bush administration believed that the Clinton government was "overly obsessed with al-Qaeda." This belief of Cofer Black that Clinton was obsessed with al-Qaeda was not true. He was furious when the Clinton administration permitted Bin Laden to escape from Afghanistan to Pakistan, and Cofer Black, who had identified and captured Carlos the Jackal (Ilich Ramirez Sanchez) while in Khartoum in August 1994, also wanted to kill Bin Laden operating out of Khartoum until 1995. If one wishes to follow the influence of Cofer Black in the CIA and his important role in recommending Blackwater, the mercenary troops, to President George W. Bush after the World Trade Center attack of September 11, 2001, one must consult the study of *Blackwater* by Jeremy Scahill.[265]

Quandt, based upon his many years watching instruments of the U.S. government, noted in his book some points that the Clinton government should have followed once the Senior Bush administration had brought all parties to the negotiating table. He proposed: (1) there must be a reasonable appraisal of the regional situation; (2) the president and his top advisers must be involved and must work in harmony; (3) the domestic basis of support for American policy in the region must be constantly developed; (4) success as a mediator requires a feeling for both process and for substance; (5) there must be a substantial investment in quiet diplomacy before deals can be cut; (6) pressure sometimes succeeds, but it must be skillfully exerted; (7) timing is crucial for successful negotiations. Quandt had hoped that the Clinton administration would be free of complications, but the reality was quite the opposite.

Milosevic's ethnic cleansing of Bosnians, the problems of Somalia, the Lewinsky affair and impeachment proceedings, the removal of the Glass-Steagall Act of 1999, which gave the banks and insurance companies the right to form trading houses—all conspired to complicate the two terms of Bill Clinton.

Thus, Clinton was only able to try a negotiated peace treaty with Arafat of the PLO and Prime Minister Barak of Israel in the last year of his presidency and was not able to make headway on the settler issue and the intransigence of the U.S. Congress for moves against the finances of Israel's expansion. If we read Martin Indyk's account of the Camp David II negotiations of President Clinton with Arafat of the Palestinian authority and Ehud Barak, prime minister of Israel, we have an almost blow-by-blow picture of the negotiations. Barak had offered Arafat between 80 and 91 percent of sovereignty over the West Bank and control over the Old City of Jerusalem, but Arafat remained firm on his demand for control of the Temple Mount and the Haram al-Sharif, one of Islam's most sacred sites. In like manner, the Israelis could not give up control of the Wailing Wall bordering the Temple Mount as the site of the Jewish temple of ancient Israel. Israel also believed it should sharply control the right of return for the great number of Palestinians who were forced to leave their ancestral homes in Palestine.[266] President Clinton attempted to bring the two parties together on a settlement until the end of his presidency, but to no avail.

11. The George W. Bush Presidency (January 2001 to January 2009)

The overall picture of what happened in this Presidency of George W. Bush is difficult to summarize because of the preemptive attack on Iraq in 2003 under the false assumption that Iraq had "caused" the September 11, 2001, attack on the World Trade Center and the Pentagon. This position was proven false at the outset when Richard Clarke, counterterrorism specialist on the NSC, met with President Bush on the night of September 11, 2001. In his speech to the nation, Bush had emphasized, "The rest of the world is either with us or with the terrorists." And Bush said to Clarke, "See if Saddam did this. See if he is linked in any way." Clarke replied, "But Mr. President, al-Qaeda did this." And the President, "I know, I know . . . but see if Saddam is involved. Just look! I want to know any shred." President Bush and his National Security Adviser, Condoleezza Rice, had the ideology of the Neoconservatives to dominate their thinking. As George Packer recognized already in 2005, "The Iraq War will always be linked with the term *Neoconservative*."[267]

The net result of the utter ignorance and arrogance of President Bush and his confidante and adviser, Condoleezza Rice, together with Vice President Cheney and Secretary of Defense Rumsfeld, resulted in the formation of a coalition of Sh'ite states about 2006: the Hezbollah of Lebanon, the Alawite rulers of Syria, the Shi'ite government installed by the United States in Iraq, and the active Ayatollah-controlled government of Iran. Because of this coalition of Shi'ite states across the Middle East, we must now consider it a major blunder of foreign policy during the Bush Presidency. The world's attention is now being drawn to the revolt of the Sunni majority in Syria against the Bashar Al-Asad government and the Iraqi government of Al-Maliki, known as ISIS (the Islamic State of Iraq and Syria). We have been made aware also of the outsize warnings from Israel's Prime Minister Netanyahu that Iran's nuclear facilities should be bombed. This policy of the Israeli government to stir up underlying Arab factions was long ago outlined during Israel's occupation of Lebanon (1982) and currently has given to Israel a free hand, as the world looks elsewhere, further to annex Palestinian land in the West Bank, occupied illegally by Israel since 1967, and to bomb and invade the Gaza Strip in 2014, where Israel keeps a million and a half Palestinians in the largest prison in the world.[268] Today the newspapers are filled with new admonitions from Prime Minister Natanyahu of Israel in his address to the U.S. Congress of 7 March 2015, warning that Iran wants to build an atomic bomb and that the United States should bomb the facilities, not negotiate with Iran.

As early as 1998, George W. Bush was thinking of running for the presidency in the year 2000. He had the name and the money and had a good chance to be reelected as governor of Texas in November 1998, so why not try for the presidency? Bush himself admitted that he did not have "the foggiest idea" about international affairs. No doubt at his father's suggestion, that summer, he began meeting with a number of foreign affairs specialists that had served his father. Former Secretary of State George Shultz and former Secretaries of Defense Dick Cheney and Donald Rumsfeld, were consulted. He also brought in his own contemporaries that had served in various capacities, such as Paul Wolfowitz, a chief policy aide of Cheney in the Pentagon; Richard Haass, a Mideast specialist on his father Bush's NSC staff; and Condoleezza Rice, also on the NSC as General Scowcroft's Soviet specialist. Bush was especially taken by Rice as an excellent tutor. Rice, with Wolfowitz, lined up a small group of friends and experts in a group they called the Vulcans, from the Roman god of fire, a statue of which stood in Rice's hometown of Birmingham, Alabama.[269] James Mann has summarized the backgrounds of six members of Bush's war cabinet, indicating how they assumed that the American armed forces were invincible and could intervene in Iraq and Afghanistan to gain natural resources and also to change their political culture to American interests. This group, apart from the war cabinet, included Stephen Hadley, Richard Perle and Dov Zakheim from the Reagan or Father Bush's Pentagon, Robert Blackwill (Rice's boss at the NSC), and Robert Zoellick, an important aide to Secretary of State James Baker. Powell, Scowcroft, and Kissinger also dutifully supported the candidacy of George W. Bush. Most of these named individuals considered themselves of the Neocon persuasion, perhaps with the exception of James Baker. When George W. Bush took office in January 2001, Rice, as National Security Adviser and later as Secretary of State, saw her role as actively supporting the President, his enabler and enforcer. I. Lewis (Scooter) Libby, Vice President Cheney's chief of staff, also was a backup for Rice in the White House. Stephen Hadley, Rice's deputy, was directed to send all copies of White House communications to Vice President Cheney. This process explains why Cheney's role became so important in the George W. Bush administration. Cheney also relied on his personal allies, Rumsfeld at Defense, Paul O'Neill at Treasury, Mitch Daniels and Sean O'Keefe at the Budget Office, Stephen Hadley at the NSC, and John Bolton at the State Department. This inner circle was supposed to work smoothly together like Scowcroft's group under the Elder Bush, but the strong personalities and ideological differences of Cheney, Powell, and Rumsfeld made Rice's life difficult. For example, the acceptance speech of Colin Powell when he was appointed Secretary of State had outshone the President to such a degree on foreign affairs that Bush and Cheney knew that Powell could only be balanced by a strong appointment in Defense; hence, they chose Donald Rumsfeld, who had the experience under Ford as Secretary of Defense and also a strong military record as a navy fighter pilot.[270]

Meanwhile, Richard Clarke, in charge of the Counterterrorism and Security Group under Clinton, had, as early as 25 January 2001, sent a memorandum to Condi Rice "urgently" requesting a Principals' meeting of the NSC. Rice ignored the request because it sounded like old Clinton business, and she wanted terrorist threats to be dealt with in the regional context of Pakistan and Afghanistan. Also, Rice demoted Clarke's terrorism group. They would report no longer to the Principals (basically, the Cabinet) but to the Deputies. Sandy Berger, as Clinton's National Security Adviser, had joined Richard Clarke in his initial briefing of Condi Rice. Berger said, "You're going to spend more time during your four years on terrorism generally and al-Qaeda especially than on any other issue." His prediction was correct. But when Clarke briefed Condi Rice on Al-Qaeda as a worldwide organization, Condi Rice remained skeptical and aloof. Clarke, who had observed the power and scope of al-Qaeda throughout the Middle East, called for a Principals' meeting "as soon as possible" to brief Bush's Cabinet Members about what to expect from Al-Qaeda. But Rice had already decided that first, the Deputies to the Secretaries should discuss the problem of terrorism as a fixed matter of procedure. Clarke probably erroneously believed that he could arrange a deputies meeting in short order because of the imminent threat of international terrorism. Not so, a meeting of the Deputies finally was arranged for April 2001! The meeting did not go well. Steven Hadley, deputy to Condi Rice, opened the meeting and asked Clarke to speak. Clarke stated that pressure should be placed on the Taliban and Al-Qaeda by arming the Northern Alliance in Afghanistan and other groups. Also, the United States must target Bin Laden by reinstituting the drone flights. Wolfowitz, Rumsfeld's Deputy from the Defense Department, asked why all the attention on Bin Laden when Iraqi terrorism might cause a threat. Clarke stated that Al-Qaeda had cells in fifty countries and asked John McLaughlin, deputy for the CIA, if Iraq had threatened the United States. McLaughlin said that the CIA had no evidence of

Iraqi terrorism in the United States. Finally, Richard Armitage, deputy for Colin Powell in the State Department, strongly supported Clarke. Hadley then agreed that the Deputies would first concentrate on Al-Qaeda and then move to other threats. The Principals' meeting on terrorism --in other words, the Secretaries of State, Defense and other government leaders—finally took place on 4 September 2001, just seven days before the attack on the Twin Towers of the World Trade Center and the Pentagon. As previously noted, Clarke was only able to brief the President directly on the evening of September 11.[271]

There exists another record of the George W. Bush administration that was buried after the war against Iraq that began on March 17, 2003. In December 1999, the United Nations Security Council had established the UN Monitoring, Verification, and Inspection Commission for Iraq (UNMOVIC) because the UN believed that there might still be weapons of mass destruction (WMD) in Iraq. The United States had fully accepted the idea of inspections, and Saddam Hussein appeared to cooperate with the inspection team, headed at first by Mohamed Baradei of Egypt and later by Hans Blix of Sweden. However, after the terrorist attacks on New York and Washington, DC, on September 11, 2001, the Bush administration wished to cajole the inspection team into a positive conclusion that the Iraqi regime of Saddam Hussein possessed a number of "smoking guns." They emphasized, among other items, purchasing "yellowcake" uranium from Niger, mobile chemical labs (supported by Secretary of State Colin Powell), drones purchased from South Africa, and aluminum tubes for centrifuges, and Condoleezza Rice conjured the image of a mushroom cloud over the United States. In spite of the fact that all these items and others were inspected or discounted by various reliable U.S. or other sources, the Bush administration and the British Blair administration had decided unilaterally on a military attack on Iraq without the support of the UN Security Council. The details of the discrediting of the inspection team are thoroughly revealed in the book by Hans Blix.[272]

Soon after the attack on the Twin Towers, Clarke was replaced in Counterterrorism on the NSC by retired General Wayne Downing, who had worked with Clarke on the Khobar apartment attack in Saudi

Arabia in 1995. Downing soon quit the government over the apparent lack of concern for terrorism and was replaced by John Gordon and Randy Beers, both men with long experience of terror threats to the United States. Beers later quit the job when the Bush administration decided to attack Iraq in 2003. Clarke and Roger Cressey, his deputy, were moved over to Cyber Security, considered the next threat to U.S. security. Clarke doubted that "anyone ever had the chance to make the case to him (Bush) that attacking Iraq would actually make America less secure and strengthen the broader Islamic terrorist movement."[273]

Clarke poses, in his final chapter, the question, What would a successful and comprehensive effort have looked like after September 11? He provides the following answer in three key areas as an alternative agenda to placing our vast resources, energies, and more than three trillion dollars into the Iraq War: (1) The President might have increased homeland security, (2) To promote a worldwide movement against al-Qaeda ideology and radical terrorism and instead promote the values of true Islam, (3) to become active in key countries to dry up support for terrorism (Afghanistan, Iran, Saudi Arabia, and Pakistan). The White House initially suggested a parallel organization to the NSC, an Office of Homeland Security. Soon Senator Joe Lieberman and others in the Senate proposed a bill setting up a new Department of Homeland Security. Finally, twenty-two agencies were placed in the Department of Homeland Security, but its organization became a nightmare for years, and the budget in recent years soared to fifty billion dollars per year. Very soon, after the new Department was formed in 2003, the FBI and the CIA would complain that their own capacities for analyzing terrorist data were being undermined by the new department. Just because an organization like Homeland Security is of giant size, it does not necessarily produce the information needed.[274]

The second item that Clarke believed the United States should deal with was Islamic ideology. When asked why this was important, Clarke advised his critiques to study the French film *The Battle of Algiers* (also available in English). In that film, the French military and the French Intelligence units eliminate the leadership of the FLN (Federation de la Liberation Nationale), but new recruits took over the leadership, and the French were driven out of Algeria. The reason that the Algerians were successful was because the French could not overcome the ideology of liberation from France combined with the Islamic Faith. Clarke believed that we faced the same problem with Al-Qaeda. How much have the United States and Europe lived up to their high principles by permitting torture, the ignoring of the Geneva conventions and taking over other nations' resources without proper compensation? Clarke also points out that the FBI and the CIA during the 1980s and 1990s had deteriorated in their assigned duties to such an extent that the new directors, George Tenet of the CIA, appointed by Clinton, and Robert Mueller of the FBI, appointed by George W. Bush, were also required to rebuild their organizations in the wake of September 11, 2001, and the formation of the Department of Homeland Security.[275]

The foregoing paragraphs have dealt with the rocky transition from the Presidency of William Clinton to the Presidency of George W. Bush and the consequences of being ill-prepared for a terrorist attack of the magnitude of Al-Qaeda attacks on the Twin Towers of the World Trade Center and the Pentagon. How deeply erroneous it seems that Paul Wolfowitz, deputy secretary in the Defense Department, in the light of new information, could state that the attacks had to have a state sponsorship. It is important now for this essay to understand how clumsily the Bush government blamed the 9/11 attacks on Saddam Hussein and Iraq when Richard Clarke and George Tenet and other important players in Washington, DC, indicated that it was Osama Bin Laden of Saudi Arabia and his network of *Al-Qaeda* (Ar., the Base) that had masterminded the attack.

The Republicans fully expected that Father Bush would win a second term in 1992. Consequently, a document known as the Defense Planning Guidance was commissioned by Dick Cheney, Secretary of Defense, and drawn up by Zalmay Khalilzad and Abram Shulsky under the guidance of Paul Wolfowitz, undersecretary for policy in the Defense Department. The document outlined the U.S. political and military strategy to be followed after the Cold War ended about 1991. Even with the document's revision in May 1992, the wording speaks of American world dominance, coalitions, and preemptive war "to prevent threats from unconventional weapons." Not surprising, the wording and many of the ideas of this original document were picked up in President George W. Bush's "National Security Strategy of 2002" and tended to reflect the ideas of Vice President Cheney. This document became the basis of the Bush Doctrine and its first test, the invasion of Iraq.[276]

Packer calls attention to the split between the foreign policy of the Elder Bush and that of his son. He asserts that the Elder Bush followed the Nixon-Kissinger school of realism; that is, they believed in the concept of "vital national interest" and the concept of "preserving the balance of power" between nations. But in the 1990s, a new current of thought attracted a number of young Republicans. As Packer noted, and I repeat, "The Iraq War will always be linked with the term *Neoconservative*." One must then logically inquire: (1) Who were the Neocons? (2) What ideas did they espouse? (3) Who would benefit from following their lead? Packer indicates that that the Neocons had not followed the ideas of their immigrant parents who idealized Socialism and Communism, ideologies so prevalent in the 1930s. Originally, the first generation of Neocons born in the United States included Senator Henry "Scoop" Jackson of Washington state; Norman Podhoretz, editor of the *Commentary*, the house organ of the Neocons; Irving Kristol of *the Daily Standard*, and Senator Daniel Patrick Moynihan of Massachusetts, all of whom did not get the message that America had overreached itself in the Vietnam War, 1965–1973. The Neocons considered that U.S. foreign policy had gone "wobbly" in the SALT treaty, the fall of Saigon, the Iranian Revolution, and the Soviet invasion of Afghanistan. In President Reagan, they found a champion: the worldwide defeat of Communism and "democracy spreading across the globe."[277] Brent Scowcroft, National Security Adviser, and James Baker, the Secretary of State to the Elder Bush, were realists, as noted by Packer. They were too attuned to American national interests to give importance to the shaky ideas of the Neocons. As President Clinton became deeply involved in his personal problems, individuals like Perle, Wolfowitz, and Dennis Ross could insinuate more Neocons into government posts. This practice persisted even more in the George W. Bush presidency. Examples of other Neocons include R. James Woolsey, Director of

Central Intelligence; Robert Blackwill on the N
the Middle East specialist on the NSC; Jeane Kirk
representative to the UN; Vice President Dick Che.
staff, Scooter Libby; Donald Rumsfeld; and other De
cronies like Frank Gaffney and William Boykin. Elliot
into the Podhoretz family, and Norman and son, J   ...oretz,
were editors of the Neocon organ, *Commentary*. Charles Krauthammer,
columnist and physician; and Francis Fukuyama, later a disavowed
follower; David Frum, speechwriter for President Bush; and Douglas
Feith, State Department adviser to Secretary Rice, had joined the club.
It is shocking how few of these individuals had expertise or training in
the Middle East, yet they became principal spokespersons, and these
individuals collectively involved the George W. Bush Presidency in
a war costing three trillion dollars (many say five trillion) in which
more than three thousand U.S. troops were killed and as many as fifty
thousand wounded, many of whom require ongoing medical care from
the U.S. government.[278]

12. Iraq and the Bremer Disaster
(May 12, 2003 to June 28, 2004)
and Major Aspects of Recent Iraqi History

The period of J. Paul Bremer in Iraq indeed belongs to the Presidency
of George W. Bush, but there were so many mistakes in this time frame
from all the Bush advisers that this author wishes to give it special
attention! While the Neocons became the hallmark and the guiding
ideologues of the George W. Bush presidency, it was the height of folly
appointing J. Paul Bremer (Jerry), a diplomat with very little Middle East
experience, to be the point man for the first year after the preemptive
war of the United States on Iraq. One of the features of the George W.
Bush administration was the reliance on outside advisers such as James
Baker, Secretary of State under George Bush Senior and a close friend
of Saudi and Kuwaiti regimes, J. Paul Bremer, Henry Kissinger, George
Shultz, Secretary of State under President Reagan, and Richard Perle,

of the Defense Department and a hawk on Iraq. When Bremer
ved in Iraq, Iraqis were thinking about drinking water and taking a
bath, not that a foreign company would privatize the water system. For
whatever foolish reason, the invasion of Iraq was deemed a success by
President Bush on May 1, 2003, as he flew on board a U.S. naval vessel;
it is clear that the war and the occupation were failures. Warfare on small
states, which the United States and Israel specialized in, became mass
torture and murder shops. In the 1991 attack on Iraq under President
George Bush Senior, three hundred U.S. Tomahawk missiles were fired
on Iraq in five weeks; in 2003, 380 Tomahawk missiles were fired in one
day. The "shock and awe" doctrine was meant to deprive the Iraqis of
sensory perception and the dislocation of their equilibrium. The looting
of museums was described by Secetary Rumsfeld as "Stuff happens."
Obviously, Rumsfeld would not give credit to General Shinseki when
he had stated that the United States needed more troops for the Iraqi
venture! Shinseki, for his effort, was removed from his post.

Peter McPherson, senior economic adviser to Bremer, was assigned
to downsizing state enterprises and privatizing state assets. His colleague
John Agresto, Director of the Reconstruction of Higher Education,
stripped the universities of their former equipment and carted in
truckloads of "the best modern equipment." He might have considered
that 89 percent of Iraqis under Saddam Hussein were literate. In John
Agresto's state of New Mexico, where he headed St. John's College,
literacy was about 46 percent.[279]

L. Paul Bremer was born on September 30, 1941. His father was,
at one time, head of the Christian Dior Perfume Company, and his
mother taught art history in the University of Bridgeport. He was
educated in private schools including Philips Academy in Andover,
Massachusetts, and Bremer graduated from Yale University in 1963.
Bremer completed an MBA at the Harvard Business School in 1966.
Thereafter, he spent a year in Paris studying at the Institut des Etudes
Politiques and joined the U.S. Foreign Service in 1967. He held a
variety of posts overseas, a short assignment to Kabul, Afghanistan, his
first year, then three years in Blantyre, Malawi. From 1972 to 1976,
he worked in the State Department for Henry Kissinger during the

era of the Mideast and China-Vietnam Negotiations of Kissinger and President Nixon. He became Chief of Mission in Oslo, Norway, 1976–1979. Under President Reagan, he was Executive Secretary to Alexander Haig, Secretary of state. Also under President Reagan in 1983, he became Ambassador to the Netherlands. In 1986–1989, he was appointed Ambassador-at-large for counterterrorism, and he retired from the State Department in 1989. He was then forty-eight years old, having been in the State Department twenty-two years. Building on his expertise in counterterrorism, Bremer became managing director of Kissinger and Associates. He and his wife became converts to Roman Catholicism in 1994, leaving the Anglican Church. During the late 1990s, Bremer took up the post of CEO at Marsh Crisis Consulting, a subsidiary of Marsh and McLennan. His office was in the South Tower of the World Trade Center when it was attacked on September 11, 2001; he lost many associates, but he was not in the building at the time. Bremer was appointed to head the Coalition Provisional Authority (CPA) in Iraq in May 2003 by President George W. Bush and Donald Rumsfeld.[280]

One must attempt to break through the verbiage and understand how the Bremer policies in Iraq had incubated in Republican ideology since the era of President Reagan, 1981–89. Some observers, for example, believe that Bremer was sent to Iraq expressly to carry out the complete destruction of the country by disenfranchising and destroying the Sunnis, who were a vital part of a government established by Britain in 1920 consisting of Sunni, Kurdish, and Shiʻi elements. Most non-ideological Sunnis and others under Saddam Hussein had been forced to become members of the Baʻath Party as in any party dictatorship. Following Bremer's orders, baring all members of the Baʻath from holding any position in occupied Iraq, many thousands of professors, teachers, doctors, lawyers, experts in every field, and more than three hundred thousand police, military, and intelligence units were driven from employment and left to join the opposition to the American occupation. Meanwhile, as a result, Bremer kept in office thousands of Shiʻites who took over from their Sunni counterparts, often without the same skill levels. There is no question that Sunni Iraqis traditionally held the senior positions over the Kurds and Sh'ites, even though they were outnumbered by Shi'ites. Israel had fostered a policy of rule by the Maronites in Lebanon in the 1980s.[281] The gist of this policy was for Israel to assist militarily to break up all Arab states into ethnic or religious divisions so they could easily be "managed" by Israel. Israel applied this policy to Lebanon in 1982, and the United States, under Neocon influence, applied this principle to Iraq under Bremer. Bremer took his orders from Washington after he arrived in Iraq on May 12, 2003; thus, one may conclude that the Middle East policies of the Neoconservative advisers of the George W. Bush White House, who had flocked to Washington in January of 2001, would follow the policies of Republican ideology that had set in since the Reagan presidency. Not surprisingly, this ideology corresponded very closely with the Israeli ideology published also in the Reagan years.[282]

When Bremer arrived in Baghdad, there were no traffic lights, no electricity, nor oil production. Bremer's solution was for Iraq to open Iraq's borders to unrestricted imports with no tariffs, no inspections, and no taxes. Pickup trucks and vans moved out of Iraq for Jordan, Syria, Iran, and Israel with stolen goods from museums and ministries, while flatbed trucks brought in Chinese televisions, Hollywood DVDs, and Jordanian satellite dishes. In September 2003, a conference was called together with notables from Russia and Poland who had applied the shock therapy of Milton Friedman and the Chicago School of Economics to their own economies. The course of action recommended by these notables was to eliminate government subsidies and to develop the private sector. A key element included in the program of the Chicago School of Economics entailed seizing new markets directly for Western Multinationals. Two hundred Iraqi state firms were privatized immediately, and new economic laws were put in place to entice foreigners. Corporate tax was lowered from 45 percent to 15 percent. Iraqi assets could be owned 100 percent by foreigners, and contracts were signed for forty years with the right of renewal. About 100 percent of profits could now leave the country. National Iraqi oil contracts, considered a sensitive issue, were untouched, but twenty billion barrels of production were set aside to pay the bills of the occupation. The British firm of De La Rue brought in truckloads of the new currency, but Iraqis lacked drinking water, traffic lights, and crime was rampant. Bremer largely followed the "snowflakes" (notes) from Rumsfeld and the President, but many disastrous decisions he made himself. There were many laudatory comments about the United States creating a new Marshall Plan, but President George W. Bush and his cabinet created an "Anti-Marshall Plan" that undermined Iraq's weak manufacturing sector, and unemployment soared. The U.S. Congress had kicked in thirty-eight billion dollars; fifteen billion dollars came from other countries, plus the twenty billion dollars from the Iraqi oil fields. Halliburton, Bechtel, and Parsons, the big contractors from the United States, preferred to import foreign workers because of racist assumptions about U.S. superiority and Iraqi inferiority. Iraqis were supposed to be awed spectators of the U.S. military, engineering, and management prowess, but this proved to be laughable. Mohammed Tofiq of the Ministry of Industry requested a number of generators to offset the frequent blackouts but was told by the Bremer organization that they were not available to Iraqi firms. Halliburton built a dozen beautiful military bases but could not supply Iraqi firms as they were supposed to have done. Basically, these U.S. companies robbed the Iraqi construction funds. The Iraqi Central Bank was also forbidden to offer loans to state-owned firms. For example, there were seventeen idle Iraqi cement plants, a key ingredient for reconstruction, while cement was imported. "Corporate Reconstruction" was considered by most Iraqis not as a "gift" but as a modern form of pillage. No one was impressed by U.S. speed and efficiency. Iraq became a nightmare of capitalist greed, but of course, all was blamed on Iraqi sectarianism, tribalism, or favoritism, not on White House incompetence or U.S. cronyism. In the original Marshall Plan, the Europeans were hired for all kinds of jobs, and they were permitted to operate their former economic and manufacturing structures.[283]

As George Packer has noted previously, "The Iraq War will always be linked with the term *Neoconservative*."[284] The early Neocon group lived on to include the Committee on the Present Danger, and the same group gave advice to Prime Minister Benjamin Netanyahu in 1998.

To top off the influence of the Neocons, Dennis Ross, a clear supporter of Israeli solutions, was considered the chief negotiator between Israel and the United States. It also irked the Iraqis that Noah Feldman, a young member of the law faculty of NYU, was brought in after the war to rewrite the Iraqi constitution. There had already been the Iraqi Constitution of 1970.

But there is also a hidden side to Bremer's disastrous effect on Iraq that has been captured by Maureen Dowd's incisive article during Mitt Romney's run for the Presidency in 2012, "Neocons Slither Back." In this article, she mentions that Dan Senor, foreign policy adviser for Mitt Romney, had also ill-advised Paul Ryan for his outlandish remarks on foreign policy, essentially following Netanyahu, the Israeli Prime Minister, to make war on Iran and not negotiate on Iran's nuclear stance.[285]

Upon Senor's advice, when Bremer summarily fired five hundred thousand state employees in his De-Baathification, he wiped out years of accumulated knowledge and greatly weakened the voice of secular Iraqis. Moreover, he fed the resistance to American rule by permitting 100 percent foreign ownership of Iraqi businesses. Bremer and his crowd also tried to lock in the changes so that future Iraqi governments could not alter them. Bremer had a staff of 150 persons to manage twenty-five million Iraqis. Halliburton, by contrast, maintained a staff of fifteen thousand. In the course of privatizing two hundred Iraqi factories, workers revolted in the soap factory, shot the manager, and threatened to burn down the factory.

Iraq already had a Universal Health Care System. James Haveman, in charge of rebuilding Iraq's health care system, was so ideologically opposed to free public health care, where 70 percent of child deaths are caused by treatable illnesses such as diarrhea, "Haveman decided that an overarching priority was to privatize the drug distribution system."[286]

In the Bush/Bremer system, only fifteen thousand Iraqis were hired to work on American projects, but many more thousands of foreigners worked on security and engineering jobs when these jobs were multisectarian under Saddam and were sources of national pride. The primary contractors subcontracted to Kuwaitis as the rebellion increased.

They, in turn, subcontracted to Saudis, who then subcontracted to Iraqi firms. Bechtel left Iraq in November 2006 complaining of violence, but their incompetence showed before the violence. Complaints rolled in about the schools they built and the open sewage in a children's hospital. Parsons received $186 million to build 142 health clinics, but only six were completed. Michael Fleischer, a deputy of Bremer, often lectured to Iraqi business leaders. Once he explained that "protected businesses never, never become competitive." He failed to see the irony that Halliburton, Bechtel, Parsons, KPMG, RTI, and Blackwater, the army of mercenaries, and all other U.S. corporations in Iraq to pick up the reconstruction goodies "were part of a vast protectionist racket whereby the U.S. government had created their markets with war, barred their competitors from even entering the race, then paid them to do the work while guaranteeing (the original companies) a profit, all at (U.S.) taxpayers' expense."[287]

To understand why the United States and the British were virtually never able to pacify Iraq after the invasion of March 20, 2003, it is important to understand "The Calamity of Nation Building in Iraq," a chapter in the important study by Gilles Kepel.[288] The Neocons wanted the American public to believe that Bin Laden and al-Qaeda were the figureheads for Saddam Hussein's secret financial support. Thus, a war on Iraq, already weakened by eight years of war with Iran, 1980–1988, and weakened by the U.S. Desert Storm of 1991, would be an easy and welcome conquest and also a means of controlling Iraqi oil production and silence a threat to Israel. There was not much thought actually given to Democratization. What the Neocon war planners failed to recognize was the nationalism of Iraqis and the complexities of three major factions: the Sunnis, who had been the dominate faction from the time of the Ottoman Empire, 1639–1918; the Kurdish faction in the north that wanted its independence and possessed a strong army (the *Peshmerga*); and the Shi'ites, the dominant majority of Iraq whose sacred cities, Karbala and Najaf, became power centers for the followers of Muqtada al-Sadr and the leading ayatollah, Ali al-Sistani.[289]

At the outset, one must firmly state that the Neocons and the President knew very little about Iraq with its complex structures and the effects of years of a dictatorship or the rise of state-prompted religiosity in the 1990s after the defeat of Iraq in Desert Storm of 1991. The George W. Bush White House listened eagerly to the picture that the Shi'ite exiles painted of Iraqis ("they would welcome an occupation"), but they did not have in their confidence Iraqis, who might have described a more realistic picture. Ali Allawi, an exiled financial expert, was a relative of Ayad Allawi and was himself a former Ba'ath official. Ayad Allawi became head of the INA, the Iraqi National Accord, formed in exile in London after his falling out with Saddam Hussein in 1970. This group of exiles, favored by the State Department and the CIA, was also close to MI6, the British intelligence service. They "emphasized the difficulties in planting democratic values in Arab/Islamic cultures; it was wary of radical change that would disrupt the delicate sectarian and ethnic balances inside Iraq, and it was concerned about the adverse effects of such change on the stability and interests of U.S. Arab allies in the area, notably Saudi Arabia and Jordan and also Turkey."

Ali Allawi was also related to Ahmad Chalabi, former head of another exile group in the United States, the INC (the Iraqi National Congress). This group was favored by the Neocons and conservative senators in the United States. The INC "called for a radical overhaul of the Middle East political culture and the vigorous espousal of democracy and human rights as the levers to modernize the societies therein. Iraq was to be a test case for this new direction in U.S. foreign policy." Their obvious agenda was also to take over Iraqi oil resources and also to make sure that Israel was secure from Saddam's animosity toward Israel.[290] Ayad Allawi became prime minister of the Interim Government of June 2004, inherited from Jerry Bremer. Ahmad Chalabi served on the governing council and fell out of favor with his American supporters when his predictions about an occupation went badly wrong. Chalabi also questioned the oil for food (OFF) program of the United Nations that had squandered billions of dollars of Iraqi money. He also had very close ties with the Iranian government, which made the Interim Government nervous.

He later emerged as the Deputy Prime Minister in the Transitional National Government on 2 June 2004 that would be headed by Ayad

Allawi. Yet many of the powers that Bremer had enjoyed now went to John Negroponte, the American Ambassador. The transitional or interim Government did maintain control of the oil ministry. Effective control of military power still rested with the MNF (Multi-National Force), which was, in effect, the United States. If we wish to understand the American military problems in the Iraq War, we must consult the important work of Thomas E. Ricks, the *Washington Post* senior Pentagon correspondent. Ricks has written the definitive books on the American war in Iraq *Fiasco: The American Military Adventure in Iraq (2003–2005)* and *The Gamble: General David Petraeus and the American Military Adventure in Iraq, 2006–2008*, wherein he has interviewed or served with most of the military commanders and civilians involved in the war in Iraq.[291]

As the U.S. government forces were heavily under attack in 2006 in Iraq from the insurrection of various Iraqi factions, it is important to mention that George W. Bush and Condi Rice had become concerned about the enhanced power of the Hezbollah in Lebanon after the Israelis had withdrawn from Lebanon in 2002 to cut their losses. President Bush had had a personal contact with Prime Minister Olmert on May 23, 2006, in which he encouraged Israel to attack Lebanon to reduce Hezbollah power and influence. The Israelis were not averse to such an attack, and the U.S. government hoped that supplies from Syria and Iran to the Iraqi insurgency might cease altogether if Israel could decisively defeat the Hezbollah. What Israel and the United States did not realize was that the Hezbollah had increased its defense capabilities through winning the hearts of the Lebanese and also gaining antitank missiles from Iran. The Israeli attack on Lebanon began on July 12, 2006, and the Israelis used their aircraft to attack areas of high population, even in Northern Lebanon where there was no fighting. In particular, the Israelis struck at Lebanon's infrastructure, as had the American Air Force in Iraq. When Kofi Annan, UN Secetary General, called for a cease-fire, John Bolton, U.S. representative at the United Nations, and Condi Rice, head of the State Department, asked how one could arrange a cease-fire with terrorists. A cease-fire only was arranged after it was clear that Israel had acted as a U.S. proxy and would not achieve the expected victory over the Hezbollah. Most observers counted the Israeli invasion of Lebanon in 2006 as a win for the Hezbollah.[292]

It took ten years to pick up Baer's story about Ahmad Chalabi as related by Bob Baer's *See No Evil*. Ahmad Chalabi was the poster boy for the Neocons. They presumed that Chalabi would soon head up the Iraqi government and would institute the so-called democratic reforms.[293] Baer's book reads like a spy novel and discusses many of his duty posts in Europe and Asia, but in the Middle East, he is greatly troubled by the blowing up of the American Embassy in Beirut on April 18, 1983, where many Americans died and also an entire contingent of the CIA.

The Reagan government and the CIA obviously had no clue about Middle Eastern realities. Baer also describes the blowing up of the Marine barracks on October 23, 1983, in which 241 Marines were killed. These events led Baer into a description of the crumbling of professionalism in the CIA and how the Clinton government showed no interest in the revolt of Saddam Hussein's military officers in 1995.[294]

On 21 January 1995, Robert Baer, the only Arabic-speaking CIA agent working on the Iraqi case, was ordered to take his team to Northern Iraq to monitor the plans of Saddam Hussein and to recruit, if possible, Iraqi military officers to overthrow Saddam. Shortly thereafter, Baer was able to meet with an Iraqi Major General in the small town of Zhuku, which had been seized in March 1987 by Kurdish troops (the *Peshmerga*. Baer asked the General, who had been in Saddam's inner circle of trusted Sunni officers, what he knew about SCUD missiles or biochemical warheads. The General, in civilian clothes, confirmed that Iraq and Iraq watchers were living under a host of myths about Saddam, especially about chemical or nuclear warheads. One such myth circulated that the United States wanted to keep Saddam in power and had made a secret deal for him to invade Iran in 1980. Another rumor entailed the United States urging Saddam in 1990 to attack Kuwait and that the United States gave Saddam a secret list of his enemies in 1991. The General made it clear: the Military wanted Saddam removed from power, but Saddam still had many Iraqis supporting him. The General explained his position. The General was sent to Kurdish territory to discover if the United States would support or oppose their planned coup. After the coup, the officers would need immediate diplomatic recognition to avoid a civil war. Baer made it clear to the General that the United States, for its support, would have to know the details. The General countered with his belief that he must know the American position before he revealed the details. "We know what we're doing, and we know the consequences."[295]

Meanwhile, the General flew off to Turkey and urged Baer to have an answer in two or three days. He also said that the United States must know what they are doing with Saddam, because Saddam's security was very good. Baer could only hope that the United States would take the General seriously. The General's credentials were unassailable. He was from a prominent Sunni upper Euphrates family. The General's defection had rattled Saddam to such an extent that the chief cleric of the General's clan was forced to denounce him. His defection brought up a major question, Were the Sunnis wavering in their support of Saddam Hussein? The General's requests brought up another glaring problem: other than Baer, the CIA had no other Arabic-speaking agents in Iraq to check on the General. Thus, the CIA and the U.S. Government were virtually blind on Iraq and elsewhere in the Arab Middle East. Baer, to meet the General's time constraints, sent a courier to Washington, DC, who brought back an expected sharp response: "This is not a plan." Baer still found the response rather bizarre since the agents in Washington never had been to Iraq, but it was very unrealistic to think that the besieged Clinton government would support such a plan. Baer was, of course, forced to ask the General for full details. When the General returned from Turkey, he provided specific details, because it was clear; there was no going back to Baghdad for him! The Iraqi Twenty-Sixth Brigade, the Fifteenth Infantry Division, and the Fifth Mechanical Division could hold off the Republican Guards, the chief element keeping Saddam in power. The General continued: Before the troops loyal to Saddam could organize and deploy troops, a tank training unit outside of Tikrit planned to move to 'Awjah, a retreat near Tikrit. The General asked for an American flyover as a signal for the operation to begin. Baer stated that such a flyover would not be possible. The General told Baer that the military plot consisted mostly of first cousins of the General in command posts and that all were from the Shummar tribe. Baer had checked the family tree, and he confirmed that the General's story rang true, but Washington was silent.[296]

At this stage of our analysis, it is helpful to bring in the observations of David Rothkopf's book *Running the World: The Inside Story of the National Security Council*. Rothkopf, in his introduction, indicates how often the inner government circle in the years since World War II (1941–1945) was trained in elite colleges such as Yale, Princeton, Harvard, and Columbia and served in the government together, or served in the armed forces together. Also, he indicates how more than half the NSC elite had deep connections with Henry Kissinger. Rothkopf also, out of false modesty, fails to indicate clearly that he was also a part of this elite group in the Kissinger organization. As noted above, Bremer worked for Kissinger and received Kissinger's blessing and guidance for his disastrous role in Iraq.[297]

What is particularly of interest here is what was said about Anthony Lake's relations with his colleagues in his role as Clinton's National Security adviser. In the Clinton White House, the National Economic Council began to play an equal part with the National Security Council. This change came about because two strong leaders were in charge of the post of Secretary of the Treasury, Robert Rubin initially and then Larry Summers. This pair of "advisers" to President Clinton during Clinton's first term fed his interest in tighter regulation of securities trading. But as George Packer in his 2012 study, *The Unwinding: An Inner History of the New America*, reported, President Clinton, at the end of his second term, completely reversed himself on the question of controlling Wall Street. He signed into law in 1999 the "Gramm-Leach-Bliley Law, which disastrously repealed those provisions of the 1933 Glass-Steagall Law that banned financial houses from engaging in both investment and commercial banking. Clinton also signed the Futures Modification Act of 2000, which abolished most meaningful restraints on derivatives trading."[298]

Sandy Berger had served as deputy to Warren Christopher at the State Department. Rothkopf tells us that Lake almost resigned in 1994 over inaction by his colleagues on Bosnia. Lake found it difficult to forge a consensus. He constructed issues so that the outcome favored his opinions. Lake and Holbrooke had fallen out after years of friendship, but Lake finally, with Berger coaxing, acquiesced in Holbrooke's negotiation with Milosevic at Dayton, Ohio, in 1995. But it is clear from this excursus that Lake would not be interested in involving the Clinton government in a serious action as Baer and Chalabi were proposing for Iraq. Clinton's China policy, the problems with Somalia, the Balkan settlement, and relations with Russia were already more than the Clinton crowd could handle. Lake even commented on the ways of American politics, "I think this is a pattern of American foreign policy throughout the Cold War and even now: the rhetoric that succeeds is the rhetoric of the shining city on the hill, morality, evil versus good, etc., whereas the realities call for pragmatism. Every president gets trapped in the difference."[299]

Ahmad Chalabi, in his book *End Game*, published in 1991, had advocated that the CIA maintain a post in northern Iraq. This idea was still a good one in 1995. The United States needed persons on the ground.

The CIA in Washington wanted Baer present in Salah ed-Din in northern Iraq to meet with David Litt, the U.S. de facto Iraqi ambassador, who was scheduled to contact the State Department's northern Gulf officers. Litt let it be known that he disliked the CIA, and thus, no word came from the State Department about his arrival. By the time Baer had reached Salah ed-Din, Litt was finishing his speech to the Kurds, at first with Jalal Talabani of the DUK (the Democratic Union of Kurdistan) and then to Masoud Barzani of the KDP (the Kurdish Democratic Party), whose father had fought Saddam until Kissinger and Muhammed Reza Shah had withdrawn their support in 1974. Litt had asked the Kurds to stop fighting one another, and then the United States would provide them with one million dollars. When Baer asked, "Whose money?" Chalabi laughed. "From the CIA!" Chalabi laughed because to him, in the United States, the right hand never seemed to know what the left hand was doing. Chalabi told Baer, "Litt has destroyed your credibility. Only a preemptive strike against Saddam could save the situation."[300]

Baer was chiefly concerned with that same distraction: the ongoing Kurdish civil war. When Baer moved to Salah ed-Din on March 3, 1995, he found a Kurdish civil war all over northern Iraq. The KDP (Kurdish Democrat Party) was on the point of bringing Saddam into the war. Baer knew that only the Sunni Iraqis, not the Kurds, could throw out Saddam. Ahmad Chalabi was, at that time, also headquartered in Salah ed-Din. Let us remember, he was head of the INC (the Iraqi National Congress). Chalabi had good U.S. credentials, an American BA, and MSc from MIT, and a PhD from the University of Chicago. He spoke Lebanese Arabic and American English. Chalabi's own Petra Bank in Jordan collapsed in 1989, and he was indicted for embezzlement. He had, according to Baer, brains, energy, and political savvy. He was a moderate Shi'ite, but Chalabi contended that the most influential Iraqi Shi'ites were in Teheran. Chalabi was closely connected to the CIA and, in 1995, was running his own Kurdish faction. Also, Chalabi encouraged the two Kurdish factions to attack Saddam's northern border and also to make intermittent attacks in Mosul and Kirkuk. Mustafa Barzani had earlier been known as the Red Mullah, father of Masoud, when he led guerrilla warfare against Saddam, 1970–1974, until the Shah Mohammed Reza and Kissinger pulled the plug on his operations. Mustafa Barzani died in McLean, Virginia; hence, Masoud Barzani distrusted the United States and especially the CIA. Masoud liked the status quo with the United States namely, air protection and smuggling. Saddam also profited greatly from this arrangement. One could see trucks lined up at the Turkish border for twenty miles. The first war with Saddam in 1991 seriously hurt the Turkish trade with Iraq; hence, a blind eye was turned toward the oil trade of Turkish truckers. Administrative procedures in the State Department also caused snafus. In official Washington, Turkey was managed by the European Bureau, while Iraqi affairs were managed by the Near Eastern Affairs Bureau (NEA).

Now Baer was faced with three rather weak plans: the General's plot, Chalabi's wish to assault Saddam's V Corps, and Talabani wishing to curb the profits of Barzani's smuggling. Baer told Talabani that Washington would do nothing. He was right! On 3 March 1995, in Salah ad-Din,

Chalabi received a direct message from Anthony Lake: "Call it off!" DC had permitted the General's and Chalabi's plans to move ahead but then pulled the plug. Republicans attacked Lake when he was appointed by President Clinton to become head of the CIA in the Clinton second term. Lake was turned down for the appointment in part because he failed to support Bob Baer's proposal to overthrow Saddam Hussein.[301] The General now escaped with his family to Damascus. Meanwhile, Baer was called back to Washington to clear his name. Baer, toward the end of his book, also indicates how deeply the Clinton government and Anthony Lake's family were involved with the Exxon, Amoco, and Mobil Oil Companies and their ties with Tansu and Ozer Ciller, the former Prime Minister of Turkey and her husband, and Heydar Aliyev, Prime Minister of Soviet Azerbaijan. It was during this time span of the Clinton administration that the United States was pushing for its share of new oil fields in the Caspian Sea that would then be shipped through pipelines across Turkey to the Mediterranean.[302]

It is, of course, easy to fault the government of President Clinton and of Tony Lake, his national security adviser, because they failed to take out Saddam Hussein by means of the General's Plot in 1995. But one only needs to remember the shock to the Clinton government and the U.S. Armed Forces of the U.S. attempt to unseat Mohamed Farrah Aidd in the Battle for Mogadishu of October 3 and 4 of 1993. This incident and the loss of eighteen of America's finest combat troops, an incident popularized by a book and a film known as *Black Hawk Down*, assured that U.S. ground forces would not be committed to a Muslim city in the near future. The subsequent involvement of the United States in the Balkan War was caused by President Milosevic of Jugoslavia in 1994 and 1995, who had practiced ethnic cleansing against Bosnia and Herzegovina. U.S. commitments involved the U.S. Air Force and also international and U.S. troops on the ground in Bosnia and Herzegovina.

Ali Allawi, the economist, has looked more deeply into the ideologies of various groups dealing with Iraq than Jerry Bremer ever could. As the point man for the Bush government in Iraq, Bremer had only time for the agenda Washington ordered him to enforce and to survive the daily attacks to the Coalition's control of Iraq. Allawi pulls no punches in his analysis. He makes no bones about the Neocons wishing to gain control of the rich Iraqi oil fields and also to protect Israel. Citing both the writings of Leo Strauss, sociologist and political theorist from the University of Chicago, and Bernard Lewis, a leading Islamic historian, who moved from the University of London to Princeton University in the 1970s, Ali Allawi assessed their influence on the Bush administration. Strauss advocated the influence of an intelligent elite who would counsel and advise leaders. They also could protect the masses from their worst instincts. These ideas follow closely the teachings in Plato's *The Republic*, advocating the guidance of political leaders by an elite of political philosophers (i.e., professors like Strauss) to maintain a society's balance. Radical Islam, in the minds of the Neocons, was the ideological replacement for the menace of World Communism to democratic states. As many of the Neocons were of the Jewish faith, they instinctively associated the threat of radical Islam as a threat to Israel. Allawi, in particular, discusses the influence of the writings of Bernard Lewis on the ideology of the Neocons and George W. Bush. To be sure, Saddam Hussein often made verbal threats regarding Israel, particularly after Israel bombed the Iraqi Osirak nuclear reactor facility on June 7, 1981. Also, Iraq and all Arab countries have been greatly disturbed by the Israeli occupation of the West Bank and Gaza and the cruel treatment of Palestinians since 1948.

In the recent past, many Muslim Empires have succumbed to the dominance of Western imperial powers. One may note the Muslim Moghul Empire of India that gradually fell under the control of Great Britain in the eighteen and nineteen centuries. Likewise, the Ottoman Empire had menaced the Austrian and Russian Empires in its sixteenth and seventeenth-century heyday. It too gradually succumbed to the military and technological superiority of Western Powers in the eighteenth and nineteenth centuries.

Ali Allawi makes a stark contrast between the traditional "liberal" view of why Islamic lands failed to cope with the challenges of Western Powers and the Lewis Doctrine. The former version of why Islamic countries fell behind in the struggle for modernity and technical progress derived from the internal meddling of European powers in the affairs of Muslim lands, thus thwarting them from adopting modern competitive systems. The Lewis Doctrine, echoed in the Neocon approach and the Bush government, emphasized that it was Muslims themselves who were to blame for their backwardness. Allawi fails to give us footnotes on his various observations except to note the Lewis essay "The Roots of Muslim Rage," to which many Muslims objected. This essay, termed initially as "Western Civilization: A View from the East," by Professor Lewis was presented as the Jefferson lecture of 1990, sponsored by the National Endowment for the Humanities. Allawi neglects to analyze the essay that is a good summary of the choke points of Muslim fundamentalist movements. Basically, Lewis calls on Muslims to recall elements of their past civilization that made them great leaders. Also, he condenses "Islamic rage" into two primary elements of Western civilization: secularism and modernity. He notes also that political freedom, together with representative government, elections, and constitutional government, is admired by some Muslim fundamentalists.[303] Citing the influence of Strauss and Lewis, and particularly Lewis, whose analysis influenced many government personnel and think tanks, Allawi observes that Lewis provided the background for Washington's "best and brightest" (the Neocons) to begin "dragging the Middle East, kicking and screaming, into the democratic and secular future." And "Iraq was the right place, and it was the right time (2003) to start the makeover of the region."[304]

But Allawi's interesting analysis does not stop here. He continues by citing the writings of two brilliant sociologists, Robert Merton (d. 2003) and Ali al-Wardi (d. 1995)—the one, American; the other, Iraqi. Robert Merton, in 1936, wrote an important essay, "The Unanticipated Consequences of Purposive Social Action." Merton indicated five factors that could interrupt the best-laid plans:

a) Ignorance of true conditions.
b) Errors of inference (that is, "a pathological obsession to consider only certain elements of a problem").
c) Primacy of immediate interests, a "willful ignoring of its effects": Allawi mentions as examples the Sunni boycott of the first

225

election, a crippling constitution forced through in record time (as required by Ayatollah Sistani, the highest Shi'ite religious authority). But since the constitution was passed, there have been few rectifications of constitutional errors in parliamentary committees, as promised by the Constitutional Committee, and also there was no consideration of the consequences of Shi'a and Kurdish federalism that would monopolize the oil wealth.

d) The ideology or *"base values" imperative*: Allawi cited President Bush's Christian faith-driven decisions that were supported by the religious right, decisions that were supposed to limit Iranian influence but actually empowered Iran by placing vindictive Shi'ites at every level of government.

e) Finally, self-fulfilling prophecy: the Bushites harped on "a war against terror" after the 9/11 attacks and bent over backward trying to link Saddam's regime with the al-Qaeda of Osama Bin Laden and Weapons of Mass Destruction (WMD), only to find no links to al-Qaeda or WMD.

The chosen standard-bearers of a new Iraq, the Shi'ites, we must assume, were not recognized by the Americans and the British as having easily aroused animosity against Sunnis. Yet the Shi'ites believed that, with some exceptions, they had been discriminated against throughout the course of Islamic history while considering themselves to be the bearers of the true faith.

Saddam, for all his backward and cruel policies and his support of Sunni domination, at least had fostered a secular state and a secular school system. With the advent of Shi'a control of the government and parliament as fostered by the Americans, the clear aspects of a state controlled by Shi'ite clerics, as in Iran, became evident. Bremer and the actions of the Neocon government of George W. Bush had unwittingly created a band of Shi'ite-linked governments from the Lebanese Hezbollah, to the Syrian Allawi regime of Hafiz al-Asad and his son, Bashar, the new Shi'ite regime of Iraq, the Iranian Shi'ites, and a number of Shi'ites in Afghanistan and Pakistan. One wonders where

Professor Lewis was when this bit of wisdom became current knowledge. It is clear that this policy of "divide and conquer" was favored by Israel.

Allawi also disclosed the writings of the Iraqi sociologist Ali al-Wardi, who, for him, came the closest to "unlocking the secrets of the Iraqi character." Allawi believes that the works of al-Wardi, who graduated with a doctorate in sociology from the University of Texas in 1950, were generally ignored by Western scholars and governments because he failed to follow the new statistical methods in the social sciences of the United States. Instead, he elucidated the character of Iraqis by older descriptive methods. Furthermore, Al-Wardi "insisted that the process of modernization and urbanization was skin-deep in Iraq and that tribal values, born of the experience of surviving the harsh environment of the desert, continued to hold sway for the vast majority of the country's inhabitants." Allawi lists in detail the intellectual baggage that al-Wardi noted about Iraqis that puts into stark relief the erroneous assumptions of Washington and the Bushites. (One might also mention in passing the lack of knowledge of the Middle East exhibited by the current Obama government and the U.S. military.)

We may abbreviate al-Wardi as follows:

a) Tribal solidarity rivals the state, promoting parochial values and local disputes and emphasizing lineage and status.

b) The tribesman disdains craftsmanship and most professions but sees prestige in government employment.

c) Property rights and rule of law contrast sharply with the glory of seizing property or imposing one's will on a neighbor.

d) Desert-based societies are rife with petty squabbles.

e) The rivalry of Sunnites and Shi'ites was increased by Sunni Ottoman Turk and Safavid Shi'a Iranian attempts to dominate Mesopotamia.

f) In Iraq, Shi'ism was linked to southern Iraq, a more urbanized area, while Sunnism was linked to the northwest steppe and desert. Baghdad, the seat of Ottoman power, became a stronghold of moderate Sunnism often linked to Sufism—that is, the mystical brotherhoods that flourished up to the occupation by the Americans.

Al-Wardi felt that there was a certain "geographic imperative" to get along with neighbors in Iraq even though one's neighbor often shared few common values or historic links. Allawi calls special attention to Al-Wardi's conclusions: "The people of Iraq are divided against themselves. There is no way of resolving this condition better than adapting a democratic system, where each group can participate in power according to its proportional number." This ideal situation may have been possible before the Americans fostered communal strife and the death squads entered the scene.[305]

The advent of oil wealth, particularly after World War II, provided funds for Iraq to make a tremendous investment in education. Very soon, students seeking higher degrees began appearing in British and American universities. A law was passed requiring all elementary students to begin learning English after grade 4, and this prevailed through high school. Even under successive governments of Nuri as-Said in the 1950s, the Shi'ites often became full-fledged ministers in education, health, and other positions. Education was free so long as one passed the exams; moreover, health care was free to all citizens. Anyone supported in studies abroad by the government for higher degrees was expected to serve in Iraq in his profession for the same time. It is not surprising that, until the Iraqi-Iranian War (1980–88) and the American invasions (1991 and 2003), Iraq actually had the best-educated population of all Arab countries.

Ali Allawi, even as a moderate Shi'ite, fails to mention in his book a number of facts about former Iraqi governments that have a bearing on the present-day sharp divisions between Sunnites and Shi'ites. This sharp division was first fostered by Bremer and the U.S. Government, not 'Abd al-Musab al-Zarqawi. Zarqawi, it appears, was more a symptom of the sharp division sponsored by Bremer and the Neocons. Naomi Klein attributes the interference of Bremer, acting on behalf of the U.S. government, to block the Iraqi drive for self-government as the immediate cause of the insurrection. "Within his first six months in the job, he (Bremer) had canceled a constituent assembly, nixed the idea of electing the drafters of a constitution, annulled and called off dozens of local and provincial elections, and then vanquished the beast of national elections—hardly the actions of an idealistic Democrat."[306]

As noted above, one does not have to delve very deeply into Iraqi history to find Sunni governments that brought talented Shi'ites and Kurds into the government. Often Kurds are found in the highest ranks of the military. Shi'ites even occupied such important posts as Ministers of Foreign Affairs and deans of the medical school and the law faculty. As oil revenues rose in the 1950s, conspicuous consumption increased among those favored by the royal family and the government of Nuri Al-Said. Also, the government took part in negotiating the Baghdad Pact sponsored by Britain in 1955, a measure viewed by Egypt to isolate Nasser and to bring the Middle East into the Cold War. Because the monarchy in Iraq had been so repressive, the New Democratic Party was not well organized to fight against a move to join Iraq with the union of Syria and Egypt. Only the the ICP (the Iraq Communist Party) was organized enough through the trade unions to fight this movement.

The army overthrew the King and his government on 14 July 1958, and the General 'Abd al-Karim Qasim took control of the army and the government. By then, Egypt, Syria, and Iraq had bought arms from the Soviet Union starting in 1955. As a result of the *coup d'état,* most of the royal family and the Nuri as-Said government lost their lives. General Qasim walked a fine line between control of the Army and the ICP (the Iraqi Communist Party), who controlled the Baghdad streets. Only then could General Qasim direct his country away from joining Egypt and Syria in the UAR and make reforms that benefitted the lower middle class. In this respect, General Qasim followed the Halpern model. In his law no. 80, the Iraq parliament nationalized most of the land owned by the British-controlled Iraq Petroleum Company. On some of the land, he built housing for the poor, known first as Madinat al-Thawra (City of the Revolution). This same suburb of Baghdad under Saddam Husein became Madinat al-Saddam but today is known as Madinat al-Sadr (Sadr City), home to the followers of the fiery Shi'ite leader Muhammad al-Sadr.

As a result of internal strife in the army, the Kurds led by Mustafa Barzani wishing for autonomy, the *Peshmerga* (the Kurdish Army), was at war with the Qasim government. Qasim's laying claim to Kuwait and the greater involvement of Communists led to Qasim's overthrow by the Ba'athist Party on 8 February 1963. The Communists faced a bloodbath, but the Ba'athists who had originally supported joining the UAR no longer sought this union. Many of Qasim's reforms such as land distribution, women's rights, and educational reform were not followed through after the overthrow of the Qasim government, but the British Iraq Petroleum Company lost 99 percent of its holdings.[307]

After Qasim, the Ba'ath Party that had previously struck roots in Syria under the guidance of the theorists Bitar and Aflaq was initially in favor of the pan-Arab ideas of Nasser (*Qawmiyah*), but by the time of the end of the Qasim government, the Ba'athists began to appeal to Iraqis not wishing to join the Nasser camp; *Qawmiyah* was replaced with *Vataniyah*, the nationalist camp. The Ba'ath Party was supposed to introduce into a country a modern secular government based on Western principles of democracy, a parliament answerable to the people and freedom of speech. But when a poorly educated, ruthless, and paranoid Sunni party hack named Saddam Hussein took control of the Iraqi Ba'ath Party in 1969, the high-minded principles that had inspired early members soon disintegrated into a dictatorship of Tikrit relatives and friends of Saddam.[308]

Thus, under the dictatorship, the delicate education and health systems began to deteriorate because the Shi'ites became the scapegoats of every foolish policy Saddam pursued. By starting a war with Iran, partly supported by Israel and the United States to ward off the spread of Khomeini popularity, Saddam broke the financial stability of Iraq by borrowing huge sums from the Gulf States. His vaunted aim was to join to Iraq the southern Arabic-speaking provinces of Iran along the Persian Gulf, particularly Khuzistan. When the war began, Iranians outnumbered Iraqis on a scale of three to one. Iraq brought Iran to a draw and a peace in 1988 because Saddam gassed their own Kurdish area of Halabja and was aided by American satellite technology and equipment. But the deeper aim of the United States and her allies,

Britain and Israel, was to weaken both Iraq and Iran, the two states that threatened the hegemony of the West in the Middle East.

We must not completely criticize the position of Bernard Lewis and his intellectual cohorts on the question of how Muslim states might improve. The idea of Salafiyya, for example, insofar as Muslims must emulate their ancestors, this approach was tried by a faction of Ottoman intellectuals in the eighteenth century. The basic idea was to return to the state the government structures of the time of Suleyman the Magnificent in the sixteenth century. This subject has been studied in its modern contexts by Henri Lauziere. Muslim countries also would be wise to emulate the principles of Mustafa Kemal Ataturk in bringing women into full civil rights regarding education, the workforce, the rearing of future generations, and freedom from male domination. Lewis also suggests freeing citizens from the tyranny and mismanagement of Muslim economies. One must not, however, fall into the trap of "the pot calling the kettle black." The Western economies and the United States, in particular, have been frightfully mismanaged in recent years, bringing the world to the brink of a worldwide depression. Bernard Lewis also accused the Iraqis of not developing their industrial base, but after the U.S. invasion of 2003, many Iraqi industries were not given the support to utilize their vast resources for rebuilding Iraq. The leading U.S. engineering firms imported both labor and materials when the work could have gone to Iraqis.[309]

One needs here to mention the problems Iraq had had with Britain after the Ottoman Empire was defeated in World War I (1914–1918). The British claimed Iraq as a mandate of the League of Nations having occupied the three Ottoman provinces of Mosul, Baghdad, and Basra by 1918. Iraq, as noted above, was divided religiously and ethnically. The British realized the difficulty of unifying Iraq when a revolt against British control broke out in June 1920. Iraq had been governed very loosely by the Ottomans, who maintained their administration in the main cities but basically permitted the tribes and factions a free hand in other areas. The revolt broke out when Britain tried to centralize the government, including the tribal areas.

According to William Cleveland, the quelling of the rebellion cost as many as ten thousand tribal Iraqi lives, 450 British soldiers, and an expenditure of forty million pounds. The British, under the Colonial Secretary Winston Churchill, struck on a formula of minimum imperial presence and shifted the administrative load to cooperative Iraqis, including Prince Faisal, the leader of the Arab revolt against the Ottomans. Faisal, the son of Sherif Hussein of Mecca, had been driven out of Damascus by the French but was installed by Britain as King of Iraq in 1921. An organic law was passed by the new Iraqi parliament in 1925 stating that the Shari'ah courts would control the Muslim judicial system and the Waqf foundations, while Jews and Christians would run their own courts, in keeping with the Millet laws of the defunct Ottoman Empire. The army also came into existence in 1921, founded largely through the efforts of Ja'far Al-Askari, a graduate of the Ottoman Military Academy at Harbiye and a military leader of the Arab Revolt against Turkish rule in World War I. The pressing need for administrators led King Faisal to invite Sati' al-Husri, an experienced Syrian Ottoman educator, to set up a secular school system. By 1930, Al-Husri had made amazing progress. In various treaty agreements, Britain accepted Iraqi independence and admission to the League of Nations in 1932 but held on to an array of military and defense arrangements that left Iraq dependent on Britain. Particularly humiliating to the Iraqis was Britain's forcing Iraq to sign away its oil rights to the Iraqi Petroleum Company for seventy-five years in 1925.[310]

Basically, the Ottoman-trained army officers, who had fought with King Faisal in WWI, were favored for administrative posts. As Cleveland points out, the officers sometimes used their special positions of power to amass wealth and property to match the older large landholders who had been favored by the Ottomans. Many of the officers basically did not work to alter the system. While there was a prosperous and skilled merchant class of Jews, Arabs, and Assyrians, the new oil royalties brought much wealth to all classes. While the favored general grade officers tended to support the British system, younger officers wanted to make Iraq free of the British Empire's military, administrative, and economic grip. King Faisal died suddenly in 1933, leaving a void at the top because his twenty-oneyear-old son, crowned as King Ghazi, took little interest in governing. This serious state left the field mostly to five generals. Some of them, namely, Al-Askari, had broad experience. Apart from Ottoman training under the Germans, he also had graduated from Sandhurst in Britain. He was prime minister in 1924 and 1932, but his rivals lacked his broad experience, except in military affairs. They now vied for the office of prime minister so they could use the power to enhance their position and that of their families. The ranking general Yasin al-Hashimi (1884–1937), unlike the other four, had served the Ottomans to the end of World War I and held much power and prestige in Iraq until his death. Ja'far Al-Askari was Minister of Defense in 1936, while Al-Hashimi was Prime Minister, but Al-Askari was soon assassinated by a fellow Kurdish officer. Nuri as-Sa'id (1888–1958), the most durable of the generals, who was married to Ja'far al-Askari's sister, was often prime minister up to his assassination in 1958. All the generals were Sunni Muslims, and true to the old Ottoman system, they often kept the Shi'a, the majority population, out of significant positions of power. Al-Hashimi and Al-Askari faced a Kurdish coup attempt by the army general of the northern district, Bakr Sidki, who had led his troops against the Assyrian Christian minority, perpetrating a major massacre, and their flight to Turkey. Some of the Assyrians seeking British employment had served in British units to quell the revolt of 1920. This service of Assyrians to Britain had not been forgotten. Bakr Sidki, acclaimed by the masses for his so-called patriotic duty, killing Assyrian Christians, brought his troops into Baghdad in 1936, murdered Ja'far al-Askari, and instituted a series of army coups that cursed Iraqi politics until the Ba'ath takeover of Saddam Husein in 1969. Apart from other problems at the outset of WWII, King Ghazi was killed in a car crash in 1939. His infant son was placed on the throne as Faisal II, but his regent was Abd al-Ilah, a Hashmite Prince of the line of King Faisal and also a close associate of Nuri as-Said. (Ironically, Nuri as-Said had not favored his choice as regent.)[311]

While there had always been pressures against British rule, a group of young officers, four colonels, taking advantage of Britain's war with Germany in World War II, appointed Rashid Ali al-Gaylani, a former prime minister, to the office of prime minister on 1 April 1941. One month later, hostilities began. Rashid Ali's government appeared too attached to Nazi Germany, and also the Iraqis (Gaylani was a trained lawyer) challenged the right of Britain to restrict Iraqi independence. Britain was too hard-pressed to argue treaty rights particularly because the Gaylani government surrounded the Habbaniyah air base and challenged the right of the British to establish a supply base in Basra. By the end of 1941, the British had marched Jewish and British troops across the desert from Palestine and defeated the Iraqi Revolt. (Moshe Dayan lost an eye in the Iraqi campaign.) The four colonels fled the country, but three of them were returned to be executed under a Nuri as-Said premiership. Gaylani remained in exile. Nuri as-Said and the Regent sided with the British again after the war, even setting up the Baghdad Pact in 1955 as a move with Britain to counter the popularity of Nasser. These acts sealed the fate of Nuri, the King and the Regent. They were all killed in an army revolt led by Brigadier 'Abd al-Karim Qasim (1958–1963). One must also mention the short-lived rule of the 'Arif brothers, who supported joining Nasser in a unified command. (Col. 'Abd al-Salam 'Arif died in a plane crash in 1966 and was replaced by his brother 'Abd al-Rahman 'Arif up to 1968.) The Kurds and the Shi'a opposed any union with Nasser's Egypt and, hence, strengthened the Ba'ath Party as a countermeasure.[312]

At this point, we may summarize the structural changes in most countries of the Middle East after World War II. The old patrician families nurtured by and supporting Ottoman policies gave way to their young people, who were often educated in Western schools abroad. These young scions of leading families filled government posts in the interim between WWI and WWII, usually working out a modus vivendi with the dominant colonial powers. The lower middle class, as in many western countries, were introduced to modern systems of organization in the ranks of semicolonial armies, whose efficiency depended on the military skills of the colonial overlords (the Halpern Thesis). Finally, as the European Colonial Powers were forced to release the control of their colonies after WWII, the new military leaders, often deriving from humble origins, took control of the emerging states and, to be sure, wished to bring the fruits of modern life to the places of their origin. This question pertains especially to Boumedienne of Algeria, Nasser of Egypt, Hafez al-Asad in Syria, Chamoun of Lebanon, Qasim of Iraq, Reza Shah of Iran, and Bourguiba of Tunisia. Mossadegh, by contrast, who replaced Mohammad Reza Shah, son of Reza Shah, was trained in Switzerland as a lawyer and was a scion of the Qajar royal family. By close analysis of the successor governments of these individuals and their interaction with the U.S. Government in the post–World War II struggle, Soviet and U.S. dominance, we have noted how far all governments have departed from their original ideals.

13. The Presidency of Barack Obama (January 2009 to January 2017)

To help us understand the Presidency of Barack Obama, we need to look at the individuals that he chose for important posts in the government. To ease the pain of her loss to the president in the election, he chose Hillary Clinton as his Secretary of State. Indirectly, he also enlisted the support of the former two-term president Bill Clinton. This choice was particularly evident in Bill Clinton's help in President Obama's reelection campaign in November 2012. The President ran afoul of his replacement for Hillary Clinton after his reelection when he appointed Susan Rice, who had represented the United States in the United Nations. She was blamed for the inaccurate picture she was given by the CIA of the murder of the Arabic-speaking Ambassador Christopher Stevens in Benhazi, Libya. She retained her post at the UN, while Senator John Kerry, former presidential candidate, became the alternate appointment to the State Department. Later Susan Rice was appointed as national security adviser to the president, which did not require Senate approval. Another important post was Obama's chief of staff, Rahm Emanuel, the son of a Chicago rabbi, who was known for his ability to get legislation through Congress. Toward the end of Obama's first term, Emanuel resigned his post and became mayor of Chicago, and Denis McDonough became the new chief of staff.

Another important appointment was Eric Holder as Attorney General, a longtime friend of the president and the first African American to hold this post.

President Obama had carried over the Secretary of Defense Robert Gates from the Republican administraton. He was replaced by Leon Panetta, from 2011 to 2013, who had served the administration as head of the CIA (2009–2011). Chuck Hagel, former Senator from Nebraska, was appointed as his replacement but ran into Republican opposition before he was eventually confirmed. The Senate Republicans did not like Hagel's independent remarks about Israel and the Defense Department. President Obama, meanwhile, had declared that he would bring our troops out of Iraq in August 2010 and all support troops by the end of 2011. In the light of later developments, notably Nuri Al-Maliki, prime minister of Iraq, had left the Sunnis and Kurds out of his government; moreover, he also did not permit a few American troops to remain in positions to advise his troops. Suddenly, as described below, the Shi'ite Iraqi troops were unable to stop another invasion in 2014 by Sunni-based fighters from the Syrian civil war under the black banner of ISIS, the Islamic State in Iraq and Syria. Apart from the Afghan surge of 2011, at the request of General Petraeus, President Obama had charted our troops to leave Afghanistan at the end of 2014. The President recently decided to leave more troop advisers in Afghanistan into the next Presidency, noting that the Afghan army still needed strengthening. The Law of Sequestration, pushed by the Republicans, basically took from the Defense Department budget about eighty billion dollars on March 1, 2013.

The Director of the Office of Management and Budget started with Peter Orszag, and he was later replaced by Jack Lew (2010–2012). After Obama's reelection, Jack Lew replaced Tim Geithner as Secretary of the Treasury in 2013. Paul Volcker came back from retirement to head the Economic Recovery Advisory Board (2009–2011), and Jeffrey Immelt, former head of General Electric, replaced him, and the name was changed to the Council on Jobs and Competitiveness. Larry Summers, recently dismissed as the President of Harvard University (basically because of remarks about women in science) and Clinton's last Secretary of the Treasury, became an adviser to the President for Economic Policy (2009–2010) and was followed by Gene Sperling. Summers apparently was the President's first choice to replace Ben Bernanke at the Federal Reserve, but Summers faced so much opposition from both parties that he withdrew his name from consideration. Hence, Janet Yellen, economist and head of the San Francisco branch of the Federal Reserve, received the Obama appointment. General Eric Shinseki, who had stated that more troops would be required for the Iraqi War, and was fired by Secretary Rumsfeld in the Bush administration, but General Shinseki was appointed head of the Department of Veterans Affairs under President Obama. He was removed from the VA in early 2014 because a number of Shinseki appointments had falsified documents about the time it took for veterans to obtain medical attention. Janet Napolitano has remained as head of Homeland Security since 2009 but was recently replaced by Jay Johnson, who served most recently in the CIA. The Republicans in the U.S. House of Representatives, as of 27 February 2015, have had difficulty in funding the Department of Homeland Security by attaching it to a bill, indicating their hatred for the President's Ruling to protect immigrants from deportation and also their dislike of the Affordable Care Act. Even the Supreme Court could have rendered the latter as unconstitutional but instead gave it their support.

U.S. Republicans had deeply miscalculated the qualifications of Mitt Romney during the election campaign for the presidency and failed to make a strong case to win Latino, African American, and American female votes. Romney hurt his own campaign by stating that almost half the American population paid no taxes and were "freeloaders" on the U.S. economy. If one wishes to dig deeper into Romney's shadow cabinet, one should consult the important article "Mitt Romney's Neocon War Cabinet" in *The Nation* by Ari Berman. Berman notes that among other appointments, he had John Bolton in mind for Secretary of State. Bolton was one of the most outspoken of George W. Bush's appointments as U.S. representative to the United Nations. In describing other Neocons that were close to Romney, Ari Berman mentioned Dan Senor, spokesman for Paul Bremer at a time when Bremer disbanded the Iraqi army and tried to privatize the entire Iraqi economy.[313]

We must count ourselves fortunate in the study of Fawaz Gerges, a professor at the London School of Economics and Political Science, on the topic *Obama and the Middle East: The End of America's Moment.*[314]Gerges has examined President Obama's Middle East record from the time of his service in the U.S. Senate and his Presidency up to the election of 2012. From Obama's record, Gerges has pieced together what he considers the weaknesses of Obama's Middle East policies. Gerges readily concedes that President Obama inherited a weak U.S. economy, a military grossly overextended, and a mixed legacy in the Middle East. The United States is undergoing challenges from the BRIC economies (Brazil, Russia, India, and China) and especially from China, which may challenge the reserve currency of the U.S. dollar with a currency based on gold. BRIC countries concentrate on creating skilled workers, research, and technology at a time when the U.S. education system is frequently attacked and appears to be in disarray. Gerges believes that the Cold War distorted American policy in the Middle East, forcing artificial relationships with Nasser, Sadat, and Mubarak in Egypt, the excessive favoring of Israel because of the strength of its army, the power of the Jewish lobby in the United States, and the dependence on Saudi oil." After 1991, the United States did not rethink its position in the Middle East, and the militant Islamic challenge caused apprehension. The Arab revolts of 2011 and 2012 fostered only partial solutions. Clearly, however, the autocratic rulers in the Middle East that had protected American interests for half a century no longer were secure. Moreover, the United States has signaled the world that the United States believes it must pay greater attention to its interests in the Pacific and Far East and less to the Middle East.[315]

The Obama administration had picked up the causes of Israel at the expense of relations with even the former U.S. allies of Iran and Turkey. Gerges noted that after June of 1967 and the so-called Six-Day War, the United States gradually dropped a balanced Mideast policy because Israel's armed forces could be used as a balance to Arab countries that had begun extensive trade with the Soviet Union. Kissinger emphasized that if Israel felt secure, it would make peace with its Arab neighbors. This proposition of Kissinger never bore fruit because Israel could always seek further privileges from the United States with greater subsidies, more weapons, and greater influence. The natural balance to Israel's "security ploy" would be the regionalist point of view that George Ball and other regionalists had advocated and Gerges supports. This position called upon the United States to advocate a balanced policy with the needs of each country taken into consideration and to seek a balance of power in the Middle East. This policy had no traction with American policy or Congress because there was very little support from an Arab, Persian, or Turkish constituency in the United States. Politicians seek *votes* and *money* because the American system requires a huge outlay of cash to gain votes. This requirement of the great amount of cash one must raise to run for public office has increased astronomically after the Supreme Court passed the Citizens United ruling in 2011, giving large corporations the right to donate large sums of cash to a designated candidate without disclosing the sum's origin. As the Constitution requires the House of Representatives to run for office every two years, basically, the incumbent Bill Owens gave up his seat to Elise Stefanik, complaining that he had to devote five hours of every day to fund-raising.[316] This system also has consequences for the U.S. Presidents. To seek reelection; an American president learns to avoid controversial domestic policies that the Congress and Senate are dead set against. Gerges notes that without a transformational strategy, which means educating people on foreign policy in order to make foreign policy in the best interests of the United States, President Obama had no chance to change course. Obama was basically stuck with an "Israel First" policy that was advocated by the Neocons and such foreign policy experts as Dennis Ross and Martin Indyk, who are known to have close ties with Israel. It should be recognized that this was a failed policy.[317]

In conclusion, Professor Gerges observed that the system rewards *conformity* and *groupthink*. The realists know that America is in decline because the United States lacks strong administrative leadership. There is little or no credibility. We have gone from a hegemonic power to a multilateral state system in less than a generation. In spite of the great favoritism shown to Israel, the Israeli Prime Minister Bibi Netanyahu has openly defied President Obama on Israel's settlement policy and also in a recent joint session of Congress (2013), to which Netanyahu spoke; the Senators and Congressmen, in a most disgusting fashion, flocked around Netanyahu after his address and ignored the President. (There was a repeat performance of Netanyahu when Speaker of the House Boehner invited Netanyahu to address Congress in February 2015 on the dangers of negotiating with Iran!) Gerges believes that whenever President Obama got into a political problem, he was too timid and failed to react in the way Israelis respect, by cutting off funds and arms shipments as President Eisenhower and President Gerald Ford had done in the past.

A recent estimate of total U.S. subsidies to Israel amounts to 130 billion dollars, but this great subsidy does not count many hidden benefits for Israeli supporters, such as tax exemption of American Jews supporting Israel wherein the United States virtually subsidies the settlements on Arab land. It is also noteworthy that under President Obama's watch, the National Security Administration not only spied on Americans but also shared its findings with Israel.[318] We have recently also been treated to Israel's "Mowing of Grass" in the Gaza Strip, Gaza being dubbed by the Press as the largest open-air prison in the world. The recent Israeli attack on the Gaza Strip started when Israel broke its agreement with Hamas, the governing entity of Gaza. Gaza retaliated with launching its useless rocket attack on Israel. Prime Minister Natanyahu and President Obama both stated that Israel has a right to defend itself, and Israel commenced artillery and aircraft assaults on Gaza, eventually leading up to a major ground attack supposedly to destroy tunnels that the Palestinians used to attack Israel or to gain supplies from Egypt. The loss of life in Gaza approached three thousand, mostly noncombatant women, children, and other civilians. Israeli troop casualties amounted to under one hundred. The wounded amounted to ten thousand souls, and there followed the Israeli destruction in Gaza of untold numbers of homes, mosques, and hospitals. A reluctant truce was negotiated after about one month of destruction. To gain some measure of the extent of the damage to Gaza, one must read the account of David Shulman's book review, "Gaza: The Murderous Melodrama," in *The New York Review of Books, or* also the article in the Sunday *Times Weekly Review* by Nicholas Kristof, "Winds of War in Gaza," describing the everyday miseries imposed by Israeli air destruction and Israeli and Egypt's blockade of Gaza.[319]

It is clear that President Obama had become more flexible in dealing with Islamic regimes, but Obama showed little regard for new policies in dealings with confrontational entities like Hamas and Hezbollah, Israel, and the new regime of al-Sisi in Egypt. Also, ordinary Americans seem blind to the Israeli annexation of Palestinian land because American leadership raises few questions or complaints. The security of Israel, a modern state fully capable of defending its vital interests and equipped with the latest U.S. and their own weaponry, outweighs enormously the security of the cash-strapped, weak entities of the Palestinians and their self-determination, even though recent Arab revolutions have tended to produce democratic institutions. If one wishes to look deeply into the failure of the Muslim Brotherhood government of Mohammed Morsi, one should consult the analysis of Peter Hessler, "Arab Summer: Will the Elections End the Egyptian Revolution?" written in *The New Yorker*, 18 June 2012, just before the election of 2012.[320]

President Obama had nourished the traditional good relations with Turkey with the regime of Prime Minister Recep Tayyip Erdogan but followed Israel's coaxing in the harsh sanctions he placed on Iran to block its suspected attempt to create atomic weapons. The latest restrictions on the Iranian economy interfered with Iran's marketing of its oil and the blocking of Iran's banking transactions; either restriction is grounds for war. Professor Gerges doubted if Obama had the leadership qualities to lead the world to a new Middle East consensus. Professor Gerges also notes that there was a dearth of Middle East specialists in the Obama government, yet President Obama had prominently appointed Dennis Ross to the National Security Council, who was a well-known supporter of Israel. In such a position, Ross was once again, as he did as President Clinton's chief negotiator, able to bring into play his losing strategy of the "Israel First" doctrine. There is also the growing influence once again of the Neocons Bernard Lewis, former Vice President Cheney,

Martin Indyk, Elliott Abrams, John Bolton, Aaron Friedberg, John Hannah, Cofer Black, Richard Perle, Paul Wolfowitz, Douglas Feith, David Wurmser, and Matthew Levitt. This group of "enlightened" leaders brought us the Iraqi War, and as a number of commanders in that war, particularly General Petraeus noted, our close alliance with Israel caused our enemies to kill many more U.S. troops. What Gerges and a number of independent observers have noted, Israel has a virtual veto on peace negotiations. Israel also has floated the idea that Islamic radicalism is trumped by Jewish settlers on Palestinian lands, yet Islamic radicalism has its roots in Israeli land grabs.[321]

Stephen P. Cohen, in his critical study *Beyond America's Grasp: A Century of Failed Diplomacy in the Middle East*, makes many good points about the United States inheriting after World War II the mantle of peacemaking with national Middle East leaders such as Nasser of Egypt, Nuri Al-Said of Iraq, or Habib Bourguiba of Tunisia, the United States, Cohen states, made the mistake of dealing with Middle Eastern states as if they were mature nation-states when, in fact, their populations held primary loyalties to their religious communities, their ethnic group or to a tribe. This problem made it difficult for the United States to promote normal relations or policies that would help the modernization of Middle Eastern states. What Professor Cohen fails to mention, however, is that Israel promotes the separation of Middle Eastern states into these primordial loyalties and uses its special relationship with the United States to gain massive subsidies and advanced military systems to keep all Middle Eastern states in a subordinate position.[322]

It should be obvious to Professor Gerges and the many other critics of President Obama that, as this book goes to press, President Obama has just finished the fourth year of his second term (January 2017). Obama and Secretary of State John Kerry have given us the outline of a dynamic new foreign policy based on diplomacy, not warfare fostered, in the past by the United States, Israel, and the Neocons as under the George W. Bush administration. We must remind our readers that President Obama negotiated the withdrawal of American troops from Iraq after an occupation lasting more than thirteen years. This same diplomatic logic has been applied to our troop concentrations in

Afghanistan. President Obama and John Kerry and other individuals have negotiated with President Hamid Karzai of Afghanistan for the withdrawal of American combat troops from Afghanistan at the end of 2014, but were occupied with saving Aleppo from the Asad government and participating in the allied push to retake Mosul from ISIS. President Karzai of Afghanistan has meanwhile witnessed a change in government goals and has asked the Taliban leadership to take part in a national debate for the future of Afghanistan.

For President Obama, the real game change was the election of Hassan Rouhani as the seventh president of Iran on 15 June 2013. He was born in November 1948 as Hassan Fereydoun and has just celebrated his sixty-fifth birthday. Somewhere in his youth, his name was changed to Rouhani. Rouhani has had incredible experience in all phases of recent Iranian history from his teen years until the present, and in spite of critics, he is considered a moderate, particularly in contrast to his immediate predecessor, Mahmoud Ahmadinejad. His father, Asadullah Fereydoun, ran a spice shop in his town of Sorkheh near Semnan and was arrested twenty times in his protests of Mohammed Reza Shah. Following the usual religious studies in one's hometown, Rouhani moved on to the Qom Seminary in 1961. In 1969, he enrolled in Tehran University and received a law degree in 1972. The following year, he enrolled in the military in Nishapur. Later, in 1990, Rouhani was earmarked for law studies abroad and gained an MPhil degree from Glasgow Caledonian University in Scotland in 1995 and later attained an PhD in 1999 from the same university. Before his university work abroad, he had spoken often against the Shah's government like his father. In 1977, he was on the blacklist of the Savak secret police for praising Ayatollah Khomeini as the awaited Imam to help all Shi'ites and was advised to go abroad to France and join Khomeini's entourage. Rouhani, after the Khomeini Revolution of 1979, having had military experience, he first involved himself in military organization. Also, he was elected to the parliament, the *Majlis*, in 1980. During the war with Iraq, 1980–1988, Hassan Rouhani, held a number of high military posts, including the head of the Iran Air Defense Force. During the Iran-Contra arms debacle of President Reagan, Robert McFarlane, our national security adviser in 1986, dealt with Rouhani. Rouhani was first secretary of the Supreme National Security Council, 1989–1997 and 2000–2005, and Rouhani was national security adviser to Presidents Rafsanjani and Khatami. Since 1991 until the present, he has served on the Expediency Council. Under Kamal Kharazi, foreign minister, a dispute erupted over atomic policies and the foreign ministry; Rouhani was placed in charge of atomic development, and hence, he dealt with complaints of the IAEA (the International Atomic Energy Agency) and met with the EU (European Union) negotiators in 2005. Since October 2007, Rouhani, until his run for the presidency, has been the personal representative of the Supreme Leader, Ali Khamenei, to the Supreme National Security Council. We have learned that during the election, Rouhani gained many votes among the middle class and young voters and also did well in the religious communities of Mashhad and Qum.[323]

I believe that the Western powers are very fortunate to be able to negotiate with President Rouhani, who has been deeply involved in the full panoply of Iranian affairs from an early age. In the last few months, John Kerry, Secretary of State, Barack Obama, and a number of Western European governments arrived at an agreement with President Rouhani. The Iranians are permitted to continue enriching low-grade uranium, but the IAEA and other experts are permitted to monitor the production of all phases of the Iranian nuclear program. In return for this program, the United States and Western Powers have agreed to relax certain sanctions in oil production and currency controls that will aid the Iranian economy. As Antony Blinken, Deputy National Security Adviser, stated that the Republicans and the Israelis who reject diplomatic negotiations must be honest in what they are proposing as an alternative. The Republicans and newly-Elected Trump and Israelis are looking at all-out war on the Iranians, which has also no sure outcome. Prime Minister Netanyahu should well consult the stress he is placing on ordinary Israelis by his vision of constant warfare because many Jews are abandoning Israel for Western Europe and North America.[324] Prime Minister Netanyahu addressed the U.S. Congress on 3 March 2015, advising against any negotiations with Iran, but he too is facing a warfare alternative.

In the Middle East, Europe and the United States face a far greater danger, not understanding the power of ISIS to recruit young Muslims into the fight for a new Caliphate. As Professor Fawaz Gerges stated on a recent interview on the BBC, "Unless we understand more fully the ideology that motivates ISIS, we shall suffer a great deal of difficulty defeating this new force."[325]

One should say a word about Samantha Power. Ms. Power has been appointed as our representative to the United Nations and then Obama's National Security Adviser. She was first known for her Pulitzer Prize book of 2003, *A Problem from Hell: America and the Age of Genocide*. She also was a Harvard professor and served on the National Security Council. She became an adviser to Obama's political campaign in 2007 but was criticized by the pro-Israeli crowd because she held that a gigantic police force was her recommendation for peace between Arab and Jew. She recognized early on that politics was the "art of the possible" and recanted her views. This realization has been characteristic of her performance and votes in the United Nations. Billed as a fighter for human rights, she has put in a milk-toast performance. This is reflected in the article *in the New Yorker* by Evan Osnos. Her recent marriage to Cass Sunstein, a distinguished Harvard law professor, may also have mitigated her former strong views.[326]

The late political scientist, much respected, from Harvard Samuel Huntington completed his very insightful book, *The Clash of Civilizations and the Remaking of World Order* in 1996, following a controversial article on the same theme that appeared in *Foreign Affairs* in 1993. Huntington's observations are singularly interesting. Huntington projects that in the near future, the peoples of the world will tend to coalesce around their original civilizations: Western Europe and North America, Latin American, African, Orthodox, Buddhist, Hindic, Sinic, and Japanese. He also believes that the fault lines between these civilizations will require special monitoring to avoid major wars. In his book, Huntington spends a good deal of time on the "crucial impact of population growth, on stability and the balance of power." Huntington also observes that "the clashes of civilization are the greatest threats to world peace." He thus advocates an international order based on civilizations to ensure world peace.[327]

Postscript

President Obama damaged his presidency by not bombing Syria after international inspectors determined that Syria had used poison gas on its own citizens in 2011, the so-called crossing of the red line. Subsequently, many Democratic Senators and Congressman in the Election of 2014 did not seek President Obama's support because in many constuencies, Obama was deemed weak on foreign policy. Fortunately, it was clear from a *New York Times* editorial of Sunday, June 29, 2014, "They Said It Couldn't Be Done," that the Organization for the Prohibition of Chemical Weapons had delivered to a Danish vessel in Latakia harbor on Monday, 23 June 2014, the last of a cache or 1,300 Tons of chemical agents that Syria had stockpiled. In the main body of my book, it was clear that Russia's President, Vladimir Putin, had suggested to President Obama that in lieu of bombing Syria, he would support the position of removing chemical weapons from the Syrian arsenal and would also support the peaceful resolution of the Palestinian-Israeli issue and work toward Iran's goal of establishing the peaceful use of nuclear materials in the fields of medicine and electricity. Secretary of State John Kerry had taken a strong position on the Palestinian issue shortly after his confirmation, which was completely rejected by Benjamin Netanyahu, Prime Minister of Israel. Ross Douthat, a columnist for the *New York Times*, has written a serious critique of President Obama's foreign policy entitled "Grading Obama's Foreign Policy," in which he indicates a rather sorry list of failures. He even indicates that the Asad government of Syria has once again used mustard gas against its own citizens.[328]

Israel was also unhappy with President Obama's desire to negotiate with the newly elected President of Iran, Hasan Rouhani, and his agent over the impasse on nuclear proliferation. To this end, Robin Wright has written an important article called "The Adversary," summarizing her interview with Javad Zarif, Iran's Foreign Minister and the chief negotiator in nuclear talks with Wendy Sherman, Under Secretary for Political Affairs in the State Department and our chief negotiator with Iran. Wright mentions that Zarif spent twenty years in the United States and holds a doctorate from the University of Denver.[329] An article also is recommended to our readers by David Remnick, "The One-State Reality," concerning the views of Israel's new President, Reuven Rivlin. In this article, President Rivlin notes that he is strongly opposed to a two-state solution on the grounds that now the Palestinians would be faced with Bantustans because Israeli settlements are encompassing most of the West Bank. The basic problem still remains, what would happen to the Palestinians who desire their own statehood? Remnick points out, and President Rivlin concurs that virtually, the Palestinian population of Palestine has been replaced by a Jewish population. President Rivlin admits that the hostility of the Arab population toward Jews is generated by the harsh treatment, historically, of Jews toward Arabs in their replacement activities and their settlement policies. But it does not help the Palestinians when President Rivlin calls for "more civilized" treatment by Israelis of Palestinians. Israel has made its settlements in the West Bank through annexation by the Israeli-erected wall or annexation by superior military force.[330]

In the Pandora's Box that President Obama opened, one must also include the problem of the Ukraine. As Eric S. Margolis has indicated in his article "Another Anschluss in Crimea,"[331] The Crimea was detached from the Russian Republic in 1954 by Nikita Khrushchev in a drunken dinner party. No sooner had Washington engineered a coup against the corrupt government of Ukraine's pro-Russian president, Viktor Yanukovych, than Vladimir Putin laid claim to the historic ties of the Crimea to Russia. Fortunately for the United States, Mr. Putin had separated the disagreement over the Crimea from Syria's chemical weapons. The Crimea has long been in the strategic sphere of Russia, and the Russian fleet was also stationed off the shores of Crimea. But with the Russian-arranged plebiscite and the reannexation (*Anschluss*) of Crimea once again to Russia, Secretary Kerry and President Obama went out of their way in supporting the right of the Ukraine to the Crimea and virtually overthrew the remaining concerns of the United States in the Middle East.

Moreover, as Margolis reported, President Bush Senior had negotiated with Russia that the United States would not extend American interests to the borders of Russia. However, President Bush Senior and President Clinton thought of Russia in their presidencies as a third-rate power after the *Perestroika and Glasnost* Reforms of Mikhail Gorbachev, who became President of the Soviet Union in 1990. Bush Senior and Bill Clinton even planned to place rockets in Poland and the Baltic States allegedly as a check on Iran. A still nuclear-armed Russia was not taken in by these foolish excuses. It is important to remember that Vladimir Putin is popular with Russians because of his attempts to rebuild the power of the former Soviet Union, the breakup of which was blamed on *Perestroika* (Restructuring of the Soviet Union). On this same enthusiasm of the Obama government for Ukraine, Stephen F. Cohen has written an incisive article called "Patriotic Heresy" in a recent issue of *The Nation*. In this article, Cohen notes how weak the opposition has been to the Obama government policies about Russia. Cohen believes that the Russian point of view has been nonexistent in the news media and the popular press. In particular, Cohen attacks the so-called EU offer to have stronger ties with the European Union without giving the Ukraine any visible economic support.[332] As Cohen notes, President Obama did not cultivate a leadership role in this problem, and Secretary Kerry acted more like a Minister of War than our chief negotiator. In affairs of the Ukraine, one should look at the religious history. The leadership in Kiev belongs to the Uniate Church allied with the Papacy. In the Crimea, this was formerly the territory of the Crimean Tatar Khan, a Muslim. The coal miners of Eastern Ukraine belong to the Orthodox version of Christianity, under the Metropolitan of Moscow.

There is no doubt that the Robert Parry article "The Neocons Have Weathered the Storm" appearing in *Consortium News* in 2013 and also in *Other Voices From the Middle East Clipboard,* appearing also in the May 2014 issue of the *Washington Report on Middle East Affairs,* cited above, had a greater long-term significance for the Obama administration and the United States in general. Parry contends that the Neocons, who provided the ideological underpinnings for the George W. Bush invasion of Iraq, are once again in powerful positions in Washington. From their strategic positions, the Neocons can and have influenced the Obama government down the path of confrontation and war in the Ukraine and the Middle East. The Neocons may have an even stronger voice in 2017. This outcome will be hard to predict under normal circumstances since the Neocons were responsible for the disastrous ten-year war against Iraq in which thousands of U.S. soldiers were either maimed or killed, and Iraqis suffered the same fate for at least a million citizens. This American tragedy cost the American taxpayers upward of three trillion dollars, not counting now ongoing medical expenses for veterans (witness the General Shinseki experience with the Veterans Administration).

The opening gambit of this "Postscript" was the statement that President Obama failed to bomb the aircraft and heavy weapons of Syria upon evidence that President Bashar Al-Asad had used chemical weapons on fellow Syrians. We are hopeful that President Obama's restraint in this instance paid off. The United States was called upon to support the Iraqi government of Nuri Al-Maliki, Prime Minister of Iraq, with U.S. aircraft and drones. The reason for this sudden turn of events is that both Syria and Iraq are faced with the new threat from ISIS (the Islamic State of Iraq and Syria) that has been organized by Sunni tribal and straight-line forces from former armed forces in Iraq and Syria that were dismissed when the Alawites took over in Syria, and Al-Maliki and Bremer and President George W. Bush, with the help of U.S. armed forces, put the Shi'ites in power in Iraq. The real problem is that the Asad government in Damascus is, on occasion, secretly cooperating with ISIS, making it difficult to bomb the anti-Asad forces.[333] It is remembered that Al-Maliki has consistently supported the Shi'ites in military and intelligence units and throughout his government and even encouraged goon squads against Sunnis as the Americans withdrew their forces. Fortunately, Al-Maliki has now been replaced by Haider Al-Abadi. The request for air support has been in the light of the fall of Mosul, Tikrit, and Fallujah to this new threat headed by Al-Bakar al-Baghdadi, the self-appointed Caliph of the ISIS movement. Ashton Carter, the new Secretary of Defense in the Obama government, after the fall of Fallujah, has stated that "the Iraqi forces do not seem to have the will to fight." They notoriously disgarded their American weapons to the ISIS fighters and retreated from wide swaths of territory.[334] While President Obama answered the call for U.S. air support in bombing troop and heavy weapons movements of ISIS, he also reminded NATO countries and local Arab governments that they should take part in the air war. The United States, the European Union, and even Saudi Arabia and Iran also insisted that Nouri Al-Maliki resign in favor of Haider Al-Abadi, viewed as a more neutral leader for Iraq. With everyone talking about the air war, it has become clear that ISIS will not be defeated by air warfare alone. This became clear when the Kurdish forces in northern Iraq, the *Peshmerga,* saved the Christian Nestorian community that had fled to White Mountain in northern Iraq. Initially, the Iraqi forces abandoned their units and heavy weapons because of the ferocity of the attacking ISIS Sunnis. With the approach to Baghdad, units of Shi'ite forces have better held their ground, and also leaders of Iran's elite force, the Quds Force, have supplied military intelligence and support forces, and fortunately, al-Maliki had resigned on 14 August 2014 and was replaced by Al-Abadi on September 9.[335]

What has been a new game changer is that President Putin has, in the month of October 2015, fired rockets from ships in the Caspian Sea. As Ashton Carter, Secretary of Defense, soon reported, the rockets mainly destroyed units fighting Asad's army. Also, President Putin committed his aircraft to flying sorties in Syria. At first, Putin's aircraft proceded to attack units that were undermining Asad's regime. These same fighter jets suddenly did a *volte-face* when a Russian aircraft full of Russian tourists was returning from Egypt and a bomb obliterated the aircraft over the Sinai Desert. Now Russian aircraft began attacking ISIS forces in Raqqa, their headquarters city.

President Putin of Russia also had his own explanations to deliver because of the downing of flight 17 of Malaysian Airways. This tragic event occurred on Thursday, July 17, 2014, in Eastern Ukraine by rockets believed to have been supplied by Russia for the rebel forces, mainly Russian coal minors from the Donets Coal fields! (The rocket that brought down the plane was later confirmed as Russian.) The pressure from Kiev, deciding to attack the rebel forces in Eastern Ukraine, and Putin not wishing to be portrayed as the American *bête noire* have, nevertheless, equipped the rebel forces of Eastern Ukraine with advanced weaponry. The net result of President Obama's apparent lack of leadership in a number of crises has greatly affected the results of the election of November 4, 2014. The Democrats have lost their leadership in the U.S. Senate and also have given up many seats in the House of Representatives. Only in the state governorships have the Democrats had a better showing. Many Democratic candidates for both the Senate and congressional elections had distanced themselves from President Obama because his overall popularity has slipped to the 30 percent level. Many Americans believed that the President should have bombed Syria and attempted to destroy the Alawite leadership of Bashar Al-Asad before ISIS complicated the battlefield. Now in Syria, for example, the U.S. Air Force, while striking ISIS forces, also is striking enemies of the Asad regime, such as the Al-Nusra rebels, who are linked with Al-Qaeda but have proved the most effective force against the Asad regime. One should read the serious account "My Captivity" by Theo Padnos of his two-year captivity in Syria by the Al-Nusra forces.[336] In Syria, there are other smaller units fighting the Asad regime, and these also have links to Al-Qaeda, such as the Khorasani Group, known for its expertise in bombing aircraft. One waits on tenterhooks to see if the all-Republican-controlled Congress will support former President Obama's desire for financial support in the air war and his desire to support tax and immigration reform. Meanwhile, the U.S. Air Force and its Allies often find it difficult to determine friend from foe. Until the Russian tourist aircraft was downed by ISIS, as noted above, Russian aircraft and tanks were deployed in Syria to prop up the Bashar al-Asad regime. The Americans felt themselves at a distinct disadvantage when the rockets rained down on Syria. One now wonders whether or not President Putin will further cooperate with the Western allies after the events that have wrecked havoc in Paris after the events of Charlie Hebdo and the theater killings in November of 2015. One of his own aircraft was downed by an antiaircraft unit working in the Hatay Province of Turkey. It was claimed that the Russian jet had violated Turkish airspace.

It is now clear in this study that we have come full circle with "12 Muslim Revolutions and the Struggle for Legitimacy Against the Imperial Powers." We started this study by analyzing the roots of Islamic belief in pre-Islamic Arabia, and we discovered that there were two legitimate strains: the followers of the Prophet Muhammad, SAS, and his Sunna and the Holy Quran, who came to be known as Sunnites, and the followers of the Party of Ali, through the Prophet's daughter, Fatimah, who came to be known as Shi'ites. *Today we witness the clash between two legitimate strains of Islam.* The United States, by attacking Saddam Husein in Iraq in 2003 and placing the Shi'ites in power, established a coalition of Shi'ite power with the Hezbollah in Lebanon, the 'Alawites in Syria, the Shi'ites in Iraq, and the Shi'ites in Iran. Formerly, Sunnite governments were dominant in Lebanon, Syria, and Iraq, and indeed, up to the Twentieth Century, the Sunni Ottoman Empire was dominant in the Middle East, with the exception of Iran. Herein lies the basic ideology of the Islamic State in the Levant (ISIL) or ISIS. There is a desire for the Sunnis to reestablish Sunni rule in the Middle East and a revulsion against the new Shi'ite dominance.

According to the new book by Ayaan Hirsi Ali, *Heretic: Why Islam Needs a Reformation Now*, this courageous writer asserts that there is a third way for Islam to choose, rather than Sunnites and Shi'ites killing one another: it is the choice to choose reform of certain basic texts of the Quran and the infallibility of the Prophet Muhammad, somewhat in the vein of Martin Luther, who founded Protestantism in the Sixteenth Century by revising basic concepts of Catholicism. To place this courageous lady in the minds of our readers, Ms. Ayaan Hirsi Ali made a film in the Netherlands about reforming Islam with

Theodore Van Gogh, the grandson of the Dutch painter Vincent Van Gogh, and for his trouble, he was murdered. Ayaan Hirsi Ali has written two other books, *Infidel* and *Nomad*, drawing deeply upon her personal experience with Islam as a young woman in which she describes the mutilation of Islamic girls' genitalia in the name of female circumcision and chastity. The foibles and the cautious note on the reform of Islam are found in the recent review of her latest book in an article termed "Refusing My Religion" by Susan Dominus, staff writer for the *NYT Magazine*.[337]

In the United States, foreign policy is deeply affected by the shallowness of domestic politics. Americans are left largely alone, in the absence of media personnel, to make clear the basic facts concerning their collective goals and assumptions.

1) About 50 percent of Americans are racists. They believe that the White Race is under threat of being exterminated or outvoted by other races. This factor demonstrates itself particularly in Southern States, where all manner of obstacles are placed in giving the vote to Blacks, Hispanics, and Asians and the current rise in antigovernment and Nazi-type racial organizations against Jews and anyone opposing such groups including police officers.[338]

2) Americans are only about 50 percent literate simply because Americans rely on television exclusively for their convictions on foreign affairs. This shocking fact derives from the poor quality of the public school system and the manner in which we select candidates for higher education. In both instances, we tend to skimp on funding for these systems. In many countries, school systems are tied to progressive examinations. If one passes the tests, then one advances to a higher degree program, and the state provides the funding. In our system, the wealthiest citizens gain admittance to the competitive universities. The inadequacy of the school system shows up in science and mathematics scores, where the U.S. scores, on an international basis, about twenty-first in a recent comparison.

3) In the United States, the Supreme Court, where judges are appointed to lifetime tenure, tends to follow liberal or conservative interpretations of the U.S. Constitution, regardless of the harm to ordinary voters. A recent example is the Citizens United decision that makes a mockery of financing of candidates for public office. In this decision, a corporation is counted like any ordinary citizen, and hence, a corporation or an individual can decide an election result by donating exorbitant funds to one candidate, with no record of how many funds were donated, foreign or domestic.

4) There is no universal health system for ordinary citizens in the United States, even though some of the poorest of countries try to give their citizens elemental health care. Can we imagine that once President George W. Bush, through Jerry Bremer, took over the Iraqi health system, he privatized medicines at Iraqi pharmacies? Only citizens over sixty-five years of age in the United States obtain medical assistance for 80 percent of out-of-pocket costs; otherwise, the hospital system is mandated to run Emergency-Care facilities at their own or public expense. Even there is a current threat for a Republican-dominated Congress to roll back this thin privilege for the poor and aged.

With these handicaps to good government in the United States, it is surprising that any President or Corporate Head can make thoughtful decisions. A recent case in point has been the Congressional Leaders wishing to encroach on the prerogatives of the U.S. President in working out an agreement with Iran on the extent Iran may enrich uranium for peaceful uses. This encroachment has been made the more suspect for an American foreign policy because the Israeli Prime Minister Bibi Netanyahu urged the United States to bomb the Iranian nuclear facilities and to increase financial restrictions on the Iranian economy. Do we need the Israeli government to tell us what we should do in our national interest? Shame on U.S. Congressmen and Senators for currying favors from Israel in their quest for election funds!

Addendum

January 29, 2017

At the printing of this book, President Trump has ordered a halt to refugees and immigration influx to the United States from the following Muslim-majority countries: Iran, Iraq, Libya, Somalia, Sudan, Syria and Yemen. It is my hope in writing this comprehensive work that America with new Administration and leadership will change in policy and actively become once again a force of strength, a beacon of peace and a true source of philanthropy in the Middle East as in days of the past. It is in the Middle East where I and my family were welcomed with open arms as Americans, bringing friendship and shared intellect into the universities and face-to-face in the community over lengthy dinners and in the coffee houses on the streets of Cairo and Damascus, Rabat, Istanbul and Jerusalem alike. It is my hope also that the Middle Eastern peoples and their governments as a whole, will be able to take an even stronger hold of their centuries of rich heritage and emerge into the future with great pride and new hope, and to stem the dismantling of their own rich individual heritage and societies in internal fighting at the expense of their own peoples and future.

Carl Max Kortepeter

Appendix A

Khalil Bendib

Adopted from Khalil Bendib's collection of cartoons, *Mission Accomplished* (Referencing the U.S. Invasion of Iraq): Northhampton, MA, Interlink Publishing Group, 2007, 110.

Index

to have seventy-five senators
sign a petition to lift the ban,
153
Al-Abadi, viewed as a more neutral
leader for Iraq, 251
al-'Ala' ibn-Mughith, 25
governor of Al-Andalus, 25
Al-Andalus, ix, xi, 19, 22–25,
27–28, 32–34
Al-Andalus (Islamic Spain), 22
al-ansar or the supporters, 6
Al-Bakar al-Baghdadi, the self-
appointed caliph of the ISIS
movement, 251
Alexius Comnenus of Byzantium
made a plea for military
support from Pope Urban
II, 51
Al-Faruqi claimed to be a member
of the *Al-Ahd* secret Arab
organization, 92
Alfonso VII of Castille, 32
al-Ghafiqi, 'Abd ur-Rahman ibn
'Abdullah
governor of Al-Andalus, 24
al-Hakim, Tawfiq, 116, 120
al-Hurr 'Abd ar-Rahman al-
Thaqafi, 24
Ali, son of the Prophet's uncle, Abu
Talib, 6
Ali ibn Buyah, 13
'Ali was implicated, 7
Al-Khalifah, 5
Allah, 1, 4, 19, 28
Al-Mahdi, the savior, x, 15
Al-Maliki has consistently
supported the Shi'ites in
military and intelligence

units and throughout his
government and even
encouraged goon squads
against Sunnis, 250
Al-Maliki has now been replaced by
Haider Al-Abadi, 251
Al-Ma'mun, x, 50
Almohad, 32–33
Muwahidun, 32
Almoravids, 31–32
Murabitun, 31–33
al-Mu'izz, 19–20
Al-Mulk, Nizam (vizier), 37
Al-Nusra forces, 252
Alp Arslan, 20, 37–38
the Seljuk ruler, 20
Al-Razi (865-925), the greatest of
the Muslim physicians, 51
al-Samh ibn Malik al-Thaqafi, 24
al-Shafi,' Muhammad bin al-Idris
(d. 820), 8
amir, 13–14, 25–28, 30, 32, 38,
43, 52, 189
roughly commander or governor,
26
'amir al-'umara (the commander
of the armed guard),
Muhammad ibn Ra'iq, 13
amirates, ix–xi, 13, 50, 74
in Egypt and North Africa, ix
Persian amirates, xi, 13
amirs, ix, 7, 11, 13, 19–20, 28, 30,
32–33, 38
another factor that played an
important role: where the
respective armies ended their
onslaughts, 131
Antalya, 96

Ceuta, 22, 25, 28

Chanson de Roland, 25

Charlemagne, 25

   invasion of Al-Andalus in 778, 25

Charlemagne of France, 25

Ch'in Dynasty (BC 221-207), 35

Ch'in Dynasty in Northern China,
   40

Christian, x, 4, 28–34, 39, 45, 51–
   52, 60–61, 72, 84–85, 90,
   128, 144, 150–51, 167, 210

Christians, 24, 26–27, 33, 49–50,
   52–53, 55–56, 58, 65, 85,
   151, 163–64, 166, 232–33

Churchill, Winston, 87, 98, 115,
   232

   head of the admiralty, 87

Churchill in the Commons:
   defended Palestine as a
   Jewish home, 99

city of Ejiha, 23

Clemenceau, Georges, Prime
   Minister of France, 96

Clinton, Bill, 187, 195, 200, 235,
   249

Clinton, Hillary, 235

Cohen, Stephen F.

   has written an incisive article, 249

Colonel Edward Mandell House, 95

Colonel Qassem had overthrown
   the monarchy in Iraq, 138

commercial development, 4

Coptic or Sunni, xi

Count Julian, 22

courier system (the *Yam*), 43

Cox, Sir Percy (British high
   commissioner in Iraq), 99

Crimea, 48, 74, 248–49

detached from the Russian
   Republic in 1954 by Nikita
   Khrushchev in a drunken
   dinner party, 248

Crimean War (1853 to 1855), 82,
   85

Crusade of Kings, 53

Crusade of Nicopolis of 1396, 61

Crusaders, xii, 20, 39, 50, 52–55

Cumans on the Desht-i Kipchak
   (Ukraine), 42

Curzon, Lord, 95

customary laws (*Qanun*), 11

Cyril and Methodius, 57

D

Dabashi, Hamid, 7

Da Gama, Vasco

   spice trade, 56

Dallin, 137

Dallin, Robert, 137

   any country acting in its own
   interest would become
   Communist, 137

Damascus, 10, 18, 23–25, 91–92,
   99, 108, 168, 223, 232, 250,
   257

   the seat then of Umayyad power, 23

Damietta, 53

Dar al-Harb, 3

Daruga was set up to manage
   taxation, 43

Daylam infantry, 13

Daylam in Northern Iran, 13

dervish orders (*Tariqat*), 37

details to their *wazirs* and military
   leaders, 10

devils or *shayatin*, 3

Diem, Ngo Dinh, 141

dissension between the
Merovingian court and the
dukes of Aquitaine, 24

distant provincial governors
('*amirs*), ix

divine charisma, 11

Diwans or centralized ministries, 10

Douthat, 247

Douthat, Ross
a serious critique of President
Obama's foreign policy, 247

Do we need the Israeli government
to tell us what we should do
in our national interest? 255

drastic changes were called for if the
Empire were to survive, 83

Dubs, Adolph, the ambassador, was
killed, 162

Duke Eudes of Aquitaine, 24

Dushan, Stephan (1331-1355): the
great Serbian leader, 58

E

Eastern Question, 83

Ecevit, Mustafa Bulent
invaded northern Cyprus in
1974, 143
ordered an invasion, 154

Egyptian El-Sisi government sided
with Israel in its current
attacks on the Gaza Strip, 129

Egyptian Mamluk State: Polovtsy,
Circassians, 39

Eilts, Ambassador Hermann, 145

Eilts, Hermann

a refugee from Nazi Germany,
like Kissinger, but an Arabist,
who often stood against
Kissinger, was the major
exception, 151

Elliott, William Yandell, xiii

El-Sisi criticized the U.S.
government for not
supporting "the will of the
people," 129

El-Sisi stood for the presidency and
was elected by twenty-two
million Egyptians on 26, 27,
and 28 May 2014, 129

Emanuel resigned his post and
became mayor of Chicago,
235

Emperors, Crusade of the (1189-
1192), 21

Era of the Amirates, ix, 13

Eric Holder as Attorney General,
236

Ertogrul, father of Osman, 42

etatist-populist revolution" on
Egypt and challenged, 120

Events in Afghanistan took a
turn for the worse with the
overthrow of the Afghan
monarchy in 1973 by Daoud
Khan, 161

F

Fatima, 6, 11, 15, 17, 19, 37
the only surviving daughter of the
Prophet, 6

Fatimid, x–xi, 15–20, 29, 50, 52

Fatimid caliphate, 15

Istanbul, Turkey, xiii
'istijarah, 3
Italians and Greeks, 95
'izzat al-nafs, 2

J

Ja'far Al-Askeri, 99
Ja'far al-Sadiq, 15–17
Ja'far had four sons, 15
Jahiliya Temper, 1
Jenghiz Khan, 40–42, 44, 47–48,
    132
    1227, 41, 132
    and his famous generals, Jebe and
        Subudey, 41
Jerusalem, 21, 52–53, 79, 118,
    147, 179, 197, 201, 257
Jewish residents, 23
Jews, 24, 26, 34, 52, 93–95, 99–
    101, 120, 155–58, 198, 232,
    240, 244, 248, 254
jinn, the malevolent creatures, 3
jizya on Christians and Jews, 26
Joanna, 21
Johnson, Jay, 237
Johnson basically neglected
    the Middle East while
    concentrating on Vietnam,
    142
Johnson had shared the ticket
    with Kennedy as a master of
    congressional affairs, 140
Johnson's wife, "Lady Bird," was of
    Greek origin, 142

K

Kalb tribe in Syria, 7
Kalka in 1223, 41
Karzai of Afghanistan has recently
    asked the Taliban leadership
    to take part in a national
    debate for the future of
    Afghanistan, 243
Kemal, Mustafa (Ataturk), 88, 97,
    103, 121, 231
Kennedy, John F.
    was friendly to Nasser's Pan-
        Arabism because of his
        familiarity with Irish
        nationalism, 139
Kennedy failed to understand
    the refugee problem and,
    consequently, the frustrated
    Palestinian nationalism:
    according to George
    Lenczowsky, 140
Kennedy government deeply
    involved the United States
    in Vietnam: it hastened the
    collapse of Ngo Dinh Diem,
    141
Kerry, secretary of state, Barack
    Obama, and a number
    of Western European
    governments have arrived at
    a provisional agreement with
    President Rouhani, 244
Kerry, John
    appointed to head the State
        Department, 235
Kerry and President Obama
    went out of their way in

L

the Prophet Muhammad and His
message, vii
the Prophet's family, vii
Lemnitzer, General
on the eve of a Turkish air attack
on Cyprus, 142
Lenczowski, George
has produced an important study,
*American Presidents and the
Middle East*, how successive
American presidents
overwhelmed Middle East
leaders, 133
Lenczowski shows how Israel,
though a second-class player
in the great-power games,
gradually gained a veto over
American foreign policy, 133
Lenczowski starts his analysis by
noting six basic facts of the
Middle East, 133
Lenczowski summarized the
damage to American foreign
affairs of President Johnson,
146
Lenczowski summarized the results
of U.S. policies under Nixon
and Kissinger, 152
Lew, Jack
replaced Tim Geithner as
secretary of the treasury in
2013, 236
Lew, Jack (2010-2012)
replaced Orszag as director of the
Office of Management and
Budget, 236
Lewis, Bernard, 224-225, 241
Liao Dynasty: Kara Khitai, 36

liberalism, 84–85
Lieutenant Muhammad Sharif
al-Faruqi
got through to the British lines,
92
lingua franca became Chagatay or
Northern Turkish, 44
London-Zurich Accord on Cyprus
was negotiated in 1959, 142
looting of museums described by
Secetary Rumsfeld as "Stuff
happens," 210
looting of the capital city of
Cordoba, 25
loss of life in Gaza approached
three thousand, mostly
noncombatant women,
children, and other civilians.
Israeli troop casualties
amounted to under one
hundred, 240
Luther, Martin, the assassination
of, 141

M

madrassas (Islamic prep schools), 9
Mahdi, x, 15–19, 25, 32
Mahmud of Ghazna, xi, 36
Maksoud, Clovis (a Lebanese
spokesman), 117
Malik bin Anas, 8
Maliki Mathhab, 8
Malikshah (1072-1092), 38
Malikshah (d. 1092), 20, 37
Mamluks, xii, 29, 36, 38–39,
47–48, 50, 53–56, 64–65,
67–68

the position of removing
chemical weapons from the
Syrian arsenal, 247
president's ruling to protect
immigrants from deportation
and also their dislike of the
Affordable Care Act, 237
President Truman
attempt to alleviate Arab hostility
at his second inauguration in
January 1949, 135
recognizing the state of Israel
fostered the opposite effect
among Arabs, 134
President Wilson, 95–96
Prime Minister Natanyahu and
President Obama
both stated that Israel has a right
to defend itself, 240
Princeton University, 4, 103, 138,
140, 224
Dr. Inalcik, Halil. *See* Bilkent
University
Hitti, Dr. Philip K., 138
Khalidi, Dr. Walid, 4
principal ideological forces,
nationalism and liberalism,
84
Pritsch, Erich, 7
Prophet died in AD 632, 5
Prophet governing al-Madinah, 4
Prophetic Spark, 15–16
Prophet Muhammad
introducing the Quran and his
commentaries (*the Sunna*),
vii
province of Dulkadir, 67
provincial governors, the *amirs*, 11

Putin, Vladimir
laid claim to the historic ties of
the Crimea to Russia, 248
Putin, not wishing to be portrayed
as the American *bête noire*,
has, nevertheless, equipped
the rebel forces of Eastern
Ukraine with advanced
weaponry, 252
Putin of Russia also had his own
explanations to deliver
because of the downing
of flight 17 of Malaysian
Airways, 252
Putin's aircraft proceded to attack
units that were undermining
Asad's regime, 251
Pyrenees, 24–25

Q

Qadi Nu'man, 20
qadis
 taqiyya, 34
Qalawun, 55
*Qarmatian and the Fatimid
 Revolutions*, xi
 philosophic underpinnings, x
Qarmatians, xi, 18–19, 37, 50
Quds Force, Iran's elite force, has
supplied military intelligence
and support forces, 251
Quran, vii, x, 1–3, 8, 171–72, 253
Quran, Miracle of, 3
Qurchis (Mongol, quiver bearers),
67

S

Shulman's book review, "Gaza: The Murderous Melodrama," in *The New York Review of Books*, 241

Sikkah wa Khutbah, 54

slaughter of Jews and Muslims in Jerusalem was never forgotten, 52

social structure of pre-Islamic Arabia, vii

Sokolow, Nahum, 94

Sourdel, Dominique, 79

southern Arabs, the Yamanites, 24

Soviets

forced Poland, Hungary, and East Germany into their own restrictive system, 132

Spanish, 23–24, 26–27, 31, 33–34, 73

Spanish-Roman population, 23

spread by the rich dynasty of the Saudis, 9

Stefanik, Elise, 239

Stevens, Christopher (ambassador), 235

strife between Berbers and Arabs, 24

Suevi, 23

Sufis, in the eleventh century, 8

Sultan 'Abd ul-Hamid II (1876-1909), 82, 86

Sultan Baybars (1260-1277), 55

Sultan Malikshah (d. 1092), 20

Sultan Mehmed II (1451-1481) proved to be a formidable leader, 62

Sultan Murad I (1362-1389), 60

Sultan Orhan (1326-1362)

supported John Cantecuzenos, 60

Sultan Selim I (1512-1520), 56

Summers, Larry

recently dismissed as the president of Harvard University, 236

Summers faced so much opposition, 237

Sunna (the sayings of the Prophet other than the Quran), 8

Sunni Islam, xi, 38, 52

Sunnis to reestablish Sunni rule in the Middle East and a revulsion against the new Shi'ite dominance, 253

Sunnite branch of the Muslims, 8

Sunnites, 11, 227–28, 253

Sunnites and Shi'ites

the clash between two legitimate strains of Islam, 253

Supreme Court passed the Citizens United ruling in 2011, 239

Susan Rice was appointed as national security adviser, 235

Sygnak in Kazakhstan, 44

Sykes, Percy

viewed as the mouthpiece of General Kitchener, 89

Sykes-Picot Agreement, 89–90, 95–96

Syria and Iraq are faced with the new threat from ISIS (the Islamic State of Iraq and Syria) that has been organized by Sunni tribal and straight-line forces, 250

Syrian Arabs, 25

Syrian troops, 25

About the Author

Professor Carl Max Kortepeter, "Max" to his family and friends, chose a different pathway than recommended by his undergraduate professors at Harvard University and accepted his first job out of college teaching biology to young Turks at Robert College in Istanbul, now known as Boğaziçi University. An avid traveller with a gift for foreign languages, Professor Kortepeter studied German at Harvard, Turkish while living in Istanbul, and learned Russian from a Russian priest. Later in his career, he studied Arabic with Professors Makdisi and Wickens at the Universities of Michigan and Toronto, respectively. In addition to teaching three decades at New York University, Professor Kortepeter held faculty appointments at the University of Toronto and Princeton University before his retirement in 1996. He has lectured around the world, often in his adopted languages. Speaking both Turkish and Russian, he acted as Tour Historian on a Royal Ontario Museum trip to to the Caucasus and Central Asia in 1985.

Kortepeter has written several other works as primary author, including Ottoman Imperialism During the Reformation and The Ottoman Turks: Nomad Kingdom to World Empire. With Mounir Farah and Andrea Karls, he co-wrote The Human Experience, a popular world history text. His edited works include, with Gunsel Renda, Ataturk and the Transformation of Turkish Culture; Alex Melamid's Oil and Economic Geography in the Middle East, and The Modern Middle East: Literature and Society. Dr. Kortepeter has contributed more than thirty articles to various journals in the U.S., Europe, and the Middle East, and he was a former columnist for <u>The Trenton Times</u>. Extensive travel has taken Dr. Kortepeter to every country considered part of the Modern Middle East, including many Muslim countries of North Africa. His personal experiences from these travels have given him a lifelong love of the Middle East, its cultures, and its people, which are reflected in Twelve Muslim Revolutions.

Professor Kortepeter holds a B.A. from Harvard University in American History, an M.A. in Islamic Studies from McGill University, and a Ph.D. in Middle East History from the School of Oriental and African Studies, London University.

About the Book

In <u>Twelve Muslim Revolutions</u>, Professor Kortepeter presents a broadly encompassing study of the medieval and modern history of the central lands of Islam over a period of centuries. Told in three parts: 1) Revolutions from pre-Islamic Arabia to the Ottoman Turks, 2) The imperial powers' establishing footprints in the Middle East in the eighteenth to the twentieth centuries, and 3) American presidents and their inability to fully comprehend the complexities of the Middle East since World War II. This narrative is told in a very personal manner, borne of on-the-ground experience in those lands, an essential read for anyone wishing to comprehend the story of the Middle East present, past and future. University students, scholars, and policy-makers alike will find Kortepeter's insights equally compelling.

Endnotes

1   For further elaboration of this doctrine and its relationship to Islamic, Christian, and Greek philosophy, one may consult P. M. Holt, Ann K. S. Lambton, and Bernard Lewis, editors, *The Cambridge History of Islam*, Volume 2, Cambridge University Press, 1970, 803 ff.

2   Cf. the article, N. S. Nyberg, "Al-Mu'tazila," in H. A. R Gibb and J. H. Kramers, *Shorter Encyclopedia of Islam*, E. J. Brill, Leiden, 1953, 421–427.

3   See the article, W. Ivanow, "Isma'iliya," loc. cit., 179–183.

4   Cf. George Makdisi, "The Marriage of Tughril Bey," *IJMES (International Journal of Middle East Studies) I (1 July 1970)*, 259–275; interested individuals should also consult the many studies by Clifford Edmund Bosworth of various amirates. On the Ghaznavids, one should consult his initial work, *The Ghaznavids:* Edinburgh, Edinburgh University Press, 1963, and a sequence, *The Later Ghaznavids,* by the same press in 1977.

5   Michael Marmura, Seminar Paper, University of Toronto, 1965; Hitti, Philip K. and Walid Khalidi, *The Arabs in History, rev. 10ᵗʰ paperback ed.*: Palgrave-Macmillan, NY 2010, 3–110; Fred M. Donner has recently published a study, *Muhammad and the Believers at the Origins of Islam*: Cambridge, University of Harvard Press, 2010, in which he has observed that one may assess the rapid expansion of Islam because in Medina, the message of the Prophet appealed also to Jews and probably Christians, who were counted "Believers" (*Mu'minun*), but with the regime of the Umayyads about 694, the concept of "Believers" was clearly defined as only those who followed the message of the Quran. Also in assessing studies on legitimacy in Islam, one should also note the important study of Ann K. S. Lambton, "Quis Custodiet Custodes, Some Reflections on the Persian Theory of Government," in *Studia Islamica* V (1956), 125–148.

6 In the *Southwestern Journal of Anthropology* 7/4 (Winter 1951), passim.

7 Takim, *loc.cit.*, 18.

8 Erich Pritsch, "Der Islamische Idea von dem Staat," *Die Zeitschrift für vergleichende Rechts-wissenschaft 53: Stuttgart, 1939, 1–19*. (Cf., translation of C. M. Kortepeter, McGill U. Library, Montreal, 1953.)

9 Takim, *Heirs of the Prophet*, 18–22.

10 Art. T. H. Weir, "Ibn Al-Arabi," H. A. R. Gibb and J. H. Kramers, eds., *Shorter Encyclopaedia of Islam*: Leiden, E. J. Brill, 146–147.

11 Takim, *Heirs of the Prophet*, ibid.

12 Hitti/Khalidi, *History of the Arabs*, 309.

13 Cf., for example, Hitti/Khalidi, *History of the Arabs, 129–239*. For a basic source for the early years of the 'Abbasid caliphate, one may consult *The History of al-Tabari, 'Abbasid Authority Affirmed vol. 28*, tr. and ed. by Jane Dammen McAuliffe: Albany, State University of NY, 1995 (hereafter, Al-Tabari/Dammen). To follow the ideological course of the early 'Abbasids, see N. S. Nyberg, "Al-Mu'tazila," in the *Shorter Encylopaedia of Islam*, ed. by H. A. R. Gibb and J. H. Kramers: Leiden, E. J. Brill, 1955, 421–427.

14 For details, one is urged to consult the standard work, T. W. Arnold, *The Caliphate*: Oxford, Clarendon, reprint ed., 2000; and Bernard Lewis, *The Arabs in History*:1950 or subsequent editions (London, Penguin Press), *passim*. One is also urged to consult the analysis of Pritsch, *loc. cit.* 7.

15 For an elaboration of the terms *adab* and *'ilm*, please refer to H. A. R. Gibb and J. H. Kramers, *Shorter Encyclopaedia of Islam:* Ithaca, NY, Cornell U. Press, 1953, 163–164.

16 Pritsch, *ibid*. The standard work for the 'Abbasid Revolution is M. A. Shaban, *The 'Abbasid Revolution:* NY, Cambridge U. Press, 1970, *passim*. For the definitive study of Wazirate (Vizirat), see Dominique Sourdel, *Le Vizirat 'Abbaside de 749 á 936*: Damascus, Institut français de Damas, two volumes, 1959–1960. On the Kharajites, one may consult the article "Kharidjites," eds. H. A. R. Gibb and J. H. Kramers, *Shorter Encyclopaedia of Islam*: Leiden, E. J. Brill, 1953 (G. Levi de la Vida), 246–249.

17 Shaban, *The 'Abbasid Revolution*, 3–26; see also the important essay "Abbasids," *E.I.²* I (B. Lewis), 15–23.

18 See the article "Buwayhids," *E. I.²* I, 1350–1357 (C. Cahen); for notes on the decay of Arab troops and their replacement by Turks, one may consult S. Khuda Bakhsh, *Politics in Islam*, a translation with additional notes of Von Kremer's *Die Geschichte der herrschenden Ideen des Islams*: Delhi, Idarah-i Adabiyat-i Delli, 1920, 1981, 100 ff. See also the specific

study, Matthew S. Gordon, *The Breaking of a Thousand Swords: A History of the Turkish Military of Samarra* (AH 200–275, 815–889 CE): Albany, State University of NY, 2001—not seen. Claude Cahen, in his article on the Buwayhids, uses the Minorsky expression "Persian Intermezzo" to describe the dominance of Persian amirates in the Eastern caliphate of the 'Abbasids. He also cites the Vladimir Minorsky study *La Domination des Daylamites* (Paris, 1932), where Minorsky must have used the expression.

[19] Abu Muslim, the hero of the 'Abbasids, was killed by the Caliph Al-Mansur in 755 because he wished to return to his followers in Khorasan after his pilgrimage. The caliph recognized his popularity among the *mawali*, the Shi'i and Sunni warriors in Khorasan that did not belong to Arab tribes. Cf. Shaban, loc. cit.

[20] H. F. Hamdani, *On the Genealogy of the Fatimid Caliphs* (publications of the American University in Cairo, School of Oriental Studies, occasional papers, no. 1), Cairo, Egypt, 1958. This document was written by the founder of the Fatimid caliphate, 'Abdallah al-Mahdi, and preserved by Ja'far ibn Mansur al-Yaman, an early Fatimid religious authority, in his book, *Kitab al-Fara'id wa Hudud al-Din*.

[21] I refer the careful reader to the monumental study on Al-Mahdi's complex document to Abbas Hamdani and Francois de Blois, "A Re-examination of Al-Mahdi's Letter to the Yemenites on the Genealogy of the Fatimid Caliphs," in *the Journal of the Royal Asiatic Society*, London, no. 2 (1983), 173–207 and the tables on 180 and 188.

[22] One should consult the article "Fatimids," *E. I.², 850–862* (M. Canard); see also the article "The Organizational *Structure of the Fatimid Da'wa*," by Abbas Hamdani, presented to the MESA Annual Meeting at Ohio State University (November 1970), 1–16. Dr. Abbas Hamdani has published a number of studies related to this subject. In fact, his succinct summation of Isma'ili doctrine is based on his major publication, Abbas Hamdani, *The Fatimids*: Karachi, Pakistan, Pakistan Publishing House, 1962. In his earlier study, he discusses the apparent meaning of the Quran (*al-Zahir*) and the hidden meaning (*al-Batin*) developed by the Isma'ilis. I give credit here to a brilliant student essay, about 1973, by William Bean, "The Fatimids and the Qarmatians," 1–39. Paul E. Walker, in his intricate article, "The Isma'ili Da'wa and the Fatimid Caliphate," in Carl F. Petry, ed., *The Cambridge History of Egypt:* I (640–1517) Cambridge, Cambridge University Press, 1998, 120–150, has traced the origins of the Da'wa up to its modern survival in the devotion to the Aga Khan.

It is also important to study Professor Sumaiya A. Hamdani, *Between Revolution and State: The Path to Fatimid Statehood: Qadi al-Numan and the Construction of Fatimid Legitimacy*: London, I. B. Tauris and Co. Ltd., 2006, *passim*.

23 Dr. 'Abbas Hamdani is the current doyen of Isma'ili studies. His daughter, Sumaiya, represents the third generation of Isma'ili studies in the Hamdani family. I give credit to Dr. Kamil Taha for a seminar essay he wrote detailing the Zanj Revolt, NYU, 1973, in which he used Al-Tabari (volumes 12 and 13, Beirut, 1962) and Ibn Al-'Athir (volume 7, Beirut, 1965) as his main sources. Above all, Cf. A. Hamdani, *loc. cit.*, 2.

24 A. Hamdani, *loc. cit., 3;* see also Bernard Lewis, "An Interpretation of Fatimid History," in *From Babel to Dragomans: Interpreting the Middle East:* New York, Oxford University Press, 66–78. One should also consult the details provided by W. Ivanow in the article "Isma'iliya" in H. A. R. Gibb and J. H. Kamers, in the *Shorter Encyclopaedia of Islam*, 1953, 179–183.

25 This abbreviated summary of the Qarmatians follows "Karmatis," *E. I.²*, *IV* (W. Madelung), 660–665 and Bean, *loc. cit., passim*. It is of interest to note that B. Lewis did his PhD thesis on *The Origins of Isma'ilism*: Cambridge, W. Heffer & Sons, 1940.

26 Cf. the basic source for this summary, "Fatimids," *E. I.²*, III (M. Canard), 850–862, A. Hamdani, loc. cit. and S. Hamdani, *Between Revolution and State, passim*. One is also urged to read, Paula A. Sanders "The Fatimid State," in Carl F. Petry, ed., *The Cambridge History of Egypt* I, 151–174.

27 S. Hamdani, *Revolution and State*, especially chapter 2, from Batin to Zahir, 33–53.

28 A. Hamdani, *loc. cit.*

29 See Michael Chamberlin "The Crusader Era and the Ayyubid Dynasty" in Carl F. Petry, ed., *The Cambridge History of Egypt* I, 211–241.

30 Philip K. Hitti, *History of the Arabs*: New York, rev. tenth edition, Palgrave Macmillan, 2002, 493–498; see also the recent study by Roger Collins, *The Arab Conquest of Spain, 710–797:* Oxford, UK, Blackwell, 1994 pb, *passim* (not seen).

31 Hitti, *History of the Arabs*, 498–499; see also W. Montgomery Watt and Pierre Cachia, *A History of Islamic Spain*: Edinburgh, Scotland, the University Press, pb. edition, 1977, largely follows the Hitti account, 14–16. For an important overview of Islamic Spain and the Berber dynasties, see Hugh Kennedy, professor at St. Andrews, Scotland, *Muslim Spain and*

Portugal, A Political History: Harlow, Essex, UK, Pearson Education Ltd./ Longmans pb., 1996 (not seen).

32 Ibid., 500–504; for further information, consult Watt and Cachia, *Islamic Spain*, 13–29.

33 Hitti, loc. cit., 504–507.

34 Ibid., 507–509; also the long standard, E. Levi Provencal, *Histoire de la Espagne Musulmane*: Paris, 1950, I, 121.

35 Hitti, loc. cit., 509–511.

36 Ibid., 511–516; Hitti also cites Ramon Menendez Pidal, ed., *Prima Cronica general, estoria de Espana que mando componer Alfonso el Sabio*: Madrid, 1906, I, 326.

37 Hitti, loc. cit., 516–519.

38 Ibid., 524.

39 Ibid., 525–530. See also for greater detail on cultural achievements, Watt and Cachia, *Islamic Spain*, 61–80.

40 Watt and Cachia, *Islamic Spain*, 86–91.

41 Ibid., 91–95. One must also consult the important article of Abbas Hamdani, "The Expulsion of Muslims from Spain," in *The Digest of Middle East Studies* (Milwaukee, 1992) I/13, 13–21 and the more detailed study of "An Islamic Background to the Voyages of Discovery," in Salma Khadra Jayyusi, ed., *The Legacy of Muslim Spain*: Leiden, E. J. Brill, 1992, 273–304.

42 Ibid., 100–111. For a summary of art, architecture, literature, and philosophy in the final two hundred years of Islamic Spain, one may consult Watt and Cachia, *Islamic Spain*, 112–146. For a study of the transition from Arab and Berber dominance of trade to Spanish and Jewish realignment, one must study Olivier Remie Constable's *Muslim Spain, the Commercial Realignment of the Iberian Peninsula*: Cambridge, UK, Cambridge University Press pb., 1996, especially 52–98 and 112–240.

43 Watt and Cachia, Islamic Spain, 147–154. See also C. M. Kortepeter, "History of the Arabian Horse," in Studi in Memoria di Aldo Gallotti, Instituto par L'Africa et LOriente, LXIV, Napoli, 2003, 38 pp.

44 Watt and Cachia, *Islamic Spain*, 147–154. See also C. M. Kortepeter, "History of the Arabian Horse," loc. cit.; for further reading, please consult Salma Khadra Jayyusi, ed., *The Legacy of Muslim Spain*, two volumes: Leiden, Brill, n.d.

45 Please consult "The Origins and Nature of Turkish Power," in C. M. Kortepeter, *The Ottoman Turks: Nomad Kingdom to World Empire:*

Istanbul, Isis Press, 1991, 1–40. There is also a very important study of the troubled and complex history of the breakup of the 'Abbasid Empire in Iran and the so-called Eastern Caliphate, by Amir H. Siddiqi, *Caliphate and Kingship in Medieval Islam*: Philadelphia, Porcupine Press, 1977, in which the author deals with the Mu'tazilites, the Zanj Revolt, the Rise of the Turkish Legions, the Tahirids, the Saffarids, the Buwayhids, the role of qadis, the Ghaznavids, the Seljuks, and the Khwarezmshahs, 1–114. This serious study was first published in *Islamic Culture* volumes 9–11: Hyderabad, 1935–1937.

46   C. E. Bosworth, *The Ghaznavids: Their Empire in Afghanistan and Eastern Iran*: Edinburgh, 1963, 227, 242–268.

47   Nicholas Riasanovsky, *A History of Russia*: NY, Oxford U. Press, 1977, 42–46.

48   Kortepeter, *loc. cit.*, 28–29.

49   Köprülü, "Osmanlı İmparatorluğu'nun Etnik Menşei Meseleleri," T. T. K. *Belleten* VII/28 (1943), 219–303.

50   G. Makdisi, "The Marriage of Tughril Bey," *International Journal of Middle Eastern Studies (IJMES)* I (July 1970), 259–275.

51   See, for example, the article "Kılıç Arslan II" (1156–1192), *Islam Ansiklopedisi* (hereafter, *I. A.*) VI, 688–703 (Osman Turan).

52   See the article "Kay Kavus I," *I. A.* VI, 631–642 (Osman Turan). Professor Turan refers specifically to the caliph's investiture on VI, 633. The Rum Seljuks and later the Ottomans laid claim to a new kind of legitimacy. This thesis was the main subject of Paul Wittek's important study, *The Rise of the Ottoman Empire:* London, Luzac, 1938. Cf. also, Kortepeter, "The Origins and Nature of Turkish Power," *Op. cit.,* 1–40 and Elizabeth A. Zachariadou, ed., *The Ottoman Amirate* 1300–*1389*: Heraklion, Crete University Press, 1993, *passim.*

53   For Khwarezmshah history, see C. E. Bosworth, "The Political and Dynastic History of the Iranian World (AD 1000–1217)," *The Cambridge History of Iran* V, Cambridge University Press, ed. by J. A. Boyle, 1968, 1–202; here, use of the Bosworth summary in *The Encyclopedia Irannica*, digital edition, Columbia University Press, NY, 1996. Cf. also, Ibrahim Kafesoglu, *Harezmşahlar Devleti Tarihi (485–617/1002–1229)*: Ankara, Ankara University Press, 1956. The above-noted description of early Mongol expansion follows the analysis of George Vernadsky, *The Mongols and Russia*: New Haven, Yale University Press, 1953, 27–45. One may also consult the new illustrated edition, Marco Polo, *The Travels of Marco*

Polo: New York, Sterling Publishing, general editor, Morris Rossabi, tr. by Henry Yule, rev. by Henri Cordier, 2012, especially 87–127.

54 The term *Il Khan* would mean in Turkish "provincial khan," to distinguish it from the "Great Khans."

55 Vernadsky, *The Mongols and Russia*, 46–50.

56 Vernadsky, *ibid.*, 51–58. For details of Batu and his successors, see article "Batu," *I. A.* II: Istanbul, the Turkish Ministry of Education, n.d., 251–253 (W. Barthold); for a full rundown of the Mongol/Turkish genealogy in Russia, see article "Batu'ids," *E. I.* I: Leiden, Brill, 1960, 1106–1108 (B. Spuler). On the Livonian knights, one may consult William L. Langer, compiler and editor, *An Encyclopedia of World History*, rev. ed., Houghton Mifflin, Boston, 1948, 211 ff.

57 Nicholas V. Riasanovsky, *A History of Russia*, 3rd ed.: NY, Oxford University Press, NY, 1977, 73–78.

58 Vernadsky, *The Mongols and Russia*, 208–237.

59 The name Timur or Demir is often used by Turks and Mongols to denote strength or toughness, but the simple translation is the word *iron*.

60 Vernadsky, *The Mongols and Russia*, 59–74. By way of justifying the use of Vernadsky, he happens to be the only writer in English who has combined a detailed study of the Mongol homeland to the various Mongol provinces. Many of the primary sources of Vernadsky are the well-known reports of a series of friars and priests sent by the papacy or European rulers to the Mongol governments and also Marco Polo's account. For the legitimacy of the future Mamluk Dynasty, it is interesting to note that Baybars invited the last surviving 'Abbasid, Ahmad Abu'l Qasim, to reside in Cairo as Caliph Mustansur l'Allah. He and his descendants lent legitimacy to the Mamluks, and this was sometimes claimed by the Ottomans after Sultan Selim I in 1517 occupied Cairo. Cf. William Cleveland, *A History of the Modern Middle East*: Boulder, Westview. 1994, 42.

61 Vernadsky, *The Mongols and Russia*, 74–92. Kubilay limited future succession to his own direct descendants, usually to the eldest son. For details on the radical sect of assassins, one should consult B. Lewis, *The Assassins: A Radical Sect in Islam*: London, Weidenfeld & Nicolson, 1967 or other editions. The standard account of Marco Polo is Sir Henry Yule, trans., *The Book of Ser Marco Polo, the Venetian*, rev. by H. Cordier: London, J. Murray, 1903, two volumes.

62 Vernadsky, *The Mongols and Russia*, 82, 163–208. In the future Russian State, it is important to remember that Moscow's claim to be the "Third

Rome," after Rome and Constantinople, derives from Ivan III's marriage to Sophia, the niece of the last emperor of Constantinople, Emperor Constantine XIII, who was defeated by the Ottomans in Costantinople in 1453.

63 One may consult for details C. M. Kortepeter, *Ottoman Imperialism During the Reformation*: NY, NY University Press, 1972, 26–49 and Kortepeter, *The Ottoman Turks, Nomad Kingdom to World Empire*, 89–103. See Vernadsky, *The Mongols and Russia*, 333–376, for an important summary of "The Mongol Impact on Russia." The Golden Horde had a profound impact on Russia that lasted almost to the twentieth century. See also Alan Fisher, *The Russian Annexation of the Crimea, 1772–1783*: NY, Cambridge U. Press, 1970, *passim*.

64 Rene Grousset, *L'Empire des Steppes*: Paris, Payot, 1952, *passim* and Dorothea Krawulsky, *The Mongol Il Khans and their Vizier Raschid ud-Din*: Berlin, Peter Lang, 2010—not seen.

65 Marshall G. S. Hodgson, *The Venture of Islam, Vol. 2, The Expansion of Islam in the Middle Periods*: Chicago, the Uiversity of Chicago Press, 1974, 386–391.

66 See the recent study on Islamic medicine of Peter E. Pormann and E. Suvage Smith, *Medieval Islamic Medicine*: Washington, DC, Georgetown University Press, 2007, passim and also Hitti, loc. cit., 363–428.

67 Hitti, 429–460.

68 Ibid.

69 For a detailed background analysis to the rise of the Mamluks, one must consult the important study of Abdul-Aziz Khowaiter, *Baibars the First, His Endeavors and Achievements*: London, the Green Mountain Press, 1978, 1–23; Hitti, op. cit., 644–655.

70 Khowaiter, ibid.; Hitti, op. cit., 671–677.

71 Vernadsky, *Mongols and Russia*, 165.

72 Khowaiter, op. cit., 24–49; Hitti, op. cit. 674–676. One may also consult the detailed articles of Linda S. Northrup, "The Bahri Mamluk Sutanate, 1250–1390," and Jean-Claude Garcin, "The Regime of the Circassian Mamluks," in Carl F. Petry, ed., *The Cambridge History of Egypt* I, 242–289 and 290–317, respectively. The V&R Unipress has published a number of studies on Mamluk History, edited by Stephan Conermann. One such study is particularly worthy of mention, Annemarie Schimmel, *History and Society during the Mamluk Period (1250–1517)*: NY, reissue, 2014. Annemarie was the doyen of medieval Islamic history.

73 For a thorough rundown of the sources for the Mamluks and other dynasties of premodern period, see Khowaiter, *Baibars The First*, 144–190; Hitti, op. cit., 677–682 and 694–705.

74 L. S. Stavrianos, *The Balkans Since 1453*: New York, Holt, Rinehart and Winston, 1958, 24–32.

75 Stavrianos, ibid., 32.

76 Halil Inalcik, *The Ottoman Empire 1300–1600*: New York, 1973, 14–16.

77 These notes essentially follow the closely argued text of Halil Inalcik, *The Ottoman Empire: The Classical Age, 1300–1600*: New York, Weidenfeld & Nicholson, 1973, reprinted by Orpheus Publishing, New Rochelle, 1989, 3–16; see also Wittek, *op. cit., passim,* where he elaborates the Gazi theory of the Ottoman frontier, and also Kortepeter, "The Origins and Nature of Turkish Power," in *The Ottoman Turks: Nomad Kingdom to World Empire*, 1–39; one should also consult Speros Vryonis Jr., *The Decline of Medieval Hellenism in Asia Minor: The Eleventh to the Fifteenth Century*: Los Angeles, University of California Press, 1972, *passim,* and Cemal Kafadar, *Between Two Worlds: The Construction of the Ottoman State*: Cambridge, Harvard University Press, 1996, a review of previous studies, including my "Origins and Nature of Turkish Power," *loc. cit.,* 1–39.

78 Inalcik, *The Ottoman Empire*, 17–26 and Wm. Langer, *Encyclopedia of World History, passim,* for precise dates. In the Islamic system of the Ottomans, the millet system left governance of community affairs of non-Muslim religions to their respective religious and community hierarchies.

79 Inalcik, ibid., and Langer, *op. cit.*, 327.

80 Inalcik, ibid., 62 and 144. See also the details of Isma'il Hami Danishmend, *Izahli Osmanli Tarihi Kronolojisi*, I, 285–286.

81 Inalcik, *The Ottoman Empire*, 27–30; the standard work on this era was published by Franz Babinger in German, *Mehmed der Eroberer und Seine Zeit* (Munich, 1953): the work was translated in 1978 for Princeton University Press, *Mehmed the Conqueror and His Time*, paperback ed., 1992.

82 Inalcik, *The Ottoman Empire*, 30–34 and Langer, *op. cit.*, 330 and 526. See also for details V. J. Parry, "Bayazid II," *E. I.²* 1119–1121, also his bibliography, and Sidney N. Fisher, *The Foreign Relations of Turkey, 1481–1512*: Urbana, Ill. Studies in the Social Sciences xxx/1, 1948, *passim.*

83 Inalcik, ibid.; V. J. Parry, loc. cit.; and S. N. Fisher, ibid.

84 Inalcik, ibid., and David Blow, *Shah Abbas: The Ruthless King Who Became*

an *Iranian Legend:* London, I. B. Tauris, 2009, 1–238. R. M. Savory, *Iran Under the Safavids*, Cambrige U. Press, 1980, 50–76.

85 R. M. Savory, "A Curious Episode of Safavid History," in C. E. Bosworth, ed., *Iran and Islam, in Memory of the Late Vladimir Minorsky*: Edinburgh, Scotland, Edinburgh University Press, 1971, 461–474.

86 Inalcik, *ibid.*, and David Blow, ibid. Perhaps the most consulted study of the Safavids is by R. M. Savory, *Iran Under the Safavids*: Cambridge, Cambridge University Press, 1980 and Savory's brilliant translation of Eskandar Beg Monshi, *The History of Shah 'Abbas the Great*, two volumes, Persian Heritage Series No. 28, Westview Press, Boulder, 1978. See also C. M. Kortepeter, "Complex Goals of the Ottomans, Persians and Muscovites in the Caucasus, 1578–1640," in Colin P. Mitchell, ed., *New Perspectives on Safavid Iran*: London & NY, Routledge, 2011, 59–83.

87 Inalcik, ibid., and for a response of the Ottomans to the Portuguese threat, see A. Vambery, ed. and tr., *The Travels and Adventures of the Turkish Admiral Sidi Ali Reis in India, Afghanistan, Central Asia and Persia during the Years 1553–1556*: London, 1899, passim and Mesut Uyar and Edward J. Erickson, *A Military History of the Ottoman Empire*: Santa Barbara, ABC-Clio, 2009—not seen.

88 Inalcik, *The Ottoman Empire: The Classical Age, 1300–1600*, 35–39 and C. M. Kortepeter, *Ottoman Imperialism during the Reformation: Europe and the Caucasus*: New York, NY U. Press, 1972, 1–2, 123–136.

89 See Kortepeter, *Ottoman Imperialism*, 39–43 and 123–160.

90 Inalcik, *ibid.*, and Kortepeter, *ibid.*

91 Kortepeter, *Ottoman Imperialism*, 1–49.

92 *Ibid.*, Halil Inalcik, "Osmanli-Rus Rekabetinin Menşei ve Don-Volga Kanal Teşebbüsü (1569)," *Belleten* XII/46 (Ankara, 1948), 349–402; C. M. Kortepeter, "Complex Goals of the Ottomans, Persians and Muscovites in the Caucasus, 1578–1640," in Colin P. Mitchell, ed., *New Perspectives on Safavid Iran* (a Festschrift in honor of Professor Roger Savory): London and New York, Routledge, 2011, 59–83.

93 Inalcik, *loc. cit.*, 41–52; Kortepeter, *ibid.*

94 Inalcik, *History of the Ottoman Empire*, 111–118 ; the first serious Ottoman population studies were done by Fernand Braudel, *La Mediterranée et le monde méditerranéan à l'époque de Philippe II*, Paris, two volumes, 2nd ed., 1967, *passim*; for a short guide to Ottoman institutions of government, see C. M. Kortepeter, "The Islamic-Ottoman Social Structure: The Quest for a Model of Ottoman History," in C. M. Kortepeter, *The Ottoman Turks:*

Nomad Kindom to World Empire, 1991, 41–64.

95   Gerber refers to the study by Theda Skocpol, *States and Revolutions: A Comparative Analysis of France, Russia and China*: Cambridge, Cambridge University Press, 1979, passim; and Barrington Moore, *Constitutions of the Modern World*: Boston, The Beacon Press, 1966, passim; we here also refer to Haim Gerber's study, *Social Origins of the Modern Middle East*: London, L. Riennar, 1987, paper ed., 1–10.

96   Gerber, *Social Origins*, 10–15.

97   Gerber, *Social Origins*, 15–45.

98   Gerber, *Social Origins, 45 ff.* The modernization of the military is discussed in the article, C. M. Kortepeter, "Did the Turks Attain Enlightenment Through Defeat in Warfare?" in *Balkan Studies* 40/1: Thessaloniki, 1999, 129–171; see also Turkish Ministry of Education, *Tanzimat* I: Istanbul, 1940, pubished to commemorate one hundred years after the proclamation by Sultan Abd al-Majid in 1839. This volume was compiled by Turkey's leading scholars at the beginning of World War II. To review the ideological advances in Ottoman and Turkish society, one could not do better than reread Niyazi Berkes, *The Development of Secularism in Turkey*: Montreal, McGill University Press, 1964, or for a fresh look at Turkish history, see Eric J. Zürcher, *Turkey: A Modern History*: London & NY, I. B. Tauris, 3rd ed., 2004, *passim*. For a modern discussion of the current Salafi movement in Egypt, see Wendell Steavenson's "Radicals Rising," *The New Yorker* (April 30, 2012), 24–30.

99   Immanuel Wallerstein, *World Systems Analysis*: Durham, Duke University Press, pb., 2004, 42–60, and see also Bruce McGowan, in the collection of studies, in S. Faroqui, B. McGowan, D. Quataert, and S. Pamuk, *An Economic and Social History of the Ottoman Empire* II, Cambridge University Press, pb., 1997, 639–758.

100 For details of the pilgrimage, one may consult C. M. Kortepeter, "A Source for the History of Ottoman-Hijaz Relations" in A. Ansari, ed., *Sources for the History of Arabia* II (Al-Riyadh, 1979), more readily accessible in C. M. Kortepeter, *The Ottoman Turks: Nomad Kingdom to World Empire*: Istanbul, Isis Press, 1991, 173–188. As the companion volume to Inalcik's *The Ottoman Empire: The Classical Age 1300–1600*, see, under a new title, S. Faroqui, B. McGowan, D. Quataert, and Ş. Pamuk, loc. cit. For Faroqui's comments on legitimacy, see pages 609–622.

101 Gerber, *Social Origins*, 48–80.

102 Bruce McGowan, "The Age of the Ayans, 1699–1812," in Faroqui,

McGowan, Quataert, and Pamuk, *An Economic and Social History of the Ottoman Empire* II, 639–758; on the question of the modernization of the Ottoman Military, see C. M. Kortepeter's "Did the Ottomans Attain Enlightenment Through Defeat in Warfare?" *Balkan Studies* 40/1, Thessalonica, 1999, 129–171. See also Virginia Aksan's *Ottoman Wars: An Empire Besieged, 1700–1870*: Harlow, United Kingdom, Edinburgh Gate, 2007, especially 306–449. Article "Palmerston," Hans-Werner Wittenberg, ed., *Meyer's Handbuch der Geschichte* I, Mannheim, 1968, 498–499. Concerning the creation of privileges for Ottoman merchants allied with foreign commercial houses, see Halil Inalcik, "Imtiyazat," in *E. I.²*, III, 1178b ff.

[103] See Donald Quataert for details of this era, "The Age of Reforms 1812–1914," in *An Economic and Social History of the Ottoman Empire* II, 759–943; see also C. M. Kortepeter, "Kemal Atatürk and the Ottoman Tradition of Leadership and Reform," in Kortepeter's *The Ottoman Turks: Nomad Kingdom to World Empire*, 305–320 and also M. Şükrü Hanioğlu, *A Brief History of the late Ottoman Empire*: Princeton, Princeton University Press, 2008, *passim*.

[104] One may gain insight into the types of reform instituted in the late Ottoman Empire by referring to the summary "Kemal Ataturk and the Ottoman Tradition of Leadership and Reform," in C. M. Kortepeter, *The Ottoman Turks: Nomad Kingdom to World Empire* (Istanbul, Isis Press, 1991), 305–320. Also, *loc. cit.*, "Did the Ottomans Attain Enlightenment Through Defeat in Battle?"

[105] See Robin Bruce Lockhart's *Reilly: Ace of Spies*: New York, 1984, *passim* and also Andrew Cook, *Ace of Spies: The True Story of Sidney Reilly*: Gloucestershire, UK, the History Press, rev. ed., 2004, Preface and *passim*. For a serious study of the "Great Game," one should consult Peter Hopkirk's *The Great Game: The Struggle for Empire in Central Asia*: New York, Kodansha America Inc., pb., 1994, *passim*.

[106] For details of the Crimean War, see William Yale's *The Near East: A Modern History* (Ann Arbor, University of Michigan Press, 1958, 73–79, and for a fuller treatment of the "Great Game," see David Fromkin's *A Peace to End All Peace* (NY, Avon-Hearst, 1989), 26–32, discussing Palmerston, Von Moltke, Commodore David Porter. For a recent biography of Viscount Palmerston, see Paul R Ziegler's *Palmerston*: London, Palgrave Macmillan, 2003 (not seen).

[107] See Kortepeter, *loc. cit.*, 261–267 and 247–260, and Fromkin, *Peace*, 28

and 75, wherin Mark Sykes warns Parliament in 1914: "The disappearance of the Ottoman Empire will be the first step in the disappearance of our own." Maps of the Ottoman Empire and of the modern Middle East will aid this analysis. Cf. also, Orhan Kurmush, *Emperyalizmin Turkiye'ye Girishi:* Ankara, Sevinch Matbaasi, 1982, pb., *passim.*

[108] No one has mastered the detail of World War I peace settlements with such clarity as David Fromkin's *A Peace to End All Peace*, 137–140.

[109] Fromkin, *Peace,* 79–87.

[110] Fromkin, ibid., 173–181.

[111] Ibid., see also Ottoman's plans to maintain Arab loyalties by supporting the Al-Rashid family; see "The Rise of King 'Abd al-'Aziz ibn Saud" in Kortepeter's *The Ottoman Turks*, 286–290.

[112] Fromkin, *Peace,* 181–187. See also "Ottoman Military Reform," in Kortepeter's *The Ottoman Turks*, 256–260.

[113] One should consult Melvin I. Urofsky's *Louis D. Brandeis:* NY, Pantheon / Random House, pb., 2009, *passim*, to discover Brandeis's contribution to law studies and the Supreme Court, apart from his well-known Zionist activities and his advice on Jewish affairs to President Woodrow Wilson.

[114] Lloyd George, by origin Welch, but a prominent British lawyer, became minister of munitions under Asquith, later minister of war when Kitchener died, and replaced Asquith as prime minister in 1916. He held strong beliefs that the Middle East should remain British, talked Clemenceau, French Prime Minister, out of French claims to Palestine at Versailles dating from the Sykes-Picot Agreement but acquiesced in a French Syria. See Fromkin, 270–283 and 629–630 for further details.

[115] Fromkin, *Peace,* 389–394.

[116] On the Greek campaign and its aftermath, ibid., 540–557. For a dramatic end to Izmir as a famous international city, see Giles Milton's *Paradise Lost: Smyrna, 1922:* New York, Basic Books pb., 2008, 3–39 and *passim.*

[117] Yale, *The NearEast*, 262–270; Fromkin, *Peace,* 521–526.

[118] Fromkin, ibid., 523, cites Kennith W. Stein's *The Land Question in Palestine, 1917–1939* (Chapel Hill, University of North Carolina, 1984), 64, noting as much as one quarter of the Palestinian leadership sold lands to Zionists.

[119] Ibid.

[120] Yale, *loc. cit.*, 384–394. Yale points out that the high concentration of Jewish voters in eleven major U.S. cities became important factors in American elections and in fund-raising that, in turn, influenced American

attitudes toward Jewish national aspirations in Palestine.

121 Ibid., 394–397. See also the study by Taysir Jbara, *Palestinian Leader, Hajj Amin al-Husayni, Mufti of Jerusalem*: Princeton, the Kingston Press, 1985, *passim;* and also on the same subject, Philip Mattar, *The Mufti of Jerusalem, Al-Hajj Amin al-Husayni, and the Palestinian National Movement*: New York, Columbia University Press, 1992, *passim.*

122 Fromkin, *Peace*, 499–517.

123 See Manfred Halpern, *The Politics of Social Change in the Middle East and North Africa*: Princeton, Princeton University Press, 1963, *passim;* another important study of modern Arab politics is Michael C. Hudson's *Arab Politics: The Search for Legitimacy*: New Haven and London, Yale University Press, 1977. This study deals specifically with problems of social change in modern Arab countries and consequently does not have the broad theoretical sweep of the Halpern study. It does, however, address the various theories of legitimacy of such theorists as Max Weber, David Easton, Ted Gurr and Robert MacIver, Dankwart Rustow and Karl Deutsch, Hisham Sharabi, Clifford Geertz, and Ilya Harik, among others, 1–30. Paul Kennedy, in his monumental study, *The Rise and Fall of the Great Powers: Economic Change and Military Conflict from 1500 to 2000*: NY, Random House, 1987, passim, in some respects, covers all bases into modern times and shows how reluctant the great powers were to give up their controls after 1945.

124 Halpern, *Politics of Social Change*, 51–58; and Roger Le Tourneau, "Le Développement d'une Classe Moyenne en Afrique du Nord," in *Development of a Middle Class in Tropical and Subtropical Countries*, Record of the XXIX session held in London, 1955, Brussels, International Institute of Differing Civilizations, 1956, 106–110.

125 Halpern, *Politics of Social Change*, 58–60.

126 Halpern, *Politics of Social Change*, 61–65; and also, Reza Arasteh, *Education and Social Awakening in Iran*, 1850–1960: Leiden, Brill, 1962, passim.

127 Halpern, ibid.

128 Halpern, *The Politics of Social Change*, 65–78.

129 Shortly after Qasim threatened Kuwait, the British landed troops in Kuwait in April 1961, and they only left in October. The United States, when Saddam Hussein threatened Kuwait in 1990, we waited until he invaded.

130 Thus, it is likely that MI6 and the CIA had a hand in Qasim's removal. See Stephen Dorril's *MI6: Inside the Covert World of Her Majesty's Secret*

Intelligence Service: New York, the Free Press, 2000, 670–676. For details of the Qasim government, it is important to consult Marion Farouk-Sluglett and Peter Sluglett's *Iraq since 1958: From Revolution to Dictatorship:* London, I. B. Tauris & Co. Ltd., 1990, 47–93, and Samira Haj's *The Making of Iraq, 1900–1963:* Albany, State University of New York, 1997, 111–150.

[131] Miles Copeland, *The Game of Nations*: New York, Simon and Schuster, 1969, *passim.*

[132] Donald Wilbur, *Adventures in the Middle East, Excursions and Incursions*: Princeton, Darwin Press, 1986, 187–195.

[133] For details of the actual planning and overthrow of King Farouk, one should consult Eliezer Be'eri's *Army Officers in Arab Politics and Society*, NY, Praeger, 1970, 76–129.

[134] Copeland, loc. cit.

[135] Copeland, ibid. See also footnote 136, Robert Dallek's note of the high dam in the U.S. Congress. For what really happened behind the scenes, we must rely on Mohamed H. Heikal, the confidant of Nasser and the head of the leading newspaper, *Al-Ahram*. Please consult Heikal's *The Cairo Documents*: NY, Doubleday Press, 1973, 5–69. He was dimissed by President Sadat when Heikal objected to relying too much on Americans.

[136] "Miles Copeland," Wikipedia and general background supplied by Copeland.

[137] Stephen Green, *Taking Sides: America's Secret Relations with a Militant Israel:* NY, William Morrow and Company, 1984, 94–122.

[138] Copeland, *The Game*, 19–33.

[139] Ibid., 34–35. In dealing with the problem of recruitment for a number of Arabic-speaking posts that the United States inherited from the former colonial powers, it is important to consult the study by Robert D. Kaplan, *The Arabists: The Romance of an American Elite:* New York, the Free Press / Macmillan, 1993, wherein the author indicates that the modern Arabists derived from the nineteenth-century missionaries who tended to center on the American University of Beirut and the State Department Center for the teaching of Arabic in Beirut.

[140] Copeland, *The Game*, 76–88.

[141] Ibid., 91–108.

[142] Copeland, *The Game*, 133–139. Nasser's book was printed in DC by the Washington Affairs Press, 1955.

[143] Ibid., 143–148.

144 Copeland, *The Game*, 132–169, 246–247. One should also consult Robert Dallek's *The American Style of Foreign Policy*: NY, Alfred Knopf, 1983, 192–205, for insight into the Eisenhower-Dulles refusal to support the high dam.

145 Heikal, 80–85.

146 Heikal, xvii–xxvi.

147 Copeland, loc. cit., 170–206.

148 Michael C. Hudson, *ARAB POLITICS: The Search for Legitimacy:* New Haven, Yale University Press, 1977, 1–30.

149 Hudson, ibid.

150 Vatikiotis, London, Croom Helm Ltd., 1978.

151 'Abd al-Fath, *L'Affair Nasser*, Paris, Hachette, 1962, 239 ff.

152 Vatikiotis, loc. cit., 225–228.

153 Ibid., 234–344.

154 Ibid., 256–260.

155 Ibid., 325–331.

156 Boulder and London, updated pb. edition (hardcover originally Cambridge U. Press), Lynne Rienner Publishers, 1988.

157 Hinnebusch, *Sadat*, 1.

158 Op. cit., 3–4. Later Hinnebusch notes, "The private sector retained a role in the economy, but high tax rates, bureaucratic red tape and the anti-capitalist climate of the sixties discouraged productive investment; although the private sector still controlled half of the GNP, it accounted for only a tenth of total investment" (p. 25).

159 Hinnebusch, 5–6. For a detailed British view of events in the Middle East during and after the era of Nasser, please consult Stephen Dorril's *MI6: Inside the Covert World of Her Majesty's Secret Intelligence Service:* New York, the Free Press, Simon & Schuster, 2000, "The Macmillan Doctrine," 652–676.

160 Hinnebusch, 35–37. See also Stephen Budiansky's *Air Power:* New York, Viking Penguin, 2004, 402–405, to learn technogical advances in aircraft and air warfare from 1967 to 1977.

161 James Surowiecki, in *The New Yorker*, March 7, 2011, has written a very important article, "The Tyrant Tax," in which he advocates free market economies for the Middle East because regimes want to stay in power and do so by keeping at least 30 percent of their citizens on government payrolls and subsidizes the entire population with important food subsidies. But young entrepreneurs receive no support from the

government or loans from banks.

162 Hinnebusch, 40–42.

163 Hinnebusch, 43–45.

164 David Rothkopf, *Running the World: The Inside Story of the National Security Council and the Architects of American Power*. NY, Public Affairs of the Perseus Group, pb. ed., 2005, 115–147.

165 Lenczowski, 126–134.

166 Hinnebusch, 46–48. For a full account of Max Weber's views on "Charisma and Its Transformation," please consult Max Weber's *Economy and Society*: ed. by G. Roth and C. Wittich, NY, Bedminster Press, 1968, 1111–1157.

167 Hinnebusch, 60–62, 97.

168 Hinnebusch, 297–298. See also Judith Kohn's well-researched paper, 1–35.

169 "Anwar Sadat," *Wikipedia*, quoting Lawrence Wright, *The Looming Tower: Al-Qaeda and the Road to 9/11*, New York, Alfred Knopf, 2006, passim.

170 Andrew Heiss, "The Failed Management of a Dying Regime," *Journal of Third World Studies*, XXIX/1 (Spring 2012), 159–174.

171 Carrie R. Wickham, *The Muslim Brotherhood: Evolution of an Islamic Movement*, Princeton, Princeton University Press, 2013. Her article appeared in the *NYT* on 28 July 2013.

172 All the above details on the rise of General El-Sisi to the presidency of Egypt depends on an excellent summary available in *Wikipedia*, 1–22.

173 See Oded Yinon's "A Strategy for Israel in the 1980s," appearing in Hebrew in KIVUNIM 14 (Winter 5742), Tel Aviv (February 1982), under the auspices of the Department of Publicity, World Zionist Org. (translated by Israel Shahak [NY, 1983], 16 pp.).

174 An enlightened discussion of Truman and the Korean War, see Robert Dallek's *The American Style of Foreign Policy*: New York, Borzoi/Alfred Knoff Inc., 1983, 180–186.

175 Ibid.

176 Lenczowski, *The American Presidents*, 7.

177 Ibid., 13.

178 Ibid., 21.

179 Henry Hazlitt, *The Illusion of Point 4*: New York, Irvington-on-Hudson, 1950, *passim.*

180 Nasser's book went through a number of editions such as the one by Public Affairs Press, Washington, DC, 1955, with an introduction by Dorothy Thompson. See also footnote 164 and the book by Robert Dreyfuss.

181 James A. Bill, *The Eagle and the Lion: The Tragedy of American-Iranian Relations:* New Haven, Yale University Press, pb. ed., 1988, 51–97.

182 Bill, *The Eagle and the Lion,* ibid., especially 72–77.

183 For further details, consult Dallek, *American Style of Foreign Policy,* 102–118.

184 Lenczowski, 31–64. On the support for the Muslim Brotherhood, see Robert Dreyfuss's *Devil's Game: How the U.S. Helped Unleash Fundamentalist Islam:* New York, Henry Holt and Co., 2005, especially chapter 4, "The War against Nasser and Mossadegh," 94–138. Also Donald N. Wilber, Reoperation Ajax, *Adventures in the Middle East: Excursions and Incursions:* Princeton, Darwin Press, 1986, 18-19,53.

185 For details, see Ivo H. Daalder and I. M. Destler's *In the Shadow of the Oval Office*: New York, Simon & Schuster, 2009, 34–38.

186 Lenczowski, 67–78. See also John Badeau's *The American Approach to the Arab World:* NY Harper, 1968, and Badeau's memoir, *The Middle East Remembered*: Washington, DC, the Middle East Institute, 1983. See Jacob Abadi's serious study of *Britain's Withdrawal from the Middle East, 1947–1971: The Economic and Strategic Imperatives*: Princeton, the Kingston Press, 1983, *passim,* and also the important but outdated study, Sir Knox Helm and the Chatham House Study Group, Royal Institute of International Affairs, *British Interests in the Mediterranean and Middle East*: London and New York, Oxford University Press, 1958, especially 101–123. Also worth consulting is Max Beloff's *The Future of British Foreign Policy:* New York, Taplinger, 1969, especially the "Retreat from Empire," 1–23.

187 Lenczowski, 79–89; Jesse Ferris, *Nasser's Gamble*: Princeton, NJ, Princeton University Press, Jan., 2013, *passim.*

188 Melissa Harris-Perry, "The Civil Rights Legislation of President Johnson," discussed on 23 November 2013 on MSNBC.

189 Lenczowski, *American Presidents*, 90–92.

190 Daalder and Destler, *In the Shadow,* 43–45; to gain insight into George Ball's warning that Vietnam was a war that we could not win and eventually the American public would not support, see Rothkopf's *Running the World*, 105–107.

191 Lenczowski, *American Presidents*, 92–104. Prime Minister Ecevit was also known as a writer. For example, After his forces invaded Cyprus, he wrote a book on foreign policy, *Dish politikasi*: Ankara, 1975 (not seen).

192 Ibid., 105; see Beshloss's *Reaching For Glory: Lyndon Johnson's Secret White*

House Tapes, 1964–1965, New York, Simon & Schuster, 2001, 188–189.

193 Robert St. John, *EBAN*, Garden City, NY, Doubleday & Company Inc., 1972, 400–427.

194 St. John, *Eban*, 428–429.

195 St. John, *Eban*, 430–449, and Kaplan, *The Arabists*, 143.

196 James M.Ennes, *Assault on the Liberty*: NY, Random House, 1979, *passim;* Lenczowski, ibid.; Robert A. Caro, *The Years of Lyndon Johnson: The Passage of Power*, New York, Alfred A. Knopf / Random House, 2012, *passim.*

197 James Bamford, *A Body of Secrets*: NY, Anchor Books, 2002, 201–237.

198 It is important to consult the new findings of Baylis Thomas's *The Dark Side of Zionism*: Lanham, MD, and Plymouth, UK, Rowman and Littlefield, pb. ed., 2011, 57–79; also William Quandt, in his *Peace Process . . . since 1967*: Berkeley and LA, University of Ca. Press, pb., 1993, 49–62, excuses President Johnson's handling of the crisis, in spite of the Israeli attack on the USS *Liberty*, not putting ships in the Straits of Tiran, the CIA assurance of Israeli victory, military supplies to Israel in spite of the weapons ban, Zionist decision-makers, etc. One should also consult the more foregiving account of President Johnson and the Six-Day War in Robert Dallek's *FLAWED GIANT: Lyndon Johnson and His Times, 1961–1973*, NY, Oxford U. Press, 1968, 425–432.

199 On this sensitive subject, see Robert Parry's "Getting Rid of 'Anti-Israeli' Presidents," *Washington Report on Middle East Affairs*, vol. XXXI/2, "Other Voices," 8–10. Please consult also the Oliver Stone Film, *JFK*, for the many unanswered questions about the assassination of President Kennedy, Warner Brothers Production, 1991. Finally, one should consult Victor Ostrovsky and Claire Hoy, *By Way of Deception: The Making and Unmaking of a Mossad Officer*, New York, St. Martin's Press, pb., 1990, 141–143. See also the article by William Boardman, "Dead Kennedys," in *Reader Supported News* of 28 May 2013, 1–4, which implicates President Johnson in the assassination of President Kennedy. On this topic, Phillip F. Nelson has written a book, *LBJ: The Mastermind of the JFK Assassination*, NY, Skyhorse Publishing, pb., 2010, and Cf. also, Mark North, *Betrayal in Dallas: LBJ, the Pearl Street Mafia and the Murder of President Kennedy*, NY, Skyhorse Publishing, hc., 2013 (not seen).

200 Lenczowski, 112–125.

201 Ibid.; a deeper analysis of economic revolutions in the key countries of Egypt, Syria, and Iraq is dealt with in the important article of Roger

Owen of Oxford University, "The Economic Aspects of Revolution in the Middle East," in P. J. Vatakiotis, ed., *Revolution in the Middle East and Other Case Studies:* Totowa, New Jersey, Rowman and Littlefield/George Allen & Unwin Ltd., 1972, 43–64.

[202] Robert Dallek, *Nixon and Kissinger: Partners in Power*, New York, Harper Collins Publishers, 2007 pb., 327, 572–623, *passim.*

[203] Lenczowski, 126–135. For details of early negotiations, see Henry Kissinger's *White House Years*: Boston & Toronto, Little Brown and Company, 1979, 341–379.

[204] Rothkopf, 147–156. Concerning Kissinger's early attitude toward Sadat, see Henry Kissinger's *White House Years*, 1276–1300. It is interesting also to review why the Israeli Defense Force was caught with its pants down with Sadat's attack. Read the account of Avi Shlaim's *Israel and Palestine*: London, Verso / New Left Books, 2009, 107 ff; Bill Quandt, on the National Security Council during the Nixon and Carter administrations, notes in his book, *Peace Process*, the neglect of Nixon and Kissinger of the period 1970 to 1973 and Sadat's interest in peace,146–147, the war on Israel, 148–182, and the ensuing diplomacy, 183–220. It is also interesting to note the neglect of the possibility of an oil boycott.

[205] Rothkopf, ibid.; Lenczowski, 128 ff. Personal interview of the author with George S. Brown, chief of staff, in the Pentagon, in 1974.

[206] Robert Kaplan, *The Arabists: The Romance of an American Elite*, New York, the Free Press / MacMillan Inc., 1993, *passim.* In the Middle East, Kissinger and Nixon believed that the Soviet Union had more power over Arab countries than actually existed according to Dallek, *The American Style of Foreign Policy*, 281. This is consistent with Dallek's critique that the U.S. government always ignored the fact that Asian and African states often acted in keeping with their own interests and were not always governed by wishes of the great powers.

[207] Lenczowski, 135 ff., 149; David Gergen, *Eyewitness to Power*(N.Y., Simon & Schuster, 2000, 107-149) has stated that the presidency of Gerald Ford was the most principled.

[208] See particularly William Quandt's *Peace Process*, 223–251, for the intricacies of these negotiations.

[209] Lenczowski, ibid., and Rothkopf, 162–165. The Carter campaign is here sharply described as running against the "Kissinger Presidency of Nixon and Ford." See also Quandt, loc. cit., 255–283.

[210] For details of Camp David Agreements and other notes, see Lenczowski,

157–184, and Quandt, *Peace Process*, 255–285.

211 Quandt, ibid., 286–331.

212 See Charles Kurzman's *The Unthinkable Revolution in Iran:* Cambridge, MA, Harvard University Press, 2004, especially 163–172. It is also important to discover how entire families inherited the ayatollah mantel in Iraq and Iran, usually with no knowledge or control from the Ottoman and Persian governments. There was also a hierarchy of madrassas in Iran and Iraq. In the twentieth century, the madrassas of Qum seem to have dominated the madrassas of Najaf. See the study of Yitzhak Nakash, *The Shi'is of Iraq:* Princeton, Princeton University Press pb., 2nd ed., 2003, especially "The Sh'i Madrasa in Iraq," 238–268.

213 Lenczowski, 184–199. Ross Perot's company, Economic Data Systems, was working on a major contract in Iran when the revolution took place. Some of his employees were jailed, and to spring them from jail and bring them out of Iran, the company had to wait until the revolution hit the streets of Teheran. These events are detailed in a book by Ken Follett, *On Wings of Eagles:* New York, New American Library, 1984. For the economic details of Volcker's bold moves to hault the inflation, see Alan Greenspan's *The Age of Turbulence: Adventures in a New World*, New York, the Penguin Group (USA), 2007, 81–87.

214 James A. Bill, *The Eagle and the Lion: The Tragedy of American-Iranian Relations*, New Haven, Yale University Press pb., 1988.

215 Ibid., 319–330.

216 Ibid., 323–324.

217 Bill, ibid., 330–378; Lenczowski, 199–203; Lenczowski also quotes Hamilton Jordan's *Crisis: The Last Year of the Carter Presidency*, New York, Jos. Putnam and Sons, 1982, 83–95; and Gary Sick, Deputy to Cyrus Vance, *The October Surprise*: London, I. B. Tauris Co. Ltd., pb. ed. 1991, 174–229.

218 Lenczowski, 203–205.

219 Ibid., 205–211.

220 George Lenczowski's *The American Presidents and the Middle East* is an important and key source for all presidents from WWII to Reagan, ibid., 212. One should also consult Victor Ostrovsky's *By Way of Deception, passim*, for multiple attacks against Israeli foes.

221 Lenczowski, 212–215. Also see Thomas W. Lippman's *Inside the Image: America's Fragile Partnership with Saudi Arabia*, Boulder, Westview Press, 2004, especially "From Swords to Missiles," 273–298.

222 Lenczowski, 215–217. See also the definitive work on the Lebanese civil war by Kamal Salibi, *Crossroads to Civil War: Lebanon, 1958–1976:* London, 1976.

223 *Lenczowski, 217–221, and also Kamal Salibi's A House of Many Mansions: A Reconsideration of Lebanese History*, London, I. B. Tauris, 2nd ed., 1998, *passim*. See also Patrick Seale's monumental study, *Asad*: Berkeley, University of California Press, 1989, "The Invasion of Lebanon," 376–383.

224 Lenczowski, 320. No one can match, not even Lenczowski, the details of this period of Lebanese history like Patrick Seale, *Asad*, 383–418.

225 Seale, 339–366, and Lenczowski, 212–226; Rothkopf, 210–221.

226 Seale, 316–338; it is important to know the basic facts of the founding of the Ba'ath Party because it inspired the young Asad and all Syrian youth of the post–WW II era. 'Aflaq and Bitar were graduated from the Sorbonne in 1934 and returned to Syria to teach at the most prestigious high school, the Tajhiz al-Ula. An earlier graduate of the Sorbonne in 1932, Zaki al-Arsuzi, an Alawi from Antioch, also played an early role in the party. By 1941, they began a campaign to overcome tribalism, sectarianism, the oppression of women, and the supremacy of landowners. The central message was Arab revival with the slogan "Unity, Freedom, and Socialism." Only after the French left Syria on 17 April 1946 did the party have a formal foundation in the Rashid Coffee House in Damascus on 7 April 1947. See Seale, 27–35.

227 Seale, 351–365.

228 Ermond Abrahamian, *Khomeinism: Essays on the Islamic Republic*, Berkeley and Los Angeles, University of California Press, pb., 1993, *passim*.

229 Dilop Hiro, *Iran Under the Ayatollahs:* London, Routledge & Kegan Paul, pb., 1985, 179–189.

230 Hiro, 357–365. One may also consult Naghi Yousefi to discover the key role that Ali Sheriati played in the years leading up to the Khomeini Revolution, *Religion and Revolution in the Modern World: Ali Sheriati's Islam and Persian Revolution*, Lanham, MD, University Press of America, 1995, *passim*.

231 Rothkopf, *Running the World*, 239–242.

232 Ibid.

233 See Deborah and Gerald Strober's *REAGAN: The Man and His Presidency, the Oral History of an Era*, Boston and New York, Houghton Mifflin and Co., 1998, 387–561.

[234] Rothkopf, *Running the World*, 225–250. Lenczowski differs slightly from Rothkopf's version, 233–243. For a clear understanding of the "Trading Arms for Hostages" and payoffs to the Sandanistas, see also Strober, loc. cit., 458–561.

[235] Lenczowski, 243–254. Apart from Lenczowski, one should also consult Richard Clarke's *Against All Enemies: Inside America's War on Terror*, NY, Free Press, 2004, "Stumbling into the Islamic World," a chapter in which the author indicates how the United States supplied the Mujahidn in Afghanistan with antiaircraft missiles and also helped Saddam Hussein defeat Iran, 1980–1988, 35–54.

[236] Clarke, ibid., and Lenczowski, 255–256 and *passim*.

[237] Lenczowski, 256–258.

[238] Lenczowski, 258–260, and citing the *NY Times*, July 11, 1988.

[239] Lenczowski, 261–263.

[240] Ibid., 263–267, 270–276.

[241] One may also consult Quandt's *Peace Process, 335–380*, to gain further details of "Cold War Revival" and a partial "Return to Realism." Sidney Blumenthal, in his important study, *Our Long National Daydream: A Political Pageant of Reagan Era* (NY, Harper and Row, 1988, *passim*), digs deeply into the foibles of an era.

[242] Avi Shlaim, *Israel and Palestine:* London, Verso Press, 2009, 114–127. Also, Shlaim deals in detail with the biased peacemaking of President Clinton and Dennis Ross, 263–276. For a detailed biography of Dennis Ross, one should consult the Wikipedia article, "Dennis Ross," to understand the complex biases of this important presidential envoy to the Middle East. Also, one must take the time to consult Dennis Ross's recent book, *Doomed to Succeed: The U.S.-Israel Relationship from Truman to Obama*, NY, Farrar, Straus and Giroux, 2015*, passim*. In many respects, my book is a foil for the book by Dennis Ross.

[243] "Dan Quayle," *Wikipedia*, NY, 2001; Rothkopf, *Running the World*, 260–274.

[244] Kaplan, *The Arabists*, 286–288.

[245] Ibid.

[246] Rothkopf, loc. cit., but also read the admonitions of Middle East specialists about choosing Dennis Ross as our principal negotiator in the *Wikipedia* article under the heading "Dennis Ross," 2; see also the book by Dennis Ross, *Doomed to Succeed: The U.S.-Israeli Relationship from Truman to Obama*, NY, Furrar, Straus and Giroux, 2015, *passim*.

247 Colin L. Powell, *My American Journey* (with Joseph E. Persico): New York, Random House, 1995, 497–499. This memoir ends with General Powell's military career. It avoids his more controversial experiences as Secretary of State under President George W. Bush.

248 Clarke, *Against All Enemies*, 55–66. See the article by Phebe Marr in Ibrahim Ibrahim, ed., *The Iraq Gulf Crisis: Background and Consequences*, Washington, DC, Georgetown University pb., 1992, 145–168.

249 Clarke, *Against All Enemies*, 66–71; Shlaim, *Israel and Palestine*, 141–151.

250 See the detailed rundown of this complex period in Quandt's *Peace Process*, 383–412.

251 Rothkopf, *Running the World*, 303–320; one should also consult the book that Stephanopoulos wrote after the Clinton campaign and four years in the White House, George Stephanopoulos, *All too Human:* New York, Little, Brown and Co., 1999. This book, widely acclaimed, starts with his life as a Greek Orthodox kid, son of a priest, and how he became a presidential adviser after graduating from Columbia University, winning a Rhodes scholarship for Oxford and serving members of Congress from Ohio.

252 Clarke, *Against All Enemies*, 73–79. See also Ivo H. Daalder and I. M. Destler's *In the Shadow of the Oval Office: Profiles of the National Security Advisors and the Presidents They Served—From JFK to George W. Bush*, New York, Simon and Schuster, 2009, 245–246, and passim.

253 Ibid., 80–84. See also, regarding the Mossad plan, Victor Ostrovsky's *The Other Side of Deception: A Rogue Agent Exposes the Mossad's Secret Agenda*, New York, Harper Collins, 1994, 277–283.

254 Daalder and Destler, *In the Shadow of the Oval Office*, 214–232.

255 Clarke, *Against All Enemies*, 84–89, 93–97.

256 Ibid., 98–99.

257 "Slobodan Milosevic," in *Wikipedia*: New York, 2012, 1–22.

258 One should consult David Halberstam's *War in the Time of Peace* (Waterville, ME, Thorndike Press Large Print Ed., 2001, 227–299) to discover why Larry Eagleburger advised against involvement in Yugoslavia, both for President Bush Senior and President Clinton. Also details of "Lawrence Eagleburger" in *Wikipedia:* New York, 2012, 1–4. See specifically William Clinton's *My Life*: New York, Borzoi Books / Alfred A. Knopf, 2004, 509–513 and 684–686.

259 "Milosevic," loc. cit., and Clinton, *loc. cit.*

260 Clarke, *Against All Enemies*, 228–249.

261   Clarke, *Against All Enemies*, 111–118.

262   "William Clinton" in *Wikipedia:* New York, 2012, 1–10; for a full account of these events, one is urged to consult daily reports in *the New York Times*. Especially relevant are the articles in the *Sunday Times* for 18 April 1999; see also Daalder and Destler, loc. cit., and Clinton, *My Life, passim.*

263   "Clinton," *Wikipedia, loc. cit.*; President Clinton also mentioned the regular bombing of Iraq in his memoirs along with the positive vote in the Palestinian Council for the official recognition of Israel; see Clinton's *My Life*, 832–834.

264   Avi Shlaim, *Israel and Palestine,* 361–365; for reliable details on the Clinton administration and Clinton's important efforts for peace negotiations, one must consult Blumenthal, senior adviser to the Clinton administration from August 1997 to January 2001, Sidney Blumenthal, *The Clinton Wars*: New York, Farrar, Straus and Giroux, 2003, 776–780, and *passim*. We should also refer to the peace negotiations in which Martin Indyk was involved for President Clinton in Indyk's memoir, *Innocent Abroad:* New York, Simon and Schuster, 2009, especially 253–306. One should mention that Indyk was no "innocent abroad." He played every tune he could for his advancement to become two times the American ambassador to Israel, April 1995–Sept. 1997 and Jan. 2000–July 2001. He obtained his American citizenship in 1993. He was able to move from Australia to a visiting professorship at Columbia University to AIPAC (the Israeli lobbying group), 1982–1985, and then founded and headed the Washington Institute for Near East Policy, 1985–1993, with Daniel Pipes. See "Martin Indyk," *Wikipedia, 2–3.*

265   Naomi Klein, *The Shock Doctine*, 423–442. To reenforce Naomi Klein's observations about Bremer's superficial attempts to control developments in Iraq, one is asked also to check another keen observer revealing an inner look at what took place in the Green Zone, Rajiv Chandrasekaran— *Imperial Life in the Emerald City: Inside Iraq's Green Zone*, NY, Vintage/Random House pb., 2007, 129–140, and the careers, especially, of Dan Senor and John Agresto, 145–192.

266   Clarke, *Against All Enemies,* 205–226. One should also consult the large file on Cofer Black amassed by Jeremy Scahill in his important book *Blackwater: The Rise of the World's Most Powerful Mercenary Army*, New York, Nation Books / Perseus Group pb., 2008, 330–358.

267   Martin Indyk, a British Jew, educated in Australia, immigrated to the United States in 1982. Later he became the American ambassador to Israel

and a valued adviser to American presidents. His memoir, Martin Indyk, *Innocent Abroad* (NY, Simon & Schuster, 2009, 288–340), is a valuable record of the Camp David II negotiations of July 10 to July 25, 2000. For a critical look at the Clinton administration, one should consult Elizabeth Drew's *On the Edge: The Clinton Presidency*, NY, Simon & Schuster, 1994, *passim.*

268 George Packer, *The Assassin's Gate,* 15, 39–40; also, Clarke, *Against All Enemies,* 205–240.

269 See footnote 27.

270 James Mann, former correspondent for the *Los Angeles Times,* has written an important book, *The Rise of the Vulcans: The History of Bush's War Cabinet,* New York, Penguin Group, 2004, *passim.* The book traces the careers of the leading members of those giving advice to the George W. Bush presidency, 2001–2009. These individuals had often served other presidents: Condi Rice, presidential adviser; Powell, Secretary of State; Vice President Cheney and Rumsfeld, Secretary of Defense; Wolfowitz, deputy to Cheney; and Armitage, deputy to Powell.

271 Daalder and Destler, *Shadow of the Oval Office,* 248–263. One should also consult the excellent biography of the Bush family, especially dealing with the problems of the two Bush presidencies: Kitty Kelley, *The Family: The Real Story of the Bush Dynasty,* New York, Doubleday / Random House Inc., 2004, 502–634.

272 Clarke, *Against All Enemies,* 227–238; Daalder and Dester, loc. cit.

273 Hans Blix, *Disarming Iraq*: New York, Pantheon Books, 2004, 3–7, 215–253.

274 Clarke, *loc. cit.,* 244.

275 Clarke, loc. cit., 247–252; Joseph Stiglitz and Linda Bilmes, *The Three Trillion Dollar War,* NY, the WW Norton & Co., 2008 passim.

276 Clarke, *loc. cit.,* 252–287. already noted by Clarke, there was a shortage of Arabic speakers in the U.S. CIA. One might also consult the serious study by Robert D. Kaplan, *The Arabists*: New York, the Free Press / Macmillan, 1993, *passim,* in which Kaplan describes the elimination of Arabic speakers in the State Department by Secretaries of State Kissinger and Baker because many of them were not pro-Israeli enough. This policy also must have affected the CIA and the FBI.

277 George Packer, *The Assassins' Gate*: NY, Farrar, Straus and Giroux, 2003, 13–15.

278 Packer, ibid., 15–18.

279 One is urged to consult the article "Neoconservatism" in *Wikipedia, 26 pp.* See also the serious study of the Iraqi War costs, Joseph E. Stiglitz and Linda J. Bilmes's *The Three Trillion Dollar War*: New York, the WW Norton & Co., 2008, *passim.*

280 Naomi Klein, *The Shock Doctrine: The Rise of Disaster Capitalism,* NY, Henry Holt and Co., 2007, 316–317, 326, 330, 331–338. Rajiv Chandrasekaran, in his important book *Imperial Life in the Emerald City* (London, Bloomsbury Publishing Plc., 2006, 45–140), often covers what Naomi Klein has mentioned, but in greater detail.

281 "L. Paul Bremer," *Wikipedia*; L. Paul Bremer with Malcolm McConnell, *My Year in Iraq: The Struggle to Build a Future of Hope,* New York, Threshhold Editions, 2006, 4–8.

282 In Hebrew, by Oded Yinon, "A Strategy for Israel in the 1980s" in KIVUNIM 14 (Tel Aviv, Feb. 1982), sixteen pages, translated by Israel Shahak (NY 1983). See FN 155.

283 Ibid.

284 Klein, *The Shock Doctrine,* 346–350. Chandrasekaran, *loc. cit.*

285 George Packer, *The Assassins' Gate,* 16.

286 Maureen Dowd, "Neocons Slither Back," NYT, 16 September 2012, 11, and "Dan Senor," *Wikipedia.*

287 Klein, *The Shock Doctrine,* 351–357.

288 Ibid.

289 Gilles Kepel, *The War for Muslim Minds: Islam and the West,* Cambridge, MA, Harvard University Press, tr. by Pascale Ghazaleh, 2004, especially 141-197. Kepel is the professor and chair of Middle East Studies, Institute of Politics, Paris, France.

290 Kepel, loc.cit. 226 ff.

291 Ali A. Allawi, *The Occupation of Iraq: Winning the War, Losing the Peace,* New Haven, Yale University Press, 2007, 77–78.

292 Ali Allawi, *The Occupation of Iraq,* 280–290; and Thomas E. Ricks, *Fiasco:* NY, Penguin Group Inc., 2006, *passim*; and *The Gamble: NY,* Penguin Group Inc., 2009, 15–37, the problem of Shi'i death squads, 43–73, Congress and Israel, and the partial success of the surge; Al-Maliki is noted as part of the problem, 243–301. Bob Woodward, in his excellent study *The War Within: A Secret White House History (2006–2008: NY,* Simon & Schuster, 2008, 40), discusses Sadr death squads and bomb making by Iranians, 402–425, where Al-Maliki, the Prime Minister, is told by Condi Rice that he is failing his people, also a discussion of Bassima al-Jaidra,

who was "anti-Western, anti-American, anti-occupation," and she was one of Al-Maliki's chief aides.

293   Consult the incisive article by Stephen Zunes, "Washington's Proxy War," in the important collection on the war by Nubar Hovsepian's *The War on Lebanon: A Reader*, Northampton, Olive Branch Press, 2008, 93–118.

294   Robert Baer, *See No Evil: The True Story of a Ground Soldier in the CIA's War on Terrorism*, New York, Crown Publishers, 2000, 72–167.

295   Baer, *bid.*

296   Baer, 374–379.

297   Baer, 379–390.

298   David J. Rothkopf, *Running the World*: New York, Public Affairs, pb. ed., 2005, 3–21.

299   One is seriously called upon to read the excellent review of George Packer's books by Chris Lehmann, in the September 30, 2013, edition of *The Nation*, New York, 33–37.

300   Rothkopf interview with Anthony Lake, 30 June 2004, and also Rothkopf, 303–343.

301   Ibid.

302   "Anthony Lake," Wikipedia, loc. cit.

303   Baer, 171–253. Baer also, on one occasion, clashed with Martin Indyk, who was then serving on the National Security Council as its ME specialist. Baer told Indyk that it was wrong for the NSC to think that Saddam could be overthrown in a bloodless coup.

304   The essay first appeared in the *Atlantic Monthly* of September 1990 but is now readily available in a collection of essays by Bernard Lewis, *From Babel to Dragomans: Interpreting the Middle East*, Oxford and New York, Oxford University Press, 2004, 319–331.

305   Ali Allawi, *The Occupation of Iraq*, 14–16, and passim.

306   Ibid.

307   Naomi Klein, *The Shock Doctrine: The Rise of Disaster Capitalism*, NY, Henry Holt and Co., 2007, 364.

308   Private nterview with Salah Al-Askari regarding his family history. Also, one must consult the seven-page summary of the al-Qasim government found in *Wikipedia*.

309   For the standard book on the pluses and minuses of Saddam's government, one should refer to Samir al-Khalil's *Republic of Fear: The Inside Story of Saddam's Iraq*, NY, Pantheon / Random House pb., 1990, *passim*, but one should also read how the Ba'ath Party tried to introduce modern legislation

apart from Shari'ah law, under "Family Relations," see especially the "Status of Women," 88–92.

310 B. Lewis, *What Went Wrong?*: Oxford, Oxford U. Press, 2002, 159. Lewis also has made outlandish claims about Iraqi shortcomings in engineering and productivity in a second book, *The Crisis of Islam: Holy War and Unholy Terror*, New York, Random House Trade paperbacks, 2003, *passim*. The Saudis also have a great deal of explaining to do in keeping with Lewis's chapter VIII, "The Marriage of Saudi Power and Wahhabi Teaching," 120–136. See also Henri Lauziere's "The Construction of Salafiyya: Reconsidering Salafism from the Perspective of Conceptual History," *IJMES* 42/3 (Aug. 2010), 369–389.

311 William Cleveland, *A History of the Modern Middle East*: Boulder, Westview Press, 1994, 191–197.

312 Ja'far Al-Askari, *A Soldier's Story from Ottoman Rule to Independent Iraq*: Bagdad, tr. by Mustafa Tariq Al-Askari, ed. by William Facey and Najdat Fathi Safwat, 1935, *passim*.

313 Cleveland, *The Modern Middle East*, 191–201; also private interviews with Dr. Salah Al-Askari. On the German influence in the Middle East in WWII, see Peter Wien's "Coming to Terms with the Past: German Academia," *IJMES* 42 (2010), 311–321.

314 Cleveland, ibid. See also Ari Berman in *The Nation*, May 21, 2012, 11–17.

315 Gerges, *Obama and the Middle East*: New York, Palgrave, Macmillan / St. Martin's Press, 2012.

316 Gerges, *Obama and the Middle East*, 1–10.

317 Letter to the editor, *The Valley News*, 31 October 2014.

318 Gerges, *Obama and the Middle East*, 11–25.

319 See the articles by Delinda C. Hanley, "NSA Not Only Spies on Americans but Shares the Information with Israel," and Shirl McArthur, "A Conservative Estimate of Total U.S. Direct Aid to Israel: More Than $130 Billion," in *Washington Report on Middle East Affairs*, XXXII/8 (October–November 2013), 11 and 45 and 22–24.

320 Ibid., Vol. LXI/18 (November 20, 2014). And Kristof describing the miserable winter in Gaza, often without shelter or proper clothing, *NY Times* (March 8, 2015).

321 Peter Hessler, *The New Yorker*, 18 June 2012, 30–36; one must also read the authoritative article by Esam Al-Amin, "Disarray in Egypt: The New Regime, the Opposition, and the Judiciary," in *The Washington Report on*

Middle East Affairs, XXXII, no. 5 (June/July 2013, 30–31).

322   Gerges, *Obama and the Middle East*, 11–25, 234–245, and *passim*.

323   Stephen P. Cohen, *Beyond America's Grasp*: NY, Farrar, Straus and Giroux, 2009; see especially chapter 7 on legitimacy and chapter 8 on Israel, 151–173.

324   This wealth of authoritative information has been collected in the article "Hassan Rouhani" in the latest references of the *Wikipedia*.

325   Even the Israelis seem to be voting with their feet in the light of the spread of Orthodox and messianic Judaism, a harsh settlement policy and a right-wing government that delivers no peace proposals. On this score, one should consult the article by Doug Saunders, "Why Jews Flee to Europe," in *The Toronto Globe and Mail*, Saturday, November 16, 2013, F2. In this seminal article, Mr. Saunders describes how each year, five hundred thousand Israelis flee to Western Europe or the United States, seeking a peace of mind and a future away from the stress of Israeli life.

326   Fawaz Gerges, *BBC broadcast* of 2 April 2015.

327   See the brilliant and critical article "In the Land of the Possible: Samantha Power Has the President's Ear. To What End?" *The New Yorker*, December 22 and 29, 2014, 90–107.

328   Samuel Huntington, *The Clash of World Civilizations: Cambridge, Harvard University Press*, pb., 1996, passim. One may also consult the small paperback collection of essays by Adam Shapiro, E. Faye Williams, Khaled Dawoud, Muhammed Kaddam, and William Martin, *Neocon Middle East Policy: The "Clean Break" Plan Damage Assessment*, Washington, DC, Institute for Research, Middle East Policy Inc., 2007, especially 46–54, wherein Professor Martin relates President Bush's challenge to Israeli general Mofaz.

329   Ross Douthat, *NYT*, May 18, 2014, 9.

330   Robin Wright, "The Adversary," *The New Yorker* (May 26, 2014), 40–49.

331   David Remnick, "The One-State Reality: Israel's Conservative President Speaks Up for Civility and Pays a Price," *The New Yorker* (November 17, 2014), 46–53.

332   Eric S. Margolis, *The Washington Report on Middle Eastern Affairs* XXXIII (May 2014), 11 and 14.

333   Stephen F. Cohen, "Patriotic Heresy vs. the New Cold War," *The Nation* (September 15, 2014), 22–26.

334   See the important book review by Steve Negus, especially his review of *ISIS: Inside the Army of Terror* by Michael Weiss and Hassan Hassan, in

the *NYT* for April 5, 2015, 11–12.

335 This news item hit the press corps on station, Ashton Carter, CNN, on 25 May 2015.

336 "Iraq" in *Wikipedia*. For further reading, one should consult the book review of two books by Brian Urquhart, Patrick Tyler's study of the presidency, and Rashid Khalidi's study of the cold world and the Middle East, "Blundering in the Mideast with Prince Bandar" *in the New York Review*, vol. LVI (Aug. 13, 2009), 44–47.

337 Theo Padnos, *The New York Times Magazine*, November 2, 2014, 34–39 and 46–51.

338 Susan Dominus, *The New York Times Book Review*, Sunday, April 5, 2015, 10. One should also consult *VOICES*, the pamphlet of the Christian dialogue on global issues, Autumn, 1994, 7–8, where it gives statistics on the proportion of males to females, child marriage, female labor, and genital mutilation in non-Western countries.

339 See any issue of the *Southern Poverty Law Center Bulletin* of Montgomery, Alabama, 36177-7459.

Made in the USA
Middletown, DE
07 July 2017